In the Ring With Bob Fitzsimmons

Part II

Three-Time Champion

Adam J. Pollack

WIN BY KO

Win By KO Publications
Iowa City

In the Ring With Bob Fitzsimmons
Part II: Three-Time Champion

Adam J. Pollack

(ISBN-13): 978-1-949783-11-7

(softcover: 50# acid-free alkaline paper)

Includes footnotes and index.

All cover colorizations by Gregory Speciale ©

Cover design by Gwyn Flowers ©

Manufactured in the United States of America.

Win By KO Publications
Iowa City, Iowa
winbykopublications.com

Contents

The Interim

On March 17, 1897 in Carson City, Nevada, at an estimated 165, 170, or 175 pounds, 33-year-old former world middleweight champion Bob Fitzsimmons won the world heavyweight championship from 30-year-old 185-188-pound James J. Corbett, coming back from a 6th round knockdown, forcing the fight with power punches throughout, until finally in the 14th round, a counter left hook to the body, subsequently known as the solar plexus punch, sent Corbett down for the full ten-count. The supreme knockout artist Fitzsimmons had struck again. Six years after winning the world middleweight title back in 1891 at age 27, he had become. the world heavyweight champion.

One of Corbett's sparring partners for the fight was emerging heavyweight contender James J. Jeffries. Over the next two years, Jeffries kept fighting regularly, obtaining experience and eventually becoming a top contender for the crown.

During that time, Fitzsimmons, who turned 34 years old two months after beating Corbett, vacillated about whether or not he was retired or whether he would return to the ring to defend his crown. Primarily, Fitz rested on his laurels, earning easy

COURT ST. THEATER
Matinee EveryDay. Good Orchestra Seat 25¢.
BOB FITZSIMMONS
Champion of Champions — and His
GREAT SPECIALTY COMPANY.
12 — Refined Acts — 12.
NEXT WEEK — 40 Theirz's Mammoth Burlesque Company and Joe Linder.

Buffalo Times, June 6, 1897

money in short exhibitions (mostly with sparring partners like Jack Stelzner, Dan Hickey, Ernest Roeber, Mike Conley, George Lawler, Yank Kenny, or James Murphy), or stage appearances, traveling across the country.[1] The fame that went with being world heavyweight champion allowed him to earn a lot of money without risking his crown.

Jim Corbett wanted a rematch. Bob sometimes told him that he was retired, and at other times told him to go win some fights and build up momentum for a rematch between them. Bob certainly had no intention of re-entering the ring to risk his title unless large financial inducements were offered. However, Corbett, like Fitz, did not fight for quite a while.

The police thwarted a potential July 5, 1897 scheduled 6-round bout in Brooklyn, New York between Fitzsimmons and former champion John L. Sullivan, who at age 39 had not fought in nearly five years, only participating in some tame exhibitions.

On July 16, 1897, in San Francisco, 212-pound James J. Jeffries fought 199-pound Gus Ruhlin to a 20-round draw, dropping Ruhlin in the 4th, 5th, and 20th rounds.

---

[1] *New York World*, May 9, 1897; *Kansas City Times*, May 16, 1897.

On November 30, 1897, in San Francisco, 220-pound Jim Jeffries fought 171-pound Joe Choynski (37-6-3) to a 20-round draw, though Jeff scored a couple knockdowns in the process, in the 3rd and 15th rounds, and was the aggressor throughout. However, some said Choynski was the better boxer, hitting and moving well.

Back in 1894, Fitzsimmons stopped Choynski in the 5th round, though Choynski had decked and badly hurt Fitz in the 3rd round. Fitz came back in the 4th round to knock down Choynski several times, and then, after dropping Choynski several more times in the 5th round, the police stopped the fight. It was declared a draw pursuant to a pre-fight agreement, but everyone knew that Bob had stopped him and it essentially was a de facto technical knockout victory. In 1889, Jim Corbett stopped Choynski in the 27th round.

On March 22, 1898, in San Francisco, 216-pound James J. Jeffries knocked out the legendary Australian black fighter 195-pound Peter Jackson (57-1-15) in the 3rd round, decking him in the 2nd before finishing him off in the 3rd. It was Jackson's first loss since 1884, his only prior official defeat.

Heavyweight champion John L. Sullivan had refused to fight Australian and Colored Champion Peter Jackson, owing to the color line. Jim Corbett had fought Jackson in 1891 to a 61-round no contest/draw in a 4-hour fight to the finish that was stopped because it appeared that neither man could knock out the other owing to fatigue and risk-aversiveness. Jackson had won the British/Commonwealth championship in 1892 with a KO10 Frank Slavin, but after he was unable to obtain a world championship fight with Corbett, he essentially had been semi-retired for nearly six years.

On May 6, 1898, in San Francisco, James J. Jeffries won a 20-round decision over Sailor Tom Sharkey (20-2-6), decking him in the 11th round.

Sharkey had fought Corbett to a June 24, 1896 4-round draw.

On December 2, 1896, in San Francisco, Bob Fitzsimmons had dropped Tom Sharkey in the 1st and 5th rounds and knocked him out in the 8th round. Referee Wyatt Earp controversially called the final punch a foul low blow and disqualified Fitzsimmons, but most believed that there was no low blow and the referee had been paid to fix the fight for Sharkey. Bob insisted that he had been defrauded out of his rightful victory and the money. Most agreed, and the result only increased the esteem for Fitzsimmons and set up the eventual Corbett championship fight.

On June 29, 1898, in Brooklyn, New York, Tom Sharkey knocked out Gus Ruhlin in the 1st round.

Many were criticizing Fitzsimmons for failing to defend the title, for it had been more than a year since he won the championship. Fitz could not make up his mind regarding whether or not he was retired.

However, in early August 1898, Fitzsimmons said that since he already had defeated Corbett, Sharkey, and Maher (1896 KO1), if Jim Jeffries wanted, he would fight him. Bob posted $2,500. "Jeffries is the only man that I have not defeated who is at liberty, and for his benefit I will say once more that, providing he is agreeable and that the details can be arranged so that the fight will take place before Oct. 1, I will accommodate him." Bob's manager Martin Julian noted that Jeff was a "reputed world-beater," and had defeated Sharkey, so Fitz wanted to fight him.[2]

On August 5, 1898 in New York City, an alleged 212-pound (but many later said he was 230 or more) Jim Jeffries won a 10-round decision over 187-pound (who looked bigger as well) 6'4" black Bob Armstrong, scoring a knockdown in the final round. However, during the fight, Jeffries badly broke his left thumb. It would require time to heal properly.

Supposedly, on or about October 4 or 5, 1898, James Fitzsimmons, Bob's father, died of pneumonia at age 90 (some say 86) in New Zealand. He had been a constable/police officer in Timaru and previously had been in the British army for most of his life until he retired on a pension. He was born in Ireland.[3]

On November 22, 1898 in New York City, Tom Sharkey defeated former world heavyweight champion James J. Corbett (his first fight since the March 1897 title loss), when Jim was disqualified in the 9th round as a result of his cornerman entering the ring to protest Sharkey's rough tactics. Most believed that he did it to save Corbett from an eventual knockout, for he was fatiguing under Sharkey's incessant attack. Sharkey had scored a knockdown in the 2nd round. Sharkey's win only made Jeffries' victory over him all the more impressive and important.

---

[2] *New York World*, August 2-4, 1898.

[3] *Boston Globe*, October 5, 1898; *Cincinnati Enquirer, Baltimore Sun*, October 6, 1898. James Fitzsimmons' gravestone says he died on August 29, 1898. However, Bob received a cable dispatch from his mother on October 5 saying, "Your father died here to-day."

CHAPTER 2

Road to a Title Defense

On January 10, 1899, in New York City, Tom Sharkey suffered two knockdowns in the 3rd round but came back to knock out Charles 'Kid' McCoy (48-2-7) in the 10th round.

On January 12, 1899, James J. Jeffries placed himself in William A. Brady's managerial hands. Brady, who previously had handled Corbett, advertised Jeff as the world's only undefeated heavyweight, who had defeated Sharkey, who in turn had beaten Ruhlin (KO1), Corbett (WDQ9), and Kid McCoy (KO10). The 10-0-2 Jeffries did not have a lot of fights, but he had high quality experience and important results, fighting top men in scheduled 20-round bouts from the start of his career, with victories over the likes of Hank Griffin (KO14), Joe Goddard (KO4), Peter Jackson (KO3), Mexican Pete Everett (KO3), Tom Sharkey (W20), and Bob Armstrong (W10), and the 20-round draws with Joe Choynski and Gus Ruhlin, dropping both in the process.

On February 9, 1899, Fitz's manager Martin Julian met with Jeffries' representatives/managers Bill Delaney and Joe Eagan (Bill Brady's representative) and made an agreement for Bob to defend his world heavyweight championship crown against Jeffries. The most relevant terms of the articles of agreement signed the following day said that the match would be to a finish or not less than 25 rounds, there would be no hitting in clinches or breakaways (a term Jeff did not want but Fitz insisted upon), neither could wear hand bandages (another term Fitz insisted upon), the gloves were to be 5 ounces, and the winner was to take the entire purse. At least, that is what they told the public.[4]

Jeffries and Brady later explained how they obtained the title shot. Upon returning to Oakland after the Armstrong fight, Jeff's manager Bill Delaney received a telegram from William Brady saying that if Jeff would put himself under his management for two years that he would guarantee him a match with Fitzsimmons. They accepted. In order to induce Bob to make the match, Brady had to guarantee Fitzsimmons 65% of the purse, win or lose. According to Brady, he also offered Bob a 25% interest in the club with which Brady was associated (the Coney Island Club), which wanted to host the fight. It was an offer that Fitzsimmons could not refuse. Sometimes, when a contender wants to win a potentially lucrative championship badly enough, he makes some concessions, as the Jeffries crew did.[5]

Initially, the deal to give Fitz the guaranteed lion's share of the money was kept secret from the public. Such an arrangement was considered a

[4] *National Police Gazette, New York Clipper*, February 18, 1899.
[5] *My Life and Battles* at 29-30; *Two Fisted Jeff* at 94-99; Brady, *Life and Battles of James J. Jeffries*, at 16-17; *National Police Gazette*, March 11, 1899.

disincentive to give best efforts, because payment did not depend on success. However, fighters were well aware that future financial success depended on victory, so Fitz had a reason to fight hard. Plus, most champions have big egos. Fitzsimmons had knocked out everyone.

On March 23, the parties accepted the Coney Island Club's offer to host the bout on May 26, 1899 [later changed to June 9] for a $20,000 purse, the winner to take all, and for each pugilist to receive 33 1/3% of the money accruing from the picture machine exhibitions, with the club to take the remaining third. At least, this is what they told the public regarding the purse-split. It also was reported that Jeffries' manager Bill Brady, Fitz's manager Martin Julian, and Senator Tim Sullivan all were given interests in the club. Both sides approved of George Siler, who had refereed Corbett-Fitzsimmons, to referee the fight.[6]

On March 24, 1899 in San Francisco, 160-pound Kid McCoy won a 20-round decision over 167-pound Joe Choynski. Choynski dropped McCoy in the 9th, but McCoy dropped Choynski in the 17th en route to the decision win. This made Sharkey's victory over McCoy more impressive.

In the meantime, Fitzsimmons kept giving bag punching and sparring exhibitions with large 200+-pound heavyweight Yank Kenny.[7]

Fitzsimmons said he was not too far from being fit. "You see, I do not dissipate, and consequently I do not have to kill myself to be well for a mill." Bob's sparring exhibitions kept him in good trim. He would begin hard training in about two weeks, after his theatrical season closed. "I have no fear of the outcome. I have never met Jeffries as of yet, but I guess he is a nice fellow. There is one thing about him that I like. He can make a match without a lot of nonsensical talk and mud-slinging."[8] The quiet Jeffries was no Corbett when it came to trash talk.

Although Fitz was the 7 to 5 betting odds favorite, Delaney opined that 220-pound Jeffries had the edge in the upcoming fight. He was younger and bigger, but that was not all. "This boy is the best man I ever handled. He is a natural born fighter, can hit as hard as any man I ever saw in a ring and is a glutton for punishment. He has never been stunned and it seems impossible to knock him out." This was a high compliment coming from a man who had handled Jim Corbett. A reporter who saw Jeffries exhibit was "fairly astonished at the cleverness of the giant. He sends his ponderous arms to all parts of the body with lightning-like rapidity, and is as light on his feet as a dancing master."[9]

In mid-May, Fitzsimmons, who had been sparring with Yank Kenny and Dan Hickey, said, "I feel in better form now than ever before…. [I]t will be all over with him after our contest."[10]

Speaking of Bob's training methods, the *National Police Gazette* noted, "Fitz is a man who trains a little all the time and is really never out of shape." Its writer observed a day of his training. In the morning, Fitz

[6] *New York Clipper*, April 1, 1899; *National Police Gazette*, April 4, 8, 1899.
[7] *St. Louis Post-Dispatch*, April 5, 1899; Boxrec.com; *National Police Gazette*, April 8, 1899.
[8] *St. Louis Post-Dispatch*, *St. Louis Republic*, *St. Louis Daily Globe Democrat*, April 6, 7, 1899.
[9] *Brooklyn Daily Eagle*, *Asbury Park Daily Press*, April 25, 26, 1899; *National Police Gazette*, May 13, 1899.
[10] *New York Evening Journal*, May 16, 1899.

walked 2 ½ miles and then ran back. After breakfast, Bob tossed the 15-pound medicine ball with Yank Kenny, who stood six feet and weighed 230 pounds. Fitz then did ball punching for 15 minutes. Following that, he hit the punching bag, which was three feet in diameter by four feet in length. Next, he worked the wrist machine. After that, Fitz sparred 4 rounds with Kenny. "Kenny, though a giant, in reality is no more than a boy in the hands of the champion, who spars, wrestles and literally roughs it with him in the course of the day." After sparring, Bob hit a baseball for an hour.

After a meal, Bob played a game called quoits for an hour, throwing a ring at a peg. Then, wearing 3-ounce gloves to prevent scratches, he and the huge Kenny wrestled for half an hour, roughing it, pushing the head back, engaging in neck holds, and generally mauling each other. After a few minutes of rest, Bob hit a bag for 6 rounds while holding a pair of small dumbbells. He then wore 6-ounce gloves and exercised his legs, feinting, side-stepping, advancing, retreating, and ducking from little rubber balls thrown at him, this lasting 20 minutes. After an evening meal, Bob ran 7 miles with his dog.[11]

Fitzsimmons discussed his skills and strategies. He liked to bluff and lay clever traps in order to get an opening to knock out his opponent.

> I guess I am the champion because I depend upon no particular blow and can drop my man with either hand. I know the spots on a man that are worth hitting. ... There was a day that I was the cleverest boxer in Australia, but I soon found that a man cannot be exceedingly showy and still punch hard. There is a difference between a boxer and a fighter. The boxer may be very pretty, but he is seldom capable of stopping things with a punch. A man who expects to beat the world must hit, and I have spent most of my time figuring how to do the most damage with a punch. ... When I enter the ring with a man I have no plans. After I shake hands I look him over in a friendly way, then I feint him. I try to figure what blow he wishes to use and which he thinks I will use. If he don't hit hard I won't mind being hit. I want him to keep working, for I am sure to find a chance for a good punch if he keeps coming. If he wants me to set the pace I crowd in with my jaw well shielded by my shoulder and jab his head back with the left. ... I have never yet got a man on the jaw fair that he did not drop and stay there for the ten seconds at least. ... I do not know exactly how I will beat Jeffries, but I will certainly beat him. Furthermore, I won't let him hit me. He is a big, strong fellow and might do damage.[12]

When discussing his initial prediction, Jim Corbett, who had sparred with Jeffries back in 1897, said, "Fitzsimmons on form should carry off the honors. He is a great fighter and has experience in his favor." Bob could hit, was game, and could take considerable punishment. Nevertheless, Jim granted that Jeffries had a good chance to win.

[11] *National Police Gazette*, June 3, 1899.
[12] *New York Journal*, May 22, 1899.

Jeffries is a good, willing fighter, who can hit a terrific blow, and, should he get one of those punches in at any time, it will be all over with the Australian. Since I trained with Jeffries, over two years ago, he has improved wonderfully and may surprise his admirers. His contest with Armstrong, who he fought with a broken hand, can hardly be considered seriously.

Corbett also said if Jeff won, he would return to the ring and fight him.[13]

Tom Sharkey, who had fought both, believed that Bob would defeat Jeffries with ease. "Fitz ought to win over Jeffries in jig time. He'll be an easy mark for Bob."[14]

Despite being the underdog, Jeffries eloquently and confidently stated his belief that he would defeat Fitzsimmons. Jeff also assessed fellow fighters:

Oh, I don't think Fitz is the hardest man in the world, and if I didn't believe I could best him I wouldn't have made the match. I have thought so ever since he beat Corbett at Carson City. You know I helped to train Corbett for that fight. Corbett outpointed Fitzsimmons as a boxer, but his strength gave out. He had no force behind his blows.

Fitzsimmons' strength is what I call natural strength. The work in his early days in a blacksmith shop gave him the foundation for a constitution which has stood by him in many a hard-fought battle. He could take a good, hard thrashing and turn around and beat a man of but ordinary strength, as he showed against Corbett at Carson.

Corbett is what I call a manufactured gymnasium boxer, and I claim that manufactured strength gained in a gymnasium is not the real thing. It comes of training for an athletic event and comes out after a few hard knocks in the ring. The clever boxer with only manufactured strength has nothing to fall back on after his stamina has gone back on him....

I am an admirer of the science of boxing, but science alone will not turn the trick when the scientific man is up against one who is twice as strong and only half as clever. Corbett whipped himself by punching Fitz, and after his wind and strength were spent Fitzsimmons finished him up....

Sharkey is naturally strong, but loses his head entirely. He isn't half as good a man as Fitzsimmons, and never will be, because it isn't in him. ... We went twenty rounds, and during the entire journey I had him on the run. ... It's hard to whip a fairly strong fellow if he refuses to fight. I believe in clever footwork, but Sharkey wasn't clever on his feet. He simply refused to fight. ... I floored him at least ten times. Alex Greggains, who refereed the bout, asked Sharkey repeatedly to

[13] *New York Journal*, May 17, 1899.
[14] *National Police Gazette*, May 20, 1899.

stand up and fight like a man, but the Sailor refused. As for Sharkey's hitting powers, they made no impression upon me. ... He can't hit straight to save his life. ...

I can whip Fitzsimmons, because I will carry fifty more pounds of weight into the ring and have the benefit of thirteen years. He is thirty-six, and I am in my twenty-third year. I know I am as fast on my feet; yes, faster, and can avoid his swings. He is a wicked puncher and dangerous man, but I have studied his methods closely.

I cannot see how he can spring any knockout surprise on me. I hold my right in reserve, and do most of my execution with the left. In swinging with the right a fighter leaves an opening for a cross punch. Fitz won't surprise me with his long, sweeping right cross. Of course, I swing the right when I have my man in a position for a straight, right jab for the body or in swinging into a clinch at short range. I don't save a right swing for a knockout as a rule.

I don't want the newspapers to write me up as a swell chest or big head. I am asked an honest opinion. I give it without boasting, and it is my honest belief that Fitzsimmons isn't big enough, strong enough, or clever enough for me.[15]

Jeff's confidence got the boxing public excited. He told another local New York paper,

I certainly expect to beat Fitzsimmons on the evening of June 9, or I would not fight him. I do not think he is easy – far from it – but I believe in my heart that I can beat the man I saw beat Corbett at Carson. ... I believe I know a few things about scientific fighting, in spite of the talk about being "just a strong, rough fellow." Fitz may know it all, but he will learn that I know a few things myself. ... I am certain that Fitzsimmons will stand punishment. ... He has got to be hit, and hit awful hard, to settle him. ... As long as he is on his feet, no matter how groggy, he is always dangerous. ... I must admit that Fitz, from his pictures, looks pretty hard to get at. Still, I will get to him. ... I can stand a punch, and expect to have to take a few to get a few in. ... I believe I know his tricks and how to discount them. ... I am stronger, heavier, and can both give and take more punishment.[16]

The *National Police Gazette* noted,

It must not be forgotten that Jeffries is one of the greatest two-handed fighters of the age. Naturally he is left handed, but he has, owing to the requirements of boxing, been obliged to learn to use his right hand so that he can now use either one with equal facility and hits as hard with the right as with the left. ...

---

[15] *National Police Gazette*, May 27, 1899.
[16] *New York Journal*, May 26, 1899.

The one thing that Jeffries needs to do, and I believe that is the reason why the services of Tommy Ryan were secured, is to get fast on his feet. If there is any man who can develop him in this direction it is Ryan, for he is the king at foot work. [17]

Some felt that Fitz's relative lack of fight activity for two years might affect his capacity for a sustained endeavor. Jeffries did not think it would last long, because neither of them was in the habit of running away.[18] Fitz argued that layoffs did not bother him at all because he always remained in shape by working out and sparring in exhibitions, and he had no bad habits.

Against common opponents, Fitzsimmons had the superior results. He had stopped both Choynski and Sharkey, while Jeff had managed only a draw with Joe and had won a decision over Tom. That said, Jeffries had decked both, and never had been down in a professional fight, while Fitz had been hurt and/or down on a few occasions, including against Maher, Choynski, and Corbett. Yet, Bob had stopped everyone who had hurt him. Both Fitzsimmons and Jeffries were punchers, having decked everyone they had fought. Both were fit. Hence, it appeared to be a great matchup.

> There cannot be the least doubt that both men are in as good condition as any two men who ever fought. The big fellow from California has done wonders in the way of work. ... Still weighing in the vicinity of 210 pounds, he can do three miles at a speed which would bother a professional runner, and can tear off the last hundred yards in close to 11 seconds. He has improved in his general foot work and boxing to a startling degree. ...

> Fitzsimmons, in turn, seems, like good wine, to grow better with age. He is a bit heavier than hitherto, and, in spite of the assertion that he will weigh but 158, it is likely he will be nearer 170. Fitz has always had people fooled on his weight.[19]

In late May, after sparring 6 rounds with current world middleweight champion Tommy Ryan (57-1-9), mostly working on his defense, Jeff again spoke of the Fitzsimmons-Corbett bout, which he had witnessed.

> Fitzsimmons didn't strike me as being particularly clever, and he certainly did not loom up as a terrible puncher in that go. He didn't knock Corbett down until the very last, and he didn't daze him. As for that famous solar plexus punch, it was simply a case of Corbett being fagged and going down from a light blow. I am sure that left-hander would not have hurt me. Poor Jim went all to pieces just as he did in his four rounds with Sharkey, and I knew that he was up against it long before that solar plexus crack came along.... I know that I have learned a whole lot about boxing, and all I hope is that Fitz will come at me the way he went at Corbett.[20]

[17] National Police Gazette, May 27, 1899.
[18] San Francisco Examiner, May 30, 31, 1899.
[19] New York Journal, May 27, 1899.
[20] San Francisco Examiner, May 27, 1899.

Sizing up the men, the *New York Sun* said Fitzsimmons had the experience, knew the scientific principles better than anyone, was the world's hardest hitter, and possessed supreme confidence. "He has knocked out more antagonists with one punch than any other fighter and is a physical freak." Bob was not a showy boxer. "He is a fighter, pure and simple, but in addition is crafty, tricky and a quick thinker." He always demonstrated wonderful recuperative powers after being hurt.

A *Sun* reporter who had seen Fitzsimmons in training was impressed. He hit the punching ball and bag. Next, Bob boxed 24 minutes straight, alternating back and forth two minutes each with Yank Kenny and Dan Hickey, taking no rest. Bob showed his blocking and feinting, together with fast footwork, and was quick as lightning in all his movements. After 18 minutes, Bob rushed at the finely built and much larger Kenny. His left shot under the chin like a bolt of lightning, and Kenny fell against some pulley weights as if a mallet had struck him. Yank then ran away, but Bob was after him and nearly knocked him out with a jolt on the jaw. Hickey then went at Bob, who "could have put him to sleep at any moment." After the round-robin sparring, Bob worked the wrist machines and the pulley weights.

When the match was made, the general opinion was that Bob had picked out an easy mark. It was claimed that in the past, Jeff's chief weakness was slowness of foot, but that allegedly was due to the fact that he often weighed too much, up to 245 pounds. However, he had trained so hard and faithfully for the Fitz fight that he was down to around 205 pounds. "With decreased avoirdupois comes increased speed in attack and defense."

Jeffries would be the biggest fighter that Fitzsimmons had met in a professional contest. Bob never had seen him box, whereas Jeff had seen the champion in action (live and on film). Despite Bob's powerful blows, Jeff really could take a punch. "He has never suffered a defeat, has never been knocked down and says that he does not know what grogginess means." Furthermore, Jeff had a "wonderful reach,

great strength and endurance." It would not be easy to defeat such a man in a 25-round bout. Fitz would be meeting a very well-trained Jeffries.[21]

After training on May 31, Jeffries told reporters,

> I may be able to keep Fitz away from me and just knock his block to pieces with my reach. I saw him fight Corbett and I got a fair line on him then. … I know that I can stand twice the punching that Corbett can and that I can also hit hard. I'll be fast, too, this time. When I fought Armstrong I weighed 235 pounds. … But this time I shall get into the ring in better shape than I've ever been before in my life. I shall weigh not more than 205 and I'll be just as speedy as Fitz.

When asked if he ever had been knocked down, Jeff responded, "Never in my life, and I've never been groggy, either. Choynski dazed me once with a right-hand swing on the cheek bone, but it only lasted a minute."

JACK JEFFRIES. TOMMY RYAN. BILLY DELANEY. JIM JEFFRIES. JIM DALY.

Jeff claimed to weigh 210 pounds stripped and would reduce to 205 by the day of the fight. He weighed 220 fully clothed.

In his afternoon sparring with Tommy Ryan, Jeffries was remarkably lively on his feet, "100 percent more so than when he met Armstrong."[22]

On Thursday, June 1, eight days before the fight, Fitz sparred 12 rounds with Kenny, Hickey, and "the other regulars in turn," including lightweight Jack Everhardt.

Jeffries was said to have been doing six hours of work every day. "It is doubtful if ever a heavy-weight was in as perfect physical condition as James J. Jeffries. … It is wonderful the amount of work he does. … He is

---

[21] *New York Sun*, June 4, 1899, discussing Fitz's training the previous week.
[22] *New York Sun*, June 4, 1899, discussing Jeff's training the week before; *New York Journal*, June 1, 1899.

better than any one believed he would be, as he has gained speed. He is fit and fast."[23]

On Friday, June 2, 1899, one week away from the fight, the hot weather had arrived. After Fitzsimmons boxed Kenny and Hickey 6 hard and fast rounds, alternating a round with each, the "spectators applauded vigorously, and declared the Australian to be the greatest fighting machine the world has ever seen." Kenny said, "I simply can't understand how a man of his weight can hit as hard as he does."[24]

Fitz claimed that he was weighing 160 ½ pounds and would weigh 158 in the ring. Jeffries questioned this weight and felt that Bob was fibbing, remarking, "He said he weighed somewhere about 156 pounds when he fought Corbett at Carson, but I'd like to find some one who saw him on the scales." Bill Delaney said Bob looked every bit as big as Corbett. The *National Police Gazette* estimated that Bob weighed at least 168 pounds to Jeff's 213 pounds.[25]

It was at that time that the authenticity of Bob's reported age was called into question. His birth certificate was found in London, and it placed him at 36 years of age, not the 37 that Bob claimed.[26]

Jeff was looking solid, allegedly 15 pounds below that which he ever had entered the ring before. "His weight is about 208 pounds...[I]t varies in a day from 207 to 211."[27]

[23] *New York Journal*, June 2, 1899.
[24] The 1st round with Hickey actually lasted six minutes. Hickey was pretty quick and unusually clever, but Bob handled him. Kenny, who was nicknamed "Jeffries" because of his size, did more slugging with Bob, but even he was about worn out at the conclusion of the 6th round.
[25] *San Francisco Examiner*, May 28, 1899; *San Francisco Chronicle*, June 7, 1899; *National Police Gazette*, June 3, 1899.
[26] *San Francisco Examiner*, May 30, 1899; June 5, 1899; *New York Journal*, June 5, 1899.
[27] *New York World*, June 3, 1899.

Regardless of Jeff's good appearance, as the fight approached, Fitzsimmons moved to and remained the 2 to 1 betting-odds favorite. This made sense, because he had stopped Choynski, Sharkey, and Corbett. He had the lengthy, impressive career, having knocked out every good fighter that he ever faced. In fact, Fitz never legitimately lost a fight to the finish. Americans had seen him score knockout victories over every opponent since his arrival in 1890, including: 1891 KO13 Jack Dempsey (world middleweight championship); 1892 KO12 Peter Maher; 1893 KO4 Jim Hall; 1894 KO5 Joe Choynski (although officially a D5 – police stoppage) and KO2 Dan Creedon; 1896 KO1 Peter Maher and KO8 Tom Sharkey (although officially LDQby8); and 1897 KO14 James J. Corbett.

Jeffries was a relative newcomer. He was criticized for not making sufficient use of his strength and weight in his fights, and therefore in a match of cleverness, it was believed that Fitz would win. Some said that Jeff lacked sufficient aggression, had an "absence of pugnacity from his temperament" and "hesitancy in mixing up." A San Francisco report said,

> When Jeffries fought Sharkey here he obtained the decision, and the award was no doubt, a just one. But in that contest Jeffries made but little use of his enormous strength and great weight. He seemed content to stand off and swing his left in when he got a chance. From the two or three rallies that did take place, Sharkey emerged groggy. It was in these mix-ups that Jeffries showed how formidable he is when he fully exerts himself. Up to the time he met him, Sharkey had hussled every fighter he met about the ring as he pleased and worn them down by sheer brute force. In Jeffries' hands, even with his tremendous strength and desperate viciousness, he was a child.[28]

However, what his critics failed to realize is that the flip side to Jeff's cautiousness was that he knew how to pace himself and not wear himself out in a lengthy bout, and he also showed defense. He may have believed

[28] *San Francisco Examiner*, June 2, 1899.

that his methods allowed him to take care not to be hit with a knockout blow. Jeff adjusted his level of aggression based on his opponent's capabilities. Not everyone could be the vicious, quick knockout artist that John L. Sullivan was, although Jeff's size caused many to expect that of him. His occasionally more cautious, methodical style kept him in good stead in lengthy bouts, but was not as awe-inspiring.

Fitzsimmons' fighting style was sized up as well.

> [Fitzsimmons is] purely and simply a fighting machine.... In action he is tricky to the last degree.... Every blow landed by Fitzsimmons hurts... He has one blow which is peculiarly his own. It only travels a few inches, and is made entirely with the forearm.... The champion's every effort is toward helping his opponent to beat himself out. He lays all sorts of traps to get his man in motion, so that he may catch him coming with a jolt.... Men have rained blows all over Fitz, and it looked that he must be dazed or at least confused, but it was only his way of finding a short route to the money and the championship. ... No one will question Fitzsimmons' shiftiness and pluck. Corbett, Maher, Choynski and nearly every fighter he has met has had him going at some stage of the encounter, but he has pulled himself together, and taken advantage of the critical moment to turn the tables. ... But Fitz himself says he does not fight two fights alike... It may be at long range fighting as he drove it into Corbett, or it may be close in with a short hook similar to the way he landed Maher. Fitz is cunning.... The faster the swings come the more closely he watches for a chance at the jaw. ... The faster his opponent goes the cooler Fitzsimmons becomes.... He will take punishment without a whimper or a sign of weakening. If his man is a mixer, he humors him into a close bit of work and drops him suddenly. If he is against a clever, elusive fellow he throws aside his caution and goes hunting him. ... That is what makes him so great. He adapts himself to his opponent's style of fighting and is so immeasurably superior that he bests the latter out at his own game.[29]

Another said,

> [Fitz] knows when, where and how to hit. He has a proper conception of the value of timing a man.... Fitz has no particular style.... No two of his fights appear to be alike. To the uninitiated he seems to be awkward and shambling, but there is a purpose in every ungainly move.

This writer described Jeffries as a man who lashed out and was a "free-arm fighter of the dashaway school.... He is also very handy with his right at the ribs. He gets beneath a difficult lead remarkably quick for a man so big and ponderous."[30]

Another assessment of the two fighters said,

[29] *National Police Gazette*, June 3, 10, 1899.
[30] *San Francisco Examiner*, June 9, 1899.

Fitz is like all great generals, as no two battles were ever fought exactly alike. … Fitz is a wonderful fighting machine, who is also shrewd to an unusual degree. He has a variety of shifts, which come perfectly natural to him, that fool the so-called clever boxers. …

Considered solely from the standpoint of physical construction, Jeffries is a marvelous man. … In fighting trim he strips at 220 pounds, and a more symmetrical man never got into a ring. … He has no hesitancy in expressing the opinion that he will win. He does it in no weak-kneed, half-hearted way, either; he says he will win in a manner which carries conviction with it. … Jeffries is a master of the left hand hook. … It is not generally known that Jeffries leads primarily with his left. His manipulation of that member is a study in itself. It is always ready and nine times out of ten when least expected. So deft is the Californian at left-handed punches that Tommy Ryan is often confused and seriously put out in his defense. … He has never known defeat. … He has never been hit with the right, or knocked down or fazed in the ring.

Although Jeffries would have a big weight advantage, Fitzsimmons was "just the sort of a puncher to check a big man." He had stopped Sharkey's rushes. Yet, "no one who has yet met the Los Angeles giant has succeeded in hurting him."[31]

On the morning of Monday June 5, Fitzsimmons hit the moving punching bag for 9 rounds. In the afternoon, Bob boxed 12 rounds with Dan Hickey, Jack Everhardt, and Yank Kenny. After a meal, he ran 6 miles. "His condition is absolutely perfect." Fitz said, "I am now in better condition than I ever was before. My course of training has been thorough and systematic. … I expect to win in short order."[32]

At one time, Professor Mike Donovan had sparred with or seen in action all of the champions: Sullivan, Corbett, and Fitzsimmons. He was an excellent prognosticator and judge of talent. Donovan observed Jeffries in training and was very impressed. He concluded that Jeffries was fast, clever, and a "marvel of physical strength and endurance." Donovan also said,

I have worked with and studied pugilists and pugilism since the time that big Mike McCool fought Joe Coburn for the championship, thirty-six years ago, and I don't hesitate to pronounce Jeffries the best, fastest and cleverest man of his size and weight I ever saw. … I had seen him once before when he sparred with his brother…and to compare the man as he was then with himself as he is now is to liken a dray horse to a thoroughbred. At that time he weighed 235 pounds, and was possessed only of the rudiments of boxing as a science. As he stands to-day, weighing 208 pounds, and stripped of every ounce of useless flesh, with the science of boxing drilled into him by capable instructors, he seems a perfect model of the heavyweight fighter.

[31] *National Police Gazette*, June 17, 1899
[32] *New York World*, June 6, 1899.

Next to McCool, I think he is the strongest man I ever saw in the ring.... [I]n this Californian great cleverness and speed are combined with the strength of a giant. Big men are generally slow...that is not the case here. ... From his actions in the bouts with his trainers he is a splendid judge of time and distance.

Donovan further said,

I had seen Fitzsimmons three days before, and had said that he was a fighting machine of the first degree...but with the ability of this man fresh before me I believe Fitz is lucky if he does not meet his Waterloo.... Fitzsimmons has no idea of what he is going up against. He imagines this fellow to be a big, unwieldy 210-pound man, totally lacking in science and one upon whom he can land when and where he chooses. He is mistaken, and...when he leaves the ring on Friday night he will be a sadder and a wiser man. I know size is not all, and that one punch in the right time and place will put the biggest man on earth to sleep, but this fellow has ideas of his own about avoiding those punches, and ideas just as good about giving them.

I had a long talk with Jeffries and was much impressed by his good sense and total lack of false pride. ... He showed his generosity by saving his sparring partners when he could have jolted them unmercifully. ... He is a plain, unassuming and sensible man. ...

Fitzsimmons's experience in his many years of fighting is a factor in his favor, but the youth and vigor of this young giant to some extent offsets that advantage. The undaunted courage and superb fighting qualities of both men will make this a battle worthy of the championship.[33]

Jeff opined that one of his famous left hooks would settle the champion.

As a novice I managed to land some good blows on Corbett, and Jim had no trouble getting in on Fitz.... My blows are harder than any Corbett delivered. ... Some people may laugh but I think I am just as clever as Fitz. They used to say I was slower than a truck horse, but I think they will change their minds when they see me in action. My work with Ryan has made me fast. In fact I'm so speedy on my feet that Ryan can't hit me, and he is pretty fast.

Bill Delaney said, "Every man who ever fought Jeffries with the exception of Peter Jackson, instead of fighting him ran away from him." Delaney said if anyone was going to run, it would be Fitzsimmons.[34]

[33] *New York World*, June 6, 1899. Another observer of Jeff's sparring said, "He put up a stiff battle with all of his trainers, and they were knocked out one after the other by a left hook. Daly received a flat knockdown." According to Jeff's autobiography, on the Monday before the fight, John L. Sullivan came to camp along with news reporters. They watched Jeff box 4 rounds each with Ryan, Jim Daly, and Jack Jeffries. John L. apparently proclaimed Jeff the next champion and said that he was the fastest big man he ever saw. *Two Fisted Jeff* at 100-101.
[34] *New York Journal, San Francisco Examiner*, June 5, 6, 1899.

Referee George Siler intended to meet with both pugilists during the week of the fight to discuss the rules. Siler noted that nothing in the Queensberry rules called for clean breaks. Straight rules meant hitting in the clinches and on the breaks. Hence the phrase, "Protect yourself at all times." However, the articles of agreement signed on February 10 called for a fight under Marquis of Queensberry rules with the exception that there should be no hitting in the clinches or breakaways, and they were to break clean upon the referee's order. Neither man could wear hand bandages. The gloves each boxer chose to wear had to be given to the referee 24 hours in advance of the fight. Jeff had unusually large hands and therefore was careful in selecting his mittens.

By the 5th, the odds in London were 3 to 2 on Bob, the favorite. He remained the 2 to 1 favorite in the United States.

Fitz's training on the morning of June 6 included running, boxing, and tossing the medicine ball. Bob hit the bag against the low board ceiling for 45 minutes, and his sparring partners went 3 rounds each. In the evening, he took the last of his long runs. Fitz was the biggest-looking alleged 158-pound man ever, if one believed he weighed that. "Nobody but Martin Julian has seen him weighed."

Julian said Fitzsimmons was a pleasure to train, because he did whatever his trainers ordered him to do. "He says he is too wise a man to play the part of his own lawyer."

Fitzsimmons was "as sure of victory as if his adversary was already prone before him." He was "trained to absolute perfection, where exertion is a pleasure and fatigue next to an impossibility." One observer called Fitz a marvel of physical fitness. "No human fighting machine was ever geared in better trim than Bob Fitzsimmons is to-day." Bob said he was tapering off in his work. The fight was only three days away.

After his training on the 6th, the confident Jeffries said, "Never for a second since I saw him win the championship at Carson City have I had the least doubt as to the outcome, should it ever be my fortune to meet him." Although Fitz had a reputation of being tricky, shifty, able to hit hard and take advantage of opportunities, Jeff still strongly believed that he would defeat him.

Jeffries was said to stand 6'1 ½" tall and weigh around 206 pounds, possibly more. Fitz was about 5'11 ½" and his weight was anyone's guess, but likely in the neighborhood of 170.

Analyzing the two combatants, the *New York Journal* said, "Both Fitzsimmons and Jeffries are fighters, pure and simple. They have science, of course, but when it comes down to bedrock, they are both sluggers. They calculate upon taking a blow in order to give one."[35]

The heat and humidity caused Fitz to do very little on the 7th. "The heat has been intolerable at the respective training quarters during the past few days." In the morning, he worked with the medicine ball for a few minutes and then punched the bag easily for several rounds. In the afternoon, Bob sparred 6 rounds in a half-hearted manner with Hickey, Kenny, and Everhardt. George Siler paid his official visit to Bob's camp to discuss the articles of agreement and the rules governing how the men were to fight.

On the 8th, Fitz took an alleged hour-long run. He then engaged in some light exercise, such as hitting the bag in a slow fashion, toying with the wrist machine, and sparring lightly with Hickey and Kenny. "The champion guards his weight with great secrecy, but his trainers think he will tip the beam in the neighborhood of 165 pounds."

Bob was wearing a bandage on his right arm, partly covering his elbow. "It will be remembered that this arm was injured in Chicago some months ago by Yank Kenny, whose powerful fist came in contact with Bob's elbow. …. Careful nursing and care have brought it into fairly good shape again."[36]

Responding to rumors that Bob was trained too fine, Martin Julian said Fitz was in wonderful condition and "has never been quicker or stronger than now."

Fitzsimmons said,

> I can truthfully say that I was never in better condition. … I have worked as hard as I did at Carson or for any of my other important battles. … I was certainly never more confident or in higher spirits. … I am only thirty-seven years old, my habits have always been good, and I feel at least ten years younger than I am. … I advise my friends to bet on me…. They will see me at my best, and they know what that is.[37]

---

[35] *New York Journal, New York World, New York Sun*, June 6, 7, 1899. On June 6, 1899, at the Lenox A.C., Bob Armstrong scored a KO2 over fellow black fighter Denver Ed Martin. Both men were tall, splendidly built, and weighed about 190 pounds.

[36] *New York Journal, New York Sun, New York World, Asbury Park Daily Press*, June 8, 9, 1899.

[37] *New York World*, June 9, 1899.

Bob also said, "There has been much talk about the title of champion going to an American. I was not born in this country, but I have adopted it. I reside here, my children were born here, and all of my money is invested here. I am as good an American at heart as any man and a good deal better than a lot of cheap alleged sporting men who are continually harping on my nationality."

When interviewed, Jeffries was just as confident.

> I am fit to fight for my life. If I lose it will not be for lack of training. But I don't mean to lose. I am certain that I will defeat Fitzsimmons. I am faster and stronger than I ever was, and I am not afraid of those famous wallops. ... All these other fellows Fitzsimmons has fought have hit him a good deal. Well, when I hit him, I'll hurt him.

A *New York World* reporter who had observed Jeffries in Carson City in Corbett's training camp said that he was a much-improved fighter.

> The Jim Jeffries of to-day and the Jim Jeffries of two years ago are as different as it is possible for two men to be. ... He has gained in speed and cleverness. I watched him this morning with the especial object of seeing how he compared with the Jeffries of two years ago who helped to train Jim Corbett at Carson City. I found him a very different man – a new man so far as knowledge of the game of fighting is concerned.

> At Carson City Jeffries weighed 225 pounds and looked strong enough to push a house over – if the house would stand and wait to be pushed. He was brisk in his foot work without being fast. ... Of course, he was going against Corbett then, a man who could make any one on earth look slow. ... He could whip across a right or left hook with great looseness of elbow motion, but he never lunged out a straight left lead or counter. ...

> Jeffries is a changed man to-day. He is down to 210 pounds and promises to go into the ring at 205. ... He used to look massive and burly. Now he looks big, strong and quick. Two years ago he was a bulky giant. To-day he is a trained athlete. It is doing him giant injustice to say that he is fifty per cent better than he was at Carson City. He is twice as good as he was on the night he fought Bob Armstrong.

This writer discussed his observations of Jeff's sparring. "Against Ryan, Jeffries came in crouching with his head held well to the right and with his right hand open guarding the jaw. The clever style in which Jeffries came in was very different from the awkward trot he used a couple of years ago. His left foot steadily advanced, the right following it up step by step." Jeff blocked and countered blows nicely. "Jeffries's left shoulder was loose and easy – nothing muscle-bound about it." As opposed to just swinging, Jeff jabbed and lunged in with his left, "something he never did in any one of the sixteen days I watched him work at Carson City." Jeff kept coming in and never broke ground, reminding the writer of John L. Sullivan.

After sparring with Tommy Ryan, both Jack Jeffries and Jim Daly took turns with Jeff for 3 rounds each. Neither could land, and Jeff just grinned, toying with them, except for one time when he landed a right under the heart which made his brother Jack gasp and reel.

> To sum up: Jeffries has a pretty good left anywhere and a mighty good right jolt for the body. His footwork is not brilliant but it is much improved over what it was two years ago. He seems quite as fast on his feet as Fitzsimmons is. He has an awkward head to get at. The way he carries it doesn't look pretty, but it is very hard to land there.
>
> Jeffries's greatest quality is his strong, steady, patient courage. When he was Corbett's sparring partner at Carson City he never gave ground. Many a time I have seen Corbett left hook him on the jaw and send him reeling against the wall. Every time Jeffries pulled himself together, gathered his legs under him and rushed in on Corbett, looking for more. That's the kind of man who cannot be beaten while he is able to move a hand. It seems to me that Fitzsimmons will find in Jeffries's youth, great size and strength, improved form, and dauntless courage a very hard combination to fight.[38]

The night before the fight, both men handed referee George Siler their choice of 5-ounce gloves.

Bob was very reluctant to prove his weight. "It is a settled fact that Bob will not go on the scales at the clubhouse so as to let the public know how much he weighs. He contends that this is his own business, and as long as the fight is for heavyweight honors he is not compelled to announce the figures." Of course, if he was not willing to prove it, then the writers did not have to believe him either.

Regardless of size, Fitzsimmons remained a 2 to 1 favorite. Kid McCoy believed that Jeffries could not win. "Fitzsimmons is one of the greatest fighters the world has ever seen, and the man to get a decision over him must be a phenomenon." McCoy said that as soon as Fitz landed a good blow, it would be the beginning of the end.

On the other hand, James J. Corbett, who could be fickle, switched his pick to Jeffries. He said the odds were false, and he would be betting on Jeff, the underdog. "Fitzsimmons is the best ring general, but Jeffries is the strongest man and should win."

> I honestly think Jeffries will win and win easily. He is a greater fighter than the public gives him credit for being…. Jeffries is remarkably fast for a man his size, and I know from experience he can hit as hard as any man in the world. If he ever lands on Fitzsimmons it will be all

[38] *New York World*, June 9, 1899.

over, and it will only take one blow to do the trick. … The Californian is one of the most underrated boxers in the ring to-day. I believe he can defeat any man in the profession. … [W]ithin the last year Jeffries's improvement has been remarkable. He is exceedingly fast, has two good hands and is fairly clever.

When I used to box with Jeffries he was a novice, but even then he showed signs of good foot-work. He is now a shifty fighter, capable of holding his own with any of the top notchers.[39]

Another quoted Corbett as saying,

The people don't know Jeffries. He can hit, and when he hits he stings. He is a real slugger. Along with being a slugger Jeffries is a very fast man. For a heavyweight – very fast indeed. Now, mind you, no one has ever accused Fitzsimmons of being fast, and neither is he. He is purely a slugger, and a mighty good one, too. He is not as good a slugger as is Jeffries, and is not near so fast. Why, I hit Fitz – well, the Lord only knows how many times. If I had Jeffries' great strength I would have simply butchered Fitzsimmons. … Now, Jeff will hit Fitz about as often as I did, and he will have his powerful strength back of his blows.

When asked if he thought Jeffries was as fast as he was, Corbett replied, "I think he is pretty close to it, and he is a very much harder hitter than I ever was."

Sam Fitzpatrick said Jeffries would knock out Fitzsimmons within 7 rounds. "I give Fitz every credit. He is a wonderful man, sure. But he has got to lick this man quick. If he doesn't, he is gone. … Jeffries is a fast heavyweight – a bit faster than Fitz. He is a harder puncher, too. When he hits he hurts. He will hit Fitz. You may depend upon that." Sam also said, "Jeffries has youth and science. He will have a 45-pound weight advantage. That wouldn't count for much if it were not for the speed behind it."

Tommy Ryan said,

I never saw a fighter improve so much as Jeffries within so short a time. He is very clever and shifty for a big fellow, and he will make a great fight. … If Fitzsimmons mixes it with Jeffries, the Californian will win sure. … I have sparred both, and I have seen them fight, so I think I know what I am talking about. Fitz won't have an easy time of it trying to feint Jeffries into a righthand blow or a knockout. Jim is naturally left-handed and he can use that member well. Most of my time when sparring with Jeffries has been devoted to feinting, and he has always handled himself well.

He is a bit cunning himself, and will show Fitz a trick or two that will be very interesting. I have pounded him hard while training and he never flinched once.

[39] *New York Sun, New York Journal*, June 8, 1899.

Professor Mike Donovan said,

> There never has been as fast a heavyweight who has the strength of Jeffries. He is the best fighter, the fastest and strongest I have ever seen. He could have whipped Sullivan any day of Sullivan's life. … I believe now that no matter how good [Peter] Jackson was this man [Jeffries] would have beaten him. … I like the champion; he is a good fellow and a great fighter, but he cannot beat this fellow, I tell you.

> Jeffries knows and uses more effective blows than any heavyweight I have ever seen. He is the strongest man that ever boxed, and I repeat I have seen them all.[40]

The *New York Clipper* opined that Fitzsimmons would win.

> Fitzsimmons, on the strength of his greater experience, and series of uninterrupted and brilliant successes within the ropes, naturally enough has the biggest following among those who are putting their spare cash on the issue, odds of 2 to 1 having so far been easily obtainable; nevertheless, there is considerable money behind Jeffries, and he will doubtless be well supported until after the battle is under way…for, with all his powerful physique, advantages in weight, height, and presumably in strength, it is pretty certain to be quickly seen that superior skill, generalship, experience, coolness and hitting power will combine to indicate the ungainly but ever-to-be-depended-upon Fitz as the eventual winner.[41]

Analyzing Fitzsimmons, another writer said that on several occasions, he had turned apparent defeat into victory, having kept opponents away when they might have finished him. Bob was a clever and dangerous man at all stages of a fight, for just one of his punches could end a contest at any time.

As the fight approached, issues threatened the bout. Earlier, the Coney Island Sporting Club had struggled to obtain a license, which had delayed the contest from May 26 to June 9. Due to the inter-club inter-borough rivalry, forces were at work to frustrate and prevent the bout from taking place at Coney Island.

Despite the fact that Fitz was the odds favorite, on June 6, Police Chief Devery said that considering the weights of 210 pounds to 156 pounds, he believed it was impossible for them to carry out a lawful contest, and, if there was any slugging or heavy hitting, he would stop the bout and arrest them. The Horton Act had legalized boxing, but nevertheless the police could interfere. Devery also said that he would terminate the contest upon the first heavy blow struck.

New York had enjoyed all sorts of fights at the Lenox, Broadway, Greenwood, and Pelican athletic clubs for two years without any police interference. Devery had seen many hard-hitting boxing contests and had not interfered. Therefore, shock was expressed at his statements and

[40] *Buffalo Times,* June 8, 1899.
[41] *New York Clipper,* June 10, 1899.

inconsistent position. "Chief Devery saw the McCoy-Sharkey fight, which was one of the hardest and fastest battles that ever took place, and he did not interfere." Bill Brady said, "As the Police Board has licensed our club I expect the same treatment from Chief Devery as he has accorded to other clubs."

It was clear that Devery had ulterior motives. "Some such obstacle to the successful completion of this big match has been looked for by those who believe they are in touch with the 'inside situation' in local pugilism. ... There has been grumbling on the part of certain politicians interested in fighting at the Lenox and Broadway clubs" ever since the Coney Island Club had secured the match. Thus, Devery, who had allowed a number of slugging matches to be fought without interference, was suddenly having a change in policy.

The press suspected that Chief Devery was trying to use his power to have the fight transferred to the Manhattan Borough, where the police had permitted several knockouts. Fitz's manager Martin Julian said, "It is very queer that Chief Devery should suddenly become so anxious about the law…. We expected something like this because of the effort that was made to prevent the Coney Island Club from getting a license."

One reporter noted that the Horton law was "a remarkably hard law to violate." It required that the boxers wear gloves weighing not less than 5 ounces, and the bouts had to be a limited number of rounds (up to 25). Formal decisions were allowed. The statute did not put any check on brutality. However, the police, "having full power to preserve the peace…can do about as they please." Devery observed that the law allowed "sparring" matches, not slugging. However, "If Chief Devery lets fights proceed unmolested at the Lenox and Broadway clubs, there is no good reason why he should not follow the same policy toward the Coney Island Club."

It was thought that Brady's political friends in Kings County would be heard from again, as they had been with the license issue, and would see to it that Devery did not interfere. "The Brooklyn politicians say that if big fights are permitted by Devery in Manhattan there must be no discrimination against Coney Island."

In the end, on the day of the fight, "big guns" in Brooklyn political matters confirmed that only the referee would stop the fight. Apparently, Devery had been called off. It was noted that he had changed his tone a bit the day before the fight. The fight was on.[42]

Another aspect of the bout that bothered some was the fact that it was revealed that the purse split was agreed-upon before the fight took place. Corbett noted that the purse would be divided between the combatants beforehand, as had been done in his own fights. Because the public might be upset and suspect a hippodrome/fake/fix, "The exact divisions of the purse can never be stipulated in the articles of agreement." Despite the articles of agreement saying that the winner was to take all, apparently the

---

[42] *New York Sun, San Francisco Chronicle, New York Daily Tribune, New York Herald,* June 7 - 9, 1899.

purse was $25,000, with 60% going to Fitzsimmons, win or lose. Jeffries initially was reluctant to admit it, saying that it was nobody's business, Corbett should mind his own business, the purse was not being split, and the fight would be on the level. Of course, he later admitted to the pre-set purse-split assuring Fitz of the big share of the purse, win or lose. It was a worthwhile investment. Of course, today, pre-set splits are typical; but back then, such was viewed with some suspicion.[43]

The *National Police Gazette's* writer offered a final analysis and prediction in Jeffries' favor.

> In my opinion Fitzsimmons is not going to have such a walkover as the records of the two men would seem to indicate. He has the fight of his life on his hands this time, and although he affects to treat the Californian's pretensions with disdain he has reason to feel a wholesome respect of his opponent's ability… I am inclined now to favor the probability of Jeffries being returned a winner. I saw him at work the other day, a great, big, strong, healthy, ambitious fellow, who knows no limit of endurance, who labors earnestly, courageously and conscientiously… His confidence in himself impressed me. … Argued from a rational, unprejudiced standpoint, everything is in his favor. He has youth, strength, height, reach, and pounds to his advantage. He may be a bit deficient compared with Fitz in knowledge of ring tactics, but it must be remembered that over two years have elapsed since Fitz has engaged in a fight, and a pugilist's knowledge of the requirements of his calling is not as keen after a long period of inactivity as it would be compared with that of a man who has had frequent opportunities to keep in practice. Jeffries has had eight fights in the interim since Fitz stood up in the ring with Corbett. …
>
> Jeffries is really a clever boxer and knows how to protect himself in a manner which will make Fitz wonder how to reach him with a damaging blow, while at the same time Jeffries, who hits equally well with either hand, and is quick, shifty and clever, may be depended upon to do his share of the fighting.
>
> It is doubtful if Fitzsimmons will enter the ring as superbly trained as he was on that eventful day at Carson City when he wrested the championship laurels from Jim Corbett. He will have to be quite as good if not better than he was then, and that seems impossible in view of the long period in which he has been in retirement. Fitz has not been as abstemious in his habits, either, as he was before he donned Corbett's mantle. … He has a big contract on his hands to defeat Jeffries, and as I said before nobody knows it better than himself.[44]

[43] *New York Daily Tribune, New York Sun*, June 8, 1899; *New York Herald*, June 9, 1899; *National Police Gazette*, June 3, 1899.
[44] *National Police Gazette*, June 17, 1899.

CHAPTER 3

A Battle Worthy of the Championship

On the eve and day of the world heavyweight championship fight, the newsmen, experts, and participants all rendered their final thoughts and analysis. Bob Fitzsimmons was certain that he would whip James Jeffries. The champion had never been given to excesses, and "I am in perfect shape." Bob said that if he could fight the version of himself which existed ten years ago, the version of today would defeat the version of yesteryear.

Jeffries said,

> That Fitzsimmons is the greatest fighter of years must be admitted. His performances warrant the belief that he is the hardest hitter that the fighting world has ever known. In his battles he has displayed remarkable skill and pluck, and for all of this I think he is entitled to great credit. At the same time I think tonight I will succeed where others failed. …
>
> Fitz can drop me with a punch on the jaw if it lands right. But when I get in the ring I'll do my best to keep away from such a punch and at the same time land a few hot ones myself. Other fighters have hit Fitz and had him groggy. Corbett had him going in the sixth round at Carson. I think I can put him out if I get over a good wallop and put it on right. Depend upon it that there'll be a real hot fight, no matter who wins. …
>
> I must say that I am not pleased with the rules. Straight Marquis of Queensberry would suit me better. But as I was anxious to fight for the championship, I accepted the changes on which Fitzsimmons insisted.[45]

Although straight Queensberry rules allowed hitting in clinches and on breaks, Fitz had wanted no punching in clinches and only clean breaks. Jeffries disliked the clause. However, as will be discussed, the rules eventually were changed on the night of the fight.

On the day of the fight, the *New York Journal* said,

> Jeffries is today the fastest and most scientific fighter who ever entered the ring at that weight. He will weigh 210 pounds. That will be fifteen pounds lighter than he ever entered the ring before. He weighed nearly 230 when he fought Armstrong. … He has been blessed with the handiest left hand ever hitched to a heavyweight. …

---

[45] *New York Journal, New York Sun*, June 9, 1899.

Jeffries's left hand knows the hooks, the jabs and the jolts perfectly. He feints savagely and with startling speed. His feet have improved until now he moves about like a shifty lightweight. His eye is wonderfully quick, and no matter how fast they come, he never blinks. His foot work resembles both Corbett's and Ryan's. He shifts about continually, is not obliged to set before he hits, and will never be caught flat-footed. ... Jeffries will likely have fifty pounds the better of the weight. He has never been knocked down or dazed in his life. He can stand more punishment than any man Fitzsimmons has ever fought, and he will give more.[46]

The fact that Jeff had handled the power of Joe Choynski and Tom Sharkey, and made these two fighters box and move when against all others they usually had attacked and mixed it up, was a sign that Fitz would have a tough time overpowering him. Jeffries had wonderful strength and stamina. Corbett again called the 2 to 1 odds in Fitz's favor ridiculous, saying that Jeff's chances were a lot better than that.

However, to most, it looked like a Fitzsimmons victory. He had a wonderful record of knockouts obtained by one terrific punch landed on a vital spot. He was rugged, powerful, and capable of standing any roughing that Jeff could give him. He had done a lot of experimenting in sparring with Kenny, who weighed as much as Jeffries did. Bob was a great ring general, a schemer, quick-witted, shrewd, and full of tricks. "For this reason Jeffries will have to fight him warily until he believes he has the Cornishman's measure." Jeff would be able to do so because of his reach.

Jeffries has such a tremendous reach that it will not be at all surprising to see him fight Fitz with left-hand jabs from the start, reserving his right-hand swings until later on. The boilermaker has been practicing defensive tactics more than attack, and believes that he can keep Fitz off. The latter is expected to force the fight from the start. In such an event it is believed that Jeffries will stand away and try to 'jab his block off.'[47]

Both were hard hitters, but Fitz had superior experience. Both were clever, but Fitz was cleverer. He was shiftier and quicker. Jeff had advantages in weight, height, reach, youth, physical strength, and perhaps ability to absorb punishment, having never been down.

Although both were confident, neither took personal cuts at the other. "A satisfactory feature of the whole affair is the absence of mud-slinging." Fitz and Corbett had insulted each other, using such terms as "cur," "yellow dog," "quitter," "stiff," "dub," and "hamfatter." Jeff had won friends by refraining from indulging in personal attacks. "It was that trait in Jeffries which helped to increase his popularity."

[46] New York Journal, June 9, 1899.
[47] New York Sun, June 9, 1899.

In his first autobiography, Jeff claimed that he was dried out, and his weight lower than it had been for any other fight before or since. He had trained harder than ever but also had dehydrated himself.

> When I came East to meet Armstrong I weighed just 245 pounds stripped to fighting togs in the ring. Now, ready to meet Fitzsimmons, I scaled exactly 204 pounds. I had run myself to a shadow. Two days before the fight I weighed just 206 pounds stripped, and let everybody around the camp see me on the scales. The day before the fight I went with a number of reporters to the baggage room at the railroad station. There on the baggage scales, in jumpers and a light sweater, I weighed an even 215 pounds. I never attempted to make such low weight again, as I know I'm stronger and have more endurance when I carry forty pounds more flesh on my bones.[48]

There is primary source support for Jeff's dehydration claims. In the days after the fight, Jeff told one reporter, "I can't get enough water. I haven't drunk any water for two weeks, and I could hardly sleep for my thirst. But they said it weakened me, and I was determined I wouldn't drink." Just imagine how much better Jeff might have been if he had not dehydrated himself and bought into the falsehood that drinking water hampered performance. Today, we know that quite the opposite is true. Lack of water adversely affects performance.[49]

The day before the fight, it was said that Jeffries would tip the scales at about 206 pounds. "In spite of the talk that Fitz will not be over 158 pounds, it is asserted that when the champion got upon the scales Wednesday [June 7] he weighed 170 ½ pounds. He has steadfastly refused to tell his weight and says he will not go on the scales to weigh in tomorrow." Often, fighters took on several pounds in the last couple days before a fight, because they did not train as hard. However, some actually lost weight as a result of restricting fluid intake.[50]

On the day of the fight, the *New York Herald* listed Jeff as 6'1½" and 206 pounds. Other local papers said Jeff weighed 215, while others estimated that he would enter the ring weighing between 210 and 212 pounds. W. W. Naughton estimated that Fitz would be 165 pounds. The *New York Journal* listed the 5'11 ¾" Fitz's fighting weight at 171 pounds. Bob insisted that he weighed 158 pounds. However,

> This is not credited by the sporting fraternity. They believe he will weigh at least twelve pounds heavier. It was stated on reliable authority today that Fitzsimmons weighed 170 ½ pounds, and men in the know declared that Fitzsimmons's fighting weight would not be less than 171 pounds.

[48] *My Life and Battles* at 31.
[49] *New York Journal*, June 12, 1899.
[50] *San Francisco Chronicle*, *New York Sun*, June 9, 1899. Another report said that "it is learned from a most trustworthy source that when the champion got upon the scales on Wednesday he weighed 170 ½ pounds."

Jeffries was weighed in his clothes before he left his training quarters. He tipped the scales at 223 pounds. "I will weigh 215 pounds stripped," he remarked. ... "Tomorrow morning I expect to be champion of the world."[51]

The reality is at that time, no official weigh-in was required for any heavyweight contest, because there was no minimum or maximum weight. Hence, their weights simply cannot be and were not confirmed officially. There always is a certain amount of speculation regarding weights in heavyweight contests in the pre- official weigh-in era.

On Friday June 9, 1899 at Coney Island, New York, over two years after he won the title, 36-year-old heavyweight champion Bob Fitzsimmons defended his crown for the first time, against 24-year-old James J. Jeffries.[52]

Tickets were quite expensive for the time: $5 for the first-come first-served seats, reserved seats being $10, $15, $20, and $25, with boxes holding six people each for $150.

That evening, those who could not afford tickets would be able to come to the Broadway Athletic Club, which would receive live telegraph wires during the fight. Two men would illustrate the bout, throwing the described blows at each other.[53]

A huge crowd of damp, steaming people stood in the pouring summer rain for hours to buy the high-priced tickets, demonstrating that "the boxing game is at its height in this country and that a set of boxing gloves and a 24-foot ring will not only get the dollars of the sporting men but the good coin of the day laborer, as well." Every large city from San Francisco to New York was represented. "It is safe to say that the assemblage was the most representative one which ever sat around a ring."

The "strangest thing of all was the great interest the women took in the affair, from the outside, of course." One-third of the crowd outside the arena was composed of women, "many of whom would have liked nothing better than to have paid some of their money as entrance fees." However, no women were allowed inside, other than Bob's wife. "There was a great crowd outside composed of those who wouldn't or couldn't pay, and who were content, apparently, to be at least near the place where a great fistic battle was taking place."

At 6:30 p.m., the arena doors were opened. The $5 crowd rushed in, because their seats were first-come, first-served. The building was a large amphitheater, "probably the largest of its kind in America." It was a "vast, roughly finished building, destitute of interior paint or ornamentation; a mere great frame, which has been rebuilt for the purposes of ring entertainments." It was oblong in shape and located on the beach, within 50 yards of the surf. Large windows around the sides and in the roof let in a

---

[51] *New York Herald, San Francisco Examiner, New York Journal,* June 9, 1899; *New York Daily Tribune,* June 10, 1899.
[52] The following accounts and quotes are the product of an amalgamation of the *New York Herald, New York Daily Tribune, New York Times, New York Journal, New York Sun, New York World, Brooklyn Daily Eagle, Brooklyn Standard Union, Brooklyn Citizen, Asbury Park Daily Press, San Francisco Chronicle, San Francisco Examiner,* all June 10, 1899, as well as *New York Clipper,* June 17, 1899; *National Police Gazette,* June 24, 1899; *My Life and Battles* at 35-36. Jim Corbett wrote the *New York World* report.
[53] *New York World,* June 5, 1899.

cool breeze. The arena was well arranged, although some spectators were annoyed by being seated behind the machine erected for taking motion pictures of the contest. The telegraph operators sat in a gallery high above. The police were close to the ring.

Directly above the ring was a scaffolding extending around the four sides. Upon this scaffolding were 24 electric calcium light reflectors, which would send a great glare of light into the ring. There were also 25 arc lights strung about in prominent places. All of these lights were designed to facilitate the taking of the motion pictures. Two film machines were shrouded in rubber covers.

At 7:00 p.m., all of the $5 seats were taken, and nearly all of the best reserved chairs had been purchased.

At 8:00 p.m., the electric reflectors were suddenly turned on, and the glare was so blinding that everyone shouted. One person said, "Put your hats on or you'll get sunstroke." The lights were quickly turned off, the operators pronouncing them to be all right.

By 8:30 p.m., at least 8,000 people present, and they were still coming. Although the seating capacity was 8,442, with the eventual overcrowding of the bleachers and those who jammed their way into the boxes and aisles, it was thought that 10,000 were present by the time the boxers entered the ring. Every seat was taken, and all available space covered in humanity. Another 5,000 or more were unable to get in but would have purchased tickets had they been allowed to do so.

The gate receipts were the largest of all time. Estimates ranged from $65,000 to $70,000 to $100,000 taken in. This beat Sullivan-Corbett, which drew $52,000, Corbett-Sharkey II at $47,000, and Corbett-Fitzsimmons at $44,000. Bob's strategy of waiting to make a big fight, creating demand for his services, and negotiating for the big end of the purse had paid off.

Fitzsimmons had been sleeping from 7 to 8 p.m. at Bath Beach. Eventually, his team drove two and a half miles to the arena. He entered the building at 9:20 p.m. and went to his private room.

At 9:30 p.m., accompanied by his trainers, Jeffries entered the building. He was wearing a black-and-red-striped sweater and long trousers. His hair was long and uncombed, and his skin was well bronzed by the sun at the seashore. As Jeff passed by, Corbett shook his hand and wished him well. Jeff proceeded to his dressing room. Both Fitz and Jeff appeared confident.

By fight time, Fitzsimmons was the favorite at 2 to 1 and 5 to 3 odds. "That Fitzsimmons was a favorite with the majority was evident from the talk." He had a knack for winning his big battles against bigger men. Bob's strength, punching power, skill, experience, and generalship were expected to win it for him. He was the real magnet, although the way that Jeffries had taken off 30 pounds and worked so hard in training had won him a lot of public confidence.

In his autobiographies, Jeffries claimed that on the night of the fight, Bill Brady told him that he wanted to try to shake Bob's confidence. Brady would intentionally get into a debate about the rules regarding clinching and breaking. He instructed Jeff to grab Bill, throw him aside, ask Bob how he wanted to fight, and then to grab Fitz and rough him a bit to show him just how strong he was, to intimidate him and shake his confidence. That evening, Jeff did just that. As they were debating the rules, he grabbed Brady by the collar and jerked him toward the corner of the room so hard that he spun around and fell. Jeff said, "You talk too much." He then asked Bob how he wanted to fight, and viciously shoved Bob back halfway across the room. Fitz said, "Straight rules. ... We'll protect ourselves at all times."

Jeffries held contradictory opinions about the impact of their ploy. At one time, he said that although he believed his display shook Bob's confidence, Bob still fought like a "cornered wild cat. He was the gamest man in the world. ... I learned to respect him as the best man I'd ever seen. It's a respect that lasts even today." However, Jeff later wrote, "Some thought that display of strength intimidated Fitzsimmons, but I do not. He was not that kind of a man. Nothing I ever saw bothered him excepting a hard punch on the jaw. But it caused him to change his demands regarding the rules."[54]

[54] *Two Fisted Jeff* at 106-107; *My Life and Battles* at 35.

The primary sources support Jeff's version of events. A couple of days after the fight, Jeffries said,

> Did you hear of the job Brady put up on Fitz? About twenty minutes before the fight Brady fixed it for me to meet Fitz face to face. The idea was for me to show him I wasn't afraid of his looks, or maybe to throw a scare into him, if you want to put it that way.
>
> We met in the dressing-room. I gave him a good, hard look. Brady said to Fitz: 'How do you want to fight?' Then along I came, as if by accident. 'Now, how do you want to fight?' I said to him, and with that I bumped up against him and shoved him clear down to the other end of the dressing-room.
>
> Well, you ought to have seen the look of surprise that lit on Fitz's face. He thought I would be paralyzed by one look at him. His eyes stuck out after he reached the other end of the room. I guess he was satisfied then that there was no scare in me.[55]

Both the *National Police Gazette* and the *New York Sun* discussed this pre-fight debate. It took place while various offers and challenges were being announced in the arena, just before the fight. In the dressing room at the back of the building, behind the bleachers, Fitzsimmons, Julian, Brady, and Jeffries indulged in an argument over the rules. Jeffries wanted straight Marquis of Queensberry rules, with hitting in the clinches and on the breakaway, while Fitz insisted on no hitting in clinches, and a clean break.

> This argument was kept up for more than twenty minutes, the crowd in the meanwhile stamping and whistling and calling for the fight to begin. ... The wrangle between the fighters was finally settled in this way: If both men were holding, the referee was to go between them. If one man was holding with both hands, the other could fight himself free.

Hence, the rules were slightly modified. Ultimately, though, the fight descriptions gave the impression that the men fought with clean breaks and no hitting in the clinches.

At 10:10 p.m., clad from head to foot in a long blue bathrobe, Fitzsimmons appeared and walked toward the 24-foot ring. Martin Julian carried a six-foot-high floral horseshoe composed of roses, with the inscription, "Good Luck to the Champion." Dan Hickey, Yank Kenny, and Jack Everhardt also accompanied him. Julian held the horseshoe aloft inside the ring. Upon Bob's ring entry, Corbett said, "He looks about the same as he has always looked in the ring."

Only a minute behind Fitz, Jeffries, wearing a garnet sweater and dark trousers with suspenders, climbed through the ropes, and the house went wild over him. Bill Delaney, Jack Jeffries, Jim Daly, and Tommy Ryan attended him.

[55] *New York World*, June 11, 1899.

Referee George Siler then entered, coatless and collarless, wearing a negligee shirt, with suspenders holding up his trousers. He was a small man, especially in comparison with the fighters.

As the boxers got ready, more challenges were announced. Kid McCoy challenged Fitz to a fight at middleweight. Tom Sharkey challenged the winner.

At this time, with the men in their respective corners, the glaring lights were turned on with a great sizzle. "The ring fairly glistened from the rays." However, Corbett was the first to prophesize that something might be wrong with the lighting and/or filming process. "I wonder what's the matter with the photographing machine. Half the lights are out; still the ring is just as brightly lighted as if it was daylight."

Siler explained the rules and noted that it was a scheduled 25-round bout. Most experts expected a relatively short contest, given that both men could punch.

Jeffries was first to strip. "His magnificent physique was looked at in wonderment. He was a giant and no mistake. He was taller, bigger, heavier, and stronger looking in every way than Fitz." He wore white trunks. "His training at the seashore had bronzed him like an Indian, and his muscular development was wonderful." Corbett said, "By George, he has enormous legs! See how Fitz is looking over at him. ... Great Scott, but he's enormous!"

Fitzsimmons removed his bathrobe. Corbett said, "He looks well. He looks great. He looks very big. I never saw him better." Bob wore black trunks with a belt of small American flags.

The fighters' weights were a point of some debate. The *Herald* said Jeff looked about 212. Corbett said Jeff weighed a trifle more than 200. One reporter said, "Fitz looked to be about 170 pounds in weight, while Jeffries was easily 206." The *Times* listed Jeff as 6'1½" and about 225. The *Sun* said Jeff would tip the scales at about 206 pounds, the lowest he had trained down to in his career. Earlier that day, Jeff had admitted that he would weigh about 215 pounds in the ring.

One wrote, "Jeffries, judging by appearances, certainly weighed considerably more than two hundred pounds, while Fitz could not have weighed less than one hundred and sixty. Neither man wished the truth to be known." The *National Police Gazette* said,

> One thing which puzzled the sports was the respective weights of the men, and while it was confidently believed that Fitz would fight in the neighborhood of 170 pounds and Jeffries somewhere about 205 yet no one except the trainers knew what the weights really were. This was an item of interest which will probably never go on record, and all that will be known was that the men fought at their best weights.

In the ring, when Fitzsimmons claimed to weigh 157 pounds, Jeffries humorously/sarcastically replied, "If Fitz weighs 157, I weigh 148." In his autobiography, Jeff said Fitzsimmons appeared to be bigger and stronger than he did in Carson City back in 1897. Neither man weighed in officially, so we'll never know for sure.

The boxers shook hands and began the fight at 10:24 p.m.

1st round

This was a feeling-out round, with no damage done. They sparred cautiously, each feinting warily for an opening. Jeffries kept his position with his body bent towards the right, with his left held out, feinting often with the left. Corbett said, "Notice how low Jeff is crouching and how far out he has his left." Fitz smiled and backed away as Jeff approached, but neither led with any blows for a while. Neither was anxious to get down to business too quickly. They had a potential 25 rounds of work ahead.

Jeffries was more aggressive, but either his blows fell short or were blocked. Fitz was good at sidestepping, dodging, and moving away, coming back again, grinning. It was evident that Jeff's appearance made Bob respect him. Fitzsimmons was on the move, keeping out of harm's way, but the smiling Jeff did not run after him. Jeff followed him around but was quick to jump back at Bob's feints. When Bob punched, he found it difficult to penetrate Jeff's crouching defense. Both were cautious.

Fitz tried a light left but Jeff ducked and clinched. They broke and feinted again. Jeff kept trying his left jab for the body, but Fitz kept stepping back. Jeff threw a left hook, but Bob jumped away. Fitz blocked another hook and they clinched. Bob showed his strength by pushing Jeff away, even though he looked small next to the Californian. Both landed lefts to the nose. Fitz tried a right, but Jeff got inside of it very handily. Fitz stepped back and swung a left, but Jeff ducked and clinched, smiling. "Now you notice he throws Fitz away as easily as if Fitz was a boy." Bob's blows mostly missed or were grazing as Jeff ducked, but he did land a few to the nose and mouth, which did no harm. Jeff landed one good left uppercut.

The *Journal* and *Daily Tribune* both called the round even. The *Examiner* said the round was a shade in Jeff's favor. Corbett said both appeared nervous, but he felt that Jeff was doing well. The *Sun* said it was Fitz's round, for he landed the most blows. Outside the arena, when the mob asked how the fight was going, the answer came back, "Fitz is killing him." The crowd, which was mostly pro-Jeffries, became downcast. Of course, the report was in error, as the round had been fairly tame.

2nd round

Jeffries seemed more at ease, crouching low and hiding his face behind his guard arm. Fitz threw some lefts, but Jeff ducked them and stepped in with heavy rights to the body. The crowd cheered with delight. When Jeff came in again, Bob clinched. Jeffries showed his great strength by pushing Fitzsimmons off with ease.

After sparring, Jeff landed a short right to the body, left to the ribs, and then right to the body again. Corbett said, "Jeff is doing well." Fitz began making the pace, throwing some hard blows, but Jeff eluded them and kept Bob off. Jeff sent a left hook to the belly but missed two lefts to the head as

Bob jumped back. Fitz bluffed with his left and swung his right for the head, but his distance was off. Jeff rushed again and shoved Fitz fully 12 feet across the ring.

Jeffries became aggressive, landing a number of quick left jabs to the body and face in succession. A left to Bob's nose brought first blood, trickling down in a tiny stream. Bill Brady called out his claim of first blood, which typically was a betting point, and referee Siler nodded in acknowledgment. Jeff bluffed with his left at the head and instead landed a good right on the head. Fitz laughed.

Fitzsimmons feinted and advanced with a left, but Jeff immediately countered by dashing in with a perfectly timed quick and powerful straight left to the nose and jaw that caught Bob coming toward him and knocked Fitzsimmons down onto his back in his own corner. The excited crowd yelled like mad at the surprise knockdown.

The champion quickly rose after being down for only two seconds. He smiled and acted as if he considered it a joke. Mrs. Fitzsimmons said, "Corbett did that too, but he did not win. One knockdown don't win a fight. Just wait until the end."

After rising, the angered Fitzsimmons attacked and tried to mix it up. He forced Jeff back by swinging both hands, but Jeffries avoided him by dancing away and cleverly blocking the blows with his arms, smiling at the champion's unsuccessful efforts. The bell rang soon thereafter.

Bob looked to all four corners of the ring before locating his own. It was evident that the knockdown had dazed him a bit. He seemed unsteady when he went to his corner. It was a "decidedly bad round" for Fitzsimmons. However, Bob told his cornermen, "It's all right. I am not hurt."

In his autobiography, Jeff said that after dropping Fitz, although he thought of trying to finish, his brother Jack told him to be careful. "That fellow is most dangerous when hurt. Look out for some trick." Jeff remained cautious, not wanting to fall into a trap.[56]

3rd round

In the corner between rounds, Tommy Ryan told Jeff to go for the body with his right and to fire his left at the head with jabs and hooks. Referee Siler later said that Jeff followed his corner's advice and landed often. "Some of course, were light, and Fitz, thinking he had no steam, did all the advancing."

At the start of the round, Bob's nostrils were bloody. Jeff landed a left squarely upon the nose. Bob clinched, laughed and pushed Jeff away. Blood ran down from Bob's nose in a stream. Jeff laughed back at him.

Bob missed a left and right for the head because Jeff got away as quickly as a cat. Jeff ducked under a left lead and clinched. After breaking, Jeff landed his left on the nose. They both rushed and landed lefts to the jaw. After clinching, Jeff threw Fitz away. Jeff rushed him and landed twice to

---

[56] *Two Fisted Jeff* at 108-113.

the cheek. As Bob threw a right, Jeff stepped inside of it so that it missed. Jeff landed his left on the ribs and followed with his right on the other side. Bob landed a left to the body, but Jeff came back with a right on the ribs. To the body, Jeff landed a left jab and left hook. Fitz closed in but as they came to a clinch, Jeff landed an awful right over the heart. In the clinch, some of Bob's blood ran onto Jeff's shoulder. At that point, Corbett opined, "Barring accidents, barring a punch like I got, it looks as if Jeff ought to win inside of ten rounds."

Fitz looked a bit worried, but nevertheless, or as a result, he began forcing the pace. He tried to mix it, but Jeff blocked with both hands and clinched, smiling while there. After breaking, Fitz feinted Jeff into ducking and then hooked his jaw hard with the left. Jeff laughed as he straightened up. He rushed in and Bob clinched. After breaking, Bob struck Jeff's forehead with the same hook. Jeff coolly got to close quarters and landed a left and right to the stomach.

Fitzsimmons rushed in again with a very hard left hook. Bob tried rushing tactics, hitting his man hard and often, particularly with his left, but seldom without return. Jeff was very fast and seemed to land his left almost at will on Bob's face. He kept in a crouching position.

Both landed some hard blows to the body and head as they exchanged. Bob tried a left for the jaw but was forced to clinch as Jeff rushed in like a tiger. They landed heart punches and rallied, fighting in exchanges all across the ring. Jeff landed his hook to the head and right to the body. "The men were now fighting very fast and both scoring effectively." Jeff landed both hands to the body and sent Bob back with a left on the chest. "The fighting was of the hottest kind now, Jeffries forcing it, until Fitz caught him with a hard right-hander on the throat. Then Jeffries backed away, Fitz following with heavy swings and jolts which landed on Jim's head and made him take the defensive at the bell."

Jeff smiled as he walked to his corner. Bob seemed a bit concerned. Mrs. Fitzsimmons could not overcome her nervousness. She withdrew into a dark passageway, and then to her husband's dressing room. Corbett said, "This has been Jeffries's fight right through up to date, even on points." Kid McCoy said, "There was great fighting in this round, but Fitz was not showing his usual form." The *Herald* said, "The fighting in this round was fast and telling, with the honors, except for a short time, in favor of Jeffries." Outside the arena, the round was announced as being pretty even.

4th round

Thus far, the fighting had been remarkably fast. Jeffries was a big surprise. However, he was a bit slower in this round, while Fitz was speedier than ever, strong and aggressive. Fitz rushed, but Jeff blocked beautifully with his elbow. Bob landed a long hard left on the jaw, but Jeff took it well.

Fitz bluffed a left for the head and missed a right for the jaw. "Jeff waits and swings in a left hook that catches Fitz under the right ear and staggers him from head to foot." Although momentarily unsteady on his legs, Bob came in and sharp infighting followed. Jeff blocked him and landed a terrific right jolt under the heart. Jeff protected himself from a right to the head and jumped in with a right on the ribs. They clinched between exchanges. "Jeff was using his immense weight to advantage in the clinches and Siler had to force his way between them to break his hold." Jeff landed a left to the body, right on the ear, and a heavy left on the cheek bone. Still, "Fitz is a game old boy. He keeps coming right in for more of it."

Fitzsimmons seemed intent on landing a knockout blow with his right, but was unsuccessful in landing it, finding more success with his left. Jeff would duck the right aimed for his head and counter with a right to the ribs. Jeff smashed his right to the belly twice more and drove Bob away. Jeff blocked some hooks, or took them with little concern, confident to a fault.

The fighting was terrific as they mixed it up in lively fashion, countering each other. Fitz landed multiple left jabs and hooks, but Jeff landed some hooks and body blows as well. "The fighting during this round was very spirited and frequently worked the enthusiasm of the spectators to a high pitch." At the end of the round, Jeff chased Fitz, but Bob's side-stepping was too clever. "It was a terrific gait, and the crowd was howling."

The *Tribune* said the round was about even. Kid McCoy said Fitz was the aggressor and won the round. The *Examiner* said Jeff looked confident and by the end of the round had a shade the better of it. The *Asbury Park Daily Press* said it was Fitz's round. Outside the arena, the round was conceded to be in Fitz's favor.

5th round

Jeffries chatted with his seconds in the corner before coming out for the round. Corbett said, "I don't see how Jeffries can lose; he is the cleverer man by far. Fitz is coming at him, though, just as if he was right in it."

Jeff met him with a left on the sore nose, bringing more blood. "Fitz dashes in with a right under the eye and raises a lump, but Jeffries meets him with a right jolt on the ribs." Fitz kept coming in, but Jeff stopped him with a left in the belly quickly followed by a right on the ribs.

As they stepped in to clinch, Jeff ducked into a vicious and quick straight left which opened a deep gash on his forehead just above his left eye. The blood flowed copiously in a stream, running down Jeff's cheek onto his breast. Although he was not hurt, Jeff bent down low more.

The aggressive Fitzsimmons forced the pace and rushed in with rights and lefts, backing Jeff to the ropes, scoring with a left to the jaw. However, Jeff ducked under most of the leads or saved himself by clinching. Fitz laughed as Jeff was nettled and took the defensive. However, Jeffries then walloped Fitz on the jaw and over the heart. Bob again rushed him back to the ropes and landed a couple of swings on the head. Bob blocked a wild blow from Jeff, laughing. However, Jeffries landed a fearful left on the neck which made Bob's head wobble. Fitz landed a return blow that stopped Jeff's advance. Jeffries stopped him with a solid left on the bleeding nose and a driving right on the ribs. "They are mixing it up very fast."

Both went to the head and body. Jeff landed two lefts to the jaw and a right on the forehead. They slugged hard, then took a rest for a few seconds, until Jeff came in again with his left on the nose. Fitz followed Jeff around. "They are both looking for a chance to land a knockout."

The majority of sources agreed that as Bob was rushing in on the attack, he slipped or tripped, and as he was falling, Jeff hit him with a right to the heart (or elbow) that sent him down. Some simply said he fell down and did not mention his being hit. In his autobiography, Jeff claimed that he hit Fitzsimmons in the ribs so hard that he went down for five seconds. Jim Corbett backed Jeff's version. He said Bob rushed in with two lefts and a right at the head, but Jeff drove a right into the ribs "that knocks him down on his knees hanging on the ropes." Bob took five seconds to get up.

After rising, Fitzsimmons landed a left to the neck and right to the body. As Fitz came in again, Jeff landed two straight lefts to the face. In the next rally, Bob landed several hard body blows, including a terrific right to the heart that made Jeffries grunt audibly.

Corbett said both seemed a little bit tired. The *Examiner* called the round even. Kid McCoy said Fitzsimmons was fighting poorly. However, during the 4th and 5th rounds, Bob's corner was aglow. They declared that Fitzsimmons was wearing Jeffries down. They did not think Jeff could handle the pace and felt that eventually one of Bob's sledgehammer blows would take him out. Certainly, the ever-confident attacking Fitzsimmons fought as if he believed that he eventually would land the knockout blow on the bigger man. Jeffries was boxing effectively, though his face was cut and marked. Bob's nose was bleeding. Both men were landing some heavy blows, but Fitz was the one who hit the canvas in the round.

6th round

The *Sun* said, "Fitzsimmons would not sit down between the rounds." However, Corbett said that Bob was up first.

Fitzsimmons was fresher and on the aggressive, landing lefts to the head and chest. He appeared to be the more confident of the two. He backed Jeff to a corner, feinted with his left and landed a glancing right to the ear. Jeff clinched. Fitz did the forcing with considerable feinting. Jeff was more inclined to retreat, duck and clinch. Bob's rushing tactics slightly rattled Jeff.

A right to Jeff's throat could be heard throughout the pavilion. Bob also landed a left to the stomach. Bob jabbed his left lightly in the face and then landed a heavy blow that drew blood from Jeff's eye again. Jeff's cut was bleeding profusely. Fitz played for the cut and hit it, but Jeff countered with a jab to the nose which again set Bob's blood flowing from it.

Corbett felt that Jeffries was resting and taking his time, mostly using his left jab. Jeff was slower but came back occasionally with a surprising spurt when the champion did not seem to expect it. Whenever Bob would think that he had Jeff cornered and swung a blow, Jeff with surprising quickness sidestepped, ducked, or blocked, or struck out and hit Bob instead. Corbett said, "[Jeff] almost knocks his head off with a left hook." Every time that Bob led with the left to the head, Jeff stopped him with a right to the ribs.

Another writer said Jeffries fought back wildly, missing with both hands. However, Jeff then used three left jabs, sending Bob's head back with each one. Although Jeff still hit him with some solid blows, he seemed to be a bit slower than before. On the other hand, "Fitz was faster than chain lightning."

The attacking Fitzsimmons was busier and landed more often. After Fitz caught him with a terrific punch to the jaw, Jeff clinched hard. After breaking, Fitz cut loose and rained blows on Jeff's face. A left to the stomach made Jeff grunt again. Jeffries responded with hard blows, but Fitz landed two to his one, "which were frightful in force and made the crowd simply wild with excitement."

Mrs. Fitzsimmons returned in time to see Bob make a desperate rush that "but for a stumble might have ended the battle." Mrs. Fitz joyously said, "He's getting stronger, Watch him. He can't lose." Jeff's face was bleeding badly. Just before the bell, Jeff countered a left to his face with a hard punch to the body.

Almost all of the sources agreed that Fitzsimmons had the better of it in this round. He was improving and coming on. John Kelly went so far as to say that it looked as if Fitz had merely to await his chance to land a knockout blow. However, the lone dissenter Corbett observed that both were tired and that Jeff's tremendous weight was telling on Bob.

After the round was over, Fitzsimmons said to his cornermen, "He is easy as sheckels," and told them to watch for a knockout.

7ᵗʰ round

Having recovered wonderfully in the one-minute rest, Fitz seemed fresh as ever. He was the aggressor, doing the rushing, seeming confident. The fight had been one of the fastest ever seen between heavyweights. As Jeffries had been fighting very fast, he seemed to be taking a rest in this, as well as the previous round. Jeff was slow in getting to ring center, and he walked backward around the ring.

Fitzsimmons took advantage of Jeff's slowing up by trying to keep the pace fast, advancing as Jeffries moved, hoping to wear out the larger man. Bob led with his left, and Jeff backed away. Bob missed a left swing and Jeff hit the body with his right as Bob was coming in. Fitz advanced and followed Jeff around the ring. Fitz was aggressive and appeared to be looking for an opening for his right. Three times Bob came in and Jeff ducked under his attack and clinched, at the same time throwing his entire weight onto the champion. Jeffries dashed in with a left on the belly, showing that he had faster feet than Bob. The next time Bob came in, Jeff landed his right to the belly. Corbett said, "That tires Fitz." However, Fitzsimmons kept coming.

As he was pressed, Jeffries landed some light lefts to the stomach and ribs, as well as the left jab to the nose and mouth, and Bob laughed. A Jeffries hook to the jaw rattled Bob. Fitz grinned and shook his head. They exchanged swings, with Fitzsimmons ducking two or three and landing two or three himself. Fitz was faster and seemed at ease.

Fitzsimmons fought hard and went at Jeffries. As Bob was advancing, Jeff led with a left, but Bob stepped inside of it and countered with his hard left hook on the jaw, which appeared to shake up Jeffries. Mrs. Fitzsimmons said, "Oh, that's it! I knew he would get it in." Bob missed a right but followed with a good left hook to the body.

Jeff was busy blocking as Fitz threw hard blows. After a clinch and break, Fitz landed a left hook to the chin but took a right on the ribs. Blood came from the corner of Jeff's mouth. Bob landed a right uppercut to the stomach and a left on the neck, both blows having tremendous power. He also nailed the eye with a right and split it open again. At the end of the round, Jeff landed a left on the cheek, but Fitz came back with a hard thudding right to the heart that made a loud sound. Jeffries was doing his best to stop the assault when the bell rang. As Fitzsimmons was walking back to his corner, he looked back at Jeffries and smiled.

The local sources agreed that Fitzsimmons had the best of the round, particularly at the end, when he landed the most effective blows. Although Jeffries was still landing, his blows were not as hard or as effective as they had been earlier. His light blows did little or no apparent damage and were not sufficient to keep Bob off. He failed to reach Fitz as well as he had in the previous rounds and was doing most of the clinching. Fitz appeared to have a chance to win. Even Corbett felt that Jeff seemed to be the more tired of the two.

8th round

Slow to respond to the bell, Jeffries looked puzzled as Fitzsimmons grinned and advanced confidently. Jeff backed away as Fitz pressed. However, as Bob moved in, Jeffries effectively countered him with lefts to the nose and mouth. Bob grinned and tried a left and right, but Jeff got inside of them, anxious to duck when Bob got close. Fitz's punches often missed around his neck. Jeff landed a hard right on the body, causing Bob to grit his teeth. Bob rushed the fighting but did no damage. After a Fitz miss, Jeff landed a left swing full on Bob's neck and the crowd cheered. Jeff was as strong as when he began and was going a little smoother than ever.

Fitz looked angry and went in with a wild rush, landing a couple of body blows and whipping up a jolt on the neck or jaw that made Jeff retreat. Jeff met another rush with a left. He then rushed in and scored heavily to Bob's body but was hit on the bleeding eye. Fitz fired in some hot jabs and the blood poured down Jeff's cheek.

Jeffries seemed a bit slower, but was game and willing to fight, doing some rushing of his own. However, Bob was able to step back and smile. The champion still looked strong. Both landed left jabs. Fitz feinted with the right, trying to coax Jeff into a right lead. They exchanged blows for a while. Jeff mostly threw lefts at the body.

As Jeffries was rushing in, both simultaneously threw straight lefts, but Jeff's left jolt to the nose got there first and sent Bob reeling back to the ropes, acting as if he was groggy, leaning halfway over them. However, Jeff's second told him to look out, that Bob was only acting. Fitz was a master at bluffing grogginess in order to set a trap. Even when actually groggy, as fighters came to him, Fitzsimmons excelled at timing them perfectly with knockout blows. Referee Siler said, "[Jeff] kept away from Fitz in the same old cautious manner." Fitz came away from the ropes acting as if it had only been a joke and again bluffed the right. However, another reporter said Bob was momentarily dazed. Fitz grinned and rushed in. Like a flash, Jeff hooked a left, but Fitz slipped away from it.

As Jeffries came forward, Fitzsimmons missed a right but countered the advancing Jeff by catching him with a frightfully hard short left hook on the cheek. One said that although it was perhaps the best punch of the fight, it seemed to have no effect on Jeffries. Another said it was an awful hard punch, but it was too high to be effective, that if it had been a couple of inches lower, it could have ended the fight. Still, one writer felt that it had to put some stars in Jeff's eyes. It was the best punch of the round, but overall, Jeff did the superior work in the round.

After having lost the last two rounds, the local reporters agreed that Jeffries had the better of it in this round. One said Jeffries had rallied astonishingly. Another said Jeff showed more strength and speed in this round. A third writer said Jeff had the best of it at this point and Fitz seemed to be growing desperate. Echoing this thought, one said that Fitzsimmons was trying to make a sensational knockout finish but imprudently forced matters. Still, both smiled at each other after the bell. Corbett said Bob looked tired, puffing a little. "Jeffries had by far the best of that round. Look at the big boy smile as he comes back to his corner."

9th round

As usual, Fitzsimmons was first up and gamely went in to do or die, advancing to close quarters. He kept on top of Jeffries all the time. They mixed it and engaged in fast exchanges of heavy swings. Fitz seemed to pick out the marks with better judgment. He landed two solid body blows, then came in close again and punched Jeff on the bleeding eye.

Fitzsimmons was the aggressor, but Jeff countered frequently. Jeffries was stronger in this round, and by the middle of the round, it was anybody's fight. They were tired and clinched frequently. Bob looked for an opening, but Jeff ducked and threw his shoulder into Bob's chest. Jeff roughed it a bit. He sent Bob backward with a straight blow to the face. Fitz continued on the aggressive but was sent back again with a left on the body. Two long jarring left smashes to the nose made Bob wince, and the crowd howled its approval. Fitz bled a good deal from his nose, the blood pouring down his chest. Later, a right to the heart had Fitz guessing.

Jeff alternated between jabs, hooks, and body blows, working up and down. After landing, Jeff would break away and begin feinting again with as much caution as in the 1st round. Bob was also bleeding from his mouth, and he spit up a considerable amount of blood. He landed a left swing on the cheek, but it was too high to do any good. When Jeff dashed in with his left and missed, he clinched. Bob spit out a mouthful of blood over Jeff's shoulder. The jabs smeared blood all over Bob's face. With his mouth open,

Fitz was a bit tired and probably wondering from where all the blows were coming. However, he kept forcing matters, always believing in his ability to score a knockout against anyone.

Jeffries occasionally smiled after landing. He knew what he was doing. However, Jeff did not get his full power into his punches because he was constantly getting away as he punched. Fitz treated his punches with disdain, constantly advancing and looking to land his power shots. However, Corbett said, "His swings are going wild. Jim is either a couple of inches away from them or else he steps in and lets the arm double around his neck."

Several times during the round, Mrs. Fitzsimmons exclaimed, "Oh!" as Jeff's blows brought blood from Bob's nose or sent his head to the right or left. Jeffries suddenly made a savage feint as if to drive in the left jab but whipped in a stiff-arm swing across the neck, then dug in an awful right to the body and roughed Fitz in the clinch. Regardless, Fitzsimmons continued infighting and leading until the bell, breaking no ground.

There was a difference of opinion regarding what this round showed. Corbett said, "Fitz is now much more tired than Jeffries. I think Jim has the fight now." The *Herald* presented different opinions. One said that this was a fierce round, and Jeff had somewhat the better of it. Another said Bob was tired and unsteady with his movements, that it was a bad round for him. Jeff was comparatively fresh. Still a third opinion said, "There is no doubt that in the ninth round Fitzsimmons thought himself a winner as nearly as in the third. He looked it, and his backers believed that he had sized his man up and would soon land the decisive blow." The *Tribune* said Jeff clearly had the better of the round. The *Examiner* said that on the whole, it was Jeff's round. The *Sun* said, "The round was even, if not slightly in favor of Jeffries." Kid McCoy said Fitz fought poorly and seemed a little weak. Referee Siler said Jeff had the better of it, but Fitzsimmons kept smiling, still confident.

10th round

Although Fitzsimmons was a bit tired in the previous round, at the start of the round, he appeared as fresh as ever. Corbett said of Bob, "He's a tough, game man." Jeff assumed his peculiar stooping position that he used throughout the fight, advancing cautiously toward Fitz. They exchanged blows, but Jeff landed the hardest and most effective punches, including his jab, a hard hook, and, after ducking a left, a right to the body. Jeff dashed in, missed and clinched. Corbett said, "Fitz turns and looks to the referee for sympathy. He's getting done up, that's what's the matter, Jim hasn't done anything wrong." Apparently, Jeff was using his weight and strength in the clinches.

Jeffries landed a couple lefts on the nose. "They don't look hard, but they are rocking Fitz's head just the same." Fitzsimmons fought back hard and reached the face with the left, but his rights missed. No matter how quick Bob was, Jeff either blocked or stepped inside of the rights. Fitz backed Jeffries across the ring. Just as Jeff touched the ropes, he used some neat footwork and slipped away.

After a few exchanges, Jeffries landed a right over the heart and straight left to the jaw that rocked Fitz's head. When Bob advanced again with a wild left hook lead, Jeff ducked, and with lightning speed, either swung his left hook or shot out his crushing stiff straight left (depending on the source), landing to the jaw with double force, dropping Bob backwards to the boards, his head striking the stage floor. As Bob lay motionless, Martin Julian tried to douse him with water. Siler quickly ordered him back to his place. Lying on his back, Bob rolled over as Siler counted four. Julian cried for him to get up.

Fitzsimmons slowly rose at eight in a dazed condition. Jeffries, watching him like a cat, crouching low with his hands poised for instant action, crept steadily towards the groggy champion. Fitzsimmons tried to step in with a body shot and clinch, but Jeffries smashed him with another left hook to the neck and dropped him again. The *Journal* said, "Jeff caught him with a vicious left hook and nearly threw him on his head. But the blow was not as good as the other and Fitz came back quicker." Corbett said, "This Fitz is a game fellow. Those two knock-downs are enough to knock the life out of almost anybody."

Fitzsimmons rose in a moment and moved about the ring, hoping to recuperate. Jeffries was cool, not excited or overanxious to finish or leave himself open to one of Bob's desperate punches. Despite the roars of the crowd, Jeff began feinting again. He was in no hurry. Referee Siler said that despite knocking him down and Bob looking a bit dazed, "Instead of rushing him novice-like he restrained himself like an old-timer, and bided his time to lick him gradually but surely. … Jeffries was undoubtedly wisely coached. Instead of cutting loose and rushing at Bob…he fought just as carefully and cautiously as he had in the previous rounds."

When Bob saw that Jeff did not come at him, he gamely attacked again, still hoping to land a knockout blow. However, Jeff was able to avoid the blows, sending in rights to the body. Still, Fitz rushed Jeff to his corner. "His last mad rush was only a bluff, weakness was fast overtaking him, and the quivering of his legs was plainly visible to all." Corbett called Fitz a splendid bluffer, rushing Jeff into his own corner, "pretending he is trying to get in on him, and we, who are outside of the ring, can see that Fitz is too weak to do any real execution."

Jeff came back, and in a rush, landed a left hook to the jaw, a left to the body, a left to the ear, followed by a right to the head, and Fitz wobbled like a dying top. Chief Devery was on his feet, waving his arms as if he wanted the fight stopped, but sat down again as the bell rang and saved Bob. Jeff had him pretty well used up.

Bob was practically a beaten man, weak, staggering, and reeling during the round and at the bell. He had managed to last the round through sheer pluck and gameness, but the end was near. The crowd was wild as Bob staggered to his corner. Fitzsimmons clearly was one of the pluckiest fighters ever, for even when he was hopelessly beaten, he once again refused to sit down in his corner during the minute rest.

11th round

Showing his gameness, Bob came out of the corner for the 11th round like a bulldog, seeming revived, fresh, and strong, advancing as willingly as Jeffries did. His wonderful recovery dumbfounded the crowd. Corbett said, "Did you ever see a man like Fitzsimmons? He comes out of his corner without a trace of blood on him, with his eyes bright and a cool, confident smile on his face as if he had just made up his mind to begin to fight." Fitzsimmons advanced quickly and aggressively. Jeff kept away, waiting for his chance. Fitz rushed in with a left and right, but Jeff ducked under and landed his straight right jolt to the short ribs, "which stops Fitzsimmons dead and actually shoves him back." Corbett credited Jeffries for not taking a chance and rushing in, despite the crowd calling on him to do so. "He knows enough not to take any risks." Jeff studied his man for a moment.

Jeffries hit the nose lightly with a left, then followed a second later with a stiff left on the nose that sent Bob staggering back. Jeff feinted his lefts, shifted to the left, broke ground, and then worked in again, drawing a left lead by Bob. Jeff blocked it, and, coming into a clinch, landed his furious right over the heart. Jeff broke and feinted again. Some clinches followed. In close, a Jeffries left to the body and right over the heart sent Fitz back. Bob did not like it, and made a desperate attempt to land a knockout blow with his right. Jeff dodged and laughed. He eluded or blocked Bob's right and lefts. Jeff landed two lefts solidly to the mouth and stomach. Corbett observed, "See how the flesh on Fitzsimmons's thighs is quivering? He is pretty nearly gone, but he is as game as a thoroughbred." The champion rushed in again with his right, but Jeff ducked low and landed his left straight into Bob's body.

Fitzsimmons rushed and fought recklessly, with Jeffries backing and getting out of harm's way before throwing some blows in return. "The game old champion is still on the rush and actually makes Jeff back away into his corner." Jeff was being careful, crouching with his body drawn in and both hands protecting his head, guarding against Bob's dangerous wallops. Fitz kept boring in, but Jeff stopped him twice with straight lefts on the mouth.

According to Corbett and the *Brooklyn Daily Eagle*, Bob kept rushing, while Jeffries quickly broke ground "as fast as an athlete can run." However, Jeffries suddenly stopped and shot out his straight left like a crowbar. Fitzsimmons ran his mouth right into it and went down on his face. Siler told Jeff to stand back.

Fitz rolled over and then arose. Still game, Fitzsimmons rushed in, but Jeffries met him with a piston-like hard left jab that stopped Bob in his tracks. Jeff then followed with a left hook as hard as a mallet on the jaw that clearly dazed him. Bob's hands dropped to his sides. He stood still, but his limbs were wobbly. Jeff waited just an instant, but quickly realized the helplessness of Bob's condition, and, raising his up his left arm as if to block, simultaneously shot out a thunderbolt sledge-hammer right squarely on the jaw and Fitz went down like an ox struck with an axe.

Bob dropped backward, his back, shoulders, and head crashing to the ground with a thud. His outstretched arms flopped out beside him. He lay motionless as if asleep. "No mortal physique could have withstood that blow." Corbett said, "It's all up with Fitz. He's gone. He'll never be able to get up." Referee Siler immediately knew that the fight was over but gave him the full count.

Jeff looked at him, and then stepped back over to the ropes, watchful as Bob was counted out. Fitzsimmons was motionless for a few moments, then vainly tried to rise, but sunk back into unconsciousness, the blood flowing out of his mouth and nose. He was out cold. After the ten-count, Referee Siler waved his hands at 1 minute 32 or 35 seconds of the 11th round. James J. Jeffries was the new heavyweight champion of the world.

Fitz had been down in the 2nd, 5th, 10th (twice), and 11th (twice) rounds, but fought gamely and confidently throughout, always believing that he would win by knockout.

At first, there was silent amazement, but then the crowd came to life and there was wild excitement. They cheered the new champion. Men leaped into the ring from all sides and danced for joy. Many men tried to kiss and hug Jeffries, mobbing him. Brady, Delaney, and Jeff's brother Jack hugged and kissed him too. The crowd was cheering incessantly, and the big fellow looked over the ropes and bowed in response. Jeff's eye and nose were cut and scratched.

Police Chief Devery and his men hustled the crowd out of the ring and told Jeff to wait to leave until they found out how badly Fitz was hurt. Back then, if a fighter died, manslaughter charges could be brought.

In the meantime, after being counted out, Julian and Kenny picked up Fitzsimmons and dragged him to his corner. Bob's eye was cut, his nose puffed, mouth swollen, and there was an egg-sized lump on the back of his head where it had struck the floor. They wiped the blood from his face, gave him restoratives, and he came to within thirty seconds. When Bob got up and walked away, the police allowed the new champion to leave too.

Fitz walked to his dressing room and lay down on the couch provided, looking like a broken-hearted man. His wife Rose stroked Bob's forehead. Julian was crying. Some said Bob wept too. After about a half-hour of recovery time, at 12:10 a.m., Fitz dressed and left, accompanied by his wife.

Praises were heaped upon both men. Although defeated, Fitzsimmons had "put up a game, hard, vicious fight against a man whom many will now regard as the greatest heavyweight in the world since the days of John L. Sullivan." Corbett said, "Well, the best man won. There is no excuse for Fitz. He was in splendid condition. Jeff was too big, strong and clever for him." The *Brooklyn Daily Eagle* said of Fitz, "He is certainly one of the gamest men that ever wore a glove." The *New York Journal* said, "James J. Jeffries is by long odds the greatest heavyweight fighter the world has ever seen. There is no man today who has a chance with him." The general feeling was that the two best men in the division had fought one another.

There were extensive post-fight summaries and analysis. The *New York Times* said Jeffries was able to absorb Fitzsimmons' attacks and return with his own powerful punches, launching counters from his famous defensive crouch which he had improved over the years. As the bout progressed, the attacking Fitz began landing more, but Jeffries' blows did more damage. Some experts thought that Jeff was done for at the end of the 7th round, but then his youth asserted itself and his reserve strength came to his rescue. The fight dispelled all doubts about Jeff's gameness and ability. He clearly was the best heavyweight that Fitz ever had met.

The *New York Herald* said Jeffries "is not a finished sparrer, but he is wonderfully quick for a man of his tremendous size – the quickest big man, sporting men are saying tonight, just as they used to say of John L. Sullivan when he was in his prime." It also said, "Jeffries was simply tremendous. He is the ring giant, and, awkward as was his stooping position, he landed on the champion with an ease which surprised his warmest admirers." As often as Fitz landed his hard blows, Jeff never really was groggy. Bob was "beaten down not alone by sheer weight and tremendous strength, but by a deceiving style of fighting which often led him to place his jaw in jeopardy."

The *New York Daily Tribune* said they both landed savage blows "powerful enough to slay an ordinary man." Jeffries "showed himself a better boxer than he had been thought to be. He dodged with an agility wonderful for one of his size and weight. His punches in the stomach and his left-handed blows in the face were terribly effective."

The *New York Journal* said Fitzsimmons had tried in vain to land his right on Jeff's jaw. Even when he landed some powerful blows, Jeff's iron chin held up. Conversely, Jeffries rarely used his right except to the body. He fought cautiously, sliding back, but he did not run. The spectators shouted themselves hoarse watching them thump each other, round after round, until the combatant's breasts were flecked with blood and shining with perspiration. Jeff's strength and youth told. Fitz weakened over time, but his courage never left him.

> There was not a dull spot in it from the first clang of the bell to the last deadening punch. Fitzsimmons, in spite of the fact that it was going against him, came and fought. He proved himself as game a man as ever boxed and took his knock-out with as good a grace as he ever gave one.

> It is likely he knew he was beaten after the second round. ... He made a fight and had a chance to win all the way to the tenth round.

> It is likely Jeffries has a respect for Fitzsimmons, for Fitz certainly landed him one or two terrific punches. Still, he out-feinted, out-boxed, out-generaled and out-fought the champion. He was as cold as ice from the beginning to the end. Never for a second did he show the least sign of stage fright, fear or hurry. Again and again, when half

the spectators were howling for him to go on, he would lightly shift his position, feint and then break ground.

He was never in a hurry. ... He had twenty-five rounds... Jeffries beat Fitzsimmons with his left hand. The right kept pounding away at his lower works and every time the jolt came it counted. But Jeffries's left hand work at the head and body was the feature of the fight. He knocked Fitz down, dazed him and all but put him out with the hand which Fitzsimmons never did know how to stop. Everybody who has ever fought Fitz has hit him with the left, but he finally induced them to use the right, then he won.

Jeffries was doing sufficiently well with his left to have no right-hand ambitions, and, in spite of Fitz's most tempting openings, Jeff never would let go. He used his right hand at the body and reached with an inside cross or two, but he never took a chance. When Fitz was all gone and did not have a punch in his right hand Jeff shot it over.

Further, the weight told. Jeffries had something between forty and fifty pounds in his favor. His rushes were savage, and whenever he came into collision with Fitzsimmons, it meant something. His quickness and ducking, his foot work and his general speed set all the wise people wondering. He was faster than Fitz. When he wanted to corner Fitz he succeeded, but had no trouble in slipping away from Fitzsimmons at will.

The *New York Sun* said Jeffries surprised the spectators the moment he put up his hands. He was cool-headed and looked so powerfully strong that everyone appreciated the fact that Bob had his hands full. Whenever Jeff got into a clinch, he pushed Bob off as if he was a lightweight. Fitz could not get to him as often as he liked, and when he did land on the jaw or stomach his punches had little or no effect.

Jeff was not only the biggest heavyweight in the world, but also one of the cleverest and fastest. He used his superior reach very well, mostly using his damaging left with wonderful speed, and only once cut loose a really hard right for the head at long range, for the knockout punch. "He watched out carefully for Fitz's hooks and kept away with religious care. He simply took his time, and with this powerful left of his swinging constantly in the Cornishman's face he slowly but surely battered Bob's countenance until it looked like a huge rosebud." Jeff worked his left hand so rapidly that at times Fitz, who did not block it, was dazed. Bob's nose bled profusely, although his nose always had been sensitive.

Fitzsimmons forced the fight, feinting, but Jeff was much cleverer than he had supposed, using excellent judgment, never losing his temper. His remarkable physique made it impossible for Fitz to hurt him. Jeff's left eye was cut, and it bled considerably, but he never was in serious trouble, despite the fact that Fitz worked at him like a demon.

[Fitzsimmons] tried every known method of attack, and landed repeatedly. He got both hands to the big fellow's body, but it was backed up with a protection of steel which caused Fitz's blows to bound off as if his gloves were made of rubber. In short, Jeffries, while reasonably clever in defensive work, showed a wonderful amount of ability to take punishment without showing its effects. ... This ability was what helped to beat Fitzsimmons, for when he found that he could not affect the giant with his punches, he began to tire from the effects of his work.

Jeffries was cautious to the end. There was just one period when he cut loose, but as soon as he found that Fitz was still dangerous, he let up. He fought the Cornishman at long range almost entirely, and when the end came he did not rush in close, but fired the left at Bob's head from a rather distant point, following with the right, which was a round arm swing delivered at full length squarely on the vital spot.

Fitzsimmons was a great fighter whose blows would have knocked out anyone else in quick order, "but he can never defeat Jeffries, who is, in the estimation of every ring follower who saw him last night, a wonderful pugilist." Bob finally had met a man whom he could not put down.

The fight was one of the fastest, considering the weight, ever seen. "There was no fiddling or fussing in trying, no light sparring of great length, and plenty of hard punching in every round. There was no faking, although the fight was photographed."

Although lauding his courage, the *Brooklyn Daily Eagle* was fairly critical of Fitzsimmons' performance. Every swing that Jeffries landed made it more and more evident that Bob had carried the pitcher to the well once too often. This writer opined that Fitz was not the same man who whipped Corbett and other top fighters, and was not even the same man seen in training the week before. "I am not trying to belittle Jeffries' victory. I think he is the greatest fighter breathing." However, "The Fitz I saw train and box during the six days preceding the fight seemed entirely different." In training, Fitz had shown "great cleverness, quickness, nimbleness and capacity for very severe exercise." The Fitz observed on fight-night "disgusted me with his lack of energy and style of fighting. He seemed stiff and stale. He lacked speed and generalship.... Perhaps his years had told against him."

In the 2nd round, the ease with which Jeff landed the blow to the nose that sent Fitz to the floor indicated to this writer that Bob had lost something. Jeff did not seem all that quick in his delivery, yet did not experience great difficulty in landing at least two out of five leads. "Fitz's once inimitable system of shifting, side stepping and blocking seemed to have gone somewhat wrong, for though he cleverly stopped many a vicious lunge, others found their way to his body and face." Bob showed a lack of energy and generalship by trying to block when he should have side-stepped or jumped nimbly out of harm's way. He also was unable to counterpunch "when Jeffries would give him a left hand jab on the face, which the latter used almost exclusively throughout the battle." Jeff landed those jabs with great frequency, some soft, some hard, but each blow brought Bob nearer to defeat. "Regardless of the weight of those terrible lefts of the Californian, Fitz kept wading in."

Occasionally, Fitzsimmons would show his old form by ducking or jumping away or blocking, causing some to wonder whether Bob was only trying to draw Jeffries into a trap. However, Jeff kept landing his left jab or left hook with comparative ease.

Throughout the fight, Jeffries crouched peculiarly, "all doubled into a knot." Jeff's right was drawn up in front of his stomach. He straightened out his long and powerful left with a cat-like smack, up and down at the stomach or nose, with a speed surprising in such bulk. It was this slightly bent blow that scored the knockdowns and dazed Fitz in the 11th, setting him up for the right. Jeff also used the Tommy Ryan moves of "pushing in the face with the straightened left and right short arm jab in the wind. Another was the double blow, wind and then face with the left." Conversely, when Fitz landed on Jeff without telling effect, he worried.

However, despite all the criticism, throughout the fight, Bob was competitive, and "the fighting was but slightly balanced in Jeffries' favor, until the tenth round." This writer also said the fight and its result was a surprise, for the crowd did not fully realize that Jeffries was everything he had claimed to be until Fitzsimmons was unconscious. "That I am amazed over the result is putting it mildly. I was certain Fitz would win."

In fact, the odds remained in Fitz's favor throughout the fight, despite the fact that Jeffries had decked him in the 2nd and 5th rounds. The *New York World* said the odds remained 2 to 1 on Fitz until the fight was half over, then changed to 7 to 5, with Fitz still the favorite. Most believed that Bob eventually would manage to land the knockout blow, just as he always had done before.

The *Brooklyn Daily Standard Union* wrote that even though Fitz was up against a man many years younger and 40 pounds heavier, taller, and stronger, nevertheless Bob's admirers were disappointed, for he did not display the science and generalship credited to him. He seemed somewhat slow and didn't use his footwork. He missed many opportunities.

> His style of fighting in the past has been to take blows, and when an opening was presented to leap forward with the fierceness of a tiger and land with telling effect. This he didn't do last night, either because his muscles would not respond to his will or because he feared to risk too much by closing in on the giant who was before him.

Fitz was aggressive but wary, particularly after getting decked in the 2nd. He often was foiled, for Jeff's guard, reach, and strength were too much. Even after being hurt badly in the 10th, instead of keeping away, Fitz continued to force matters. In the 11th, left swings to the head brought him to a standstill, and Jeff cooly landed a terrific right to the jaw to finish him. It was several minutes before he recovered.

Jeffries proved to be the biggest pugilistic surprise. Although not a marvel of science, he knew a trick or two. His crouching position was perplexing and proved too much for Fitz to solve. Jeff astonished the spectators by drawing blood from the champ's nose and then knocking him down. His left was dangerous. Later, he showed his right to good effect as well. He was not the ice wagon he was said to be. "He avoided Fitz's rushes in good style on a number of occasions and skipped about the ring like a middleweight."

In the dressing room, Bill Brady exclaimed, "I told you so! Jeffries is a corker, and there is not a man on earth that can beat him. He's a wonder, and no mistake. Let them all come to him now. None of them can class with him."

Bill Delaney said, "Fitz was beaten fair and square, and, although he put up a game fight, my man had his measure taken from the moment they shaped for the first round."

Jeffries said, "Fitz fought a good and game battle and hit me harder than any man whom I have been up against. He can whip Sharkey in two rounds. … I will defend my title as champion at all times and against all comers." Jeff also said, "At no time in the fight did I feel any misgivings as to my ability to win. I am satisfied that I have well earned the right to be called champion by beating Fitzsimmons, who was undoubtedly the greatest fighter of the age."

The *Asbury Park Daily Press* said Jeff never was at any time in serious danger, and after the early sizing up, took the lead. They fought before a huge crowd in a great beam of blinding white light. Jeff was a veritable giant, marvelously speedy for his immense size. It disagreed with the *Eagle's* assessment of Fitzsimmons, feeling that he was as good as ever.

> Less than a year ago [Jeffries] appeared in New York a great, awkward, ungainly boy. Today he is a lithe, active, alert, trained athlete. The men who prepared him for his fight worked wonders with him. They taught him a nearly perfect defense, instructed him in the methods of inflicting punishment. The transition since he appeared last has been little short of miraculous. …

> The defeated man was just as good as when…he lowered the colors of the then peerless Corbett. He was just as active, just as clever, just as tricky and just as fearless of punishment.

The *New York Clipper* report summarized,

> It was a case of superior skill, experience, cunning and ring generalship, handicapped in a measure by advancing years, being pitted against great advantages in weight and muscular power, combined with the freshness of youth, and backed up with a fair amount of scientific knowledge and no end of laudable ambition. …

> After [Jeffries] had sent the favorite to the floor in the second round, the first round having been without incident, he was regarded with

greater favor, and as he continued to land on head and body with comparative ease, and his blows were observed to be full of steam, while those landed by Fitz seemingly were without effect, save at long intervals. ... [T]o the majority it was apparent that his triumph was simply a matter of time, provided Fitzsimmons did not manage to deliver one of those finishing punches for which he was famous. ... [T]he tactics employed by Jeffries when clinched, legitimate but very damaging, were clearly taxing Fitz's strength greatly. ... Nevertheless, [Bob's] courage never wavered, and he assumed the offensive round after round, always wearing a smile on his battered and bleeding countenance as he dashed upon his foe, who generally met him with more pepper than he was able to give. ...

Throughout it was a clean, satisfactory fight, unmarred by anything approaching foul tactics.... The fact that the victory of the brawny Californian was largely due, as above stated, to the manner in which he made his extra avoirdupois tell upon Fitz's strength when clinched, does not detract in the slightest degree from the credit due him; the weight of his tremendous blows certainly proved a most potent factor, while a great deal of his antagonist's strength was wasted in deliveries that either missed their mark or proved ineffectual when landed upon Jeffries' massive frame, so apparently impervious to injury. ... It may truly be said that after the opening Jeffries had the best of the fighting in nearly every round. He depended mainly upon straight left hits, with an occasional hook with the left, principally on the body, varied at intervals, when a good opportunity offered, with a swinging right, and he seldom failed to land, although, at times, his hits were light, but generally they were unwelcome guests. He certainly surprised his warmest partisans by the comparatively easy way in which he got onto his opponent.

The *National Police Gazette* called it one of the most viciously contested fights in pugilistic history, before the largest and most representative gathering of men ever amassed together in a pugilistic arena. Jeff was superior to Fitz in every round, demonstrating that he could reach him effectively with either hand. Bob fought courageously and gamely in the hope of turning the tide in his favor, but never had more than a remote puncher's chance to win.[57]

A week later, the *Gazette* writer further analyzed the fight.

It's up to me I suppose to tell why I fancied Jeffries and ventured to express the opinion that he would win. ... His weight alone was an advantage.... The victor put this forty-pound advantage in evidence every time the two clinched and the lighter man was borne down and wearied beneath the ponderous load of flesh, muscle and bone which he was forced to support until Referee Siler pushed himself wedgelike between them and broke them apart. There is nothing in the rules

[57] *National Police Gazette*, June 24, 1899.

which prohibited Jeff from doing that sort of thing as often as he could and he availed himself of the privilege much to Fitz's discomfiture and disadvantage. ... Jeffries' arms are so abnormally long that he found it a comparatively easy matter to...hit at the Australian without fear of counter blows. When his sturdy left landed full on Fitz's nose, Fitz's fist, with his arm fully extended, was a couple of inches away from the objective point of his return blow. It was only when the fighting was at short range that Fitz demonstrated that he was equal, if not superior, to his long-armed opponent. ... [Bob] was quick and resourceful in getting away from the Californian's punches during the earlier rounds of the battle, and really forced the issue until he began to grow weary from the impact of Jeff's ponderous rushes and clinches. ... Fitz tried every trick he knew to get Jeffries in position for one of his famous blows. ... He might as well have been punching away at the steel belt of an armored cruiser. ... When he subsequently tried and failed to reach Jeffries' jaw, owing to the ease with which the latter could block up and throw the blow off, he was utterly powerless, and was forced to depend upon a chance opportunity. ... Jeffries...was as firm and steady as the proverbial rock, fighting a carefully planned battle. He had demonstrated his ability to hit the champion and likewise demonstrated that he had nothing to fear from the latter's punches. ... He was as sprightly as a featherweight as he danced in and out, trying to draw an opening, or rushed into a clinch. Fitz was marvelously game and willing.... Jeffries never omitted a chance to rough matters.... By hanging his weight upon the Cornishman's neck and shoulders he was wearing him down. ... Jeff had been schooled to be wary of leaving an opening and he elevated his left shoulder and used a high right-hand guard to keep out of danger. ... He could wait, which was a great thing in itself; and he could afford to wait. ... He had been told that his opponent's only chance lay in a single blow and he guarded well against that. With his handy left and his strong guard he met the champion's rush and both punished him and hugged him into weakness. ... All the hard punching [Fitz] received only served to inspire him on to greater endeavor. He refused to believe that he was beaten. He fought heroically and well, and if I never had any admiration for him before, I had it then, when I saw him fighting so desperately, with defeat staring him in the face, to get in a blow that would turn the tide in his favor. ... Every time he was knocked down or dazed and tottering against the ropes he returned to the fray with a determination born of a fresh hope that the long-deterred change would come. ... Fitz certainly deserved the admiration of the mad thousands about him.[58]

---

[58] *National Police Gazette*, July 1, 1899.

The *San Francisco Chronicle* said Jeffries "fought with the coolness and precision of a veteran and at no time was he in danger of defeat." "He was as lively as a lightweight on his feet and repeatedly ducked under the cutting swings of his opponent. ... He punches and hooks and swings with the precision of a finished boxer." Still, Jeffries was punished throughout, "for no man can engage the wonderful Australian…without being hit hard and often, but he stood up to it with lion-like courage and never faltered." Jeff was a finished fighter, alert for openings and swift to take them. His condition was superb and the fierce fighting did not affect him. Jeffries "showed himself a master at every point in the game and won as he pleased after he had taken the measure of his opponent."

Referee George Siler said it was one of the best fights he ever had witnessed, and "if the fight had been stopped at any time previous to the knockout, the decision would have to have been in Jeffries's favor."[59] He said it was the same old story of a man fighting once too often. Bob had met a younger, stronger, and faster man. "There was no time during the fight that Fitz looked as though he could win. Jeffries out-boxed and out-fought him from start to finish, having the best of every round." He also said, "In my opinion Jeffries had a shade the best of it for the last seven rounds. Jeffries is unquestionably a young man of remarkable strength. It was a good fight from start to finish and the best man won."

Siler believed Fitzsimmons thought that Jeffries could not hurt him, because often Jeff would touch him only lightly with the left, and then Bob would smile and bore in. However, Jeff "avoided his swings in the easiest manner possible." Fitz was off in his judgment of distance and probably should have utilized more straight blows. Jeffries was able to counter continually with his left and hooked him often without return.

Siler called Jeffries clever for his quickness on his feet and for his ability to duck Fitz's leads. "I knew that he was shifty on his feet, but did not think he was so clever with his head and hands, as time and again he ably ducked out of reach of Fitz's left and right hand leads." He thought that Bob should have used more uppercuts when Jeff ducked.

Siler felt that Jeff's crouched position gave him an advantage, guarding well against the right, with his jaw close to his shoulder. Fitz mostly missed his right crosses. A right did land to Jeff's left eye and caused a gash, but mostly the right went over his neck or landed on the back of the head.

Fitzsimmons generally was first up at the gong and went in on the attack. However, he did no damage. Jeff remained cool, whether being attacked or after hurting Fitz. He took his time and acted like a master.

Another expert, John Kelly, said,

> There is no similarity between the James Jeffries I saw attempt to knock out Bob Armstrong…in August, 1898, and the James Jeffries who put Robert Fitzsimmons to sleep…. One was a big, soft,

---

[59] Siler meant that if the police stopped the bout before its natural conclusion, he would then award a decision based on the merits up to that point.

painfully slow chap that didn't appear to know the first rudiments of boxing…. Last night he was big, strong, shifty, quick and scientific. A faster or a more scientific big man I have never seen. He hit like a battering ram and took hard blows in return without flinching. He used right and left hand with equal force, both hands seemingly being alike to him, and he wanted to fight all the time. His foot work was simply a revelation, his improvement in this respect in less than a year being really marvelous…. Jeffries today is a great fighter. His youth, great strength, science, quickness of hand, eye and foot, and, above all, his fearlessness, make him a champion worthy of the title. He should be champion for several years to come.

Kid McCoy said Jeff had shown wonderful improvement and had proven to have more science, speed, and judgment than anticipated. "Fitzsimmons, who is one of the cleverest fighters and best generals in the ring, should have won the fight. It was a magnificent battle and at the start it looked like Fitzsimmons would win it … If I were asked what made Fitzsimmons lose, I would say, simply – Jeffries. He proved himself a great fighter and will defend his title." Jeff was very clever, and at a rock-solid 210 pounds, too big and strong for Fitz.

From San Francisco, Tom Sharkey was surprised at the result, for he thought that Fitzsimmons would win. Tom said he could defeat Jeffries.

Bill Brady said,

> I told you so! Jeffries is a corker and there is not a man on earth that can beat him. Jeffries is one of the greatest fighters the world has ever seen. He defeated a great fighter and only won the championship after one of the hardest fights witnessed in this country. He has a wonderful left hand that will defeat any fighter in the world. Jeffries will go on the road for a time.

Brady said Jeff would be ready for Sharkey next.

Bill Delaney, former Corbett trainer, said, "I have again brought a champion-beater from California and am naturally proud of it."

Yank Kenny said Bob was in excellent shape, proven by the fact that he quickly recuperated from knockdowns and hard blows. However, Jeffries was a surprise.

Fitzsimmons gave multiple statements to different newspapers. He said,

> I fully expected to win, but I didn't. Jeffries won because he was the best man. … He is young, strong, quick and clever. I have no excuse to make on the score of condition and over-confidence. I was in perfect trim, better, really, than I ever was before, and fought the best I could. … Jeffries is now the champion of the world beyond question, and is entitled to all the praise that may be showered upon him. He won the title fairly and squarely.

Fitzsimmons said Jeffries was the best man he ever had met and was too big and strong. "I fought my hardest, but he reached me in spite of all I could do. Jeffries made a great fight, far greater than I believed he could ever do. ... I knew it was a hard game after the second round, and toward the last I was too much dazed to avoid him." Bob further said of Jeffries, "He's a hard hitter and clever. I did not seem to be able to get at him effectively. I was not prepared for his peculiar crouching style of fighting."

Mrs. Fitzsimmons claimed that Bob had gone into the ring with a bad right arm. Fitz said he had no excuses to make. "Well, I got licked, and what is the use of complaining now." However, Mrs. Fitz said Bob's arm had been injured a year ago punching a bag and it never healed properly. Bob said, "My right arm was not in shape, but that is neither here nor there." Continuing to discuss the arm, Fitz said,

> [T]he result would not have been different had it been in good shape. Jeffries is a hard puncher, and I think he is fully as clever as Corbett. He may not be as quick, but he knows how to hit from the shoulder. ... I did not weigh enough to have the strength to cope with this big fellow. My kidneys are sore and my stomach is badly used up.

Continuing, Bob said,

> My wife told me I would get licked, and as soon as I saw Jeffries in his dressing room I knew I'd have a good time. Jeffries was a hard man to get at. I sometimes think that if he had stood up I could have reached him better and the fight might have been different in its results. ... I have no excuses to make. I forced the fighting, took my punishment like a man, got licked and that's all there is to it.

There were tears in Bob's eyes, and he seemed to be on the verge of breaking down.

> Jeffries is a wonder. I never saw a fellow get away so well from a punch or show so much speed on his feet. He was as quick as a flash, and his light footwork made me guess a great deal. ... I made desperate leads; I tried every ruse at my command to beat him, but it was of no avail. He got away with such surprising skill that I wondered whether I was getting slow or whether I had before me a man whom I could not hurt. Jeffries's weight was against me. Every time we got clinched he fell against me and this impaired my chances. I don't want to have it inferred that he fought against the rules. ... I got licked on the level. ... My wife told me not to make this match...but I still clung to the belief that I was as good a man as I was two years ago and that my lay-off did not do me any harm, but now I realize that my wife was right. I know I must have been slow, for I could not use that speed that I used to have.

Fitz's face was puffed up considerably, and there was a large bump on the back of his head from striking the floor. His eye was slightly cut, and his jaw was swollen.

Bob said he would not bother Jeffries, and had not decided what he would do, but did leave open the possibility that he might one day ask him for another chance. However, when told of Kid McCoy's challenge for a fight at middleweight, Bob said that he was out of the game. "As for me – I will never fight again." Of course, Bob had claimed to be retired after beating Corbett, so one never knew what he might do.

Discussing potential Jeffries opponents, Bob said, "No man in the pugilistic arena can stand against Jeffries. He is without a serious rival. In two punches Jeffries would kill Sharkey."

In an interview with the *Brooklyn Citizen*, Bob attributed Jeff's victory to his fine left plus his superior weight. "I don't think there is a man in the world that can beat him. He can lick them all." When asked about Sharkey, Bob said, "Why, he'd kill him. I could lick Sharkey myself in two rounds." At that time, Fitz only had a slight discoloration under his right eye.

Yank Kenny, one of Bob's sparring partners/trainers, said Fitz was too old and small compared to a young Jeffries in his prime. "Jeffries' left bothered him greatly. It was the thing that did the trick. ... His showing was a surprise to us. One could hardly believe that he has improved so much." Kenny said Jeffries could beat Sharkey, McCoy, Corbett, Maher, or anyone.

Dan Hickey said, "Jeffries proved himself a wonderful fighter. I don't believe that there is a man living who can beat him."

Jeffries said he never was in danger or distress at any time, although Fitzsimmons hit him with some terrific blows. "Fitz fought a good and game battle and hit me harder than any man whom I have been up against." However, "Fitz never hurt me but once, and that was a hard blow in the left eye. His body blows did not have near the force they may have seemed to. In my estimation I had the best of every round." Jeff never had any real trouble landing his blows. "The fight was never for a moment in doubt so far as I was concerned. I had learned considerable since I fought Armstrong."

> I have trained as few men ever trained for a fight. ... I expected to win. ... I gained a lot of knowledge from my connection with Tommy Ryan. He is certainly a wonderful fighter, and what he does not know about the game is not worth knowing. ...
>
> In the first round I just sized my man up. ... I got many a good crack in the wind, but none of them even seemed to make me puff. ... In the second round, when I knocked him down, I felt more confident than ever. I was convinced then that my punches hurt. ... I thought I had him out. ... Fitz was extremely groggy, and only recovered because he was in such good shape. ... His vitality was too great and he fought as hard afterward as he did before. ... By the way, this fellow, Fitz, has a remarkable way of coming back, and this saved him many times. ...
>
> As the fight went on I became more and more convinced that I would get him directly. There was not much time to think, but it did occur to me to be thankful for the hard work I had done and the

good training. ... [I] give Fitz great credit for his splendid fighting ability. ...

Some of my friends say that my way of crouching my head to one side was somewhat instrumental in causing Fitz's defeat. Well, I puzzled him, to be sure, and I did the trick by playing for his wind...it was just the spot to play for. ... In the tenth, when I knocked him down, I knew I had him licked, for when he got up I could see that he was gone.

I did not care to take any chances, because he is noted for a foxy fellow who is liable to do some terrible damage with a chance swing. That is the reason why I did not go after him and settle matters then and there. As soon as I saw him standing up I realized that it was all over.... I defeated him with a left hook, which I followed up with a full right swing on the jaw.

Jeff had few marks of the battle. The skin over his left eye was cut up, but his body was not bruised. "One cut on the eye is all I got, but he opened that several times." Both eyes were slightly discolored, with red within, and with just a tinge of black and blue over the lids. Jeff "laughingly pointed out on his head a few knobs about the size of walnuts – evidence of Fitz's prowess."

The next day, Jeffries was quoted as saying,

The fight last night was the hardest I had ever had. It was a hard one from start to finish. Fitz never sized me up for a moment. I had him puzzled throughout. He could not reach my body because of my peculiar attitude. He reached my head often and heavily, but he did not jar at all. I did not feel his blows. I did not know that my eye had been cut until the blood came, but that blow was by long odds the heaviest that he gave me. ... Fitzsimmons is a game man, a clever man and a good fighter. He could not understand my method. He expected me to do more right hand work. I fooled him all through, and I think he will admit that he was puzzled all the time he was in front of me. I owe my success, I feel, to Tommy Ryan. He put me through the paces that were fast and furious. I went through six tough rounds every day with him and you know what that means.

A couple days after the fight, Jeff said that his body punches licked Fitzsimmons, in particular his rights to the body. Delaney told him to use his right to the body, but not to the head, fearing Bob's counter right. Jeff granted that Fitz could punch hard. "He can punch.... Fitz was as strong as hades, I tell you. He's one-third stronger than Sharkey." Jeff thought that Fitzsimmons could lick Sharkey.

Although Fitzsimmons hit him harder than anyone he ever had met, Jeffries laughed at him every time he landed, just to discourage him. "I am not afraid of punishment in a fight. ... I took all the iron out of him when he hit me hard and found it didn't hurt." Still, he did not allow Bob to reach his chin, ducking effectively. "I was always very handy at that. It comes natural for me to duck."

Jeff estimated that Bob weighed 180 pounds, while Brady thought he weighed about 170. "I weighed 210 pounds. Fitz refused to weigh. His people wanted to announce him at 158 pounds, I think it was, but Brady said if they did that he'd have me announced at 147, and they backed out." Because of his smaller size, "I was a little surprised at his hard hitting."

During the fight, Jeff took his time. He did not run, but he did not take undue chances either, employing Delaney's advice to be cautious and careful against a great ring general. Jeff said that Bob was good and strong right up to the very end.[60]

Others quoted Jeffries as saying, "I think Fitzsimmons is the hardest hitter I ever met, and he is certainly the best fighter I have fought." As a result, he took no chances, took his time, and paced himself, fighting carefully. He could have fought much faster, but there was no need for it.[61]

Jeffries later gave his analysis of Fitz's style and fighting abilities from his first-hand view:

> He's a big, strong, healthy fellow, with a long reach, and is constantly coming. What I mean by coming is that he shuffles into his opponent and is on the advance much oftener than he breaks ground. I never did consider him a skilled boxer, because he swings too much…. But there is no denying his ability as a ring general. He is a deceptive feinter with his feet and hands. He pays little or no attention to his defense, but stands ready to take a chance at getting hit if he can return the blow. He figures that he can hit twice as hard as his opponent and can stand more punishment. He is always studying to locate a certain spot on which his terrific punch can find lodging…. I like the action of Fitzsimmons' feet better than his hands. While he is not shifty of foot, still he has an awkward and puzzling way of shifting about in sidesteps, this scheme having a knockout punch for its object. He is constantly sneaking to the right or left of his opponent, as he figures that by these maneuvers he can locate the jaw or body easier with his swings. He tried this dodge on me, but I was looking for it, and either blocked his swing or stepped inside of them, his arm and glove encircling my neck as I closed on him…. You probably noticed that I slammed against him without hitting a blow, allowing my weight to lean on his body. I could see that he was puffing from the effects of this collision, and this trick of leaning and slamming the body against him took the wind out of his bellows. I got a fair sample of his hitting ability when he copped me with a double swing in the fourth round. These blows jarred me for an instant, and I felt them more than any other punch delivered during the fight…. Even after I had floored him in the tenth round he was still as confident as ever…. After all, when you sum up Fitzsimmons

[60] *New York World*, June 11, 1899.
[61] *Pittsburg Press*, June 11, 1899.

you must give him credit for having the greatest powers of recuperation that were ever bestowed by nature on a boxer.... Combined with his cool head, ring generalship, punching powers and foot work, you have the qualities that make him a great fighter.[62]

A year and a half later, Jeffries discussed the effectiveness of his crouching position.

I adopted that crouching position for many reasons.... In the first place, it presents an almost perfect defense against body blows. It discounted Fitzsimmons' solar plexus, you remember. In the second place, it makes it hard for any one except a man with a very clever left to hit me in the face, and even then he can land only lightly. And in the third place, it gives me a longer reach.... I developed my left arm long ago, so I could hit very hard with it – harder even than with my right.[63]

Former champions all lauded the new champion. Jim Corbett said, "Jeffries possesses all the qualities of a great boxer. ... He does not lack ring science or generalship." Corbett won a bundle of money, supposedly $6,000 in profit by betting $3,000 on the underdog Jeff.

John L. Sullivan called Jeffries one of the greatest fighters who ever lived. He did not see how he could lose. John L. predicted that Jeff would defend the title for many years to come and could be champion for ten years if he took care of himself.

Sullivan said Jeff was wise to keep away early, confident that his opening would come later. "Jeffries took my advice. He played a waiting game, without losing any chance. He figured out Fitzsimmons in the first few rounds. Then he started in to worry him with that terrible left of his." Fitzsimmons simply went against too much weight and power combined with cleverness. "The talk about his being old is all nonsense. ... He has taken good care of himself and will be heard from again." John L. would be proven correct.[64] Continuing, Sullivan said,

Never in my mind have I thought the Californian would fall. As I said some time ago, Jeffries is Fitzsimmons's superior in strength, and last night showed that he has skill as well. He displayed great head work throughout the battle and beat Fitzsimmons at his own game. That man Jeffries is a wise one. ... Jeffries relied solely on his left and a powerful left it is. It must have been a shock to Fitzsimmons when he first came in contact with it. All along I thought that the Australian underestimated the lad from the West. ... While I knew that Jeffries had improved wonderfully, I did not think he was as fast as he proved to be. He moved with the speed of an engine when he began to fight good and hard, and poor Fitzsimmons must have been sorely puzzled as the swings and jabs from the husky Californian began to shower on

---

[62] *National Police Gazette*, July 1, 1899.
[63] *Louisville Evening Post*, January 22, 1901.
[64] *New York World*, June 11, 1899.

him. And Jim showed himself to be clever, too. From the time he began to stir things up in the fifth round he feinted and dodged and shifted like a veteran. It was this display of caginess that enabled him to first land on Fitzsimmons, and once he got in one or two, why the end was in sight. No man living, Fitzsimmons or any one else, can withstand the blows of that mountain of muscle. ... The young American will be the champion for many years to come, or I am no judge.

There was a phenomenal amount of betting, one estimating at least $250,000. "Everybody bet on the fight." Another estimate of the betting claimed that $1.2 million changed hands. "Most of the talent wanted to see Jeffries win, but they could not figure out how Fitz was going to lose."

One said Fitz earned $25,000 to lose the championship and Jeffries $15,000 to win it. "Jeffries could not get Fitzsimmons into the ring except by agreeing to give Fitzsimmons the larger share of the money." However, "The real profit of a championship comes in the 'show' business, boxing tours and plays." Jeff's training expenses were $2,000.

They also were supposed to split into equal shares the receipts accruing from the motion picture exhibitions. Unfortunately, although attempts were made to film the indoor fight, and at first, the films were reported to have been taken successfully, for whatever reason, the films did not turn out and were useless. The fighters lamented the loss of hundreds of thousands of dollars in potential profits.

However, promoters released fake films of the fight as being the actual films and profited from them. Really, two actors put on a show, but most of the viewing public did not realize that the two were not Bob and Jeff. "Nobody who saw the actual fight could be misled or easily fooled by the fake exhibition, but unfortunately there are thousands of people who did not see the actual fight." This writer attended an exhibition of the fake pictures, and said, "Not an incident of the genuine fight was correctly reproduced."[65]

During his subsequent exhibition tour, Jeffries often was asked to discuss his fight with Fitzsimmons. Jeff said that Bob was a good game fighter who took many hard punches but kept coming all the way up to the end, earning his admiration. Fitz could deliver a very hard blow. "Ugh; you bet he can. I was sore for many a day after the fight." "He hit me harder than I was ever hit before – much harder – but they never hurt me at that. He can punch about three times as hard as Sharkey can." Therefore, Jeff took his time with him. He could have knocked Bob out sooner but wanted to be careful. "There was no use in sticking my head out to get it punched off with a right." "I wasn't taking any chances with such a shifty man."[66]

Speaking of his wonderful improvement as a fighter, Jeff credited Delaney and Ryan. Sparring with Ryan was of great benefit, for Tom taught him many new tricks. He mastered the left-hand feint for the body, which

---

[65] *National Police Gazette*, August 5, 1899. Apparently, some of these fraudulent films still exist.
[66] *National Police Gazette*, August 5, 1899; *Louisville Courier-Journal*, June 24, 1899.

often set up his left hook for the jaw. Jeff attributed his success in part to his ability to anticipate and elude Bob's blows. "My crouching position was also the result of Ryan's tuition. My failure to fall a victim to Fitz's feints was also due to careful practice with Ryan." However, Jeff later said that he always had a crouch and knew how to duck, for it came naturally to him, but Ryan helped him to perfect it.[67]

THE NEW HEAVYWEIGHT CHAMPION.

[67] *St. Louis Daily Globe-Democrat*, June 25, 26, 1899.

CHAPTER 4

Not Done Yet

JEFF THORNE.

HE FIGHTS BOB FITZSIMMONS AT TATTERSALL'S TOMORROW NIGHT.

"BOB" FITZSIMMONS.

(The Cornish champion who meets Jeff Thorne at Tattersall's tonight.)

Four and a half months after losing the title, in late October 1899, Bob Fitzsimmons was scheduled to take on English or South African middleweight Jeff or Geoffrey Thorne. In early September, Kid McCoy had stopped Thorne in the 3rd round. Thorne's manager Sam Fitzpatrick said Thorne held a KO2 over 'Harlem Coffee Cooler' Frank Craig and also had defeated Fred Morris and Dick O'Brien. Fitzpatrick also said, "Thorne is much faster and cleverer than Fitzsimmons, but the Cornishman excels in punching power. ... [Thorne] cannot hit as hard as Bob, but he can hit plenty hard enough to drop that fighter if he lands right."

Thorne said his sparring work with Tom Sharkey, "and it has been hard work at that, has put me in better physical condition than I ever was." He got some inside advice from Sharkey as well and intended to surprise Bob. "I see that he says in the papers that he intends to put me out in a round or two. I mean to do the same if I am able." Sharkey predicted that Thorne would put up a good fight against Fitz.

Fitzsimmons said, "I'm coming back to the ring with the intention of fighting my way back to the championship. If I knock Thorne out, and I will knock him out, I will issue a challenge, backed up by a big forfeit, to the winner of the Jeffries-Sharkey fight. I have reason to believe that the winner of that fight will give me a match, and that's all I want, simply a chance to prove to the public that I am still a champion."

Regarding the upcoming Jeffries vs. Sharkey championship contest, Fitz said it was a "toss-up," although his words also implied that he thought Jeff would win. "I am satisfied that when Jeffries and I meet again there will be a different story to tell. My right arm is in good shape again, as I intend to prove tonight when I stack up against Thorne. The Englishman is all right, they tell me, and he will need to be, for I am in good condition, and I have a great deal at stake on the outcome of the bout." Fitz said he had been training for the past 2 months with a view towards getting a chance with Jeffries or Sharkey. He claimed to weigh 170 pounds with clothes on.

On Saturday October 28, 1899 at Tattersall's Athletic Club in Chicago, Illinois, before a crowd of 6,000 or 7,000, in a scheduled 6-rounder, the longest distance allowed there, Bob Fitzsimmons took on purported English middleweight champion/light heavyweight Jeff Thorne.

The fight began shortly after 10:25 p.m. Fitz was accompanied by manager Martin Julian and sparring partner Yank Kenny. Bob bowed to acknowledge the cheers. Thorne was attended to by Sam Fitzpatrick, Buffalo featherweight Patsey Haley, and Joe Sullivan. Fitz sat smiling in his corner as various introductions and announcements were made.

Referee Malachy Hogan called them to ring center to give instructions. When he stripped off his black overcoat, trousers, and undershirt, Bob wore white trunks, topped with an American flag belt. Thorne, who wore black trunks, insisted on a clean break, and Fitz agreed.

1st round

At the gong, they fiddled and feinted, and Thorne twice ducked in anticipation of a blow that did not come. Fitz missed a left swing, just grazing the hair. Thorne landed a light left jab to the body. Fitz, after missing left and right, sent his left to the breast. They sparred, and Fitz sent his right to the ribs. He then sent a left hook to the jaw, and Thorne fell flat on his face.

At the count of ten, Thorne had just risen to his hands and knees, but fell over onto his side, out cold. Fitz took him around the waist and helped him up to his corner. He was badly shaken and did not leave the ring for several minutes after Fitzsimmons had left.

Another writer said Fitz knocked out Thorne in 1 minute 10 seconds of the 1st round. After a couple of light exchanges, Fitz feinted with his right, and, as Thorne ducked, Bob landed a left hook to the jaw which dropped him down face first for the count. The spectators cheered wildly.

Another version said Bob feinted a lot and advanced, jabbing the head. Thorne moved his head a fair amount, but a hard left jolted him a little. Thorne then landed a left lead on the chest, which he repeated. Bob smiled, then hooked his left to the jaw, and it was all over.

Many said Bob was himself again and capable of defeating any man in the world. "The knockout blow was an admirable illustration of Fitzsimmons' ability to pick out the vulnerable point. In this Fitzsimmons probably excels any other man who has ever lived."

In an interview a couple days after the fight, Thorne remarked, "You know I didn't see much of Fitz," which brought laughter. "Say, but can't he hit? That was the worst punch I ever got in my life. Why, that man Fitz is as far above me as a fighter as I am above a blind cripple. He is so blooming fast that I couldn't tell whether he was leading at me with his hands or his feet. ... He'd whip McCoy easily." After the fight, Fitzsimmons had told Thorne, "You see, I had to beat you more quickly than McCoy did, for reasons you yourself can figure out." Thorne had lasted into the 3rd round with McCoy.[68]

Between fights, Bob returned to vaudeville, as was his custom.

LYRIC—WASH.-ST., Opp. City Hall.
Matinees Wed. and Saturday.

BOB FITZSIMMONS

AND HIS BIG VAUDEVILLE CO.

Matinee Today and Tomorrow by IMPERIAL JAPANESE DRAMATIC COMPANY.

Friday night—Reading of special returns of Jeffries-Sharkey contest from stage by Bob Fitzsimmons, who will illustrate blows by practical demonstration. Mr. Julian, manager of Coney Island Athletic club, and Lyric insures absolutely correct description of fight.

Next Sunday Mat.—"ON THE WABASH."

"I JUST FEEL SORRY FOR JEFF RIES, THAT'S WHAT I DO."

[68] *New York Clipper*, November 4, 1899; *Chicago Tribune*, October 23, 28, 29, 1899; *Daily Inter Ocean*, October 27, 28, 29, 1899; *New York Sun*, October 30, 1899; *New York World*, October 31, 1899.

Six days after Fitz-Thorne, on Friday November 3, 1899 at the Coney Island Athletic Club in Brooklyn, New York, in the same arena that he won the title, a 210-215-pound 24-year-old James J. Jeffries first defended his title against 185-195-pound 25- or 27-year-old Tom Sharkey in a scheduled 25-round bout. Competing directly underneath extremely hot lights, necessary for filming, which made the inside-the-ring temperature over 100 degrees Fahrenheit, Jeffries scored two knockdowns in the 2nd round en route to a grueling, rough, fast-paced 25-round decision victory. Sharkey had been very aggressive, leading and firing many more punches, but Jeffries, with greater height and reach, had countered and landed more cleanly and effectively, and finished stronger, leading to the close decision win for the champion. Many thought it should have been a draw. From Chicago, Bob Fitzsimmons, who had not seen the fight, said he knew that Referee George

Siler was a good and honest referee, and would back any decision he made. "He knows the game, and if he said Jeffries won – why Jeffries did win." Jeff had a left arm injury coming into the bout, and aggravated it during the contest, hampering his performance.[69]

Bob Fitzsimmons believed that he could defeat Jeffries and wanted another chance. "I have been training lightly for several weeks in anticipation of a match with the winner, and you can bet I will be better prepared for a battle next time I enter the ring."

Fitzsimmons challenged Jeffries and posted $2,500. Martin Julian contended that Fitz was not in shape when he met Jeffries. In support of the argument, he noted that Sharkey made a much better showing against Jeffries than he did against Fitzsimmons back when Bob was sharp.

Jeffries was willing to fight Fitzsimmons again, provided that "I receive the biggest end of the receipts, win or lose, as I was forced to give him when we fought before." Jeff noted that after Fitz beat Corbett, everyone challenged him, but he did not fight for over two years. One writer opined, "Fitz has no good excuse for complaining because Jeffries chooses to give him a strong dose of his own medicine."

Jeffries was scheduled to fight former champion Jim Corbett next. Some felt that Fitzsimmons and Sharkey should fight each other for the next opportunity. Jeff said, "It is only right that these two should have it out before coming back at me. I defeated them both, and am now ready to meet whichever one is the better. I don't care which one it is."[70]

Unfortunately, it was rumored that New York Governor Theodore Roosevelt, via assemblyman Lewis, was going to initiate legislation to repeal the Horton law, which would once again severely restrict and limit boxing New York. The pro- and anti-boxing factions were gearing up for a potential legislative battle.[71]

New York was where the money was. It had a big population base that could afford to pay high prices to see the fights. According to the 1900 census, the U.S. population was 76.2 million for the 45-state union. The largest population in the United States was in New York City, which contained 3,437,202 people. The next closest in population size were less than half as big - Chicago at 1,698,575 and Philadelphia at 1,293,697. After that, no U.S. city broke the 600,000 mark. San Francisco was the 9th most populous city in the U.S., with only 342,782 people. Jeff's hometown of Los Angeles only had 100,000 people.

What was so wrong with boxing? After all, football was gaining increased popularity and was very big in major colleges. Jeffries saw a football game on November 11, 1899. He commented,

> I never looked at so much lively slugging and roughing in all the years I've been in the fighting business. ... If I had to take my choice

[69] *New York World, New York Sun, Brooklyn Daily Eagle, New York Herald, New York Times, New York Daily Tribune*, November 4, 1899, and *National Police Gazette*, November 18, 25, 1899; *Asbury Park Daily Press, San Francisco Chronicle, San Francisco Examiner*, November 4, 1899, and *New York Herald*, November 5, 1899; *New York Sun*, October 31, 1899. Corbett wrote the *World* account of the fight.
[70] *New York Journal*, November 11, 11, 1899; *New York Sun*, November 12, 1899; *New York Clipper*, November 18, 1899.
[71] *New York Journal*, November 11, 1899.

between having a man punch me as hard as he could or run ten yards and jump on me with his shoulder against my stomach I think I'd take the punch. ... But I don't kick about it as lots of these football supporters kick against fighting.

Jeff said that boxing was not one-half as rough as football.

I notice that under these football rules they give a knocked-out man three minutes to recover and get into the game. Do you know what that means? It means that he has a chance to get hurt eighteen times as much at football as he has at fighting. Under Queensberry rules a man who can't go on fighting within ten seconds after he is knocked down is out of the game. That's a merciful rule. But at football they give a fellow three minutes and he can come back and get knocked out half a dozen times in a game. ... Next time the good people make a roar about prize-fighting I'll know what is their idea of a pleasant, easy, safe sport.[72]

Still, by the end of 1899, seven men had perished in the ring that year. John L. Sullivan said rules should be adopted to reduce the killings. He felt that a physician should examine a fighter a week or so before the fight and on the night of the fight. Referees should stop a fight when it was evident that one boxer was unable to defend himself anymore. Seconds or club doctors should not be allowed to give "dope" to a man when he is almost out. "Whiskey or brandy is all right, but strychnine and such drugs make the knockout a lot worse when it comes." Ring floors should be padded. However, he did not want to see the sport tinkered with too much.[73]

Martin Julian said Jeffries caught Fitzsimmons when he was not right. Jeffries recognized the fact that he was lucky, and therefore was loath to take another chance with Fitz, "whom he knows in his heart is the best in the business." Such was the kind of talk that managers engaged in so they could advertise their man and obtain another lucrative fight.

Fitzsimmons was training again, and said,

When Jeffries fought me at Coney Island he did not meet Bob Fitzsimmons; at least, not the same Bob Fitzsimmons that he will face in another contest. I was not myself. ... My senses seemed to have failed me and I am sure that all this was not from a blow. I don't believe Jeffries can hit hard enough to defeat me when I am in my proper shape. [74]

From February 7 to 8, 1900, the state capital at Albany, New York was the scene of a debate about the potential repeal of the Horton law. A large delegation of ministers and representatives of law and order leagues backed Assemblyman Lewis, who had proposed an anti-boxing bill that would limit fights to only 10 rounds (as opposed to the 25 to which fans and fighters had become accustomed), with no points decisions allowed any more, and

[72] *New York World*, November 12, 1899.
[73] *New York World*, December 16, 1899.
[74] *National Police Gazette*, December 16, 23, 1899, January 13, 1900.

restricting attendance only to members of the sponsoring athletic club, not the general public. The lawyer for the opposition noted that since the Horton law had been in effect, over 600 contests had been pulled off in Erie County without difficulty, with relatively few injuries, all under the supervision of the police in a lawful and decorous manner, and attended by the "best people."

Eugene Comiskey, President of the Broadway Athletic Club, quoted statistics to show that football was overall worse than prizefighting. During the past 7 years, there were 127 deaths from football, along with 210 permanent injuries, 1,000 seriously injured, and 1,420 minor injuries. Boxing had 142 deaths, but only 4 had occurred since the 1896 Horton law went into effect. Governor Roosevelt had attended the 1896 Peter Maher KO6 Joe Choynski fight and declared that it was not a brutal exhibition. "If that was not brutal, Mr. Comisky said, no fight ever was."

The Lewis bill, as amended, proposed that the repeal would go into effect as of September 1, 1900. Thus, even if the bill was passed, boxers would have until then to complete whatever fights they wanted.[75]

Bob Fitzsimmons made an announcement claiming that he was drugged (or doped) when he fought Jeffries. It was an "eleventh hour excuse which excites ridicule among the followers of ring happenings." One opined that it was a little late for Bob to be making excuses. Still, Fitz claimed that after the 2nd round, "I took a long drink of mineral water, and following that I have only a hazy recollection of one or two incidents of the fight." A *Police Gazette* reporter responded, "My opinion is that the wallop on the head in the second round which landed him upon his back in the southwest corner of the ring was hard enough to make him forget he was alive." No one gave Bob's claim any credence. Even Martin Julian did not back him.

Fitzsimmons posted $5,000 and challenged Jeffries, Sharkey, and Kid McCoy. Eventually, on March 5, Fitz and Sharkey met and agreed to box 25 rounds on or about August 1, 1900, to settle which one was best entitled to another crack at Jeffries. Fitz was happy to prove that there was something crooked about his first encounter with Tom.

Although Fitzsimmons thought it was a "cinch" to beat Sharkey, many experts felt that he was underestimating Tom's improvement. "He has become a really clever pugilist." Sharkey had just gone 25 rounds with Jeffries in a close and competitive contest, losing a decision, whereas Fitz got stopped by Jeff in 11 rounds.

Regardless, it was good that Bob was becoming an active fighter again. "Only fighting can keep a man at the top notch. Exhibitions are all right and practice sparring serves its purpose…but the real thing is what is wanted, even if the man in front is a sucker of the greenest type. A fighter realizes that his mission is to beat him and he throws his heart and soul into the proceedings."[76]

[75] *National Police Gazette*, February 10, 17, March 3, 10, 24, 1900; *New York Times*, February 9, March 2, 1900.
[76] *National Police Gazette*, February 17, 24, March 3, 10, 17, 24, 1900. Fitz and Sharkey agreed to wear no hand bandages, and purportedly for the winner to take the entire receipts.

Final negotiations of the details for Fitz-Sharkey were ongoing. There was even talk of Bob facing Kid McCoy instead.

In the meantime, as a tune-up, on Tuesday March 27, 1900 at the First Regiment Armory in Philadelphia, Bob Fitzsimmons fought 178-185-pound Jim Daly (40-15-10) in a scheduled 6-round contest. The experienced Daly had sparred hundreds of rounds with both Jim Corbett and Jim Jeffries.[77]

In Fitz's corner were Jeff Thorne (former opponent and now sparring partner) and Matt Dooley. Jack Hanley and Isadore Strauss cared for Daly. It was a relatively light house, most feeling that Daly had no chance. Daly requested clean breaks, to which Fitz acceded.

1st round

As soon as the bell rang, Fitz attacked and never permitted Daly to move more than ten feet from his corner. Bob missed a left and they clinched. He then landed a left on the wind, and Daly missed a similar response. Daly ducked some blows, and after an exchange of several hard blows in rapid succession, Daly was forced to the ropes and clinched. After breaking, Daly landed lightly on the face.

According to the *Philadelphia Inquirer*, Bob landed two lefts to the face, the second of which dropped Daly. The *Philadelphia Times* version said Bob landed an awful right swing on the jaw that sent him down for nine seconds.

The *Inquirer* said that after Jim rose, Bob feinted a right, and then whipped his left to the belly, and Daly went down again. The *Times* version said it was a terrific right on the heart that sent Daly down for another nine-count. Perhaps it was both a right and left.

---

[77] Jim Daly's record included: 1886 L4 Pete McCoy; 1889 D6 Jack Fallon; 1890 LTKOby7 Denver Ed Smith; 1891 LKOby2 Frank Slavin; 1891 LKOby1 Peter Maher; 1896 LKOby3 Kid McCoy; and 1899 LKOby2 Al Weinig.

From that point on, the *Inquirer* said Fitz landed as he pleased, although he did not appear to be putting his full force into his punches. Just before the gong, Bob landed another left on the jaw, dropping Daly for the third time in the round. The *Times* version said Bob followed him, landed some blows on the cautious Daly, and, feinting with his right, whipped his left over, catching Daly on the jaw and he went down with the sound of the gong. His seconds had to help him to his chair.

Although the bell had saved Daly, Referee Walter Schlichter wisely and properly declined to permit the bout to continue. If he had not stopped it, they would have needed to call in the coroner. Daly was game but overmatched. With little exertion, Fitz had punched him into partial unconsciousness in 1 round. It was several minutes before Daly could leave the ring without assistance.

Locals noted that the bout demonstrated that Fitz had lost none of his cleverness as a boxer or any of his prowess as a hitter. "Three of the blows that he landed on Daly were terrific and of sufficient force to have put any of the big fellows out of the business."[78]

The next day, on March 28, 1900, the New York Senate passed the Lewis bill repealing the Horton law by a party vote, 26 to 22, once again making boxing quite limited in New York. The Republican majority were against boxing, with the exception of only one senator, who voted with the Democrats against the measure. New York Governor Theodore Roosevelt subsequently signed the bill. The repeal would go into effect on September 1, 1900. Therefore, anyone who wanted to fight in New York and earn real money needed to do so before the repeal went into effect.

Ironically, the upcoming semi-de-facto ban/severe legal limitation of boxing in New York stimulated the making of many fights in New York up to the end of August. Fighters wanted that New York money, and there were not a lot of other options. Either boxing was illegal in other states, or legal in remote locations without large populations and hence not conducive to a big gate attendance, or it was limited to shorter lengths such as 6 rounds, which was insufficient for big championship fights.

The *National Police Gazette* lamented, "The action of the Legislature in its illogical view of the boxing situation means the loss of a large revenue to local promoters of the game, and will incidentally curtail the coming into the Metropolis of a vast amount of money which was put into circulation by visiting sporting men, who were prodigal in leaving it behind them." An unhappy Senator Tim Sullivan said, "It required a special messenger from the governor, the calling of a Republican party caucus and an exhibition of treachery which was justifiable under the pressure brought to bear to pass the Lewis bill and to practically eliminate professional boxing from this State." Still, boxing would be hot until the repeal went into effect.

Jim Jeffries said all of the top fighters were afraid of Fitzsimmons and dodging him. "To tell the truth, I would rather fight ten Sharkeys, a dozen

[78] *Philadelphia Inquirer, Philadelphia Times,* March 28, 1900. On March 21, the *Philadelphia Times* said Daly weighed in the neighborhood of 185 pounds. On March 23, the *Times* said Daly was at 178.

Corbetts and all the McCoys you could bring before me than fight Fitz again. … They do not think they can beat him, and have a fear that he may wind them up in a hurry, as he can do." In response, Gus Ruhlin also made a match with Bob. So, Fitzsimmons had potential summer matches with both Ruhlin and Sharkey. If they wanted to fight in New York for potentially large purses, they needed to do so before September 1.[79]

Five months after his Sharkey defense, on April 6, 1900 in Detroit, Michigan, in a bout scheduled for 10 rounds, 220-pound Jim Jeffries fought Pittsburg's 180-pound "Irish" John/Jack Finnegan. Jeff almost immediately decked Finnegan, four times in all for the very quick 1st round knockout victory in only 55 seconds. Jeff earned $1,200.

Jeffries again spoke highly of Fitzsimmons, and also claimed to be badly injured and ill-prepared going into the Sharkey fight.

> I think Fitz is one of the hardest men to beat the ring ever knew. … If Fitzsimmons had caught me in the same shape Sharkey did, he would have beaten me. When I fought the sailor at Coney Island my left arm was bad – much worse than many suppose, and if I were to tell just how bad it was people would not believe me. I was not up to the standard… I have no hesitancy in saying that it was a lucky thing for me that I was not in the same condition when I met Fitz as when I met Sharkey. My left arm has mended nicely and is as good as ever. The trouble I had with my blood is also a thing of the past.[80]

On Sunday April 29, 1900, at New York's Madison Square Garden, 6,000 fans attended a benefit held in John L. Sullivan's honor. Jim Jeffries, Tom Sharkey, Gus Ruhlin, Peter Maher, and Bob Fitzsimmons all participated in separate sparring exhibitions.

Fitzsimmons boxed Jeff Thorne for 3 rounds. Bob was in total control for the first two rounds, but in the 3rd, Thorne dropped Fitz twice, Bob dropped him once, Bob got decked again, and then both went down at the same time, and they were counted out. "Then for the first time did some of those present realize that they had been witnessing a really clever fake." Fitz and Thorne popped up and shook hands. They had just pulled a goof on the crowd, which loved the entertainment anyway, applauding and cheering.

The main event was a friendly sparring exhibition between Sullivan and Jeffries. The 41-year-old Sullivan was very fat, while Jeff was trained to the hour, his muscles evident everywhere. They boxed 3 tame half-minute rounds with two minutes of rest in between. The crowd applauded.[81]

The next night, on Monday April 30, 1900 at New York's Hercules Athletic Club in Brooklyn, before a crowd of 3,500 to 4,000, Bob Fitzsimmons took on the experienced and durable "Human Freight Car," Ed Dunkhorst, in a scheduled 20- or 25-round bout. Most recently,

[79] *National Police Gazette*, April 21, 1900. Fitz and Ruhlin agreed to a 25-round contest, which was to be filmed, for the fighters to receive a 67% share of the gate with a like share of the picture receipts, with 75% to the winner and 25% to the loser. They agreed to George Siler as the referee.
[80] *National Police Gazette*, April 28, 1900.
[81] *New York World*, April 30, 1900.

Dunkhorst was a Jeffries sparring partner, taking a brief hiatus to go box Bob. In 1898, Dunkhorst had lasted 22 rounds against Gus Ruhlin (and was still on his feet at the time of the referee stoppage) and he held an 1899 10-round decision win over black Bob Armstrong.[82]

JEFFRIES LANDS A HARD ONE

The huge Dunkhorst got gay with the champion and started a right straight for Jeff's kitchen. You can see by looking at the snap shot taken by the Journal photographer what happened to Dunk.

What most distinguished Dunkhorst was his durability and massive size. Estimates of his weight ranged anywhere from 225 to 260 to 300 pounds. Jeff thought he was about 287. He stood about 6'4". Given that the 215-220-pound Jeffries looked much smaller than Dunkhorst in photographs of their sparring, it probably is safe to say that Dunkhorst weighed in the uppermost range of those estimates. However, Dunk claimed (likely falsely) that he weighed only 218 pounds, his lowest ever. He "looked three times as big as the lank Australian." Fitzsimmons likely weighed at least 170-180 pounds.

Dunkhorst was so big that he "looked like a week's output of a sausage factory rolled into one convoluted and corrugated gigantic link." However, Dunk could fight. Regardless of the fact that he was the heaviest and fattest fighter in the business, "he has shown considerable agility and also plenty of punching power."

Dunkhorst said, "I expect to come back here with the big end of the money. I have never been knocked out and I have met many bigger men than Fitz." He had boxed 6 rounds with champion Jeffries the day before.

The *Brooklyn Daily Eagle* said of Dunkhorst, "He is very active for such a monstrous big fellow and his endurance and ability to stand punishment are nothing short of remarkable. He is apparently absolutely impervious to body blows and as he manages to keep his chin well under cover he makes it very lively with his big fists."

---

[82] Significant Dunkhorst bouts included: 1897 D15 Jim Hall; 1898 D10 Bob Armstrong, LTKOby22 Gus Ruhlin, W20 C. C. Smith, D10 Armstrong, L6 Peter Maher, and L6 Joe Choynski; 1899 KO5 Charley Strong, L8 Frank Childs, LKOby6 Joe Butler, L25 Yank Kenny, D6 Jim McCormick, LDQby7 Peter Maher, W10 Bob Armstrong, and D20 Jack Stelzner. Boxrec.com.

Champion Is Putting on the Finishing Touches.

How the Big Fellows Spar While at Practice.

Despite the huge size difference, 100 pounds or more, Fitz expected to knock him out in less than 10 rounds and was willing to wager that way.

Upon his ring entry, Dunkhorst received little applause, while Fitzsimmons was cheered. Ernest Roeber, Dan Hickey, and Jeff Thorne, the English middleweight whom Bob had stopped in 1 round but had taken on as a sparring partner, seconded Fitz. Dunk's seconds were Tommy Ryan, Jack Jeffries, and Dan Johnson.

Fitzsimmons was stripped to the buff, only wearing his white knitted breech clout for trunks and an American flag for a belt. Dunk work blue trunks that reached half-way down his thighs. Fitz was a 4 to 1 favorite. It was even money that the bout would not last 10 rounds. They shook hands at 10:20 p.m. Charley White refereed.[83]

1st round

Dunkhorst was several inches taller but crouched down in Jeffries style. After some sparring, Fitz shot his left hook to the ear with jarring force. Bob feinted swiftly and played for Ed's head. "He wanted to get Dunkhorst's hands up about his face so that he would protect it and forget that he had any lower works." Bob strategically set up debilitating blows. He landed a heavy right to the ribs and a hard left jab. It was mostly a feeling out round, but Bob hooked him on the jaw with lefts whenever he wanted and landed the right with equal ease, causing Dunk to retreat. Fitz followed, forcing Dunkhorst to mix it until the bell rang. However, Dunk never landed. Fitz ducked, side-stepped, or blocked. One said Fitz already had raised a lump under Dunkhorst's right eye.

2nd round

Fitzsimmons was grinning and started in to end the fight. Bob sent his stinging stabs to Dunk's face, causing Ed to protect there. Dunk landed a left on the nose. Bob jabbed him on the eye and ducked a right swing. He went in close and missed an uppercut. Fitz then poured in body blows and drove his right to the jaw.

Grinning, Fitzsimmons feinted his right for the head and then ripped the left into the stomach. The glove dug into the fat until it disappeared to

---

83 The fight account is taken from *New York Journal, New York Sun, New York World, Brooklyn Daily Eagle, New York Daily Tribune, Philadelphia Public Ledger,* May 1, 1900, and *Brooklyn Daily Eagle, New York World,* April 30, 1900.

the wrist. The surprised Dunkhorst cried out with pain and hugged with both arms. After being separated, Fitz followed with a hard right to the jaw and vicious right uppercut. Bob once again hit the wind with the left, which sounded like "a pig of lead striking a ton of lard." The punch could be heard all over the building. As he was doubling over, Bob quickly followed with a tremendous left hook to the chin that dropped Dunk to the floor on his face like a log.

Dunkhorst "wriggled about on the floor like a huge jellyfish. His motions were convulsive." However, he soon became motionless, stretched out. Fitz wore a broad grin and circled around until Referee Charlie White counted Ed out.

The crowd heartily congratulated Bob, but initially the police surrounded him, fearful for a moment of some serious consequences. If Dunk died, Bob would be arrested.

One source said the fight was over at 1 minute 45 seconds of the 2nd round, while another said that the time of the round was 2 minutes 45 seconds, and yet another said 2 minutes 25 seconds.

Stopped only twice before, this was the first time in Dunkhorst's career that he was put to sleep, out cold for the full count. With a huge effort, his seconds lifted and dragged him to a chair. As usual with a Fitz fight, it was at least a minute before Ed was cogent again. They poured water on Dunkhorst in order to revive him. When he awoke, he put his hand to his right jaw and groaned. He asked, "What happened?" His cornerman Tommy Ryan, said, "Why, the roof fell in." With a far-away look in his eyes, Dunkhorst replied, "Then it must have hit me."

ROBERT FITZSIMMONS.

Thought the Roof Had Fallen on Top of Him.

EDWARD DUNKHORST.

One newspaper said Fitzsimmons was far from being a "dead one," that he had accomplished a feat which others and bigger men had found impossible. (Dunk had lasted the distance with men like Bob Armstrong, Peter Maher, Joe Choynski, and Frank Childs.) Fitz's "wonderful hitting powers have not forsaken him, and he was as lively on his feet as ever." Another said Fitzsimmons was in prime shape, fast and clever, and "best of all he hit with all of his old-time vigor." Others said, "Surely this is not the same man who met Jeffries." He definitely was not a has-been. He had quickly and decisively knocked out a man who was 100 pounds larger and had proven durability against others. Referee Charlie White said, "There never was a colder knockout."[84]

James J. Corbett was sparring with Gus Ruhlin in preparation for Jim's upcoming fight with Jeffries. Many who saw Ruhlin were tipping him to beat Fitzsimmons in their upcoming contest. Corbett's manager George Considine was willing to bet thousands of dollars that Ruhlin would beat Lanky Bob, saying he never saw so much improvement in a fighter as Ruhlin, in part because of what he had learned from sparring Corbett.[85]

On May 11, 1900, at Coney Island's Seaside Athletic Club in Brooklyn, New York, 25-year-old 210-218-pound James J. Jeffries defended his world heavyweight championship against former champion 33-year-old 188-pound James J. Corbett in a scheduled 25-round bout. Although the speedy and clever Corbett boxed brilliantly for most of the contest with his fast hands and feet, outpointing the champion, the increasingly aggressive, harder-punching Jeffries eventually wore him down, decking Corbett in the 19th round with head blows, until knocking him out cold in the 23rd round with a savage left hook or uppercut to the jaw.

Many praised Corbett as a "regenerated pugilist" who put up "the best fight of his career," for 17 rounds landing at will and eluding blows with ease. "A prettier exhibition of the art of hit, stop and get away it would be impossible to find within a squared circle." However, Jeffries' strength, toughness, durability, condition, and power came through for him.

John Eckhardt said Corbett was at his best, and no back number, outboxing and outfighting Jeffries with far superior ring generalship to such a degree as to make Jeff

[84] *New York Journal*, May 3, 4, 1900.
[85] *Buffalo Enquirer*, May 11, 1900.

seem like a novice by comparison. Nevertheless, Jeffries excelled at rushing and constantly boring in, his bulldog tenacity and perseverance eventually producing results. "The fight proved that the skillful light-hitting boxer cannot cope with the rugged heavy hitter who is willing to take all kinds of chances to land a knockout blow." Insufficient punching power was Corbett's one weakness. "Had Bob Fitzsimmons or Tom Sharkey been able to land one-half as often as Corbett did, when they were up against Jeffries, Mr. Brady would have to remove the words 'undefeated champion of the world' from his banners."

Jeffries said,

> Corbett's work was a revelation to me. Jim never fought better in his life. He was very fast, and that may have made me appear at a disadvantage, but I got the money, and that's the main thing. They can all criticize my style of fighting, say that I am a cart horse and all that sort of thing, but none of them I have met beat me, so I can't be such a bad fighter. I knew Corbett was a clever fighter and recognized the fact that I would have to land a knockout. ... Had Corbett employed the same tactics he used [tonight] in his fight against Fitzsimmons he would never have lost the championship to "Lanky Bob." He fought me with the idea of staying the limit. He sprinted a lot and that made it hard for me to reach him.

Jeffries also was quoted as saying that Corbett was in far better shape than he had been against either Fitzsimmons or Sharkey. "Sharkey and Fitz were easy compared to him." Yet, he also said that neither Fitz nor Sharkey ran as Corbett did, and they hit harder than Jim. "Corbett is still the shifty man of old, but agility and cleverness are not all in this game. I am not slow by any means, but I rely far more on my ability to administer severe punishment than on showy side-stepping and jabs that have not got the strength to back them."

Corbett said,

> I thought I would win sure. I was landing my blows in good style and surely felt I would last the 25 rounds and get the decision. How I got the knockout blow I don't know. I have no recollection of it landing. It must have been a corker, however, to have put me out.

Attending the fight for the *New York Journal* was Bob Fitzsimmons. During the 1st round, Fitzsimmons said, "This fight demonstrates one thing so far, and that is Corbett's cleverness. It is surprising how little he knows about actual hitting." Bob noted that Corbett landed a lot. "If Corbett could only punch hard." Jeffries focused on body shots and pressure, trying to force Corbett to fight him more. But Corbett was in great shape, so it took a while to wear him down. In the 18th round, Fitz said, "Corbett's coy tactics diminish considerably. He has already taken more punishment than I thought him capable of. It is beginning to be a great fight." Bob said Jeff decked Corbett in the 19th with a right and left and severely punished his body. "I tip my hat to his gameness." In the 22nd round, Jeffries staggered

Corbett and had his legs quivering. Frightful smashes nearly lifted him off the floor. Jim clinched and used his legs and jab. "Jeffries had him to the bad toward the close." In the 23rd round, Bob said, "Bang, a left on the jaw swung like a catapult. Corbett had made the fatal mistake of overconfidence. He is down and out. He should have won. The cart horse wears the smile again." Fitzsimmons also said, "Jeffries was too heavy for him."

"Right Cross," writing for the *New York Journal*, said that Corbett's fancy boxing, with all his blocks, slips, and side-stepping, was pretty to look at, but the real fighter needed a wallop in order to take home the money. Big Jim Jeffries might not have been pretty, but he had the punch.

Right Cross further said that Bob Fitzsimmons occupied a middle ground. He was able to both give a punch and take one. He had stamina and cleverness, and probably the best "ring head" around. Summing up, "The cleverest blocker at the game must take the loser's end when opposed to the man who has the knockout blow." This was especially true in a long fight when the puncher had the stamina to keep punching hard and could avoid damaging blows while attacking. Eventually the slick boxer had to get hit, and Jeffries and Fitzsimmons had the power to put out a Corbett, who was a very fast, brilliant boxer with footwork, but he could not punch hard enough to take out really hard men like Fitz and Jeff, although he had decked Fitz.[86]

Jeffries was complimented for having defeated the three cleverest, toughest, and greatest fighters in the world – Fitzsimmons, Sharkey, and Corbett, all within one year. Very few heavyweights throughout history, including up to the present day, could say that they fought the three best men in the division in the span of one year.

[86] *Brooklyn Times, Brooklyn Daily Eagle, Buffalo Enquirer, New York Journal, New York World, New York Sun, New York Tribune, New York Times,* and *Brooklyn Daily Eagle,* May 12, 1900; *New York Journal,* May 16, 1900.

CHAPTER 5

Establishing a Right

Owing to an injury to his left hand suffered in the Dunkhorst bout, which hand still hurt, Bob Fitzsimmons required a postponement of his scheduled contest with Gus Ruhlin.[87]

Both Ruhlin and Sharkey were looking for opponents, so they agreed to fight each other.

Since the Jeffries fight, Tom Sharkey had been on a six-fight win streak, all of them by knockout, including: 1900 KO4 Joe Goddard, KO2 Jim Jeffords, KO1 Jim McCormick, KO2 Stockings Conroy, KO3 Joe Choynski, and KO1 Yank Kenny. Sharkey had the prior victories over Corbett and McCoy as well.

Gus Ruhlin's record included: 1897 D20 Jim Jeffries; 1898 L20 Kid McCoy, LKOby1 Tom Sharkey, WTKO22 Ed Dunkhorst, WND6 Joe Goddard, and WND6 Joe Choynski; and 1899 WDQ5 Goddard, D20 Peter Maher (brutal war), and L20 Joe Kennedy.[88]

Subsequent to the Kennedy loss, Ruhlin had been on an 8-0, 7 KOs win streak that included: 1899 KO7 Jack Stelzner, KO5 Jim Jeffords, W6 Jack McCormick, and KO7 Stockings Conroy; and 1900 KO4 Jack Finnegan and KO6 Yank Kenny. Ruhlin had been a Jim Corbett sparring partner prior to Corbett giving Jeff hell over 23 rounds. Gus had been getting plenty of good press from sparring with Corbett, who lauded his improvement. Observers liked what they saw. Naturally, the fact that Ruhlin had fought a 20-round draw with Jeffries also put his name in the spotlight. He was a big, strong, muscular, skillful, and experienced 200-pounder who looked

---

[87] *National Police Gazette*, June 2, 9, 16, 23, 30, 1900.

[88] *National Police Gazette*, March 25, 1899, April 8, 1899, May 20, 1899, October 14, 1899. On May 2, 1899, Ruhlin and the hard-punching Peter Maher fought a 20-round draw in what was called the hardest heavyweight fight ever. Both were badly punished. Gus was dropped in the 1st, but both men went to their corners bruised and wobbling. Ruhlin staggered Peter in the 2nd. Gus took the lead in the 5th and backed Maher up. From the 10th to the end, Ruhlin was the aggressor, but Maher countered hard and took punches well. Maher and Sharkey had fought to a 7-round draw. On September 26, 1899, the 175-pound Maher had scored a KO2 over 190-pound Joe Kennedy. However, in January 1900, Kid McCoy knocked out Maher in the 5th round. Sharkey held a knockout victory over McCoy.

the part. Gus wanted to avenge his prior LKOby1 defeat to Sharkey, which he considered to be a fluke, having been caught cold.

Born of Swiss and French descent (not German), Gus Ruhlin was 29 years old. Noted for his strength, it was said that Ruhlin's weightlifting feats overshadowed the great Sandow, the former strongman.[89]

On June 26, 1900 at Coney Island's Seaside Athletic Club, "Akron Giant" Gus Ruhlin knocked out "Sailor" Tom Sharkey in the 15th round, having decked him in the 8th round en route. Ruhlin coolly outboxed the ferociously attacking sailor, landing stiff jabs and right uppercuts, combining skill, generalship, and heavy hitting to break down the sailor.

The victory made Ruhlin the man of the hour, for he had stopped Sharkey, the man whom Jeffries had not knocked out in two contests. A *Police Gazette* writer said, "Ruhlin, in my opinion, is just the man to defeat Jeffries. He has size, bone, substance and gameness, and under Corbett's tuition has improved in boxing ability, and is the boilermaker's master in matters of ring technique. He is unquestionably more clever than the present champion."[90]

However, Jeffries' left arm, which he badly re-injured in the Corbett contest, was still healing, and he was not ready to fight any time soon.

In the mad rush to make big fights prior to boxing going out of business in New York, Bob Fitzsimmons made two matches – one with Gus Ruhlin, and another with Tom Sharkey, both fights to be held in August 1900.

Fitzsimmons vs. Ruhlin was scheduled for 25 rounds, to be held on August 10. Madison Square Garden had the winning bid to host the fight,

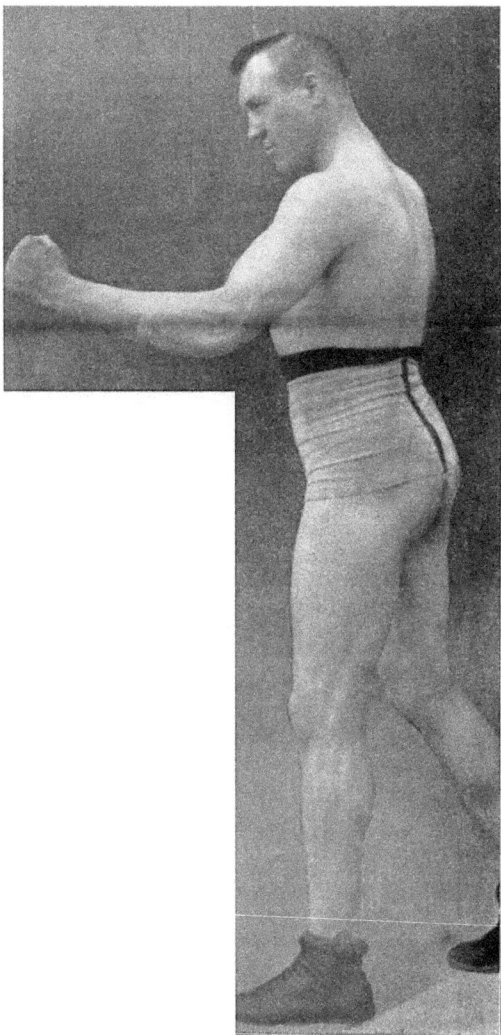

[89] *National Police Gazette*, April 8, 1899, February 3, 1900.
[90] *National Police Gazette*, July 14, 1900.

offering the fighters 50% of the gate receipts, which was to be split 75/25% winner/loser. Soft bandages were to be allowed, and Charley White would referee.

The Fitz vs. Sharkey fight was scheduled for August 25 at Coney Island.

The press opined that Ruhlin "will give [Fitzsimmons] a better fight than he bargains for. [Ruhlin] is cleverer than Sharkey, with youth and physical advantages which will be a factor in determining the outcome of his battle with the Australian." Fitzsimmons was called courageous for taking on such a tough fighter.

Sizing up Ruhlin and Fitzsimmons, one writer noted that Fitz had Sharkey in a state of total collapse in 8 rounds, while it required Ruhlin 15 rounds to stop Tom. But, then again, Ruhlin fought a better, more experienced version of Sharkey, and had avenged his prior knockout loss to Tom. Ruhlin drew in 20 rounds with Jeffries, whereas a more experienced version of Jeff stopped Fitzsimmons in 11 rounds. Ruhlin's "experience with Corbett was invaluable; he has a better knowledge of scientific fighting than he ever had and is able to execute blows with rapidity and effect." "He will give a good account of himself in the ring, and I certainly believe he has the best chance of winning."[91]

MEASUREMENTS OF FITZ AND RUHLIN.

Fitzsimmons.		Ruhlin.
5 feet 11¾ inches	Height	6 feet 1¾ inches
168 pounds	Weight	195 pounds
16 inches	Neck	17 inches
44 inches	Chest	41¾ inches
48 inches	Chest expanded	45¾ inches
28 inches	Waist	35 inches
75 ¼ inches	Reach	79 inches
14½ inches	Biceps	13½ inches
11¾ inches	Right forearm	13½ inches
7½ inches	Wrists	8 inches
23½ inches	Thighs	23¼ inches
14 inches	Calves	17 inches
9¾ inches	Ankles	10 inches

Since his loss to Jeffries in June 1899, Fitz had boxed in three bouts: October 1899 KO1 Jeff Thorne, March 1900 KO1 Jim Daly, and April 1900 KO2 Ed Dunkhorst. Although the fights were short, by remaining in active training and having legitimate contests, Fitz got himself fight sharp and maintained his fitness.

Results against common opponents included: Maher – Fitz KO12 and KO1, Ruhlin D20; Sharkey – Fitz KO8 or LDQby8, Ruhlin LKOby1 and KO15; Jeffries – Fitz LKOby11, Ruhlin D20; Dunkhorst – Fitz KO2, Ruhlin TKO22; Choynski – Fitz TKO5 or D5, Ruhlin WND6.

[91] *National Police Gazette*, July 28, August 11, 1900.

Training at Bergen Beach, Fitzsimmons was "in as fine fettle as any man I ever saw." On the morning of August 7, three days before the fight, he ran 6 to 7 miles, alternating between brisk walking and sprinting. In the afternoon, first he boxed 6 rounds with Bob Armstrong, the big 6'4" 190-pound black fighter who once went 10 rounds with Jeffries and often had sparred with Sharkey. During the 6 rounds of sparring with Armstrong,

> Fitz did not strike a single blow. He simply stepped in and out of hitting distance and feinted Bob [Armstrong] into leading. Then Fitz started a blow for the opening thus obtained, but stopped it before it landed. Ordinarily this sort of thing would be very dull entertainment, but with Fitzsimmons doing the work it was very exciting. He sidestepped around…. He bluffed him again and again into awkward dilemmas, so that he created a chance to put in one of his famous little knockout punches as Armstrong laid himself open by an unprotected lead. Fitz is one of the greatest men living at this sort of thing. To see him putting it all over a clever big fellow like Armstrong was a treat. The black man tapped him with his left on the cheek now and then, but Fitz always shifted his head and let the blow glance off harmlessly. Often he worked Armstrong into such a position that it would have needed but half a second of time to throw in one of his bombshell punches that are always fatal. This is the sort of battle that Fitz always fights. A great test awaits Ruhlin on Friday night. If he ever lets Fitz step around him and feint him into a tangled position or an unprotected one he will vanish from the scene with awful rapidity. Of course Ruhlin is preparing to avoid the calamity, but he cannot be too careful, no matter how good he is.

Fitzsimmons showed himself to be in fine condition, while Armstrong was puffing and often asking if time was up. "Fitz's footwork was of its former quality, awkward looking on the surface, but wonderfully effective in taking him just where he wanted to go."

After sparring Armstrong, Bob boxed in a similar manner for a couple of rounds with Jeff Thorne. After that, Bob practiced clinching and breaking from clinches for five minutes each with both Armstrong and Thorne. Fitz appeared to weigh about 172-174 pounds.

W. O. Inglis opined, "Ruhlin will have to fight the keen, shrewd, calculating, puzzling fellow who beat Corbett, and not the cocky, overconfident champion who quickly fell beneath the fist of Jeffries. So it appears that not only is Fitz's bodily condition perfect, but his mental attitude is perfect, too."

Back in April, speaking of his then future summer fight with Ruhlin, Fitzsimmons said, "I will not fight Ruhlin as I fought Jeffries. He, like Jeff, is bigger than I, and I'll have to be careful not to let his weight tell. I'll just smash and bang him from a distance, safe from hugging."

James Jeffries came to New York for the big fight. Jeff said, "I find that my arm is improving steadily." However, he still was nursing it. His left elbow had been hurting since the Corbett fight. "I have been advised by my physicians not to take a chance until they declare it has completely recovered." Regardless of that advice, Jeff still wanted to fight and initially said that he was willing to take the risk and fight despite doctors' advice not to do so. "I now stand ready to make a match for the world's championship with the winner of tonight's battle, the bout to be decided in or about New York City before Sept. 1."

If Fitzsimmons won, Jeff was ready to give him a chance only if Fitz accepted the same financial terms that Jeffries had accepted when he obtained his title shot. Jeff also said that if Fitz or Ruhlin did not meet him prior to September 1, they would have to wait at least six months, for his time would be occupied with other matters until May 1. "I defeated Fitzsimmons in a most decisive manner, and therefore do not consider myself bound to meet him again, but will give him another chance if he agrees to box before September 1."[92]

There was a real question regarding whether Jeffries could or would be physically ready to fight any time soon, with less than a month of serious training time and arm still bothering him, and whether Fitzsimmons would fight under such financial terms. Bob was well aware of his value in generating a big gate in a championship fight. It also was doubtful whether Fitz could fight three times in a month. However, talk helped hype fights.

Heading into the Ruhlin contest, Fitzsimmons was confident, as always.

> I am as good a man as I ever was. I am certain I will whip Ruhlin, and I expect to defeat him before the limit. He is a good, strong, clever fighter, but he will surely be added to my list of victims. I think that a lot of people will be surprised when they see me in action. It's all very well to call me an old man, but when I land a couple of good ones on Ruhlin they will see that I have lost none of my speed or hard-hitting powers. As Jeffries has promised to meet the winner of this fight, I can almost see myself the world's champion again.[93]

Ruhlin was positive that he would defeat Fitzsimmons. "I am in excellent condition, and if I don't knock Fitzsimmons out I will be able to go the whole twenty-five rounds at a fast gait and will win on points." Ruhlin also said that he would be the world's champion before the end of the year; for he was sure that he could defeat Jeffries. "In fact, I consider Fitz harder game."

The experts made their predictions. Jim Corbett said Ruhlin should win easily and would end the fight within 10 rounds. "Ruhlin should stop any heavy weight in the ring today." He said Gus was faster, stronger, more scientific, and had youth on his side. However, John L. Sullivan said, "Fitz ought to win. He has the experience, and is a hard hitter." Those picking Fitzsimmons included Tom Sharkey and Peter Maher (both of whom had fought both), Jimmy Carroll, George Siler, Bob Armstrong, George Dixon, and Joe Walcott. Those picking Ruhlin included Jack McAuliffe, Spider

[92] New York World, August 8, 10, 1900; New York Journal, April 21, 1900; National Police Gazette, August 25, 1900.
[93] New York Journal, August 10, 1900.

Kelly, Kid McCoy, George McFadden, George Considine, Billy Madden, and Tom O'Rourke.[94]

The day of the fight, W. O. Inglis of the *New York World* picked Ruhlin to defeat Fitzsimmons. Gus was about 30 pounds bigger (165 vs. 195), significantly younger (28 vs. 37), had the height advantage (6'1 ¾" vs. 5'11 ¾"), 4 inches of reach advantage, and was coming off his biggest victory, in which he had shown improvement as a technician. Ruhlin had shown great ability at blocking, both in sparring with Corbett and in the Sharkey fight. "Tom Sharkey, who is as fast as any fighter that ever lived, rushed at Ruhlin like a whirlwind, but Gus coolly stuck out his left time and again and uppercut the Sailor with his right until he stopped him. Certainly he showed coolness."

Still, Fitzsimmons "undoubtedly knows more about ring generalship than any other fighter in the business." He had the superior experience, and had taken care of his body, making it younger than his chronological age. Although Ruhlin had been defensively sound against Sharkey, it was quite another thing "to hold that form in a fight with a man of Fitzsimmons's terrific punching ability."

Summarizing, Inglis said,

> It seems to me that the issue comes down to whether or not Ruhlin will be able to keep cool and avoid being flurried by Fitzsimmons's great name and foxy tactics. If he can do this he is certainly big enough, strong enough and fast enough to win the battle. I think it is reasonable to believe that Ruhlin will keep cool and take care of himself. I expect to see him win.[95]

Lanky Bob Is a 10 to 8 Favorite Now, but Experts Think Even Money Betting Will Prevail When Fighters Enter the Ring.

RUHLIN AND FITZ IN FIGHTING ATTITUDES IN THE RING

MEASUREMENTS OF FITZ AND RUHLIN.

[94] *New York World*, August 9, 1900; *New York Journal*, August 10, 1900; *New York Sun*, August 11, 1900.
[95] *New York World*, August 10, 1900.

One source said Fitz was a close 6 to 5 odds favorite. Another said that Bob had been the betting favorite at 10 to 8 odds, but on fight night, so much money came in on Ruhlin that Gus wound up being the slight favorite. Certainly, it appears to have been a pick 'em type fight.

On Friday August 10, 1900 at New York's Madison Square Garden, for the Twentieth Century Athletic Club, Bob Fitzsimmons fought "Akron Giant" Gus Ruhlin (27-5-2) before a huge crowd (with estimates of 9,000, 10,000, 12,000 or 15,000). Jim Jeffries was in attendance. Tickets sold for $3, $5, $7, $10, $15, and $20.[96]

It was a hot, humid day, the thermometer reaching 105 degrees, and it still was quite hot in the evening. A howl was made for more air from the fans, but they already were working at their limit. The crowd had to suffer in the heat.

A picture machine was at one end of the building, and it was understood that an attempt would be made to film the fight using ordinary light.

At 9:45 p.m., Fitzsimmons entered the ring wearing a light bathrobe. Ruhlin followed a moment later, his shoulders covered with a towel. Gus wore a canvas breechcloth. Upon removing his bathrobe, it was seen that Bob was wearing a pair of pink trunks and a belt made of American flags.

The *New York Herald* reported that Fitz weighed 168 pounds to Ruhlin's 190. Bob claimed to weigh 162 pounds, but the *Sun* said it was a good bet that he really weighed about 172. It said Gus tipped the scales at 194. The *Brooklyn Daily Eagle* said Ruhlin admitted to 195, but its writer felt that Gus weighed at least ten pounds more, at 205+. Their size difference was most noticeable. "He was bigger than Fitz in every way. He towered above him half a head and looked powerful enough to twist the Cornishman in two in a wrestling match." The *New York Tribune* said Fitz contended that he weighed only 160 pounds, while Ruhlin admitted to 190. As usual, neither took the scales officially.

[96] *New York Herald*, August 10, 1900.

Fitz's seconds were George Dawson, Jeff Thorne, Bob Armstrong, Dan Hickey, and Percy Williams. Attending to Ruhlin were Jim Corbett, Billy Madden, Charley Goff, and Matty Matthews.

Fitz had brought his own gloves, and he took them over to Ruhlin's manager Billy Madden for inspection. Jim Corbett insisted on putting on Fitz's light red gloves for him, "a proceeding which the Australian didn't seem to relish." Corbett held the glove while Fitz shoved his hand into it.

The bout was scheduled for 25 rounds. Charley White refereed.

Joe Humphries was the announcer. He introduced Tom Sharkey to the crowd, who walked over and shook hands with Fitz and Ruhlin. Jim Corbett also was introduced. Humphries introduced the fighters to cheers. They were ready to go at 10:10 p.m.

1st round

Early on, it looked as though Fitzsimmons would be an easy victim. Ruhlin forced matters and landed a number of hard jabs, as well as a left to the body and a right to the jaw. Fitz seemed listless and lethargic, and some wondered what was wrong with him. Ruhlin landed straight punches as well as hooking blows. One particularly hard jab shook Bob considerably. "There's nothing to it. The old man is all in." Gus was very fast and tried to stay close.

However, Fitzsimmons suddenly came to life and landed a couple rights to the jaw that slightly staggered Ruhlin. Fitz mixed it up with a left and right to the jaw. Gus came back with a straight left to the nose and right to the jaw. Bob landed a hard left uppercut to the body that made Gus grunt, but Ruhlin with his great strength rushed Bob to the ropes and smashed him with both hands to the face and body.

Blood "spurted from Fitz's face." His left eye had been cut. They mixed it hotly, and both landed heavy smashes on the head. Gus staggered Fitz with a left, but Bob feinted and landed a good counter wallop to the mouth that drew blood.

Ruhlin landed a left hook to the jaw and Fitz clinched. Either Bob slipped down or Gus wrestled him down, depending on the source. Blood was flowing from Bob's left eye. There was something wrong with the bell. It was barely audible, and when it went off as Bob rose, Fitz stopped fighting, but Ruhlin hit him with a right before the referee intervened. The spot over Fitz's eye where Ruhlin had landed his jabs became blue and swollen as big as an egg.

Most thought Ruhlin would defeat Fitzsimmons just as he had done with Sharkey. Bob had been clearly jarred by several lefts. One gambler offered 5 to 1 odds, with Ruhlin the favorite.

2nd round

Ruhlin immediately went in with rapid swings and cut open Fitz's eye again. However, Fitzsimmons had woken up. After taking a jab, Bob stood in close and landed a terrific right to the jaw that staggered Ruhlin. "A shift with the left and a hook on the nose and the lower part of Ruhlin's face was a splash of blood." The blood poured out of Ruhlin's mouth and nose in a stream, smearing his chest with huge red patches.

Fitz hurried matters, and a left to the stomach made Gus back away. Bob was quick and strong, his blows falling with the rapidity of an avalanche. He feinted often and crashed his gloves into the face, sending the blood flying. Gus was surprised and seemed tired and dazed by the fast pace and hard blows. Instead of wilting from all the hard punches that he had absorbed thus far, Fitzsimmons was fighting faster.

Bob rushed and they mixed it up, both landing terrific punches to the head. Bob landed a hook that made Ruhlin tumble back into the ropes. Gus responded with jabs, but "he might as well have tried to stop the coming of tomorrow as make any halt in the now fighting Fitz. Old man, eh?" Both were bleeding, but Gus was backing away. Fitz rushed and with left and right on the head made Gus stagger. When Bob came in, Ruhlin lowered his head and clinched. Fitz landed a short stab in the ribs, which caused Gus to bend forward. Bob then straightened him up with an uppercut to the chin. Gus missed a wild right and clinched. Bob shook him off.

Both seemed tired. Ruhlin landed some light jabs and hooks to the face. "He landed them so easily that Bob looked silly." Fitz was not trying to block or evade Ruhlin's punches at all.

However, Fitzsimmons rained in the blows again and a left on the jaw knocked Ruhlin against the ropes, and he staggered away dazed. Bob landed a left and right. When Gus threw up his guard to block a hook, Bob shifted his feet and "for the first time Ruhlin knew what a Fitzsimmons shift and solar plexus blow meant. It landed fairly and solidly, sending Ruhlin to the floor." Another version said Bob bluffed the right, landed the left hook to the head, and then dropped the left hook down to the body. Ruhlin went down on his hands and knees, doubled up like a jackknife, with a look of agony on his face. Fitz smiled as he walked away.

After Gus rose from the knockdown, Bob went to finish him, but the bell saved Ruhlin. "If there had been a half a minute left to this round Ruhlin would have surely been put to sleep, for when he got to his feet he was scarcely able to stand and was about to pitch forward on his face when the bell rang and his seconds caught him."

The body punishment had taken all of the steam out of Ruhlin. It seemed as if it was just a matter of time before Fitzsimmons ended matters.

3rd round

Bob Armstrong, Fitz's sparring partner, said that between rounds, in the corner, a Fitz handler who was very nervous got ammonia into Bob's eyes. It nearly blinded him, and he was almost beside himself with pain. After boxing a little at the start of the round, Fitz managed to come around all right before anyone realized that something was wrong.

Ruhlin recovered fairly well from the previous round and opened on the attack, mixing it blow for blow, but Fitzsimmons got the better of it. Bob's terrific smashes beat Ruhlin back and had him in trouble. Fitz's punches raised a lump over Gus's left eye. Bob landed a number of short heavy hooks that had Ruhlin's nose and mouth bleeding again. Gus used his left jabs to the mouth and eye, drawing blood, but Bob never weakened and kept smashing the big fellow on the head and body. Gus grew fatigued and began clinching. Bob showed some signs of weariness, too. They clinched and wrestled around.

Ruhlin jolted Bob's eye with a left, but Fitzsimmons responded with a left hook to the jaw that sent Gus staggering across the ring. He followed with a left to the stomach that caused Gus to clinch. Ruhlin landed a right but Bob responded with a left and right to the head that made Gus stagger. In close, Ruhlin landed a blow to Bob's neck with his left elbow. The referee briefly stepped in to warn him. Both were tired at the bell.

4th round

Fitzsimmons tried to end matters, forcing the fight. Willing to take chances, he held his face out and let Ruhlin hit him at will. Bob never broke ground. He took punches, either to show Gus how weak they were, or to allow Gus to wear himself out, or, by allowing Ruhlin to punch, Gus would expose himself to one of Bob's brutal counterpunches. Perhaps Bob was just resting. Corbett and Madden warned Ruhlin to be careful, feeling that Bob was faking in order to set a trap.

Eventually, Fitzsimmons retaliated and again put it all over his man, landing a number of hard smashes to the head and body. Ruhlin jabbed but had little effect. Bob chased him around. Ruhlin was unsteady, but in the clinches, he laid his weight on Bob. Fitz took his time, appearing to be tired. "He was faking, however, for the next moment he let loose a left for the stomach that made the big man retreat." Gus was slow with his punches and seemed to be weakening.

Fitzsimmons rained in the blows and knocked Ruhlin down again with right and left smashes to the body and head. Particularly effective were the right to the jaw and left to the body.

After he rose, a Fitz right split open Ruhlin's eye. "Corbett made a demonstration in his corner and was warned by the police to keep quiet." Some feared that he would try to enter the ring to lose the fight for Ruhlin on a foul in order to save him from punishment.

> Just what Corbett's idea was nobody could tell, for Referee White thoroughly understood that no foul would be allowed should a second enter the ring during a round, as Corbett's handler, McVey, did when Jim was 'getting his' from Sharkey at the Lenox Club last year. But a cool-headed policeman prevented any possible unpleasantness by reaching over and shaking a club in Corbett's face with the remark, 'Don't get gay or I'll throw you out of the building!'

At the bell, Ruhlin was in bad shape, bleeding, groggy, and weak.

5th round

Ruhlin was still groggy and had no strength in his punches. Fitz was strong. He walloped Gus with a double left, first to the jaw and then down to the body. Gus hung on. After breaking, Ruhlin tried his left with all the force that he could, but Bob ignored it and sent in smashes to the face that left Gus covered in blood. Ruhlin had a lump on the right eye the size of a hen's egg.

However, once again, Fitzsimmons allowed Ruhlin to hit him. Gus landed half a dozen blows to Bob's face. All those hard punches that Bob was throwing had to tire him. However, Ruhlin's blows did no damage. Fitz took matters very coolly, and after they clinched, Bob laughed at the spectators over Ruhlin's shoulder. Corbett gave constant frantic advice from outside the ring, and upon one occasion, the police had to suppress him. Jim wanted Ruhlin to watch out for one of Bob's smashes.

Fitzsimmons took his time, stalling for a while, but then finally hurried matters with body blows and facers that made Gus clinch hard. Shortly thereafter, Bob again slugged him into a groggy state. With a right on the jaw, he made Gus drop his hands and lay against Bob's breast.

Ruhlin rallied gamely, but his blows missed, and at the end of the round, Bob was once again punching him into a state of distress. Ruhlin walked unsteadily to his corner, his face covered with bruises. Both of Bob's eyes were swelling.

6th round

Fitzsimmons came out briskly and drove a left to the stomach. Ruhlin responded with a left and right to the body but Fitz ignored them and landed a left hook to the mouth that opened up "the floodgates of blood again." Gus ran away, but Fitz followed and hooked him hard in the stomach. Gus came back with a stiff jab to the nose and short jolt to the chin.

Ruhlin was awkward and wobbled around. Bob followed, and in an unconcerned manner, took all the face punches that Gus threw. Ruhlin's punches had little force, while Bob hit like a trip-hammer. Fitz simply slugged Ruhlin about. Gus did not have enough strength to hold up his hands and was blind from the blood that flowed from his eyes, nose, and mouth. Fitz got him to the ropes and shook him up with a right smash to the jaw. Gus clinched to stop the follow-up onslaught.

After breaking, Fitzsimmons rushed and knocked Ruhlin down with a storm of blows, including a right to the jaw and left in the stomach.

Ruhlin rose at nine, reeling about. Fitz threw caution to the wind and went after him. He almost dropped Ruhlin with a left to the stomach, but Gus held around his neck.

After breaking, Fitzsimmons put on the finishing touches. He cut loose with a succession of punches that landed all over the head and body. Ruhlin tottered, and Fitz landed a left hook to the body that caused Gus to pitch forward. Bob followed with a final tremendous left hook/uppercut under the chin that raised Ruhlin off the floor and made him drop heavily on his head, limp and lifeless. He was knocked out so cleanly that the count was not even necessary. Gus Ruhlin was out cold.

Ruhlin's seconds dragged him to his chair in an unconscious condition. In his corner, Ruhlin vomited blood. Because he was bleeding from his ears as well, his handlers were concerned. They feared fatal results. His eyes were closed. His face was very badly bruised and his body severely punished.

Fitzsimmons came over to his corner and, taking Ruhlin's head in his hands, he turned up his face and said in a low voice, "Brace up, old fellow, I didn't mean to hurt you so bad!" But the moment Fitz let go, Ruhlin's chin fell to his heaving bosom, and there was no response. "Ruhlin was too far out to know where he was." It took Madden and Corbett five to ten minutes to bring him out of unconsciousness.[97]

The *New York Times* noted that Fitz conceded about 32 pounds but was equal to the task. He won with his terrible solar plexus blow, which shook Ruhlin from head to foot every time it landed. From the start, they worked with hurricane force. Both were wild at times, but Fitz always steadied himself more quickly. Ruhlin clinched a good deal, and for 3 or 4 rounds was the aggressor, landing some hard straight lefts to the face and rights to the body with fearful force. Several blows staggered Fitz, but none landed on the mark of his shifty foe, who dodged many blows in clever fashion.

[97] *New York Sun, Journal, Tribune, Herald, Brooklyn Daily Eagle, New York Times, Brooklyn Daily Standard Union, Brooklyn Citizen, Brooklyn Times, New York Evening World, New York Tribune,* August 11, 1900; *National Police Gazette,* August 25, 1900; *New York Clipper,* August 18, 1900; *New York Sun,* August 12, 1900.

Fitz forced Ruhlin to break ground, and in the hot mix-ups, the Ohio man always was first to ease up and take refuge in a clinch. Bob often forced him to the ropes. Fitz was very quick with his feet. When Ruhlin's nose began bleeding from a stiff left, he was discouraged and Fitz encouraged. Bob began attacking the body, making Gus wince with pain.

The only time Fitzsimmons touched the floor was when he slipped down in a clinch. Ruhlin was slow to come to time in the 6th, and Fitz jumped at him. Gus jabbed hard lefts, but Bob sidestepped and landed lefts into the body and rights to the head. A volley of blows, followed by a fearful left to the solar plexus sent Ruhlin down in a heap. He rose at nine, groggy. Fitz rushed in, sending lefts to the face and a right to the jaw. Gus pitched forward as if struck with an axe and fell on his face to be counted out at 2 minutes 10 seconds of the 6th round. It took Ruhlin 12 minutes to come around sufficiently to enable him to walk out.

The *Brooklyn Daily Standard Union* said 6 rounds of slugging ended in a clean knockout. They pounded on one another, but Fitz grew stronger under punishment, and he had that deadly left. He gave Ruhlin, a young, strong heavyweight, a terrible beating, the worst whipping a fighter ever received. Fitz looked so good that he likely would be backed at even money against Jeffries.

After a poor 1st round, either from taking too many chances or because he was shamming, the veteran cut loose in terrific fashion. He closed in and banged away with both hands, exchanging blow for blow. He was a glutton for work and a prodigal of punishment. It was the old-time Fitz, the fighting demon who could take punches in order to land just one terrific blow. Ruhlin started off strong and eager, but Fitz cut out the pace and led all the way after the 1st round. "No one could look at the savageness with which Fitzsimmons mixed it and say that this man was a back number or even on the decline." Fitz's dogged gameness stood out. He beat Ruhlin into bewilderment. His blows were as wicked as ever. In the 6th, Bob's left to the jaw decked Ruhlin. He again jolted his left with all his power flush on the jaw and Ruhlin went down as if falling off a roof.

The *Brooklyn Citizen* summarized, "The fight can be said to be one of the most brutal that has taken place between heavyweights in this vicinity in some time. During five of the rounds Ruhlin was covered with blood, and Fitz also shed considerable while he was fighting his way on to victory." Ruhlin's nose bled. He was annoyed by the flow of claret in his throat and was busy clearing it. His corner was trying to staunch the flow of blood from a wound over his right eye as well. Bob decked him in the 2nd with hooks to the jaw and stomach. He dropped him again in the 4th round. In the 6th, both were tired, but a left hook to the jaw ended matters.

The *Brooklyn Times* said despite the victory, Fitz took a beating. Ruhlin showered him with blows in the 1st round, cutting his mouth and opening a gash over his left eye. Fitz seemed surprised by the onslaught and missed his punches. When he returned to his corner, it looked bad for him. But from the 2nd round on, the situation changed. Bob attacked and cut Ruhlin's nose and drew blood from behind his right ear. He had Ruhlin groggy and down for nine seconds. He put him down again, with a lump gradually growing bigger on the side of his right eye. At times, both seemed tired and vulnerable to a knockout blow, but Fitz's better judgment and condition helped him win. This writer believed he should stay away from Jeffries.

Terry McGovern said Fitz won, just as he thought he would. Ruhlin made a big mistake by mixing it. He was game, but the fight essentially was over after the 2nd round, for Fitz was better in every way. "It was a great fight, and the gamest man, with the best punch, won."

After the fight was over, Fitzsimmons greeted Jeffries, who came over to congratulate him. Bill Brady asked Bob if he would fight Jeff. Fitz said that he would after he was through with Sharkey. Brady said, "Jeffries will meet you before the 1st of September, on the same terms which characterized the battle which you indulged in at Coney Island last year."

The *New York World* printed quotes from various observers. John L. Sullivan: "Fitz won because he knows too much for Ruhlin." Matty Matthews: "Ruhlin had no business mixing it with Fitz. That's Fitz's long suit." Arthur Strong: "Ruhlin is not in his class. Neither is Jeffries, for that matter. Yes, Jeffries should fight him again." The general view was that Fitzsimmons was a great fighter and clearly entitled to another contest with Jeffries.

THE KNOCK-OUT BLOW.

The *New York Tribune* said Ruhlin had made a big mistake, thinking that since he was the bigger and stronger man, he should be able to take it to Fitzsimmons and knock him out, when he should have boxed and been cautious. Bob not only had terrible blows but science as well.

> While it was a brutal, nasty exhibition and a disgrace to New York or any civilized country, the best man won. Fitzsimmons will now fight Sharkey, and his friends say that he will thrash the thicknecked ex-sailor just as easily as he did Ruhlin. Then the management of the Garden will do its best to bring Fitzsimmons and Jeffries together before the Horton law is a dead letter in the statutes of New York. This most desirable condition will arrive with the birth of September, and then the prizefighters and their managers will have to travel elsewhere to gather in the money. They will never get it elsewhere in such large quantities as they are now raking it in at Madison Square Garden.

When speaking with a reporter, Jim Jeffries said,

> It was an easy victory for Fitzsimmons. The result was just as I expected. Fitz simply waited for a chance to send in his good left. Ruhlin's blows did not seem to have any effect on Lanky Bob. I am ready to meet Fitz to arrange a match at any time. If he wants the championship he can fight for it, but he must accept my terms.

Jeffries went to visit Ruhlin in his dressing room. Ruhlin's right eye was nearly swelled shut, and his left eye was badly discolored and swollen. "His face was the color of uncooked liver." His mouth was so swollen that he could not be understood, and he could hardly speak above a whisper.

When Jeff left the Garden, he said with a gleeful smile, "I am still champion, and what is more, I know I can beat those two fellows who fought tonight."

Ruhlin was in a bad way. While in the dressing room, he passed out and lay unconscious for an hour. When Gus finally left his dressing room, two men supported him by the arms. He hardly could walk and twice staggered as if about to fall.

The *Brooklyn Citizen* said that after the knockout, it required 10 minutes to wake up Ruhlin. However, as soon as he arrived in his dressing room, Ruhlin became unconscious again. It was not until an early hour in the morning that he was able to leave the building. He was taken to a Turkish bath and lost consciousness once again.

Another report said that even into the early morning hours, Ruhlin's situation was precarious. "Ruhlin talked incoherently and lapsed occasionally into unconsciousness." A doctor said Gus was in a state of total physical collapse. He was fearful that Bob's blows had caused a blood clot to form on the brain. There was concern that he might die.

When the doctor tried to examine his body, Ruhlin winced with pain. His breathing was irregular. After about an hour, Gus vomited and said that he felt better. He then went to sleep. "Both of his eyes were almost closed and his face appeared as if he had passed through a threshing machine. His right arm is all black and blue where Fitz's gloves landed, and his breast is one mass of bruises." Blood trickled from his ears and nose. Physicians worked over him all night, and it was not until 3:30 a.m. that full consciousness returned. Despite the concern, by the next morning, at about 10 a.m., Gus seemed to be all right.

Jim Corbett said that Ruhlin made a great fight but was not himself. After the 2nd round he was all out and no longer had the steam in his punches. Jim claimed that Gus was not in the condition that he was for the Sharkey fight.

Ruhlin's manager, Billy Madden, concurred, claiming that Gus was stale and sluggish, but game, for he took ferocious punches. "The smashes which Gus received in the body did more damage than anything else. It made him forget his cleverness and he started in to slug. That was just what Bob wanted and you know the rest."

Ruhlin had hurt Fitzsimmons with lefts in the 1st round, but Bob's shift and tremendous left hook to the body in the 2nd, which dropped Gus, essentially won the fight and took Ruhlin's strength. After that, Gus had no more steam and forgot about his science and the instructions he was receiving. In the 6th round, Ruhlin "received a body punching, together with a series of jaw breakers that has seldom been seen."

The blow that put Ruhlin to sleep was a left hook that might be called a half swing. It shot in under the chin and ear and reached the jugular. Had Fitz used a big mallet he could not have administered a more tremendous blow. Though Ruhlin said he weighed 194 pounds, and he was probably heavier, he was lifted off his feet as he fell head down, it is a wonder that he did not break his neck, as his head bent under him. The Akron man was unconscious, however, before he reached the surface of the ring, as the hook acted like an electric current of high voltage.

The next day, Ruhlin said he did not remember much after he received the heavy blow in the stomach in the 2nd round. "I didn't know what was the matter with me. I could not hit hard enough to kill a flea. I must have been stale." Gus thought he might have been fighting and training too much over the past year. "The hot weather hurt me. After the first round, I gave out. I was like a dead one. Why, in the sixth round I hit Fitz four times and he never put up his guard. I couldn't move him. That shows how weak I was."

> I did my best, but Fitz proved too much for me. I looked for an early victory from the start and thought I had my man beaten several times, but he came back strong. Fitzsimmons is unquestionably the greatest fighter in the ring today. He is a cool, calculating proposition, and despite his years had a punch – well, everybody knows when it lands.

Ruhlin said Fitzsimmons was the hardest hitter on earth and was just as clever as ever. This was coming from a man who had fought both Jeffries and Sharkey. Often during his career, Bob Fitzsimmons did not simply knock his opponents down for ten seconds; he knocked them out cold, for substantial periods of time. To say that he had freakish power is an understatement.

Ruhlin felt that Bob had fought a better battle against him than he had with Jeffries. Tom Sharkey agreed, saying that Fitz would defeat Jeffries in his current shape.

Another quoted Ruhlin as saying the day after the fight, "I see I am dead or dying … Well, I am not. I am sore all right, for Fitz gave me lots of fight, and I think he can punch the heaviest blow that ever landed on me." Gus said he was stale going in, and the body blows in the 2nd round took the steam out of him, particularly a right over the heart. Regarding the knockout, he didn't know what punch hit him. There was a dazzling flash of light, and he was down. He was paralyzed on the ground and could not move.

John L. Sullivan said, "Fitzsimmons is still a great fighter. He can defeat a whole lot of these good fellows yet." Sully said Ruhlin put up a good fight, had the making of a great fighter, and might do better later on.

Honest John Kelly said, "Fitz is generally a safe fellow to bet on. The fight by the way, was one of the best I have ever witnessed."

It had been a ferocious, exciting, and damaging battle. The *New York Journal* and *New York Sun* agreed that in terms of punishment and slugging, it was the fiercest and bloodiest fight between prominent members of the fistic arena ever seen in the East since the Horton law went into effect.

Fitzsimmons literally beat Ruhlin into a state of unconsciousness. Bob showed that he could take any kind of punches without weakening, and although cut and bruised, he never was anxious to retreat. He forced the fight from start to finish and sometimes rushed in with blows delivered so quickly that they could not be counted.

Fitz alternated between vicious punching and sometimes appearing tired, perhaps bluffing, but he always quickly recovered after stalling for a bit. Ruhlin's cornermen at times yelled, "He's fakin', Gus! Look out for one o' them quick swings or a drive in the body!" Regardless of the blows that Bob took, "Fitzsimmons inevitably cut loose all of a sudden with some kind of a smash that had danger in it." Fitz's sudden recovery with quick advances and fearful belts led some to believe "there was no doubt about the fake." Bob liked to set traps.

The *Brooklyn Daily Eagle* said that given their huge size disparity, Fitz's victory was even more creditable. "To mow down such a giant, the victor needed his claim to being the hardest hitter in pugilistic history and last night he added a strong claim to being able to stand as much punishment as anyone." Fitz willingly allowed Ruhlin to hit him with the same punches that Gus used to beat Sharkey down, took them well, and landed vicious punches in return that sent Ruhlin down and out.

On all sides, Fitzsimmons was given "unlimited credit for his remarkable showing," for stopping the man who had drawn with Jeffries and knocked out Sharkey. Bob demonstrated beyond a doubt that he was not played out as a fighter and was a "pugilistic phenomenon." He had retained all of his hitting powers, was young in point of strength and condition regardless of his numeric age, and "stripped in magnificent shape, never having looked better in his life."

Amongst the sports, "there was a prevailing impression that had Champion Jeffries been in Ruhlin's place the Cornishman might have regained the laurels lost."

> Against Jeffries it will be recalled that Fitzsimmons was slow, and used only one style of assault, a rush with double swings. The latter was whipped chiefly because he continually ran his head into Jeffries' stiff left hand, which went to the mark repeatedly with damaging effect. But against Ruhlin, Fitzsimmons was as fast as chain lightning and varied his style of attack so much that he had the Akron man puzzled.[98]

---

[98] *New York Sun*, August 12, 1900. Also, against Jeffries, Fitzsimmons did not attack the body consistently or use his shifts, but "went after the head with wild swings, after the style displayed by Sharkey against Ruhlin." Of course, Jeffries had a harder punch than Ruhlin, better defense, and apparently could take it better as well. Forgotten was the fact that Jeff used his crouch and tight guard to make it difficult for Bob to land his body shots, all the while nailing Fitz with his long and powerful lefts.

The victory put Fitzsimmons next in line to meet Jeffries. "Fitz showed that a man must not always be a giant to whip another."

Interestingly enough, Bob's success also "served to boost Jeffries quite a bit." Jeff had defeated Fitz convincingly, so the fact that it had become clear that Bob wasn't old or shot made Jeff's victory over him all the more impressive. He was the only man to have legitimately knocked Fitz out, besides having defeated both Corbett and Sharkey. Ruhlin had defeated Sharkey, and Fitz had defeated Ruhlin, as well as Corbett, and for all intents and purposes, Sharkey too. That "makes Jeffries a real champion. But Fitz's return to earth has caused a universal demand for another fight between the Cornishman and Jeffries."

Fitzsimmons spoke with difficulty, owing to the fact that his larynx was badly swollen due to blows and elbows. "My throat hurts and my left hand will not close tight, but beyond a pain in my 'Adam's apple,' I feel all right."

Bob complimented Ruhlin. "That fellow is a terribly hard puncher and he is clever, too. ... It was the hardest fight of my career and I think it was the greatest and fastest that ever took place." Bob said Gus was a wonder who put up a game fight from the start. "He gave me lots of trouble in the first round – I don't know how, but he did." "He hit me repeatedly in the early rounds, but I was willing to take his punch for an opening to send a good one in. I was never in danger."

Fitz's left eye was badly swollen and blackened, and his right eye was marked. Speaking of the left eye, Bob said, "I got that from Ruhlin twelve seconds after the bell rung at the close of the first round. Ruhlin probably didn't hear the bell." That punch hurt, and Bob admitted to being shaken up by it. Other than that punch, Ruhlin's blows did not hurt him, but Bob admitted that Gus's punches made him tired, so tired that he did not know what to do for a minute.

> As I stood there and let him swing on my jaw, I thought to myself, 'what a fool I am to do this,' but I wasn't a bit frightened and I did not feel that he could hurt me. I had my wits all of the time and heard all of the bells, even when Ruhlin didn't. He was worse than I at every stage and I knew it. ..... His blows were so hard that they took some of my steam in the first round, so I went in to store up enough for the rally. ...

After the first round tonight I had no fear of the result. Ruhlin was a very fast fellow. He landed very often on me, but his knocks lacked steam and force. In the opening rounds I took things decidedly easy, doing this to size my man up. I made it look as though I was slow and heavy, but it was just the manner in which I mapped out the contest. The bell hampered me more than once. The sound was too faint for any one to hear it. For this reason I had to be very careful at times. Ruhlin is a game fellow, but he was susceptible to my body blows. These punches really licked him.

As soon as I realized that I could get to him with my left shift and right cross I knew I had him. … Only once in the fight did my right arm hurt me. That was in clinches, for Gus is very strong and roughed it with all his might. …

That blow I landed on his solar plexus at the end of the second was a corker and Ruhlin never got over it. He is a monstrous big fellow, but you know the old saying, 'The bigger they are, the further they have to fall.' Yes, he is a good man, better than I thought, but he isn't good enough to do the old man yet awhile.

If I had fought like that with Jeffries I would never have lost the championship, for this fellow is a better man than the champion and can lick him any time they meet.

Another article quoted Bob as saying,

I won the fight by fighting, and it was an awful hard fight. Ruhlin certainly had the better of it in the first round, and for a while I didn't know but he'd got me. I was tired in my legs, but I was never dazed.

After that though, I knew I had him all the way through, but it was about the hardest fight I ever had.

Ruhlin is a clever, big, strong man and he's a tough man to fight. I weighed only 165 pounds in my clothes…

I gave him some awful punching in the stomach. That's how I won the battle. I punched him five or six times in the pit of the stomach and how he groaned every time I punched him. I must have hurt him awfully. But it was like hitting a stone wall. …

He surprised me. I thought I'd beat him in two rounds and I think he'll give any other man living a great fight.

In clinches, Ruhlin's elbow crowded my Adam's apple and my throat is sore from it, and both my hands are swollen and discolored by the punching I gave him.

But you, who saw the fight, can tell how I licked him better than I can. I didn't even know how many rounds I'd fought. I felt like it was fifteen at last. All I know is I punched him in the stomach and hit as hard as I could.…

I wasn't dazed, but just as I was starting for my corner, with my hands down, Ruhlin gave me a stiff punch on the left eye. I got that cut then. You see, Ruhlin didn't hear the bell. The blow sent me whirling, but I wasn't dazed.

I got Ruhlin in shape by the punches in the stomach. Then I watched for my opening, and when it came I put him out with a left-hand shift. I thought Corbett was going to teach Ruhlin how to stop that shift.

The next day, Bob said,

My throat bothers me a good deal and I still feel the effect of some of the blows I received. Ruhlin caught me in the neck several times with his elbow, but he could not help it. It happened, you know, in clinches. I could not swallow very well last night, but I'm all right this morning. I got a couple of smashes on the Adam's apple, and I tell you it hurts when you get struck there. ...

Billy Madden states that Ruhlin was stale, and that he was overtrained. I don't think so. Any man who can stand the smashes which I gave him must have been in good and sound health. He got to me pretty often, and in the first round I was a bit unsteady; but I was in fine condition. In fact, better than when I fought Jim Jeffries or Corbett.

Bob spoke of his improved sharpness, how some underestimated him after the Jeffries fight, and how he wanted another title shot, feeling that he would do better in a rematch. He asked, "I'm too old, am I? Well, I guess I am young enough to make things hum for some people. ... I was not in good trim when beaten by Jeffries. To tell you the honest truth, I took things very easy in that mill and had to pay the penalty."

Bob's plan was to go after Sharkey next. He would rest for about a week and then return to training. "My ambition is to regain the championship. I have no doubt as to my chance with Sharkey, and if I defeat him Jeffries cannot fail to give me first chance."

One report said Fitzsimmons earned $15,750 and Ruhlin $5,250 (75/25% split of the $21,000 fighters' 50% share of the $42,000 generated). Another said Fitz earned $12,000 to Ruhlin's $4,000. However, others said it was learned "on good authority" that the boxers actually had agreed to split $20,000 evenly, $10,000 each. Another said $75,000 was generated by about 15,000 people who paid from $3 to $20. Ticket speculators made a great deal of money as well.

Bob's wife Rose said, "I knew Bob would win. ... The championship, I know, will be his again before long." She was not there but heard about the bout from her hotel. She wanted to go, but Bob wouldn't let her. The 1st round report scared her, because it said Bob had been staggered. But the 2nd round report of the hard left to the stomach sending Ruhlin to the floor brought her joy. She thought Gus was a beaten man after that.

Apparently, the Fitzsimmons vs. Ruhlin fight was filmed successfully. Showings were advertised in local New York newspapers. Unfortunately, the films have been lost in time.

Bill Brady said if Fitzsimmons failed to make a match with Jeffries before September 1, when the repeal of the Horton law went into effect, he would have to wait at least a year. However, such a match seemed unlikely, given that Bob had a late-August match with Sharkey already scheduled. Both Fitz and Sharkey had posted forfeit money. Plus, Jeff's arm status was questionable, and certainly he could not be put into championship condition in such a short period of time. Hence, it looked like a rematch would not be held any time soon.

Having attended the Fitz-Ruhlin fight, Jeffries said,

> Robert Fitzsimmons, who demonstrated last night that he is a wonderful pugilist, and for whom I have an intense admiration, has often stated, since I defeated him, that he would sacrifice anything for another chance to regain the championship. When I fought him his manager forced me to give Fitzsimmons 65 per cent of the purse, win or lose, and in order to obtain the chance I agreed to this unheard of arrangement. Since that time I have held that I was entitled to a similar division of the purse, if I agreed to meet him again, as there can be no question that my victory over him was clear and decisive.[99]

However, Jeff (or Brady on his behalf – managers often spoke for their fighters) also said that if Bob fought him before September 1, he would agree to either a winner-take-all fight, or a division of 75% to the winner

---

[99] *New York Sun*, August 12, 1900.

and 25% to the loser. Furthermore, if Bob called off his fight with Sharkey, Jeff would agree to fight both Fitz and Sharkey before September 1 – Fitzsimmons on August 25 and Sharkey on August 31. This way, Sharkey still would have a match and not be harmed by Bob pulling out of his bout with him. "If by Tuesday [August 14] I have received no favorable answer from Fitzsimmons I shall discontinue training, and refuse to meet any one until on or about June 1, 1901."

Quite frankly, this sounded like a bluff. Jeff knew fully well that he was not going to fight either of these two men in the next two weeks, and the fact that he was not going to fight again until the middle of the following year demonstrated that he really had other plans in mind. He was not in fighting shape, and his arm still was recovering.

J. C. Kennedy, the Twentieth Century Athletic Club's manager, said he thought that Jeff's proposition was spectacular and impracticable.

Perhaps to call his bluff, Fitzsimmons immediately said that he would fight Jeff. He had posted $2,500 to meet Sharkey on August 25. He said he would honor his contract to fight Sharkey and then fight Jeff the following week. He would allow Jeffries whatever terms he wanted, "he to take 65 per cent, win or lose if he is afraid to meet me winner to take all. I know I can beat him."[100]

However, Jeffries insisted that Fitz and/or Sharkey immediately post a $5,000 forfeit or he would cease training and not resume. He did not want to train for a fight that might not take place if one boxer was injured in the Fitz-Sharkey fight. He wanted them to demonstrate their sincerity and commitment with money.

The *Police Gazette* opined that it was Jeff's way of getting out of a possible fight. "A blind man could see that this was only a subterfuge to evade the issue, and it is not surprising that both Fitz and Sharkey laughed at this unreasonable proposition and questioned Jeffries' sincerity." It called Jeff's demand "preposterous."[101]

On August 13, while riding from his training quarters at Loch Arbour, Jeffries fell off his bicycle again and wrenched an ankle. It was painful, but after Jack McCormack attended to it, Jeff declared that the injury would not seriously interfere with his plans. However, "shortly after the mishap Jeffries was in bathing, his ankle swathed in as many bandages as a baby in Iceland." Some questioned whether it was a genuine injury, or whether Jeff was seeking a way out of a fight with Fitzsimmons, surprised that Bob had accepted his offer.

> There are skeptical folk hereabout who hint that Jeffries will next be taking milk baths or discovering live sea serpents in the ocean off Bradley's resort. Others, also unbelievers, wish to know if Jeffries's manager, Brady, whose theatrical methods are known, has been in the vicinity lately.

[100] *New York World*, August 12, 1900.
[101] *National Police Gazette*, September 8, 1900.

One report said Fitzsimmons was disgusted with the off-and-on hot-and-cold Jeffries. Bob said Jeff was crawling out of a match which Jeff offered, and he had accepted. "The truth of the matter is that Jeffries is afraid to meet me again." Bob said that each time he had accepted an offer to fight Jeff, "he has made some silly excuse to get out of the match." Jeff or Brady should have known that they were going up against a master of the mouth. When he wanted, Fitzsimmons could match even Corbett when it came to a sharp tongue.

The *New York Journal* said Jeffries, or his manager Brady in speaking for him, was "as coy and uncertain as the sun in April. Jeffries says he will and then he says he won't. From his lofty perch he can dictate terms, and he knows it." It felt that Brady did not want to risk a loss and wanted to capitalize further on Jeffries (via stage work) before taking another risk. With Jeff's arm and ankle troubles, and being less than perfectly trained, going against a sharp Fitz with such little time to train was a risk that Brady did not want to take. Such would be foolish.[102]

The *Police Gazette* said Jeff was not going to fight the winner of the Fitz-Sharkey battle before September 1. "I never believed he had any such intention, but he had to do something to pose before the public, and the effort he was compelled to make to keep from being lost in the shuffle was really pathetic." No one believed in Brady's proposition to have Jeff meet the winner of Fitz-Sharkey six days after their fight. "Jeffries conveniently came to the aid of his embarrassed manager with a notification that he was not satisfied with the conditions demanded by Fitzsimmons and Sharkey for a meeting with him, and he did not wish to lose time training for an uncertainty." The real "fact of the matter is that his injured arm will not stand the strain of training again and he isn't going to take any chances of losing his title. . ... And nobody can blame him."

The *Gazette* also opined that Brady simply wanted to keep Jeff's name in the newspapers so that he would not be forgotten. It sarcastically remarked, "Two whole days have gone by and Jim Jeffries, the champion prizefighter, has not sprained his leg, fallen off his bicycle, captured a runaway horse or snatched a beautiful young woman from a watery grave. There'll be a press agent out of a job if he doesn't get a hustle on himself pretty soon!"[103]

[102] *New York Journal*, August 14, 16, 17, 1900.
[103] *National Police Gazette*, September 1, 8, 1900.

CHAPTER 6

Settling a Score

Amazingly, Bob Fitzsimmons was scheduled to fight Tom Sharkey just two weeks after defeating Gus Ruhlin. Talk about confidence and toughness. He likely wanted more of that New York money before the game was shut down there. Bob said victory surely would entitle him to another fight with Jeffries. Certainly, defeating both Ruhlin and Sharkey would increase demand and strengthen his position in negotiating better financial terms for a Jeffries rematch. Plus, he had a score to settle with Sharkey. In their 1896 contest, Fitzsimmons was disqualified in the 8th round for a purported low blow which he and most others insisted was a legal body shot. Bob even took the matter to court, claiming that the fight had been fixed and referee Wyatt Earp and the Sharkey crew were in on it. Fitz felt that he had proven his case but lost the decision and the purse on a technicality, the court holding that boxing was illegal, which barred any suit pertaining to money won or lost in such a contest. Bob firmly believed that had had knocked out Sharkey cleanly and would do so again.

Sharkey said he was in great shape and Fitz would meet the same Sharkey that Jeffries met. "Both are as fit as two men ever were, and each is supremely confident of success."[104]

Tom O'Rourke, who was Sharkey's manager, explained why his man would win.

Sharkey is stronger physically than Ruhlin and can take more punishment than the latter. He is also the harder hitter. Now, if Fitz

[104] *National Police Gazette*, September 1, 8, 1900.

fights Sharkey the way he did with Ruhlin and swaps punches with him, it would not surprise me a bit to see Tom put him away. Ruhlin had Fitz to the bad even with his inferior blows, so Sharkey ought to make a better impression.[105]

Although admitting that Sharkey was a tough customer, Fitzsimmons said, "I'll whip that fellow inside the limit, and when I do so then Mr. Jeffries can come along and I will talk business with him. I believe that I am just as good to-day as when I won the heavyweight championship and I propose to do a great deal more fighting before I retire from the business."[106]

Sharkey said he was a much better version than the one who fought Ruhlin. He said the rib injury he suffered in the Jeffries fight had healed. "I do not see how I can fail to whip Fitzsimmons." He appeared to be in grand shape. His trainers said he would fight at about 190 pounds. Tom admitted that Bob hit hard.

> That's one thing about this fellow. He will hurt you if he hits you anywhere – on top of the head or anywhere else. He is an awful puncher, but I figure on keeping out of his way for a time at least. If he gets tired with me the way he did with Ruhlin the fight won't go six rounds.[107]

Bob's three sons, Bob Jr., Martin, and Charles, with Bob Armstrong, watching Bob make horseshoes.

There was some discussion about a purported attempt to bribe Fitzsimmons with $100,000 to throw the fight, which offer Bob revealed. He said that he also had been offered $75,000 to lie down to Corbett back in 1897. Bob said he was willing to fight Corbett again at Carson City if Jim was successful in his upcoming bout with Kid McCoy.[108]

[105] New York Sun, August 21, 1900.
[106] Brooklyn Citizen, August 21, 1900.
[107] Buffalo Times, August 22, 1900.
[108] Buffalo Express, August 22, 1900.

On August 22, 1900, two days before the fight, Fitzsimmons wound up his training at Bergen Beach, New York, exhibiting before a paying crowd that included 100 women. Bob punched the bag 3 hard rounds and then sparred with Bob Armstrong (who previously worked with Sharkey) and Professor George Dawson. The very tall and large Armstrong "slugged, sprinted and feinted for three rounds, and Fitz caught him unawares a number of times. Once Armstrong was punched over the heart and he almost fell." The "women spectators were fairly beside themselves with delight. They stood and applauded vigorously." After sparring George Dawson, Bob wrestled for 13 minutes with Jack Neary. Following that, he tossed the medicine ball with Neary and Joe Knipe, the amateur champion.[109]

Heading into the contest, the *Buffalo Commercial* said, "Whatever the result may be, it will be a contest worth seeing. Confidence, science and strength on Fitzsimmons's side; bull-rushes and the gameness to continue them as long as his feet will work on Sharkey's side."

Sharkey said, "It is my opinion that the fight will be a short one, because Fitz will undoubtedly try to force matters, something that I may do myself."

Fitzsimmons said, "This man Sharkey is a strong, rugged fellow, and I have no doubt that he has greatly improved since I met him in 'Frisco. Still, I want to add that after I have finished with him, then I will go after Jim Jeffries .... Sharkey, in all probability, will be harder to get at than was Ruhlin, but I will land that left on him and then it will be all over." Current wagering had Fitz the favorite at 10 to 8 odds, although others claimed he was an even bigger favorite, by as much as 2 to 1.[110]

x-Champion Has the Call with the Bettors, Odds of 2 to 1 on His Chances Being Easily Obtained.

Fighting attitudes of Fitzsimmons and Sharkey as they appear in the ring, anxious to begin battle at the sound of timekeeper's gong.

[109] *New York World*, August 23, 1900.
[110] *Buffalo Commercial, Brooklyn Citizen*, August 23, 1900.

Sharkey's record included: 1896 W8 Joe Choynski, D4 James J. Corbett, and WDQ8 Bob Fitzsimmons; 1897 D7 Peter Maher and KO6 Joe Goddard; 1898 D8 Choynski, L20 James J. Jeffries, KO1 Gus Ruhlin, and WDQ9 Corbett; 1899 KO10 Charles Kid McCoy, KO2 Jack McCormick, and L25 Jeffries; 1900 TKO4 Goddard, KO2 Jim Jeffords, KO1 McCormick, TKO3 Choynski, KO1 Yank Kenny, and LTKOby15 Ruhlin.

The day of the fight, assessing the rematch, the *New York Sun* said Sharkey's chances should not be held too cheaply, given his improvement over the three and a half years since Fitz stopped him in 8 rounds, and given how well he did the previous year against Jeffries (as well as top men such as Corbett, McCoy, and Choynski). However, against Jeffries, "Sharkey received a pretty severe grueling from which it took him a long time to recover." Tom once had stopped Ruhlin in 1 round but got handled and knocked out by him in the June 26 rematch two months ago. Some wondered whether the beatings Tom had absorbed from Jeffries and then Ruhlin had taken something out of him. Still, Sharkey said that he had not trained properly for Gus because he thought Ruhlin would be easy, given his prior 1st round knockout of him. He was taking Fitzsimmons seriously. (Plus, Sharkey had gone 6-1 with 6 KOs since the Jeffries contest.)

Sharkey argued that he could take a lot more punishment than Ruhlin could, and he would be able to exchange with Bob longer and with better results. "There is no doubt that Sharkey is a more rugged fighter than Ruhlin both in physique and in punching power. It has been said of him that barring Fitzsimmons he has no equal as a hitter."

Regarding Fitzsimmons, the *Sun* said that as far as physical strength and speed were concerned, judging from his work in training over the last ten days, he had not gone backwards at all.

Fitz's habit has been to go to a man, mix it up and beat him down as quickly as possible. He relies

almost wholly upon his craftiness and his heavy hitting. He can take punishment and a lot of it, and still come back with blows that cannot be resisted. Sharkey, while not so clever, is just as willing and just as game. Against Ruhlin, Sharkey could not get to the big man because the latter was too shifty on his feet and too quick with his defence. Ruhlin also met the Sailor's advances with a remarkably fast left hand, which had power enough in it to not only shake the Sailor up, but put him down when he had lost much of his vitality.

Fitzsimmons has a better left hand than Ruhlin, but he does not use it in the same manner. Fitz seldom adopts a straight jab for the face as an opponent comes in, but he hooks that hand or swings it for the jaw or body with a shift that has been widely talked about. ... Fitz is one of the quickest fighters in the world in changing the course of his blows. He may start a left apparently for the body and yet shift it so that it will land upon the jaw in the twinkling of an eye. He does not have to swing a punch...but he can use a six-inch jolt with just as much effect because of the accuracy with which it is landed. Fitz has an eye for openings that cannot be excelled.[111]

The *World* said it was a match between the world's greatest ring general (Fitz) and the world's most courageous and aggressive heavyweight (Sharkey). Describing Fitzsimmons, its writer said,

His pose and motions in the ring are awkward and seemingly slow. His long strides and shambling gait draw the attention of spectators from the lightning swings and jabs of his arms and hands. In each of his fights he appears at one time or another to be groggy, but many good heavyweights say that right at that time he is most dangerous. As he reels around about to fall any opening left by the other man revives Fitz more than a five-minute rest. More than one ambitious fighter has rushed into a hook that put him out because he foolishly thought that old Fitz was gone.[112]

Those picking Fitzsimmons to win included both Jim Corbett and Gus Ruhlin (who had fought both Fitz and Sharkey), Kid McCoy (who had fought Sharkey and sparred Fitz), Jim Wakely, John Kelly, Jimmy Carroll, and John Considine

Tom O'Rourke, Sam Fitzpatrick, and Spike Sullivan picked Sharkey.

On Friday August 24, 1900 at Coney Island's Seaside Sporting Club in New York, Bob Fitzsimmons took on Tom Sharkey (36-5-6) in a rematch, scheduled for 25 rounds, for a large $25,000 purse, with 50% or $12,500 going to each, win or lose (although the public initially was told the division was 75/25%).

Seats were expensive, at $3, $5, $7, $10, $15, and $25. Estimates of crowd size ranged from 4,000 to 5,000, which normally would be very good

[111] *New York Sun*, August 24, 1900.
[112] *New York World*, August 24, 1900.

but was surprisingly relatively low given the two combatants' popularity. There had been some uncertainty about the date. At first, it was scheduled for the 24th. Then it was moved to the 25th because a great crowd would be drawn to the island on that date to see the Futurity Stakes run. However, since the contract called for the 24th, after further discussion, it was moved back to the original date of the 24th. Perhaps the high ticket prices for a non-title fight kept many folks away. It also could have been diminished demand as a result of the sheer volume of fight cards as the termination of the Horton law approached. Some said it was the heat. Allegedly, the house was about $25,000, equal to the fighters' guarantees.

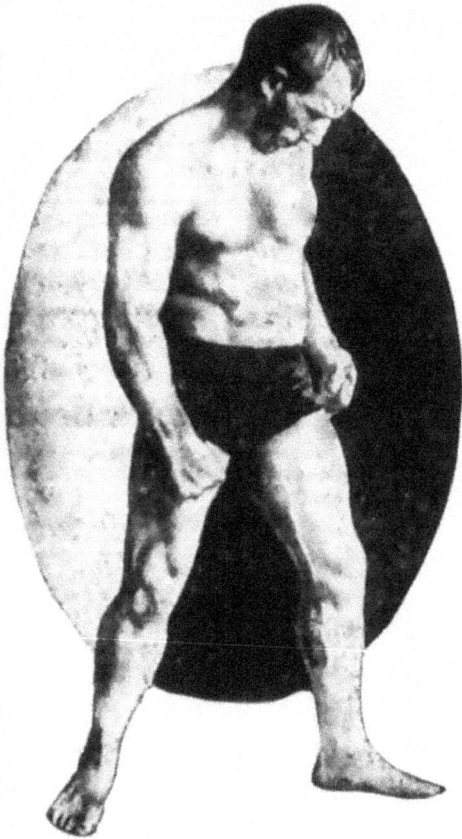

The crowd gave a great reception to John L. Sullivan. James J. Corbett and James J. Jeffries were present as well.

Some thought Fitzsimmons would weigh about 170 pounds to Sharkey's 185 pounds. The *Journal's* day-of-the-fight report said Fitz was 175, while Sharkey was 190. Jeffries thought Bob weighed about 170 pounds. The *Eagle* said Sharkey was about 190 pounds. The day before, the *World* reported their weights as 163 Fitz, 178 Sharkey, likely based on self-reports. It listed Bob as age 38 to Sharkey's 29.

At first, there was a big delay, because referee Charley White refused to work until he received payment (either $250 or $500).

After that issue was settled, at 10:40 p.m., Sharkey entered the ring wearing an elegant and expensive-looking blue bathrobe. Because it was hot, he immediately pulled it off. His seconds fanned him. Tom wore green trunks. His hands were well protected with bandages. According to Jeffries, who was reporting for the *World*, Sharkey looked first-rate and strong as a bull. Still, Fitz was the 10 to 6 and 10 to 7 favorite.

There was yet another lengthy delay because Fitzsimmons also wanted to be paid before he would enter the ring. The sweating crowd fumed. Finally, after receiving payment, Bob approached the ring at 11:05 p.m. to a great number of hisses, jeers, and groans. The crowd was angry with him for having made them wait in the heat. However, he refused to enter until the Club lived up to its contract and produced the $25,000 purse offered for the fight, which was to be split between the combatants.

Bob removed his long white bathrobe, looking very confident, ignoring the hissing and hooting, which then turned to cheers and applause. He wore white trunks with an American flag belt around his waist.[113] He brought his own gloves with him. Like Sharkey, his hands and wrists were wrapped in bandages. Jeff said, "Fitz's hands are thoroughly bandaged, and even the fingers are wrapped in adhesive tape." Sharkey's manager Tom O'Rourke examined Bob's gloves and bandages and pronounced them to be all right.

With Bob were Bob Armstrong, Dan Hickey, Jeff Thorne, and Jack Neary. Sharkey had Tom O'Rourke, Spider Kelly, Jim Buckley and Jack Sullivan.

Fitz towered at least three inches above the stocky Sharkey. Bob had wide shoulders and chest, set upon narrow hips and long slender legs. Sharkey had short, knotted muscles all over his body, very thickly built.

Fitz walked over to Jeff and told him, "I got my whack before I went on," meaning that he got his money. Jeffries said Fitz was "the coolest, shiftiest fighter that ever got inside the ropes and he has the hardest punch of the whole lot."

Sharkey remained seated while Tom O'Rourke sponged and rubbed him down with a towel and gave him a lemon to suck on. Tom's seconds also fanned him. Bob remained standing.

The men shook hands at 11:12 p.m., ready to begin the fight, and returned to their corners.[114]

1st round

Typical of his style, Sharkey ferociously attacked Fitzsimmons, rushing in with swings, but Bob was able to hit and move, back away and sidestep to avoid him. Tom rushed, while Bob felt him out, taking his time.

Eventually, Fitzsimmons held his ground more. They went at it, but Fitz seemed too clever for him, showing his craftiness and generalship. Timing Tom on the way in, Fitz would dip, step inside of Sharkey's hard rushing wallops and counter, or he would use his nimble footwork to evade him

---

[113] Another source said that Fitz entered the ring wearing a pale lavender robe and pink tights.
[114] The following account and post-fight discussion is taken from the *New York Journal, New York World, New York Sun, New York Herald, New York Tribune, Brooklyn Daily Eagle, New York Times, Brooklyn Citizen*, August 24, 25, 1900.

altogether. Bob landed relatively easily, focusing on the body. mostly with hard rights and right uppercuts to the ribs.

Bob landed powerful blows, but Sharkey remained anxious to mix it up. Fitz backed out of reach whenever Tom rushed, but he always came back with solid punches to the head and body.

Sharkey kept swinging, and amongst their mix-ups, landed a number of hard blows to jaw, nose, and ribs. However, Fitz's right was like a triphammer, and he landed his hard left shift to the solar plexus, as well as a left uppercut. Fitz landed a right to the stomach and Sharkey began backing away.

Perhaps as a result of his ability to land so easily, Fitzsimmons grew even more aggressive. However, Bob's attack perhaps was a bit premature, for in a careless unguarded moment, Sharkey knocked him down, each local source giving its own version.

James Jeffries (for the *World*): "Sharkey lands a wild left swing on the jaw and sends Fitz down backward and falls down over him." Jeff also said, "It was a holy terror – that left swing on the nose."

Referee Charlie White: It was a left to the jaw that decked Fitz.

Journal ('Right Cross'): Tom became wild and Fitz ducked a left smash, but Sharkey followed fast with a right to the jaw that staggered Bob. Sharkey shot another punch to the same place, Fitz toppled over onto his back, and Tom fell over him from the force of his own blow.

Gus Ruhlin (reporting for the *Journal*): "It was all Bob's round up to the very last, when Sharkey put him down."

Sun: Tom went in to mix it and Fitz slugged him right and left until Tom clinched. As they broke, Tom landed a terrific left on the jaw. Another punch knocked Fitz down, but before he rose, the bell rang. "The Cornishman was unquestionably in some distress from the effects of that punch, but the bell came to his rescue."

Times: Sharkey landed his left glove on the Australian's shoulder, and he went down, with Sharkey stumbling over him. Fitz seemed dazed and took the full count before he rose.

Eagle: Fitz pressed Sharkey back to the ropes and missed a vicious right uppercut. Sharkey countered with a terrific left jab in the mouth that sent Bob's head back and followed it with a powerful right to the shoulder that dropped Fitz. He went down on his back and Tom fell and rolled over him from the force of his own blow.

Brooklyn Standard Union: Several vicious blows sent Fitz down.

Fitzsimmons rose and the bell rang. Neither man heard it amongst the roars of the crowd. Sharkey attacked and they both threw punches and clinched. Their seconds, who had heard the bell, entered the ring and brought the men to their corners. After a few seconds in the corner, Bob looked as well as ever, having revived quickly.

2nd round

Encouraged by his round-ending knockdown, Sharkey again attacked like a bulldog, rushing in. Fitz backed up, blocked, and clinched. However, Bob was "as fresh as a rose," clever and cunning, and had gauged his man.

After breaking, to the sailor's surprise, Fitzsimmons began to do some rushing of his own. He sparred and feinted, got within distance and then landed awful uppercuts. Fitz stepped inside a Sharkey left swing and shot a right to the lip that drew blood. Fitz feinted a left for the head and then shot a right to the body. Sharkey's rushing wallops were in vain, as Fitzsimmons easily avoided them, sending in uppercuts to the body. Bob sidestepped and counterpunched hard, jolting Tom with his short shots. Fitz caved in his body with ripping blows and then straightened him up with a few lefts and rights to the chin.

They went at it, both landing good blows, but Fitz had the best of it. Ruhlin said, "Look at the way he is lacing it into the sailor's ribs. That was a nasty uppercut, too, wasn't it?" He staggered Tom with a right smash to the heart, catching Sharkey as Tom was advancing. The sailor threw his arms around Bob's neck.

After that, they both mixed it up, swinging right and left heavily for the head and body until Fitz landed a right to the jaw which made Tom hang on. Sharkey kept throwing wild and inaccurate blows, while Fitz piled in with short effective jolts that made the sailor reel backward to the ropes.

This time it was Fitzsimmons who knocked Sharkey down:

Jeffries: Sharkey missed a left for the head but sent in a hard right to the body that shook Fitz. Sharkey rushed in and ran into a right hook on the jaw that shook him up. He rushed in again and Fitz landed left and right hooks on the jaw that sent Tom to the floor.

Ruhlin: Fitz kept hitting him and Sharkey seemed all at sea. Bob landed another hard shot to the body and Sharkey went down.

Journal: Tom rushed in, but Bob dropped him with an uppercut to the wind.

Eagle: Fitz dropped Sharkey with a left hook on the chin.

Sun: Tom fought desperately until Fitz landed a heavy right to the jaw which knocked him down.

Times: Fitz's left landed on the side of the jaw, and he followed with a rain of other blows, a left finally sending Sharkey to the ground.

Summarizing the accounts, some said the blow that dropped him was a left hook to the head, some a right to the head, while others said it was a body shot. Another local account said Fitz dropped Tom with a series of rights and lefts to the body and head, which appears to have been the case.

Sharkey showed his toughness by rising (some said before five, others said at eight). Fitz then finished him off, with each source giving its version:

Jeffries: Sharkey rose after eight seconds. Fitz rushed at him with left and right hooks on the jaw four or five times in succession and Sharkey fell down on his face.

Ruhlin: Ever the finisher, Fitz was on top of him, reigning in the blows, forcing Tom to hold. Bob landed another stunning left. Fighting like a demon, Bob landed terrific lefts and rights to the face and body. One landed square in the solar plexus, and then the left crashed to the jaw and Tom went down and out.

Journal: Tom rose and missed a right. Bob ended matters by using his shift, bringing his right foot forward, sending the left to the stomach and then shooting his left up to the jaw, twisting his left leg into the punch. "No one of that big crowd who saw it will forget that punch." Tom's head dropped forward as if his neck had been suddenly broken. His legs bent and he sank to the floor face first on his hands and knees.

Sun: After he regained his feet, Tom swung away again. Fitz brushed aside the blows and dashed in with a volley of smashes that blinded the sailor. Bob landed all over until Tom's hands dropped. A double body punch almost ended him as Tom groaned. In another mix-up, Bob landed a close-in left swing that did not travel very far, landing on the point of the jaw and sending Tom down on all fours, the blood running down his mouth. Fitz had a little blood trickling down his lips too.

Eagle: After Sharkey rose, Fitz bore down upon him. Tom threw blows hard enough to turn the tide of the battle had they landed. Fitz was merciless, landing right and left to the face, and Tom hugged. Bob pushed him off and threw in the finishing blows. Bob hooked the left to the jaw and right to the temple. Before Tom fell, another left hit him, but it was not necessary.

Times: Sharkey met another rattle of blows, left and right, and went down again. He jumped up quickly and closed in on Fitz in an attempt to clinch. Fitz stepped back and delivered a right on the side of the jaw, and he went down for the third time, unconscious.

Sharkey's efforts to rise were in vain. He could not lift his head. He swayed and rolled on his side while his hands felt around on the floor as if looking for something he could not find. One supporting hand gave way and his shoulder bumped down to the canvas. He drew a leg up as if to get it under him, but it slid back. The instinct to rise was there, but it was only a flicker, and it went out. Referee Charlie White counted him out at 2 minutes 6 seconds of the 2nd round.

Bob Fitzsimmons had quickly knocked out in a mere 2 rounds the man in Sharkey who twice had gone the distance with James J. Jeffries (L20; L25) and had beaten Jim Corbett (D4 and WDQ9), Kid McCoy (KO10), and Joe Choynski (W8, D8, KO3). Fitz had stopped Corbett in 14 rounds, while it took Jeffries 23. Fitz had stopped Choynski in 5, whereas Jeffries had a D20 with Choynski. However, Choynski, Corbett, and Sharkey had decked Fitzsimmons, but not Jeffries. Bob also had knocked out in 6 rounds Gus Ruhlin, a man who had drawn in 20 with Jeffries and had soundly beaten Sharkey (WTKO15, although prior LTKOby1). This clearly made Fitzsimmons *the* big fight for Jeffries, despite Jeff's prior decisive KO11 victory over Fitzsimmons. It appeared that Fitzsimmons was a more impressive puncher or finisher than Jeffries, but Jeff could take it better than anyone, and the champion could both attack or box, with excellent endurance and heavy, effective blows.

Gus Ruhlin said, "Just look how Fitz wins. He's a wonder, isn't he?"

Fitzsimmons walked over to Jeffries at ringside and said, "Get up, Jeff, and shake hands." They shook cordially. Bob said, "I want you next." The crowd cheered Fitzsimmons, who had squared accounts with Sharkey.

After Tom was brought to his senses, Bob walked over, and they shared some water from the same bottle.

The *Sun* said that Sharkey grew too confident after dropping Fitzsimmons. Fitz once again showed his tremendous hitting powers and science in avoiding many dangerous smashes. He stepped inside of Tom's swings with short, accurate hooks to the head and body. "It is safe to say that there was not a punch delivered by Fitzsimmons that did not take effect." Whether it was a right or left, to the body or head, "there was enough power behind every punch to take away the phenomenal strength of the muscular Sailor, who was outclassed in headwork, generalship, speed and hitting." Fitz literally beat him down as if he had a hammer in each hand. In every respect, Fitzsimmons was Sharkey's master.

The *World* said Fitzsimmons had landed three blows to Sharkey's one.

The *New York Times* said the bout was as fast as it was short. While it lasted, the combatants were in a whirl of rapidly exchanged blows, hitting as hard and as viciously as they could, neither shirking when it came to standing punishment. Sharkey went down and out from a right in the 2nd round, and it took more than a minute until he was able to rise again.

The *Brooklyn Daily Standard Union* said Fitz, the marvel of the prize ring, outclassed the sailor in every way, and hammered him into helplessness in quick order. "He still has that same fearful punch and the quickness and ability to place it at the desired spot the same as when he came to this country many years ago." His blows had tremendous force, but also with so much accuracy such that little strength was wasted. Sharkey was known for having the finest physique and the ability to absorb punishment, but he had to succumb to such a barrage of powerful blows.

At first Sharkey moved, but then he fought in his usual style. However, other than the knockdown in the 1st round from a blow on the chin, he could not land his swings and had no defense for Bob's blows. In the 2nd round, Fitz played defense for a bit, then met the rushes with straight blows. A right sent Tom down. Bob piled in blows, finishing with a right to the body and left to the jaw, ending matters.

Fitzsimmons displayed more cleverness than ever. He always could take a punch and have one in return. "His recuperative powers are amazing." Sharkey beat him down with terrific blows at the close of the 1st round, but Bob came back in the 2nd, seeming cool and calm as ice and just as fresh as he was at the start.

The press complimented Fitzsimmons for knocking out in the span of two weeks two men whom Jeffries had failed to knock out. It stood to reason that Bob was in better shape to take on Jeff than he was the previous summer. "Fitzsimmons stands today as the only rival to Jeffries. There is no other pugilist in his class." He had fought his way to the top again and had earned his shot. Bob "clearly proved his right to another chance at championship honors, the lines of parallel being shortly drawn."

Fitzsimmons told the *Sun*,

> In the first round he caught me lightly on the jaw and knocked me down. It was not exactly a hard blow, but it was enough to jar me. The punch that did the business was the left. I made a feint with the right and as he came forward I nailed him with the left.

I observed as soon as my glove landed that the smash had dazed Sharkey, for he began to sway back and forth like a drunken man. Quick as a flash I hit him on the jaw again, and this was the knockout.

In other interviews, Fitz claimed to have slipped down in the 1st round. He agreed that Tom hit him hard once or twice, but that was before he got going. Another quoted Bob as saying, "That was a great blow Sharkey gave me in the first round." Bob told the *World* that he hit Sharkey whenever and wherever he pleased.

Fitzsimmons said that Sharkey was not as good a man as Ruhlin, for Gus was shiftier and cleverer. The only thing Tom did better than Ruhlin was hit harder. "Tom certainly can hit a terrible wallop." However, in another statement, Fitz gave Sharkey more credit for his skill. "I was lucky to defeat him in two rounds. He was cleverer than I ever saw him, and far and away better than when he fought Ruhlin." "Sharkey blocked and ducked better than I thought he could, too." Either way, Fitz said the fight proved conclusively how affairs really stood when they had fought the first time in San Francisco in late 1896.

Another quoted Bob as saying,

> Notwithstanding the fact that he knocked me down in the first round I felt that I had him. All I wanted him to do was keep rushing me, because then I knew that I must get an opening to land a knockout punch. And if he had tried to stand off and box I think I would have beaten him at that game, too. I have done pretty well in the last two weeks and made enough money to tide me over for a while, but I am ready to meet Jeffries at any time. Of course, I don't think there is a chance for us to meet before the expiration of the Horton law, but I am ready to meet him at any time, if he says the word, and I hope to get into a ring with him some time within the next six months. I'm 38 years of age. They say I'm an old man, but I want some of them to trot out a young fellow that can beat me. Sharkey has met all the big fellows, and not one of them ever put him away as I put him away to-night. I'm just a bit proud of finishing off in two rounds a man who stayed twenty-five rounds with Jeffries.

Sharkey took his defeat good-naturedly. He had a puffed lip and a bruise over his left temple but otherwise was unmarked. He said,

> Fitz surprised me. I thought I had him sure in the first round, but he came back strong and beat me out in the lead. Fitz is a great fighter. He has a wonderful punch and can inflict great punishment. I hit him repeatedly in the opening round and felt confident that I would end matters in the next. Although defeated, I have no complaint to offer. I was beaten fairly and squarely in a hard battle. I may have been a trifle careless after I thought I had Fitz going, but that was my own fault. ...

I made a mistake in mixing it up. If I had followed the advice of my seconds and fought the second round the way I did the first everything would have been all right, but I thought otherwise and I was licked. Fitz is a wonderful fighter for an old man. Why Jeffries is not in it with him, and if the two ever meet I will put my money on Bob. He is the greatest hitter in the world. When he landed on me I did not know what hit me. The blows came so fast that I did not know how to fight him at all. ... Fitz is the toughest customer I ever faced. He has two good hands; you don't know which one is going to land first. ... I simply wish to say that Fitz can beat them all and is really the champion. He'll whip Jeffries as sure as you live, if they ever meet.

Sharkey further said, "I never knew anybody could hit such blows." "As a marksman Fitz is without an equal in the world. He can hit straighter and harder than any man I ever fought. Every blow he hit hurt me. They did not seem to come hard, but they fairly lifted me off the floor and took the life out of me."

Another quoted Sharkey as saying, "Look at that first round; why, I had him going sure. The bell saved him. Then when I came up for the second round I was too anxious. I wanted to have the job over in a hurry. Fitz kept away from me until he got a chance to send in a straight left that made me see stars. Then I was all up in the air."

Referee Charley White said,

The fight, though short, was the best I ever saw. Both men displayed great gameness. Each man had a hard punch. It was a hard, fast, furious fight from the first tap of the bell. ... Sharkey landed a heavy swing on Fitz just as the gong sounded at the end of the round. The blow knocked Fitz down, but it was a trifle too high to be effective.

Fitz and Sharkey mixed it up from the opening till the finish of the second and last round. Fitzsimmons got in a number of hard punches on Sharkey that would have knocked out a less courageous man than the sailor. When the end came Sharkey stood the rain of blows like the stoic he is. When nearly gone Fitz got in his famous left hook to the jaw that won the fight.

Fitz proved by his fight that he is a clever, shifty man with a hard punch. No man in pugilistic circles has anything on Fitz in any shape. He is right in line for a return match for the championship. Should he and Jeffries come together again in the squared circle the sport-loving people of this country will have a chance to see the greatest fighters of the age struggle for supremacy.

Another quoted White as saying,

Fitzsimmons is a great fighter, and a battle between him and Jeffries would be the best fight ever seen. Sharkey did well in the first round and seemed to have a chance, but when Fitzsimmons got in that

stomach punch it was easy to see that the fight was almost over. It was the same punch that beat Ruhlin. No man can take it and still fight.

Discussing Fitzsimmons, James J. Jeffries wrote, "He is the best man of all of them that I have met. I like Fitz and I'm perfectly willing to fight him within six months before any club in this country offering the greatest amount of money." "I hope Fitz will be as well when he fights me as he is tonight. It ought to make an interesting contest."

When asked what his future plans were, Fitzsimmons said, "I'm going to take a rest. I think I need one. I have engaged already in two battles inside of two weeks. ... I am not as young as I used to be, but I am as strong as I was when I was 21 years old. I took care of myself, and that is the secret of my success." However, Bob also said that he wanted to become world champion again, and after his time off, he wanted to fight Jeffries.

He whipped me once, but I don't think he will do it again. When we met I had not fought in a couple of years, and naturally I was not in the best of condition. But I am in great form now and really think that if we were to meet again soon I would come out on top. In fact, I held Jeffries too cheap. I learned a lesson and will not be caught napping the next time. If they give me enough money I guess I will be ready to fight Jeffries some time inside of the next six months.

Bob's hands were tender. His knuckles were a little swollen and bruised. He did not remove his hand bandages until the following day. He had a couple body bruises, a tiny scratch under the right eye, and a little abrasion of the inner lip. Bob also claimed that he hurt his right arm in the fight. Therefore, it seemed that both he and Jeffries were content to wait a bit before fighting one another again.

Still, Fitzsimmons issued conflicting statements. In one interview, Bob said, "I'm not yet ready to say what I'll do in regard to a fight with Jeffries." However, Fitz also was quoted as saying, "I stand ready to meet Jeffries before September 1, but he does not seem to want any of my game." He also said he would fight him in one week, on August 31. This sounded like promotional talk rather than a genuine desire to fight again in a week. Neither one was ready to fight that soon, and both likely knew it.

The *Sun* wanted Fitz and Jeff to fight the following week and said it was up to the boxers to prove whether they "prefer the pleasantries of a theatrical tour to a mix-up inside the ropes." However, Jeff said the fight could take place in about six months.

Fitz's three children congratulated him. The girls brought their father big bunches of wild flowers. Bob, Jr. said, "You're all right, dad. I guess you're a wonder."

The next day, Fitz said, "I want to explain the delay last night. There wasn't money enough in the house to pay the purse and I demanded my share before I went into the ring. I have been in the game long enough to look out for Fitz and I have learned a few lessons. I got my money." Bob

thought the weather kept the crowd away. Few wanted to endure that heat. He did not think the pre-arranged 50/50 purse split had anything to do with it, for all big fights for the last two years had the same split.

The following day, Referee Charley White said the contest was unquestionably the hardest hitting affair ever seen in the ring. It was excellent while it lasted, and the man with the best judgment and the heaviest punch won. Sharkey was a surprise in the 1st round with his side-stepping, avoiding many dangerous blows. "That blow he landed on Fitz's jaw with his left was a corker." It sent Bob down to the floor. At the count of 7 the bell rang to end the round.

At the start of the 2nd, Fitz was fully recuperated and Sharkey, perhaps under bad advice, rushed in to finish, which was a mistake. Fitz was at home in a mix-up, and the hard body smashes were the start of Tom's undoing. Two right and left blows sent Tom down. He was pretty bad when he got up. Fitz sent his trusty left hook over and finished him. "It was a great fight while it lasted."

Jim Jeffries had an exhibition tour scheduled and was not interested in fighting any time soon. Therefore, the day after the fight, perhaps for show, aware of the fact that Jeff was not ready or really interested in fighting that quickly, Fitz signed a contract with the Twentieth Century Athletic Club for a fight with Jeffries in one week. Bob said, "I've changed my mind about not fighting again in six months, and if Jeffries is satisfied I will meet him next Friday night." He also said, "I had serious intentions of quitting the ring, but as I have a good chance of becoming the champion again I want to fight Jeffries." Of course, he could afford to seem eager, given that he was well aware that Jeff was not going to fight him in a week.

A battle between them so soon was "rather improbable." It was said that Bob's willingness to fight again so quickly was a surprise, given that he too had said that he would not fight again for six months. Both Jeff and Fitz intended to make money in theatrical tours.

Jeffries replied, "I have defeated him once and, judging from his last two battles, I can do it again, and quicker than before. … [B]ut I reserve the right to set aside sufficient time to train and to leave the bids for the contest open long enough to secure the best financial inducements."

Bill Brady on Jeff's behalf responded to Fitz's challenge:

> Fitz can make all the bluffs he wants to now. He has the upper hand, but Jeffries is the champion and will dictate terms. Jeffries quit training about ten days ago, and is in no condition to meet anybody next Friday night. Why didn't Fitz give us his assurance about two weeks ago when we asked him, that he would take on the champion? No, he did not care to because he did not mean to fight. Now that Jim is in no condition and would be at a decided disadvantage if he agreed to battle with Bob inside of a week, Fitz tries to make a grand stand play. …

He can have a mill with Jeffries, but it will not be next week. There are plenty of places outside of this State where the pair can settle their grievances. And what's more the world is not coming to an end right away. When Fitz was the champion he only fought once in two years. Jeffries on the other hand has met two men since he knocked Fitz out. And what's more Fitz can thank Jeff for his victory over Sharkey. The boiler maker gave the sailor such a hard beating that he has not recovered from it to this day. Sharkey before Jeffries met him and the Sharkey of Friday night are two different individuals as far as physical condition is concerned.

If Fitz is so desirous of meeting the man who licked him so squarely last year why does he not post a forfeit? It will be covered in a hurry.[115]

Fitzsimmons responded to Brady by saying that he would post a $2,500 forfeit to fight next Friday night. When told that Jeff would not be ready by then, Fitz replied, "Well, then he can't get on a scrap with me." When asked about Carson City as a possible location for a later fight, Bob said, "The devil with that. The East is good enough for me. Brady told me to put up my money, didn't he? It's up." Of course, Brady was talking about a forfeit for a fight in the next six months.

Some thought that Fitz did not really want or need to fight Jeffries, because his popularity had boomed owing to his recent performances, so he, like Jeff, could make money on a theatrical tour. However, by seeming more willing to fight, he could gain an upper hand over Jeffries in public opinion (which helped swell theatrical receipts), and perhaps in future financial negotiations.

Jeffries was in Norfolk, Virginia on August 27. He said that he would not recognize Bob's challenge to fight within one week because he was making money on a baseball umpiring tour. "I will, at the proper time, give him ample opportunity to redeem the drubbing I gave him." He was willing to negotiate a Fitz fight to be held later in the season. "Pugilism needs a rest at present."[116]

Interestingly enough, Fitzsimmons said if Jeffries did not consent to a fight the following week, before the Horton law was repealed, that he would retire from the ring for good and not fight any more. Fitz again claimed that Jeff licked him because he was doped. Brady responded that the dope was in Jeff's fists.

Brady noted that if Fitz really was anxious to regain the title, he would consent to a later meeting. "The world is not coming to an end next week. There are plenty of other places where we can fight." Jeffries was weighing over 250 pounds and not ready to fight immediately. On Jeff's behalf, Bill was willing to post a forfeit and sign an agreement to hold the bout within

---

[115] *New York World*, August 25, 1900; *New York Sun*, August 26, 1900. As time passed, the point of view that Jeff had softened Sharkey up for others gained greater acceptance.
[116] *New York Journal*, August 28, 1900. Cyberboxingzone.com.

six months' time. Brady felt that Carson City or San Francisco would be suitable locations.

Brady also argued that the deluge of recent bouts meant the public needed a rest. Fitz-Sharkey II did not have the hoped-for attendance, and the club actually lost money. Plus, Jim Corbett vs. Kid McCoy already was scheduled for the 30th. The market had been flooded/saturated. Brady felt that waiting to fight would mean more money for everyone. Furthermore, "Suppose something happened at the Garden on Thursday night when McCoy and Corbett meet, would it not hurt the attendance the following night?" That was an interesting thought.

Fitz responded, "I will not go in the ring with him within six months' time. It is now or never. It is no use of talking any further on the subject." Bob said he was going out of the business along with the Horton law and was retiring. Brady said the fact that Fitzsimmons was retiring demonstrated that he really had no intention of fighting Jeffries, because Bob did not want any more of the Californian's smashes.[117]

Opinions varied as to who had the best of the argument, if one did. The *National Police Gazette* harshly called Jeffries discredited and meriting disdain for failing to take on Fitz the following week. It said that such an astute manager as Brady would not allow him to risk losing his title in another fight until he had been exploited as a theatrical star. It argued that the original offer to fight the winner of the Fitz-Sharkey fight a week later was an unadulterated bluff, "made for no other reason or purpose than to obtain the usual cheap notoriety which prize fighters are prone to seek." To make the offer in a face-saving way, so that he would not actually have to fight, Jeff "arbitrarily fixed a certain day when the $5,000 forfeit must be posted, announcing his intention to quit his training camp if this extraordinary condition was not complied with."

However, those were Jeff's terms, and when the forfeit was not posted on time, Jeff ceased his training. When the forfeit was posted after the deadline, it was less than the required amount, something the *Gazette* failed to acknowledge.

Still, the *Gazette* felt that Jeff's refusal to fight immediately, after initially making the offer to do so, had brought him some humiliation. It noted that Fitz did much better against common opponents: Sharkey, Ruhlin, Armstrong (in sparring), and Corbett. "While Fitz never actually fought Armstrong, what he did to him in training bouts every day demonstrated his ability to beat him in short order any time they started."[118]

The argument in Jeff's favor was that Fitzsimmons had the opportunity to fight him within the next six months and declined, choosing to retire instead, if one believed his retirement claims. This made it seem that he did not really want to fight Jeffries. Jeff already had defeated Fitz, Sharkey, and Corbett in the span of a year, so it was a bit of a stretch to imply cowardice. This was the type of gamesmanship that Fitzsimmons had engaged in with

[117] *New York Sun*, August 28, 1900; *New York World*, August 25, 1900.
[118] *National Police Gazette*, September 15, 1900.

Corbett for years prior to their fight. Fitz also was repeating a pattern that he had established after defeating Corbett – win a big fight, capitalize on his popularity with a theatrical tour for a lengthy period of time, and then come back and make big money with another huge fight when public demand was at its zenith. Hence, his retirement might have been a negotiating ploy as well, to obtain better financial terms. Fitz was not just a fighter, but a businessman. He was a *prize*-fighter.

The truth was that Jeff still was nursing his injury and was not in shape to fight on such short notice. Furthermore, he was looking to make easy money on a theatrical tour. Fitz had just fought twice and was nursing bruised hands, and he did not really want to fight any time soon either, given his booming popularity and ability to make money on the road as well. It was in both of their financial interests to wait and build up the fight, particularly since there was a glut of New York bouts leading up to the Horton law's termination. Furthermore, by waiting, Fitz could compel Jeffries to relent on his financial demands. Jeff needed a big-name opponent to draw a big crowd.

On Wednesday August 29, 1900, at New York's Madison Square Garden, a benefit for John L. Sullivan generated $15,000 in ticket sales. About 5,000 to 6,000 were in attendance, including a dozen women. In separate 3-round exhibitions, Jim Jeffries, Bob Fitzsimmons, Gus Ruhlin, Tom Sharkey, and Peter Maher all sparred. The most popular fighter who attended was Bob Fitzsimmons. He engaged in a 3-round comedy with Jeff Thorne, each mock dropping the other several times each round. "It was the best fake fight in many moons, and the crowd laughingly enjoyed it." The two "showed how easy it is to fake grogginess, falls and knockdowns." "It was the cleverest kind of a fake."

Jeffries sparred 3 friendly short rounds with 41-year-old former champion John L. Sullivan. Sully, wearing black trunks (instead of his usual green), was gray, very fat, and out of shape. The announcer said Jeffries was ready to defend his title at any time, which statement was met with mixed applause and hisses. Jeff appeared to be no more than 220 pounds, much less than his manager claimed. None of the 3 rounds lasted even a minute.[119]

On Thursday August 30, 1900 at Madison Square Garden, the final fight held under the Horton law era was James J. Corbett vs. Kid McCoy (61-4-9). The very fast and clever but hard-hitting Kid McCoy had victories over Ruhlin, Maher, and Choynski, amongst others. McCoy's career highlights included: 1896 KO15 Tommy Ryan (world middleweight title at 154 pounds) and KO3 Jim Daly; 1897 KO1 George LaBlanche and KO2 Australian Billy Smith; 1898 W20 Gus Ruhlin and WDQ5 Joe Goddard; 1899 LKOby10 Tom Sharkey and W20 Joe Choynski; and 1900 KO5 Peter Maher and KO4 Choynski. His real name was Norman Selby, and he also was known as the Corkscrew Kid. He had fought as a middleweight and a

[119] *New York Journal, Sun, Herald,* August 30, 1900; *National Police Gazette,* September 15, 1900.

heavyweight, but really was more of a middleweight, typically weighing in the high 150s or low 160s. But he was good enough to take on heavyweights. Corbett was coming off his impressive performance in a 23rd-round loss to Jeffries several months earlier, in May, so he was fight-sharp.

Fitzsimmons thought Corbett would win because he was taller, heavier (by at least 20 pounds), stronger, and cleverer than McCoy, and the theory that Corbett could not punch was erroneous. Given that Jim was used to fighting big, strong men like Jeff and Sharkey, it would be a welcome break to fight someone smaller. (Of course, Fitz had been smaller too, but Bob was special, and Kid McCoy, though very good, was no Bob Fitzsimmons.)[120]

Regarding the fight, after three rounds of clever, competitive boxing, in the 4th round, Corbett attacked and hurt the Kid, and in the 5th round, Corbett knocked McCoy out with body blows.[121]

Some called it a very scientific fight, while others called it a fake, based on rumors before the fight. The experts did not think it was a fake. Tom Sharkey said Corbett won on the merits. Fitzsimmons said Corbett was too heavy for him and was as fast as ever. Gus Ruhlin said he knew Jim's weight would tell and thought he would win easily. Corbett won on his merits by superior cleverness.

Bob Fitzsimmons visited Corbett's café to congratulate him. Bob said, "You're the cleverest man in the world." Corbett replied, "Yes, and you are the hardest hitting fellow in the world." Of course, Jeffries had defeated both, so what did that make him?

Jeffries was anxious to arrange a match with Fitzsimmons, or at least eager to show that Bob was not really interested in meeting him. He offered to cancel all of his theatrical dates to take Bob on at either Carson City or San Francisco. All he asked for was a month's time for training. However, Bob responded, "I have retired and will not fight any one. ... I have all the money I want. I am going to be an actor and star in a play called *The Honest Blacksmith*." Fresh off the Ruhlin and Sharkey victories, Bob had plenty of money in the bank, a booming reputation, and could make more easy money on the stage, without fighting.[122]

Two days after the Corbett-McCoy bout, on September 1, 1900, the repeal of the Horton law went into effect and a new anti-prize-fight law (the Lewis law) greatly limited boxing in New York. Boxing essentially was dead in the most populous state in the nation. Large cities like Chicago and Philadelphia only allowed 6-round bouts, too short to determine a champion. Nevada and California were on the other side of the country, in less populated areas. The large New York purses had spoiled boxers, and they feared that they never would see such bounty again. Perhaps that also informed why Fitzsimmons no longer was interested in a Jeffries match.

[120] *New York World*, August 1, 1898.
[121] *New York Herald*, August 29-31, 1900; *New York Daily Tribune, New York World, New York Sun, Brooklyn Daily Eagle, New York Journal*, August 31, 1900.
[122] *New York Sun*, September 1, 1900.

It was estimated that during the Horton law's four-year existence (Sept. 1896 - Sept. 1900), 1.76 million boxing patrons at New York clubs paid nearly $3 million dollars ($2,657,800) to watch 3,350 fights. 1898 and 1899 were the banner years, with 900 fights taking place each of those two years. The fighters' share of the purses was $998,186, while the promoters made $1,677,120. Sharkey cleared the most, at $92,000, with Jeffries coming in second at $90,000. The largest gate receipts were for Jeffries-Corbett, which brought in $60,000. Corbett-McCoy was said to have generated $55,310.[123]

The Lewis law would not be touched for over a decade, until the Frawley law 1911 opened the fights up to the general public again, but left the other provisions of the Lewis bill intact – limiting contests to only 10 rounds with no decision. It would not be until 1920 that the Walker law once again allowed formal decisions and increased the allowed bout lengths to 15 rounds.

On September 5, 1900, at S. S. Lubin's laboratory in Philadelphia, Corbett and McCoy reproduced their battle for the *Evening Journal* cameras. They wanted to make some money from fight films. That idea had been abandoned for the real fight because the lighting was so poor. Therefore, they essentially acted out their fight again.[124]

In a bombshell, the wives of both Corbett and McCoy, who were estranged from their husbands, angry, and on the cusp of divorce, claimed that the Corbett-McCoy fight was fixed. Some thought the women were fabricating their claims, for the fight appeared genuine. Others believed them. Those who believed the wives thought such a fake only served as further evidence for boxing's abolishment or strict limitation and a telling final farewell to a sport they were glad had been badly harmed in New York by the Lewis law. Legally, boxing was on the ropes again throughout much of the United States, and proper championship fights were totally knocked out of New York by both the rules and economic limitations.

---

[123] *National Police Gazette*, September 22, 1900.
[124] *New York Journal*, September 3, 6, 7, 1900.

CHAPTER 7

"Retirement" and Boxing's Western Shift

Bill Brady, hopeful that Bob Fitzsimmons would agree to fight Jeffries after all, said that he would give Bob until December 1 to accept Jeff's challenge. Brady declared that Jeff's arm was back in shape and well enough again to stand vigorous training. Fitzsimmons responded by saying that he was retired, and Jeff and his manager could not use him for advertising purposes. Either he really was retired, or it was a negotiating ploy.[125]

Jeffries said,

> I am tired of splitting the money with my opponents. In my fight with Corbett I was compelled to consent to split the money with him before he would enter the ring. Before the match was made he said he only wanted one-third of the money, but when it came time for us to enter the ring Corbett sent for Brady and told him that unless he got half the money he wouldn't fight. I don't intend to ever fight again under those conditions unless, of course, I should be successful in getting on a fight with Fitzsimmons. If Fitz will only agree to fight I will make an exception in his case and box him on terms of 75 per cent to the winner.
>
> If Fitz continues to refuse my offer then it is open to Gus Ruhlin, who I think is the next man entitled to a fight with me. Ruhlin beat Sharkey in as decisive a manner as ever a man was beaten, and he has a draw with me, too.[126]

Despite initially having refused to enter the ring again, a published statement said that Bob Fitzsimmons was willing to fight Jim Jeffries at the close of his theatrical season.

However, fickle Fitz again changed his mind. "Several days ago Fitz startled the sporting world with a statement declaring that he would re-enter the ring and if possible get on a match with Champion Jim Jeffries. Now Fitz, with his customary inconsistency, makes another statement." Bob again claimed that he had no intention of returning to the ring and was retired no matter what. "Fitzsimmons, by his refusal to fight again, has injured himself to an immeasurable extent in the estimation of the public."

Fitz claimed that he never had changed his mind, that the statement issued claiming that he was willing to fight again was unauthorized, false, and likely put forth by Brady. Bob said it was just another way for Brady to

---

[125] *National Police Gazette*, October 13, 1900.
[126] *National Police Gazette*, November 3, 1900.

advertise Jeff and his show. "Jeffries isn't drawing very well on the road, and Brady wants to get the people talking fight to advertise his champion. … Jeffries wasn't so anxious to fight me last August, was he?"

On December 8, 1900, an agreement was signed for a 20-round fight between Gus Ruhlin and Jim Jeffries to be held in Cincinnati, Ohio on February 15, 1901.[127]

On December 17, 1900, at the Penn Art Club in Philadelphia, before a crowd of 4,000 or 5,000, Gus Ruhlin fought Peter Maher (119-8-6) to a fierce 6-round no decision. The local *Inquirer* called it a draw. The local *Times* said Ruhlin won every round and did all the leading. The Associated Press said the consensus of opinion was that Ruhlin had by far best of the bout and clearly outclassed the Irishman.[128]

On December 19, 1900, in New York, *New York World* writer E. A. Roth saw Fitzsimmons in the melodrama/play *The Honest Blacksmith*, performing with his wife Rose, acting and even singing, as well as boxing with 419 ½-pound Ed Dunkhorst. "Fitz is the best pugilist-actor the writer has ever seen." "Bob is an actor, whether he knows it or not." "Fitz likes the game – the glamour of the footlights has caught him…" He even had a pleasant tenor singing voice, which was a surprise.[129]

Unfortunately, on February 2, 1901, Ohio Governor George Nash declared that the Jeffries-Ruhlin bout would not be allowed to take place in Ohio and the entire power of the state would be used to prevent what he called a public nuisance. Another world boxing title defense was thwarted.[130]

On February 25, 1901 in Galveston, Texas, before the Galveston Athletic Club, 32-year-old Joe Choynski knocked out 22-year-old black Jack Johnson early in the 3rd round of a scheduled 20-round bout. Both combatants were arrested afterwards, jailed, and charged with prizefighting.

During February, Fitzsimmons and his wife Rose were performing in *The Honest Blacksmith* in Boston. Bob still was boxing with Ed Dunkhorst in conjunction with the play, which traveled around the country.

In early May 1901, Fitz switched sparring partners and now was working with 6'4" 220-pound white Sandy Ferguson, continuing performances in *The Honest Blacksmith*. The *Boston Evening Transcript* noted, "[Fitzsimmons] certainly is a better actor than John L. Sullivan was in his palmiest days, and James J. Corbett never showed such versatility as did the star of last evening. Neither pugilist-actor mentioned attempted to present such a family party as is done in this play, and when the final curtain fell one had a pretty good idea of the entire Fitzsimmons household."[131]

---

[127] *National Police Gazette*, November 17, 24, December 1, 8, 15, 29, 1900, January 19, 1901. The contract that Brady signed said that he would receive 70% of the gross receipts – to be split between the fighters via whatever agreement they arrived upon. News reports said the split of the fighters' share would be 75%/25%.

[128] *Philadelphia Inquirer, Philadelphia Times, Scranton Tribune*, December 18, 1900. Before the fight, Tom Sharkey entered the ring and said, "I want to say I will fight any man in the world, barring a nigger; I never fought one and never will."

[129] *New York World*, December 20, 1900.

[130] *Cincinnati Enquirer*, February 3, 1901.

[131] *Boston Evening Transcript*, May 7, 1901.

Despite his far superior size, Sandy Ferguson eventually had to take time off from being Bob's sparring partner in order to heal up. "While boxing the other night Sandy started in to mix it up with Bob. The result was a smashed ear, a bloody nose and several other catastrophes for Sandy, followed by his sad departure for his home in Boston."[132] In subsequent years, the durable Ferguson would hold his own with the likes of Jack Johnson (L10, L20), Gus Ruhlin (D15), Bob Armstrong (KO1), Klondike Haynes (TKO6), Marvin Hart (L20), Sam Langford (L12 and D12), Joe Jeannette (L12, L20, W12, and LTKOby8), and many more.

Because the boxing business was in a lull (and mostly illegal), Fitzsimmons was considering taking up wrestling. Engaging in wrestling bouts was a way that boxers could perform in places like New York and make money without worrying about legal impediments. Eventually, a wrestling match was made between Fitz and Ruhlin.

On July 9, 1901, at New York's Madison Square Garden, Gus Ruhlin defeated Bob Fitzsimmons in a Greco-Roman wrestling match. They were scheduled to wrestle the best two out of three falls. In their first bout, Ruhlin got Bob on his back in 12 minutes 45 seconds. After a 15-minute rest, Ruhlin defeated Bob in their second bout in 12 minutes 24 seconds to win the match with two falls. The smaller Fitz could hold his own at wrestling but was much better at punching and fighting. Ruhlin simply had too much brute strength for him.[133]

Eventually, it was announced that Jeffries and Ruhlin would box 20 rounds in mid-November 1901 in San Francisco, in a fight sponsored by the Twentieth Century Club. It agreed to pay the fighters 62 ½% of the gate receipts. At that time, California appeared to be the only semi-reasonable location (or one of the very few) in terms of population in which a legal boxing match of championship length could be held.[134]

On September 6, 1901, while standing in a receiving line at the Buffalo Pan-American Exposition, an anarchist named Fred Nieman shot U.S. President William McKinley twice. He died eight days later, on September 14, from complications related to the gunshot wound. On that day, Vice President and former New York Governor Theodore Roosevelt, who had signed the Lewis bill, became President.

On September 17, 1901, at Hazard's Pavilion in Los Angeles, California, James J. Jeffries boxed black Hank Griffin in a 4-round exhibition, decking Griffin several times in the 1st, 2nd, and 3rd rounds, though Hank survived throughout the 4th round to earn a monetary bonus for lasting. Two months later, Griffin would win a 20-round decision over fellow black fighter Jack Johnson.

A week after Jeffries-Griffin, on September 24, 1901 at the Reliance Club in Oakland, California, in another scheduled 4-round bout, Jeffries took on big 220-225-pound Joe Kennedy, who held a June 1899 W20 over

---

[132] *Boston Globe*, May 24, 1901; *National Police Gazette*, June 15, 22, 1901.
[133] *New York Clipper*, July 27, 1901; *National Police Gazette*, July 6, August 3, 1901. In Philadelphia, Tom Sharkey wrestled Peter Maher in contest that was declared a draw.
[134] *National Police Gazette*, August 10, 1901, September 14, 21, 1901.

Ruhlin and fought Hank Griffin to two 20-round draws. The aggressive Jeffries knocked out Kennedy in the 2nd round with a powerful left hook to the jaw.

Perhaps owing to the shorter bout lengths and conditions, or perhaps because he was modifying his style and utilizing his natural talents more, Jeffries had fought both Griffin and Kennedy in a much more aggressive manner than usual.

Training for Ruhlin, Jeffries said that he was in the business for money, and, realizing that Fitzsimmons would be the greatest draw, he wanted a fight with Bob. Jeff was concerned that Fitz felt there was more money in the theatrical business than boxing. Ruhlin was the next best option.[135]

On November 15, 1901 in San Francisco, California, before a crowd of 6,610 to 10,000 that paid from $2 up to $20, an alleged 212-215-pound James J. Jeffries dropped 201-202-pound Gus Ruhlin (27-6-3) in the 4th and 5th rounds, and generally pounded on him with a methodical, consistent attack, particularly left hooks and uppercuts to the body and head, a left hook to the body decking Gus in the 5th, causing his second, Billy Madden, to throw in the sponge to retire Ruhlin following the conclusion of the 5th round. The fight was successfully filmed by the Edison Manufacturing Company.

[135] *San Francisco Call*, November 6, 7, 1901; *San Francisco Bulletin*, November 10, 1901.

Since it appeared that Gus could have continued, Billy Madden took some criticism for stopping the bout rather than allowing Ruhlin to fight to the finish. Many thought Ruhlin fought as if afraid, and they called him a quitter and the fight disappointing. Nevertheless, Madden said, "What was there to be gained by letting Gus get beaten to death? He was cut all to pieces by Fitzsimmons, and after that fight I said I would never let him be punished like that again."

Offering his thoughts on the fight result, Bob Fitzsimmons said, "It is always the man behind the wallop who carries off the money and all that goes with the winner."[136]

Billy Madden was disturbed by the public/press desire for a complete knockout, saying that it was inhuman and would have only further fueled the anti-boxing folks. One writer supported Madden, saying,

> Ruhlin was knocked into unconsciousness by Fitzsimmons, and it was 6 o'clock the next morning before Gus knew what his name was. Then and there Madden declared that that would be the last time he would let his protégé be 'cut to ribbons.' If there were more managers like Madden there would be fewer accidents in the ring and fewer sermons delivered from the pulpits on the brutality of the prize ring. "If Gus had been carried out of the ring in a helpless condition and remained unconscious for several hours, what a splendid opening it would have been for the preachers today," remarked Madden. "As I

[136] San Francisco Examiner, San Francisco Chronicle, San Francisco Evening Post, San Francisco Bulletin, San Francisco Call, November 16, 1901.

ended the fight there was nothing brutal to it and it will be an easy matter to hold another championship contest."[137]

The Twentieth Century Athletic Club said the total receipts were $32,700. The *Evening Post* said over $40,000 was taken in. It said Jeff received about $22,000 and Ruhlin $5,000. Referee Harry Corbett was paid $500. The *Chronicle* said 62 ½% of the receipts went to the fighters. Of that, Jeff's share was 75% (about $13,950) to Ruhlin's 25% (about $4,650). The *Call* and *Bulletin* said the total gate receipts were $30,487.50. Jeff earned $14,056.52 to Ruhlin's $4,685.54. Most laborers at that time earned about $2 a day. New York's governor made $4,000 less in annual salary than what Jeff earned in one night. More money could be earned from the films.

The World's Champion and Four Heavyweights He Has Laid Low.

[137] *San Francisco Bulletin*, November 18, 1901.

CHAPTER 8

Road to a Rematch

The fighter with whom the press and the public most wanted to see Jeffries do battle, the only one perceived as having any chance against him, was Bob Fitzsimmons. Therefore, Jeffries stood to make the most money by fighting him.

Bob Fitzsimmons was "retired," but reportedly said that he was considering returning for a fight with Jeff. He again claimed that he was 'dosed' with poison before their fight. Bob said, "Jeffries is not what might be called a knockerout. He is too slow and deliberate, too, and at the same time does not care to take too many chances. Does anybody believe I was myself when he put me to sleep?"

Fitzsimmons was keeping fit, punching the bag and engaging in outdoor exercises. He did not drink. He was weighing about 180 pounds and said he would not have to do much to get back into fighting trim.[138]

Others felt that neither Fitzsimmons nor any other established fighter would have a chance with Jeffries, that only a newly developing crop of boxers eventually possibly could give him a real test. But it would take them time to mature properly to be ready for a monster like Jeffries. Ironically, the increasing perception of Jeffries as being vastly superior to all others was making it difficult to market future fights.

> Not in many years has a champion stood in such lonesome glory as the immense person from Los Angeles. ... Red Robert Fitzsimmons, a few days ago, was thought to be the one man that the public would fancy as Jim's foe. The feeling has veered around. It is now admitted that the terrible Jeffries of today would whip the aged Bob far more quickly than when they first did battle. Bob is in the sere and yellow – a wonderful boxer, but certainly no better than a year ago, while Jeffries is now in the very zenith of his sturdy vigor. ... Jeffries, bigger than anybody else and with a strength surpassing even his enormous size, has no competitor. Fitzsimmons is verging toward the edge of Hasbeen hill. ... If the champion is to be whipped, a new heavyweight must be caught young and properly educated. And that will take time, a great deal of time.[139]

Just past midnight in the early hours of Sunday December 15, 1901, at the Theatrical Business Men's Athletic Club at 139 West Forty-First Street in New York, at a members-only smoker, wearing 8-ounce gloves, Bob Fitzsimmons and Tom Sharkey boxed a friendly and light 5-round

[138] *National Police Gazette*, December 14, 1901; *San Francisco Evening Post*, December 19, 1901.
[139] *San Francisco Evening Post*, December 2, 1901.

exhibition bout for points only in a 15-foot ring. They went at each other at a hot pace in the final round, the blows coming so quickly that they could not be counted. When it was over, the referee declared it a draw.[140]

When asked whether Fitzsimmons had gone back, Sharkey answered in the negative.

> You can just bet Fitz is the same old fellow. Gone back? Anybody who talks that way of Bob should call at Bellevue Hospital and have his sanity tested. It was the same old Fitz I boxed on Saturday night. He was just as quick as he ever was; he had his old punch and he stepped around like a youngster. … Understand, our bout was only a friendly one, but once in a while Fitz would sneak in a jolt just to show that he still had that punch. He side-stepped in his own old-fashioned way, and altogether it does not seem to me that he has in the least forgotten a thing he knew about the fighting game. …
>
> Honestly, I believe he is as good as he ever was in his life. With the necessary training, I do not believe that Jeffries would have anything of a walkover. In fact, Fitz would have an even break, but just how such a battle would terminate I would rather not say. But Fitz is the same old clever fellow with the punch.[141]

Fitzsimmons was expected to come out of retirement and make a match with Jeffries. Bob had been training quietly for several weeks and had remarked that he was the only man in the world with a chance to defeat Jeffries. Fitz knew that he would be a big draw and therefore could insist on more money.[142]

The press noted, "A second battle between Fitz and Jeffries would excite more public interest than any other that could be arranged, and it is to be hoped that the former champion can be induced to forgo his determination to quit fighting."

Fitzsimmons said he would come back and fight again provided that sufficient money was involved. The confident Jeffries wanted to make the fight winner-take-all. He noted, "When I fought Fitzsimmons I was compelled to give him 75 per cent, win or lose." Fitz once again required a guarantee. He would not enter the ring unless it was made worth his while. He knew that their fight would be the biggest draw in boxing, and he wanted a guaranteed taste of those revenues, win or lose. Jeff said he would split the purse 65% winner/35% loser. Fitz said that was fair but wanted to see Jeff in person to consummate the deal. No one was certain whether Bob was serious or not, because his "mind was as changeable as a chameleon's colors." Negotiations were ongoing.

Eventually it was announced that Jeff and Fitz would fight. Bob was guaranteed $7,500 plus a significant portion of the fighter's share of the

[140] *San Francisco Evening Post, Buffalo Evening News, Brooklyn Times, New York Sun*, December 16, 1901.
[141] *San Francisco Evening Post*, December 26, 1901.
[142] *Kansas City Star, New York Clipper, San Francisco Chronicle, Evening Post*, December 28, 1901.

gross receipts, even should he suffer defeat, a sufficient inducement for him to fight.[143]

On February 15, 1902, Jim Jeffries and Bob Fitzsimmons signed articles of agreement. Allegedly, they were to box 20 rounds before the club offering the largest purse, to be divided 60%/40% to the winner/loser, with the winner receiving all of the moving picture profits. The contestants would be permitted the use of soft surgical bandages, subject to the referee's inspection. The bout was tentatively set to take place in mid-May. Fitz already had been doing some training.[144]

Despite their agreement, word was that apparently Bob Fitzsimmons had changed his mind, and wanted 50% of everything from his fight with Jeffries, win or lose, and refused to sign final articles with a date certain otherwise. Fitz knew that he was the only opponent whom the public really wanted to see in the ring with Jeff, and he wanted to capitalize on that fact. Jeffries would not agree, saying that the public would not stand for such terms.[145]

Still, it was looking like the fight would happen, because in March, Bob was training and sparring hard in New York with Gus Ruhlin, who was preparing for a fight with Peter Maher. Fitz took long daily spins on the road. He and Ruhlin wrestled a bit and then sparred in lively fashion. "Fitzsimmons several times shook up Ruhlin with a stiff whack on the head and once sent him staggering back with a left thrust to the body." Ruhlin returned with a punch to the nose that brought blood.

It was said that Bob would be in great shape when the fight came off. "Fitzsimmons seems to have lost none of his speed, and he is regarded as the most marvelous 'old man' in the fistic world. Ruhlin declares the lanky Australian can hit as stiff a punch as ever." Bob and Gus were mixing it daily in rough-house style.[146]

On March 21, 1902, in Philadelphia, Gus Ruhlin scored a KO2 over Peter Maher. Gus still was a top fighter.

When Fitzsimmons attempted to negotiate the location of the Jeffries match, and essentially threatened to pull out of the fight, he began taking heat from the press, which called him a flunker. Apparently, this made Bob become more reasonable. He finally agreed that California was the only state in the nation where they could legally fight a championship-length bout and maximize ticket sales. Nevada would allow a fight to the finish, but its isolation made it less attractive. Of course, all of the ongoing discussion about the final details caused the bout's date to become less certain.[147]

On April 21, 1902, at Wood's Gymnasium at West 28th Street in Manhattan, New York, Bob Fitzsimmons and Jim Corbett sparred 3 lively and fast rounds. They were not trying to knock out one another, as it was a friendly set-to, but still furnished a grand exhibition of boxing.

[143] *National Police Gazette*, January 18, 25, February 1, 8, 15, 1902.
[144] *New York Clipper*, February 22, 1902; *National Police Gazette*, March 8, 1902.
[145] *National Police Gazette*, March 1, 1902.
[146] *Los Angeles Times*, March 15, 1902; *National Police Gazette*, March 22, 1902.
[147] *National Police Gazette*, May 3, 10, 1902.

In the 1st round, Jim was as fast as ever, dancing around, jabbing, side-stepping, and swinging. Fitz retaliated and they engaged in pretty exchanges. A Corbett left to the lips left its impression, and another blow puffed up Bob's nose, but he took it well and good naturedly.

Corbett was a little slower in the 2nd, for his wind was not good, but still he was as clever as ever. Fitz landed a few stiff body punches and Corbett clinched. On the break, Jim tapped Bob on the ear with a left and hit him hard in the ribs. Fitz sidestepped twice and puzzled Jim with some feints. Neither lost their heads.

In the 3rd round, Corbett moved well, left and right, and landed on the face and mouth. Bob hit the jaw and body with his right. They went at it during the final minute with many quick blows. Corbett was puffing at the finish, while Bob seemed fresh as a daisy.[148]

Hank Griffin, whose record included LTKOby14or17 Jim Jeffries, W20 Jack Munroe, D20 Joe Kennedy (twice), LND4 Jeffries, LTKOby7 Denver Ed Martin, and W20 and D15 Jack Johnson, accepted a position as Bob Fitzsimmons' sparring partner.

> Hank thinks he is the right man to train with Fitz, as he stood up twice before the big fellow, once for seventeen and once for four rounds. Hank will find that posing as Fitz's sparring partner is no sinecure. Fitz has an unpleasant habit of putting out about three trainers a day when he is feeling well.

Fitzsimmons claimed to be weighing 168 pounds (unproven) and said that he was better now than at any other time in his career. He always had taken excellent care of himself, which was the secret to his longevity.[149]

In early June, Jeffries and Fitzsimmons finally ironed out the final details of their fight. They agreed to box on July 25, 1902 in San Francisco. Each made some concessions. Jeffries withdrew his objection to hand bandages. He had noted that Fitz did not allow either Corbett or Jeffries to wear bandages when they had fought him, so Jeff wanted to give Fitz the same treatment. However, Bob made hand bandages a requirement because his hands were becoming fragile. He noted that in the original articles, they indeed had agreed that hand bandages could be worn. Fitz said, "All I want is a little bit of sticking plaster on my hand where it was hurt before." Jeffries responded, "I have no objection to that. It will be subject to the inspection of the referee, of course." "Certainly," responded Fitzsimmons. In return, Jeff was able to name the club where the fight would be held. The purse split would be 60%/40% to the winner/loser. Both agreed that the winner would fight Jim Corbett, who wanted another crack at the title.[150]

[148] Buffalo Evening Times, Buffalo Review, Brooklyn Times, April 22, 1902; National Police Gazette, May 17, 1902.
[149] Los Angeles Herald, May 7, 11, 1902.
[150] National Police Gazette, June 14, 21, 1902, August 9, 1902.

In June 1902, Fitz stationed his training camp at Skagg's Springs, which was north of San Francisco. Bob boxed with Hank Griffin (23-3-7) and Soldier Tom Wilson, as well as Chicago's George Dawson, who had trained Bob for the Ruhlin and Sharkey fights.

According to the *Police Gazette*, Fitzsimmons rose daily at 6:30 a.m. He would walk 2.5 miles and then run back. In the gymnasium, he tossed the medicine ball with his trainers. He punched the ball for 15 minutes, and also hit the "funny fellow," a bag three-feet in diameter by four-feet in length. Fitz then sparred George Dawson, who was described as a

Robert Fitzsimmons as a Huntsman.

giant. Despite his superior size, Dawson was a boy in Bob's hands. Fitz boxed another 4 rounds with 23-year-old Soldier Tom Wilson, who stood over 6 feet tall and weighed over 200 pounds. Hank Griffin was also "there to take a punching, and it is safe to say that he gets all that is coming to him." Often, each sparring partner would box a round, alternating, while Bob remained in the ring. Fitz also hit baseballs for an hour.

After dinner, Fitzsimmons would rough it and wrestle with Dawson and Wilson, pushing their heads back, grabbing their necks, and generally mauling each other for half an hour. Next, Bob hit a bag for 6 rounds. He then exercised his legs, feinting, side-stepping, advancing, retreating, and ducking little rubber balls thrown at him.

Jeff's former trainer Tommy Ryan anticipated that Fitzsimmons would put up a much better showing this time. "If he can only stay away and fight clever, like Corbett did, he can get Jeffries. I suppose, though, he will fight the same old way – carry it to the other fellow until he wins or loses." When Jeff won the title, Ryan had told him to fire the right for the body every time that Fitz advanced.[151]

On June 20, 1902, at Hazard's Pavilion in Los Angeles, Hank Griffin fought Jack Johnson to a 20-round draw.

Two days after the fight, Griffin returned to Skagg's Springs in Northern California to resume the arduous task of being a Bob Fitzsimmons sparring partner. "Hank is authority for the statement that posing as the boxing aide

[151] *New York Clipper*, June 7, 1902; *National Police Gazette*, June 28, July 5, 19, August 23, 1902.

to the Cornishman is anything but a sinecure." Griffin, along with heavyweights George Dawson and Soldier Tom Wilson, sparred with Fitzsimmons in late June and throughout July 1902, helping to prepare Bob for the Jeffries rematch.[152]

On June 25, 1902, at the National Sporting Club in London, England, in their rubber match, Gus Ruhlin scored a KO11 over Tom Sharkey.

Fitzsimmons was working hard. On the morning of June 28, he ran, then boxed 12 rounds, 4 rounds each with Wilson, Dawson, and Griffin. "The way he goes at these men is really surprising." His sparring partners fought him hard, but he always gave them better than they sent in. Bob could take punishment without the slightest notice, and it looked "as if it would take a battering ram to put him out of business." When his manager Clark Ball advised him to let up a little on his work and not take so many hard knocks, Bob said, "Why, this work is not bothering me in the least."

On the 30th, Fitz ran 10 miles up and down the hills at a 9-minute mile pace.[153]

Fitzsimmons jogs with Hank Griffin while George Dawson follows on horseback.

On July 1, Fitz ran another 10 miles – the first 5 easy, and then 5 miles hard. Over the course of one of those miles, he sprinted 100 yards, and then walked 100 yards, alternating this way for the entire mile.

---

[152] *Los Angeles Herald*, June 23, 1902.
[153] *San Francisco Bulletin*, June 29, 30, 1902.

At a 4th of July celebration, Fitz sparred with George Dawson and Soldier Wilson. He also punched the bag.

Bob showed better form on the 8th than he had since he started training. Discussing Bob's pace on the run, Hank Griffin said,

> Well, Lord, you should see him go. He didn't know when he was going up the hill. It was all level to him. Why, I guess I must have lost my wind before I had gone two miles…. When I came in I was all done up. While Mr. Fitzsimmons, he looked as if he had just done a cakewalk around the barn.

In the afternoon, Fitz hit the bag and then sparred Dawson, Wilson, and Griffin 2 rounds each for a total of 6 rounds. A blow that Bob tried to hold back dazed Wilson.

Fitzsimmons liked working with Hank Griffin the most because he could engage and mix it up and Bob could let himself out more with him and not have to hold back so much. Griffin was the snappiest and most earnest worker of the bunch and made a good impression. "He is a willing worker and exceedingly shifty." "It is give and take and he is right after Fitz all the time."

On the 10th, wearing a costume of a baby pink hue, Bob punched the bag, cutting it a bit short on account of the summer heat. He sparred alternating rounds with Dawson, Soldier Wilson, and Griffin, and then repeated the circuit.[154]

Unfortunately, the parties were unable to negotiate an agreement regarding the fight films, which might have been short-sighted of them. Fitzsimmons was not happy with the biograph company's offer and rejected the idea of the fight being filmed. Initially, Jeffries did not worry about it too much, but said that he was sorry because he would like to have everyone see just who the better man was.

Robert Fitzsimmons Punches the Bag.

However, several days later, it was reported that the Jeffries camp was upset by Fitz's "bullheadedness" and "cussedness," which prevented an arrangement with the biograph folks to film the fight. Delaney said, "The whole thing in a nutshell is that Fitz wanted Jeff to put up all the money that was necessary to carry the thing out. He wouldn't give up a cent."

---

[154] *San Francisco Bulletin*, July 3, 5, 9-11, 1902.

Responding to the Jeffries camp, Bob said, "Delaney thinks I am overlooking a business proposition. Yes, but it was one for the biograph people, but not for me. ... By that agreement we had all to lose, while they were protected to the fullest extent without guaranteeing anything in the way of results." He noted that under the proposed agreement, the biograph company would not have to pay for expenses, while the club and the principals were expected to put up a great deal of money in financing. So, sadly, the fight would not be filmed, and it likely meant the loss of a great deal of potential revenue as well as a potential historic film record.[155]

Fitzsimmons was training hard and seemed tireless. Harry Corbett noted,

> If Fitzsimmons can fight as well as he can work, he has a great chance. ... The way that fellow runs on the road and then punches the bag and boxes a half dozen hot rounds with Wilson is really wonderful. ... Age seems to have had absolutely no effect upon him. He's as frisky as a little child.

Hank Griffin said there was nothing to the fight, for Fitzsimmons would win. This was coming from someone who had twice been in the ring with Jeffries.[156]

Jim Jeffries shifted his training quarters from Harbin Springs to Oakland's Reliance Club, beginning work there on July 14, sparring with Joe Kennedy and brother Jack Jeffries. At 212-213 pounds, Jeffries had taken off 20 pounds during his training. Bill Delaney said, "I have been with Jeff a long time, but I never saw him in such perfect condition as he is at the present time." Onlookers marveled at Jeff's speed and the lightness of his footwork. Owing to his superior size, remarkable quickness for a big man, youth, condition, great chin, and undefeated record, Jeffries was a 2 ½ to 1 and 10 to 4 betting odds favorite.[157]

That same day, the 14th, Fitzsimmons did his morning run with Griffin. In the afternoon, he hit the bag. Then he boxed Dawson 1 round. Wilson was up next, and a relatively light blow dropped him. In the next round, Bob banged Griffin hard and often, but Hank took it and fought back. During the next circuit of 3 alternating rounds, Fitz asked each man to fight in a crouch, like Jeffries, which they did. Bob boxed the 7th round against Wilson again, and then Griffin ended the 8 rounds. Fitzsimmons "hammered the colored boy good and plenty. ... Bob sent a short jolt into his jaw that gave him a dizzy spell." After the round was over, Hank said, "Did you see him give me that jolt? ... It was a dandy. What would it have been if he had meant it? Oh, Lordy!"[158]

Joe Kennedy said Jeffries had improved wonderfully. "He's quicker, stronger, more shifty and it's twice as hard to hit him. When you try to push him away, it's like moving a house."

[155] *San Francisco Bulletin*, July 8, 13, 14, 1902.
[156] *San Francisco Evening Post*, *San Francisco Bulletin*, July 14, 1902.
[157] *San Francisco Call*, *San Francisco Evening Post*, July 14, 1902; *San Francisco Bulletin*, July 15, 1902.
[158] *San Francisco Bulletin*, July 15, 1902.

Bill Delaney said not only could Jeffries dish it, but he could take it too. In their first fight, Fitz hit him with some cracking shots and expected Jeff to fall, but when he was right there grinning at him, it broke Bob's heart. Others said Fitz exhausted himself with his own output in trying to knock Jeff out, but Jeffries was the first man whom he hit but could not drop or stop.[159]

Jeff's camp strenuously denied rumors that there were two sets of articles of agreement, one for the public, in which there was a 60/40 split, and a private agreement in which they were to split the purse evenly. Delaney said he never had been accused of faking in his life and would pay $1,000 to anyone who could prove otherwise.[160]

At Skaggs Springs on July 16, Fitzsimmons ran 10 miles. He boxed 8 fast rounds with Wilson and Griffin, dropping Wilson several times. Griffin was also knocked down, the first knockdown that Fitz had given him.

On the 17th, Bob banged Wilson and Griffin around for 6 rounds. Fitz said, "I never was better in my life. … I will go into the ring in perfect condition." Dawson agreed that Bob never was better.[161]

Fitzsimmons kept claiming that he was doped in their first fight, that he could not see Jeffries or tell where he was. Most experts believed that Jeff's fists had made him groggy.

---

[159] *San Francisco Call, San Francisco Evening Post*, July 16, 1902.
[160] *San Francisco Bulletin*, July 16, 17, 1902; *San Francisco Evening Post, San Francisco Call*, July 17, 1902.
[161] *San Francisco Evening Post, San Francisco Bulletin*, July 17, 1902.

Robert Fitzsimmons.

About a week from the fight, both Jeffries and Fitzsimmons started tapering their training and sparring less often. Bill Delaney said that as a result, Jeff would gain some weight and enter the ring as strong as a bull at about 220 pounds. Bill said that when Jeff was out of training, he weighed close to 300 pounds but did not look it because it was well distributed over his body. Delaney said Fitzsimmons was an easier man to fight than Corbett because he was easier to hit, but at the same time, Bob was the more dangerous fighter because he hit so much harder.[162]

Bob's son, Fitz, Tom Wilson, Eddie Graney, and George Dawson

---

[162] *San Francisco Evening Post*, July 18, 19, 1902.

Ed Graney had been selected to referee the fight, and he met with the fighters to discuss the rules. Referee Graney said that in case of a knockdown, the other man must go to his corner until the man on the mat had regained his feet. The men could hit in the clinches while the other held on, but once he commanded a break, they were required to step back. He noted that the articles of agreement allowed the men to use soft surgical bandages.

In Fitz's 6 rounds of sparring on the 18th, Bob dropped Wilson to the mat, while a blow to the jaw dazed Griffin and caused him to stop working for a few seconds. Both men worked hard and at a fast pace. Griffin gave Bob some pretty hard raps, but none of them had any effect.[163]

At the end of his workout on the 19th, Jeff allegedly weighed in at 210 pounds. George Siler said Jeffries was faster than ever, and his condition was superb. The next day, Jeff sparred 8 rounds.

On the 20th, Fitzsimmons transferred his training quarters from Skaggs Springs to San Francisco, where he would work out at the Olympic Club.[164]

Bob commended Hank Griffin as an excellent sparring partner. Hank stood 6'2", weighed 180 pounds in top condition, and had a very long reach of 81 ½ inches, even longer than Tom Wilson's 80 inches. Fitz said it was no easy task to subdue Griffin, calling him a wonder.

Bill Delaney said of Jeffries,

> The big fellow has all his forces under control, and does not get rattled, no matter how fast the fight, nor how dangerous the surroundings. He knows his powers of administering and receiving punishment. He is aware that he can punch harder than any man that breathes, and knows that he can digest rougher knocks than any other man. He is so strongly built that he is, compared to Fitzsimmons, like a heavily armored modern battleship.[165]

On July 21 at the Olympic, Fitz took his morning run, boxed with each of his three trainers, and punched the bag. He mostly played defense against Griffin, for 4 rounds allowing him to slug away, while Bob blocked and eluded blows. In the last round, Fitz showed what he could do if he so desired, slugging Hank and keeping him trying to survive. He then wrestled for 30 minutes with Dawson and Griffin and seemed fresh afterwards. Soldier Wilson showed reporters his cauliflower ear, which he said had become misshapen as a result of Fitz's pounding.

Fitzsimmons appeared to be in excellent condition, and those who saw him were of the opinion that he was dangerous and would give Jeffries a real battle. Another paper said Bob was a freak. At an age when most were retired, he was at the height of physical perfection, showing no signs of decadence. He was bigger and stronger than at any time in his career. He appeared to be weighing 180-185 pounds. Still, he was going up against "the biggest, strongest and most powerful man known in the history of the

[163] *San Francisco Bulletin*, July 19, 1902.
[164] *San Francisco Call*, July 19-21, 1902.
[165] *San Francisco Evening Post, San Francisco Bulletin*, July 21, 1902.

ring." "Jeffries certainly ought to win, but there is always danger in an opponent of Fitzsimmons' class. He has a deadly punch, which if put in with precision, ought to be destructive enough to rock even a Jeffries." Fitz hit hard enough to hurt anyone, regardless of size.[166]

The consensus of opinion was that Jeffries ought to win, but that Fitzsimmons had a chance. Jeff had advantages in age, height, weight, strength, and a wonderful chin which could assimilate Fitz's power. He was perhaps the only man who could take Bob's punch. The *Police Gazette*'s expert wrote,

Fitz's admirers may claim that their man is more scientific, but this fact I dispute, for in Jeffries' more recent fights he has demonstrated the possession of a well-developed knowledge of the finer points of the fistic game. He blocks and counters superbly and is faster with a lead than any big man I ever saw except Corbett. He is cool and courageous and has the additional advantage of having beaten Fitzsimmons. ... Fitz has been on the shelf two years while Jeff has had four or five fights in that time. ...

In my opinion Fitz himself has no idea that he can win. Reverses in theatrical and other speculative ventures have left him in a position where ready money is a necessity, and a big losing end (probably an equal division of the purse if the inside facts were known) has tempted him to try it again.[167]

Still, Bob Fitzsimmons was a fighter with a lot of pride, who had been training diligently for over six months. He clearly wanted to reverse his only legitimate loss.

Approaching the fight, Jeffries said,

I can truthfully say that I feel bigger and stronger than at any time during my career. I have trained long and faithfully for the event and have reached a state of perfect condition. I do not think that the man

[166] *San Francisco Evening Post*, July 21, 1902; *San Francisco Call*, *San Francisco Evening Post*, July 22, 1902.
[167] *National Police Gazette*, August 2, 1902.

lives who can whip me. ... I have made a study of Fitzsimmons and think I know his methods better than he does mine, for I feel that during the past three years I have improved greatly while he has but little.

Jeff also said, "I guarantee that the battle will be fast and furious from start to finish. I think I know Fitzsimmons' style of battle and believe I can easily conquer him if I do not allow him to play in and out with me. I shall therefore hurry matters, feeling confident that in such a style of warfare I can stand the better chance of success."

Delaney said Jeffries was weighing 214 pounds.

Fitzsimmons was confident as well. "I will win the fight on Friday night. If I did not think I would be able to reverse the decision awarded to Jeffries on our first meeting I never would have signed for a second. ... I am huskier and stronger than ever."

On the 22nd, three days before the fight, Fitz took his morning run. In the afternoon, he boxed 3 rounds with Griffin, 3 rounds with amateur heavyweight Andy Gallagher, and 2 rounds with Al Ahrens, a clever Olympic Club welterweight.

That morning, Jeff ran 10 miles. In the afternoon, he weighed in at 217 pounds. Jeffries worked the pulley weights and wrist machine prior to sparring 8 alternating rounds with Jack Jeffries and Joe Kennedy. He went at Kennedy harder than usual. At one point, a punch on the jaw completely turned Joe around. Kennedy came back and landed a right to the nose, drawing blood.[168]

Although Jeff was the favorite, many felt that Bob had a fighting chance. "That he is trained to the hour is beyond question."

On the 23rd, two days before the fight, with San Francisco Mayor Eugene Schmitz watching, Fitz boxed 4 fast rounds with Griffin. "He hammered Griffin hard and blocked all the heavy blows Hank sent in." The mayor was impressed.

Afterwards, speaking of Griffin, Bob said, "That fellow is one of the hardest men I have ever tried to hit; he has a way of smothering up that leaves nothing but bones in sight."

Griffin complimented Bob as well. "When I first came to the camp Mr. Fitzsimmons had hard work getting at me, as I used the crouching position, but now it does not bother him in the least. ... I have been up against Jeffries, and I know how he can hit, and I tell you I am pinning my money on Bob."

Fitzsimmons said of Jeffries, "When I fought him some years ago I held him too cheaply. I thought he was an overgrown amateur, and I attempted to beat him quickly. He proved strong and caught me with a lucky punch. ... I am in better condition than I was when first we met and I feel confident I can beat him."[169]

The night before the fight, Jeffries said,

[168] San Francisco Evening Post, San Francisco Bulletin, San Francisco Call, July 23, 1902.
[169] San Francisco Call, San Francisco Bulletin, July 24, 1902.

There is in my mind no doubt but that I shall win. … I am not going into the ring underrating him. I know he is a very dangerous man to crowd, and I am not, I assure you, going to make him fight by taking unnecessary chances. … [In our first fight], I was then hit as hard or harder than I had ever been struck before. Anyone who saw the New York fight will bear me out in the assertion that I was punished as hard as Fitzsimmons could lay it on. Yet I survived. In the midst of his shower of blows I was unrocked. What I then went through I am ready to take again tomorrow night.[170]

[170] *San Francisco Evening Post*, July 25, 1902.

CHAPTER 9

One for the Ages

On Friday July 25, 1902, in San Francisco, 27-year-old world heavyweight champion James J. Jeffries (16-0-2) fought 39-year-old former world middleweight and heavyweight champion Bob Fitzsimmons (60-4-1) in a scheduled 20-round rematch. This was the second time a former gloved world heavyweight champion was granted another crack at the title, and both times it was Jeffries granting the former titlist the opportunity.

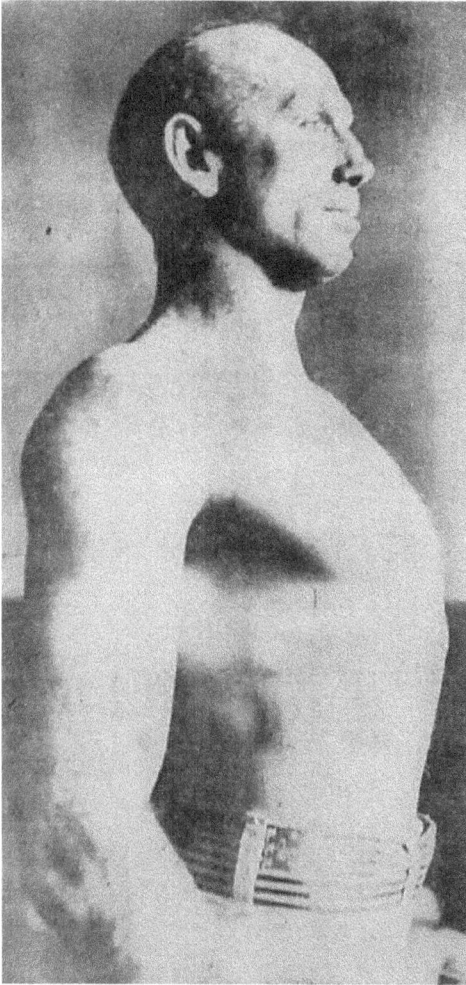

The day of the championship fight, Fitzsimmons said, "I never felt better in my life nor more confident of winning a fight. I feel that I am as good now as when I last fought Jeffries. I was in good condition then as ever in my life, but I was doped." He also said he held Jeff too cheaply the first time, underrating his strength and skill. Fitz predicted that he would do better this time, for he would fight more carefully. "I know Jeffries' style now and by making a different kind of fight, I am positive that I can turn the tables." "This time I am going to dodge his strength and play to his weakness." Fitz was not bothered by his underdog status. "Odds don't win a fight."[171]

Bob's sparring partner/trainer George Dawson said, "Fitz is in better shape than he ever was, and I think he will win sure. He is a cleverer man than Jeffries and I think he can hit harder, and there is no doubt that he is a better general." Hank Griffin said Fitz was a sure winner.

[171] The report of the fight, as well as pre- and post-fight discussion are taken from the *San Francisco Call*, *San Francisco Bulletin*, *San Francisco Evening Post*, *San Francisco Chronicle*, and *San Francisco Examiner*, all July 25-26, 1902; and *National Police Gazette*, August 9, 1902.

Jeffries said Fitzsimmons would find a greatly improved man from the one he met in 1899. He was then practically a novice by comparison, and still he knocked out Bob in 11 rounds. Jeff expected to knock him out more quickly this time. "He has a hard punch; but I have yet to meet a man who can hurt me or knock me down."

Fitz's KO6 over Ruhlin (after Ruhlin knocked out Sharkey in the 15th round) and KO2 over Sharkey (after Sharkey went 25 rounds with Jeffries and had a KO3 over Choynski, but had lost to Ruhlin) clearly made him the most deserving title challenger. However, once again, Bob had not fought in almost two years, not since late August 1900. Still, all of the training reports said Fitzsimmons was fight sharp and ready, and he had remained physically well and active in the intervening two years. He had been training steadily for over six months.

The new outdoor pavilion for the fight had been built on the corner of Fourteenth and Valencia streets. It measured 200' x 215' in the open air. The fighters would box on an elevated platform which was well lit by strong lights placed by the Independent Electric Light Company. Nearly 200 policemen would be on hand to handle the crowd.

The arrangements of the San Francisco Athletic Club and the police were perfect. There was no trouble or any arrests.

When the arena doors were opened at 6 p.m. there was a line of ticket holders that extended around the block. The arena was practically sold-out a half-hour earlier. "All the $7.50 seats were disposed of early in the afternoon, and then a raid was made on the higher priced ones." Only a few $10, $15, and $20 tickets could be obtained.

The crowd contained folks who had traveled from all over the country to be there. The *Call* said more than 5,000 people crowded the arena. The *Bulletin* estimated 6,500. Some later said 7,000 were in attendance. Scores of ushers were present to assist ticket holders and direct them to their seats.

High-power electric lights were strung all over the arena so that it was well lit. The ring was bright enough that the men could be seen clearly from the furthest part of the outdoor arena.

The sky was clear, and it was a delightful night to witness a fight outdoors. It was much better than sitting in a stuffy arena breathing in clouds of tobacco smoke and impure air.

Close to the ring were news correspondents from all over the country. During the fight, the clicking of telegraph machines could be heard.

Fitzsimmons arrived a few minutes after 7 p.m. and went to his dressing room. He was rubbed down, and to warm up, he boxed a couple of light rounds with George Dawson.

Jeffries arrived nearly two hours later. He wore a long black overcoat and a Panama hat, which he did not remove until after he entered the ring.

Owing to his great strength and vitality, the odds were 10 to 4 in Jeff's favor. Betting was very light, given that most thought Jeff would win. After all, he never had been defeated, or even dropped, including by Bob.

Shortly after 10 p.m., accompanied by trainers George Dawson, Hank Griffin, and manager Clark Ball, Fitzsimmons was first to arrive in the ring, wearing a flashy blue bathrobe. The howls and plaudits of the crowd were loud enough to be heard blocks away. The shouts attested to his popularity. Bob bowed in acknowledgement to the deafening applause and then took his seat in a corner. He was presented with a floral horseshoe, but Fitz was evidently disgusted by it. Most boxers felt it was bad luck to receive a token of esteem in the ring.

Jeffries entered the ring a few minutes later, fully dressed in an overcoat, knee pants, sweater, and Panama hat. With him were Jack Jeffries, Joe Kennedy, and Bill Delaney. The crowd gave the champion a hearty and cordial greeting as well, but not as great as that given to Fitzsimmons. Jeff bowed in acknowledgement to his fans. Despite the fact that Jeffries essentially was a California native, the underdog Fitz was the decided crowd favorite during the fight. There were plenty of Jeffries admirers, but they were in the minority.

Chewing gum, Jeff nonchalantly walked over and shook hands with Fitz, who rose to his feet from his chair/stool. At that point, Jeffries critically and carefully examined the bandages on Bob's hands. He apparently found no fault with them, for he made no objection, and walked over and took his own seat. Jeff wore no hand bandages.

Stakeholder Sam Thall returned the forfeit money that the respective parties had deposited - $2,500 to each of the fighters, and $5,000 to the promoting club, the San Francisco Athletic Club.

Harry Corbett on behalf of his brother James J. Corbett announced Jim's challenge to the winner. A challenge from Tom Sharkey was announced as well, but it was greeted with groans and jeers from all parts of the house.

Referee Ed Graney appeared in a Tuxedo and black satin bowtie.

When they stripped, Jeff was wearing black trunks, while Fitz wore lavender ones. Both men wore silk American flags for belts. Jeff's gloves were very dark red, while Bob's gloves were a light maroon.

The men were photographed shaking hands at ring center.

The *San Francisco Chronicle* said Jeff admitted to weighing in the neighborhood of 218 pounds. Fitzsimmons claimed to weigh only 160 pounds. The *Police Gazette* said Bob weighed 168 to Jeff's 218. Another *Gazette* writer listed Fitz at 180 pounds. The *Examiner's* W. W. Naughton questioned Fitz's reported weight, feeling that he actually was closer to 190 pounds. As usual, no one knew for sure, because heavyweights were not required to weigh in. In *Two Fisted Jeffries*, Jeff said Fitz later told him that before their rematch, he weighed 185 pounds. "Weight, however, had little to do with Fitz's great hitting power. He hit as if he weighed three hundred."[172]

Referee Ed Graney said hitting in the clinches and hugging would be prohibited, which was not in Jeffries' favor, given his style. Apparently, the rules had changed. After the referee gave them instructions about the rules, they returned to their corners to await the bell. The gong rang at 10:20 p.m.

1st round

Jeffries began the fight in a half-crouching attitude. Fitzsimmons broke ground as Jeff followed, both feinting rapidly. Although Jeff was the aggressor, Bob was the first to lead, sending in some quick lead rights. Jeff crouched and rushed, but Fitz side-stepped out of the way. Both feinted a lot. "The spectators sat breathless, and watched the two trained boxers fiddle and dance, strike out with the force of piston rods and with the skill of experts."

The aggressive Jeffries anxiously bore in, but Fitzsimmons eluded or neutralized his attacks. As he retreated, Bob shot his left into Jeff's face. Fitz was faster on his feet, his quick leg work getting him out of the way of many rushes. Bob was still willing to exchange though, landing his blows to the head and then moving away. Jeff landed a hard left to the body, but Bob quickly countered to the head. Whenever Jeffries landed to the body, Fitz came back like a flash with one of his hard counters to the head.

One of Fitz's lefts to Jeff's nose started the blood flowing from it in a stream. The quick Fitzsimmons hit him fairly easily, and eluded and countered most of Jeff's blows. Jeffries rushed in, but Bob nimbly hopped out of the way, his hit and move tactics working well. Jeff was repeatedly short with his blows. In a clinch, Jeff sent a right to the body. Bob landed a left to the ear. Jeffries landed a stiff left to the heart. The round concluded with the men sparring, until Jeff landed a right to the breast that momentarily knocked Bob off balance. At the bell, although Jeff's nose was bleeding, he still looked confident.

2nd round

Jeffries kept forcing in determined fashion, going right after Fitzsimmons, but Bob was inclined to retreat. Jeff missed a left and Bob countered with his own jab. Jeff smiled and forced him to a corner, but Bob quickly side-stepped out. Jeff blocked a right. Fitz broke ground from Jeff's

---

172 *Two Fisted Jeffries* at 220.

lefts, but eventually Bob stopped and landed a stiff left to the face. Jeffries crouched lower, landed a stiff left hook on Fitz's jaw, and then forced Bob back to the ropes with terrific body blows, particularly his left to the body.

Jeffries kept up such a fast pace that he forced Bob to make a stand and fight back. Fitz landed two left hooks to the face and eluded a left. Jeff went after him and landed a left to the head and Bob clinched. Jeff sent his left to the body and Bob shot his left into the head. The champion landed three lefts to the body before Bob stopped him for a moment with a left jab to the nose, followed by a left to the body and right to the head.

Fitzsimmons landed a stabbing left jab on the nose that brought out the blood again in a stream. The crowd cheered vociferously. Bob's long absence from ring competition had not impaired his judgment of distance, for he seldom missed. He was cool and calm, fighting intelligently. By the end of the round, Jeff's nose was badly bleeding, the blood flowing down freely. At the bell, Jeff gave Bob a look of mingled surprise and disgust.

The *Bulletin, Call*, and *Chronicle* all admired Bob's boxing skill. The *Evening Post* said that honors were easy at this point. However, the *Examiner's* W. W. Naughton felt that the round was slightly in favor of Jeffries, "his body blows being telling ones."

3rd round

Jeffries resumed his aggression, forcing matters even as his bloody nose annoyed him a little. He changed tactics just a bit by standing straight up. It left him in less of a defensive stance but allowed him to move and advance more quickly.

Bob blocked two left leads and countered with a left jab on the sore nose. Jeff tried another left, but Bob stopped him with a left jab to the face. After they clinched, Jeff pushed him back. Fitz landed a stiff left on the nose and Jeff bled freely. Bob also landed a left hook. Jeffries landed the second of two lefts. However, Fitz landed a staggering left counter on the jaw. Jeff fell short with a body blow and received a left and right on the nose.

Fitzsimmons landed a stiff left hook on Jeff's cheek which opened up a cut under his right eye. The blood flowed from the gash, as well as from Jeff's nose. Bob had no marks. Despite Jeff's rushing, Fitz often landed his lefts. Undeterred, Jeffries rushed and swung left and right. Bob blocked those punches, but Jeff landed a hard left to the stomach. Fitz twice jabbed his left to the face and coolly danced away.

Jeffries twice sent his left to the head. Bob hit the injured nose a couple times. In response, Jeff rushed and landed a hard blow on the neck, then sent both fists into the body. Fitzsimmons countered to the nose, causing the blood to flow in a lavish stream at the bell.

As he returned to his corner, Jeff's face was covered in blood. One said his eye was closing. Another said there was a cut both under and over his right eye as well. Between rounds, Delaney busied himself over Jeffries.

The *Examiner* said it was Fitz's round. "Jeffries' face was bathed in blood. His nose was swollen and his right eye puffed and cut." The *Evening*

Post said, "At this point of the contest honors were easy so far as punishment was concerned. Jeffries, however, appeared to be the greater sufferer, as his face was the recipient, while Fitzsimmons' body did not give evidence of the blows which had landed there."

4ᵗʰ round

Jeff crouched and clenched his lips with a look of angry determination. He went in and set the pace, landing a left to the head while trying to stay clear of Bob's left jabs. Bob blocked and eluded some blows. They exchanged lefts to the face. Fitz landed a short right to the head and Jeff landed a left on the chest. Bob snapped Jeff's head back with a jab and started the blood flowing again. He also landed a right to the head. Jeffries came in with two left hooks, one for the head and another for the body, but their force was diminished because Fitzsimmons was moving back away from them. Bob landed a stiff left to the body, but Jeff countered with a right to the head. Twice Bob blocked Jeff's lefts.

Jeffries landed a strong right to the body, left to the jaw, and another right to the wind. Bob responded with three lefts on Jeff's sore eye. Jeff landed a straight left to the body, a strong left to the jaw, and then shifted back down to the body again. He landed yet another left to the wind. He kept poking at the body with his left. Bob missed some blows as Jeff ducked, and they clinched.

After breaking, Jeffries landed a hard right to the body, but Fitzsimmons countered him with a half-dozen jabs to the mouth and eye. Fitz boxed carefully, landing clean left jabs. He cleverly ducked and sidestepped Jeff's blows.

Fitzsimmons actually took a turn forcing the fight, landing two hard lefts to the face, causing Jeffries to duck and move away from him. However, soon thereafter, Jeff once again forced Fitz across the ring and landed a hard straight left to the body which made Bob slightly double up.

Fitz again shot out his accurate left to the nose, and Jeff countered with a right on the jaw. Both landed lefts to the body, but Jeff followed with a left to the body and right to the head that rocked Bob's head back. Fitz landed three lefts to the nose and body. He also landed under the heart. "Jeffries took his medicine as if he liked it, and came back with left on body and right on face." Fitz moved back away out of danger, and then made a stand, shooting his right as Jeff came forward, but the champion ducked.

Between rounds, in the corner, Jeffries looked determined, but a bit worried as he listened to Delaney. It seemed as if he felt that Bob was putting up a much tougher fight than he had expected. Jeff's nose and right eye were still bleeding. The *Examiner* said it was another Fitzsimmons round. "He was boxing very neatly, and showed excellent judgment in drawing out of range."

5ᵗʰ round

Jeffries was determined to give Fitzsimmons no rest, so he led for the body. Fitz countered the champion with a left on the face. Jeff's nose was bleeding profusely, and the gore was pouring from the cut under his right eye. Despite his bad facial appearance, Jeffries was not at all discouraged, and he kept after Bob, repeatedly punishing him hard on the body. They fought rapidly. Fitz pasted Jeff's face with left jabs and occasionally landed his right to the head. However, Bob's body was sore.

Jeff eagerly rushed, forced Fitz to the ropes, and landed two lefts to the face and a hard left to the stomach. Fitz clinched tightly. The *Bulletin* said this was a turning point. Jeffries' blows were having an effect. After they broke, Jeff went after him again and swung his left, but Fitz ducked and countered with a right smash to the face and left and right body blows. However, as hard as Fitz hit, Jeffries was undeterred and kept coming, hurrying matters. He seemed to enjoy the rapid pace. He landed a left to the jaw and then shifted it to the body.

With a straight left, Jeff slightly cut Bob's right cheek, just under the eye. Fitz missed a left and clinched. Fitzsimmons could not punch him off, so he resorted to clinching more often. They clinched repeatedly. The problem with holding Jeffries was that he could wear opponents out that way too, because he was so strong and knew how to lay his weight on them so that grabbing him did not get them much rest. However, it was a way to avoid Jeff's punishing blows. The referee warned Bob for holding.

Fitz landed a terrific right on the jaw, and a moment later, a left on the nose. Bob's cutting jabs kept landing. Jeff was bleeding badly. A right to the mouth had Jeff spitting blood. They exchanged blows to the head and body on the inside. Jeff's smashes seemed fierce, but Bob countered well. Jeffries landed a series of hard blows to Bob's body but received two raps on his bleeding nose. Jeff again smashed Fitz's aching ribs with his left.

Just as the round ended, Fitzsimmons landed a right to the left eyebrow, cutting it open. Jeff's entire face was bleeding freely. He was bleeding from his nose, left eye, right cheek, and mouth. Another said Jeff's left eye was closing. The only mark on Fitz was a slight abrasion on the right cheek from the cutting jab that he received in this round. However, Jeff's body punches were doing their damage internally.

The *Bulletin* felt that Jeff's pace and body punches were starting to turn the tide of battle in his favor. The *Evening Post* said this round was the first time that Fitzsimmons showed signs of distress. The *Examiner* opined that the round was slightly in Fitz's favor but noted that he seemed to be the more tired of the two.

6th round

Bob's right eye looked slightly swollen as he came up to start the round, and he seemed a bit tired.

Jeff crouched low. He rushed, but Fitz cleverly avoided the blows by blocking and using fast footwork to get out of the way. Bob's defense held up well. Jeffries continued to rush, but Fitzsimmons either smothered, countered, or eluded him with sidesteps. "Fitz's foot work was marvelous."

Bob kept landing well and doing the better work. His left to the nose made Jeff's face more swollen. Jeff's eyes were in bad shape. They exchanged lefts on the head; Bob's being the more damaging. Jeff rushed multiple times, but Fitz smothered him and landed three lefts and a right to the head and face. Jeffries forced Fitzsimmons to the ropes, but received a right and left on the face, which started the blood running again. He could not corner Bob, who seemed a veritable will o' the wisp. He was using Jim Corbett tactics. Jeff was a fright from the blood which covered him.

Others described a more competitive round. Jeffries twice landed to the body, but Bob blocked the third attempt. Jeff landed a left to the body and Fitz landed a hard right to the head. Jeff landed a left to the jaw and then smashed his left into the body as Bob backed away.

Bob broke ground but then gathered himself and attacked in a quick rush, landing rights to the head, body, and nose. Jeff broke ground and moved away for the first time, ducking blows. Fitz again swung both hands with terrific force; hard enough to put out any average man, but Jeffries ignored them and hooked Bob with his left to the eye and followed it up with a body blow, causing Fitzsimmons to clinch.

After they broke, Jeff hit Fitz with the left to the head and body. Fitz then landed his right to the jaw. Jeff answered with a left to the jaw and followed with another smash to the body. Jeffries fought like a mad bull. Bob returned with a left and right to the head. Jeff followed him around the ring, trying to get at him.

Fitzsimmons showed remarkable cleverness in eluding Jeff's rushes. He continued landing cutting left jabs, and just as the gong sounded, landed another on the sore mouth and nose. In terms of points, it was Fitz's round.

7th round

This round was full of hard work. Jeffries resumed his rushing tactics, covering up well as he attacked in determined fashion. Jeff landed a couple hard lefts to the body and one on the head but received a left and right to his head in return. Jeff landed a left and right to the mouth and drove Bob back to the ropes, where he hit Fitz with a left on the body and face, both hard blows.

Jeff's body shots were getting to Fitzsimmons, which stirred up his fighting spirit to retaliate and not allow Jeffries too much momentum. Fitz rallied and landed both fists to Jeff's jaw. He threw a right uppercut and left across. Bob came on again with a right to the body and a right to the nose. The blood poured out from Jeff in a stream. Fitz jabbed him three times on the mouth and forced Jeff back to the ropes, scoring right and left to the jaw. Jeff clinched and Bob's friends cheered.

During the round, Fitz often ducked and retaliated with a right and left on Jeff's bleeding face. He also landed many jabs. Jeff looked terrible, but he was not tired.

Bleeding from all over his face, Jeffries came at him like an enraged bull, forcing Bob to the ropes, landing a left to the body and a right over the heart. Fitz tried to keep him off with left jabs.

Jeff landed a left to the head before they clinched. Jeff hit him in the clinch, which drew some hisses from the spectators. While still clinched, Bob complained about Jeff's hitting in the clinch, and Jeff responded by telling him that it was an accident.

In his autobiography, Jeffries said that during their vicious exchanges, Fitzsimmons grinned and asked, "Well, how do you like it?" Jeff replied, "Suits me all right. You're pretty good for an old fellow." Fitz was smiling, while Jeff was bleeding and looking terrible from the cuts. However, he was still strong on his feet. Jeff's rally at the end of the round showed that he had not lost any of his steam.

It was pretty fighting, and the crowd cheered both at the end. It was, however, another Fitzsimmons round. Both men went to their corners looking weary.

8th round

One writer said, "Jeffries came up strong in the eighth, while Fitzsimmons acted as a man who had had enough of the game." However, they went at it, each landing well. Jeff repeatedly struck the head and body, although his primary focus was the body. Fitz mostly hit the head. Jeffries kept attacking, keeping the pace fast. Bob began to show signs of tiring, as well as discouragement, for he had been punching Jeff squarely on the face and jaw without dazing him. Still, few expected this to be the last round.

Fitzsimmons feinted and broke ground as he drew Jeff in. Jeff forced the fighting, crouching low, carrying his right high and left held far back. Fitz landed a stinging right uppercut. He followed up with a number of quick jabs. Jeffries smiled through his bloody features, ducking a left swing and landing a hard counter left on the ribs. He next swung a left for the jaw and they clinched. After breaking, Jeff went after him. Fitz landed a left jab to the nose but received a terrific left wallop in the wind. Bob landed a left on the face but took a left on the head and one on the ribs. Bob backed away and landed a right to the body. He missed a right and took a stiff punch on the body. Jeff crouched and landed two left jabs to the face.

Jeffries tore into Fitzsimmons and forced him to the ropes, landing a left on the wind and a crashing right to the jaw. Bob fell into a clinch. He tried his uppercut and Jeff landed to the body. Fitz landed a couple blows to Jeff's ribs before they clinched again.

Each local source gave its version of how matters ended. The *Bulletin*, *Evening Post*, and *Chronicle* gave substantially similar accounts.

Jeff forced Bob back into a corner. Fitz missed a left hook, and Jeffries countered by whipping in a punishing, sledgehammer left just to the right of the navel, one of the terrific body jolts that had made him champion. Bob wobbled, and Jeffries followed up with a right to the jaw that sent Fitzsimmons down to the ground.

While the referee was counting, Fitz's face showed clearly that he was suffering excruciating pain. His eyes were bulging from his head like pigeon eggs and there was agony in every feature. As the referee counted to eight,

Bob struggled to his hands and knees, trying to rise, but was still down when the ten seconds were counted off. Referee Graney declared Jeffries the winner.

Some other local sources, including the *Call, Examiner*, and another *Chronicle* version of the knockout mentioned some talking by Fitzsimmons, either before or after he received the big left to the body. This later became the subject of some controversy.

Call: As Fitz stepped back from the clinch, he smiled and spoke to Jeff, a fatal mistake. Before Bob could get out of the way, Jeffries quickly hooked his left on the body and sent a right to the jaw. Fitz went down, clutching feebly at the lower rope, shaking his head in signal of defeat. The referee counted him out before he could stand erect.

Chronicle (2nd version): "As Fitzsimmons stepped back he smiled and spoke to Jeffries. Before he could get out of reach Jeffries hooked him lightly with his left on the jaw, and as Fitz half turned to slip away, he caught him again with a terrific left swing in the solar plexus." Fitz went down on his back, and slowly rose, but did not beat the count.

Call (2nd version): Jeff attacked and backed Bob to the ropes. For an instant, Fitz was off his guard, and Jeffries whipped in a short half-arm left hook that caught him in the lower ribs. Bob bent over, shook his head, and as he fell, said to Jeffries, "You've got me." Bob clutched the lower rope. He steadied himself on the rope, partially leaning outside of the ring. Referee Graney counted him out as Bob slowly drew himself up to a standing position. At the end of the count, he was still supporting himself by the top rope. There was no strength left in him.

Examiner: Jeff forced him to the ropes, and,

> [He] swung a left which seemed to catch Fitz above the right hip. Fitz drew away and a second later dropped his hands and spoke to Jeffries. Fitzsimmons' eyes were bright and steady, and he did not seem to be distressed. Suddenly Jeffries let fly the left for the cheek, and Fitzsimmons swung half way round on his feet and went slowly to the floor on his hands and knees…. It was a weird looking thing, for it seemed inexplicable that Fitz should lower his guard when his manner did not suggest that a damaging blow had been delivered.

Various sources noted that after the count was over and Fitz had struggled to his feet in a doubled-up condition, his eyes were still wobbling in their sockets. Bob walked toward Jeff to shake his hand. Jeffries had started to leave the ring right away but was called back to shake hands with the beaten man. Fitzsimmons could not stand erect for several minutes.

Answering the cries for a speech, Bob said that the best man in the world had beaten him fairly. "The best man won. I can't whip Jeffries and no one else can. This is my last fight." The crowd cheered. He then removed his gloves and threw them to the audience, which scrambled to secure the souvenirs.

It was said that the battle would go down in prize-ring annals as one of the greatest ever. The two had thrown powerful blows that would have knocked out any other fighter in the world. Fitz had fought more intelligently and skillfully this time, but he still could not beat Jeffries.

Jeffries said Fitzsimmons gave him the hardest fight of his life. He told the *Chronicle*,

> He seemed faster and stronger than when I met him before, and he reached my head much oftener, but I always had my jaw covered and I knew he could not hit me hard enough on the body to put me out. I am so much bigger and heavier than he is that I knew I would wear him out and win in the end.

> It was a body punch that finished the fight… I simply caught him off his guard after he missed a hook at me, and that was the end.

Jeffries told the *Call*,

> Well, I won, but I'll have to give it to Fitz for being the best old man in the world. He certainly gave me the hardest run for eight rounds that I have had in my career. Gee, but I look pretty well cut up. Say, fellows, does it add to my beauty? This fellow Fitzsimmons has the right material in him. He can go out as old as he is and beat all the other heavyweights in the country. I felt confident that I would win. The blows Fitz landed on me were good and hard, but never made me groggy. He did not knock me down nor did he stagger me. He certainly can wallop some. … The blood flowing from my nose bothered me at first, but I got used to it. The jab I got in the eye did not help me much, but my seconds soon had that patched up. Fitz is game and certainly has cleverness. … When I entered that ring I knew

I would win. I took my time and at the right moment ended things. The blow I caught Fitz was a left in the stomach. We were about to clinch and Fitz stepped back into his own corner. He never expected me to follow him up and I must have surprised him. The blow was a left rip and as soon as I let it go I knew I was the winner. I took no chances, however, but followed it with another in the solar plexus and then walloped him on the head as he was falling. ... Again I say Fitz is the goods and I have to give it to him.

The *Evening Post* quoted Jeffries as saying,

Well, I won, as I knew I would, but I must admit that the victory brought with it some disagreeable features in the shape of a broken nose, a battered eye and other bruises too numerous to mention.

Fitzsimmons is without doubt the greatest man in the ring outside of myself. ... I had no idea that any man could stand the blows I landed on the body without going down and out before he did. I struck him often with all my force, but he took the gruel and kept coming at me by shooting left and right at my nose and eye. The blood bothered me for a time, but I eventually got used to it and went right in and took his punishment, knowing my ability to withstand his assaults and fully conscious that in time he would have to wilt under my punches.

In his first autobiography, Jeffries mentioned that the new ring platform was built too lightly, which affected him. The lighter Fitz could skip about quickly, but whenever the heavier Jeff moved, the boards bent under him. "It made my footing uncertain and awkward and took away half my speed." He said it was worse when he crouched, so he stood up more. He later said that he walked right into and through Fitz's punches just so he could get close enough to have a chance to land one of his own blows. Jeffries did not mention the ring troubles in his immediate post-fight comments. However, his claim could have been true given that the ring had been built recently.[173]

Fitzsimmons told the *Call* that he was beaten fairly, and he announced his retirement. Bob complained of broken hands but otherwise had no excuses. He hit and moved but also attacked when appropriate.

I had to go in. If I'd stayed off he'd have followed me up and beaten my head off. He's always right after you. He'd have killed Corbett if Corbett had fought him as I did. Jeff's a grand fighter. No one can beat him if I can't – and I can't. I thought I had him all the way along. ... It was a left hook that did it – one of my own. The smash on the jaw that followed it did not hurt me. ... I told Jim I was gone as soon as I got that smash.

Speaking about Jeffries with a *Chronicle* reporter, Bob said,

---

173 *My Life and Battles* at 49.

He is a wonder. He had me going in the seventh…. It wasn't that last biff in the eye that did it; it was the smash in the wind. I thought my short ribs were broken. When I went down I said with all the wind that was in me, 'Jeff, I'm gone.' On the straight, I might perhaps have pulled out and gone on, but I would have only been chopped to pieces, and I've fought long enough to know when I or any other man has had the finishing punch.

He did me, but if it is the last word that I ever say I will tell you that I wasn't right the first time he put me out…. This time I was as fit as I ever was in my life. Then he was a novice. Now he is a finished fighter….

But ain't I all right for an old man? I don't think that I ever punched anyone harder than I did him in the first four rounds, but he kept coming back. There is no one fighting in the world that has a chance against him. I couldn't do it, and if I can't there is no one that can.

A few years later, Fitz said of the knockout,

He had been bringing his left hand up from a position at his side and I had prepared to block it. But this time he raised his hand high above his head and making somewhat of a circle he brought his hand up into my stomach. It was a terrific blow, for I felt the effects of it for a long time. I lay on the floor trying to get up, but my limbs refused to support me. I said to myself, 'fooled by my own blow.'[174]

Fitz had lost the first time by attacking, and he had seen Corbett try to outbox Jeffries to no avail. Bob had tried a modified version of the two extremes this time, trying to both box and punch him out, but, when even his best punches had no effect, Fitzsimmons realized that Jeffries was invincible. No one could keep this Jeffries away, and eventually the champion was going to wear his opponents down and land the big one. Fitz realized this despite all of his effective work and superior points boxing.

In his first autobiography, Jeff backed Fitz's claim that he had hurt hands. "I knew his right hand was gone, for once when he landed a very heavy smash on my forehead I could hear the bones crack, and, although he went right on hitting with it, there wasn't the same weight in the blows." The first two knuckles were broken. Bob later told him that after hurting his hand, he landed his right differently, turning it to land with the knuckles that had not been broken. "And yet he was hitting almost as hard as with a sound hand." Also, "The joints of Bob's left hand were buckled toward the end of the fight, but he didn't hold back his punches."

Fitz trainer and sparring partner George Dawson commented,

I don't see how Bob got beaten. He put up the greatest fight that any man ever fought. … I thought he would win sure as the fight progressed. Bob did wonderful hitting. He hurt one of his hands

[174] National Police Gazette, February 5, 1905.

Thursday while boxing Griffin, and that was against him, but he was in fine condition otherwise. Jeff is too big for him, that's certain. ... Fitz put up the best fight that could have been made, and the way he mixed it was marvelous. ... Jeff is a giant, and he took smashes that no other man living could have taken and not gone out. That was an unlucky body punch that Bob got, but it happens to the best of them.

Referee Eddie Graney said Fitzsimmons was as quick as a cat and displayed intelligent ring generalship. "He danced about the ring so fast sometimes that it was difficult to keep an eye on him, and his blows were aimed with marvelous accuracy." However, his punches did not take the steam away from Jeffries, who was strong and confident throughout.

It was the greatest fight I ever saw in my life. Fitz was beaten by a left-hand hook in the solar plexus – the very blow that won him the championship from Corbett at Carson. The men fought fairly and squarely. Neither man hit in the clinches. They started to rough it at one stage of the fight and I told them I would take off my coat and give them a good rough house if they did not break when I ordered them. ... Jeffries did not throw his weight on Fitz or resort to hugging. When they clinched each man stepped back and fought nicely. ... It was a clean fight and the best man won. ... When Fitz went down on his knee Jeff moved over to his own corner as provided for in the rules. Fitzsimmons' showing surprised me. I felt satisfied that he would give Jeffries a hard tussle, but I never thought for a moment that he would do so wonderfully well. He certainly is a grand old man.

The experienced George Siler gave his views as well. Jeffries took a "terrible mauling" and his face was "beaten almost to a pulp." Fitz hit him often, especially with the left. Bob would feint Jeff "into a knot," and then stab him with a left jab and dance away. After jabbing him to pieces, in the 5th round, Bob used his right more, and "some of the blows that he landed on Jeffries' jaw with that useful member appeared to be hard enough to fell an ox." However, the blows had no effect on Jeff.

It was only his weight, strength, stamina and capacity of taking punishment that won for him. True, the blow, a left hook which landed directly under the solar plexus, had everything to do with his victory, but, had he not been of cast iron he could never have withstood the blows that Fitz landed on him throughout the fight.

During the bout, Jeffries lunged with many hooks and fell short. After trying unsuccessfully for the head, he switched his focus to the body and found more success. Siler described the end:

Just before the knock-out came Jeffries rushed Bob to the south side of the ropes, and Fitz, as he had done scores of times before, propped him up with the left, and then, as upon previous occasions, attempted to dance out of distance with his back partly turned, then turned suddenly and fetched Jeff coming head on. This time he missed with the left, and as the force of the blow turned him partly around the champion was on top of him like a flash, hooked his left over Fitzsimmons' solar plexus and as the old fellow dropped his hands he crossed him with the right on the jaw, sending him on the lower ropes of the ring.

According to the *Examiner*'s W. W. Naughton, the crowd went home talking about Bob's magnificent showing. "Fitz fought more on the defensive than ever he did in his life, and put up a very effective exhibition." During the fight, the spectators were electrified by the smaller, older, underdog Fitz's performance, and cheered him wildly in each successive round. Fitz was cool, calm, fresh, and never fought better. "He was light on his feet and faultless in his judgment of distance." He outboxed and outpointed Jeffries, who seemed unable to escape his cutting blows. Jeff's nose was bloodied in the 1st, his right eye cut in the 3rd, and both eyes cut in the 6th. He was a sight, bleeding profusely, covered in blood. His crouching attitude did not save him from punishment, and at times, he abandoned it. Fitz landed hard and often. Conversely, Jeff's judgment of distance was off, falling short with most blows, and he was made to look "clumsy and inexpert." Fitzsimmons did not appear distressed by his own exertions. He held the points lead throughout, having the best of the fight up until the knockout.

Jeffries was given his just due credit though. He forced a fast pace, and when he got Fitzsimmons on the ropes, he hit his body hard. Although Bob landed a number of crushing rights and lefts on the jaw, they seemed to have no effect on the Los Angeles giant. He took three punches to one but could have taken a lot more and still kept going. "His strength and vitality are enough to keep him champion for many a long day." In the 8th, Jeff landed a hard left to the body. Fitz dropped his arm and spoke to Jeff, who then swung for the head and sent him to the floor. Bob rose after the ten-count concluded.

The *National Police Gazette* said Fitzsimmons for 7 rounds fought "as he had never fought before, cleverly and scientifically, and he surprised even his most faithful adherents. He had the champion cut, bleeding and confused." Jeff's defense seemed off, and he had difficulties landing.

The *Call* said the fight had been 8 bloody and fiercely contested rounds. Although Jeffries earned the victory, the "honor and glory of the battle rest with the vanquished." For 7 rounds, Fitz had made a "pitiable spectacle" of Jeff, landing at will, cutting his face to ribbons. But then he got knocked out by the same blow that Fitzsimmons had used to knock out Corbett. The fight ended so abruptly that the spectators were surprised.

The battle resembled Corbett-Fitzsimmons in many respects. Fitzsimmons fought both aggressively and defensively, drawing blood from Jeff's nose in the opening round and making him look like "a Sioux brave in full war-paint." Bob blackened both of Jeff's eyes, cut him deeply on the right cheek, and kept his nose and mouth bleeding continuously. He outboxed and outpointed Jeffries, dancing around, jolting, jabbing, and crossing him as he liked.

However, the champion took it all with bulldog courage, and landed the harder and more internally damaging blows, particularly to the body. Fitz was the superior boxer, but Jeff applied the determined pressure, looking to land knockout blows, until finally he landed that one fearful body punch. His right to the jaw completed the job. Jeffries had landed the one punch that wiped out all of Fitz's good work. His youth, strength, and vitality proved too much for Bob's wonderful science. Fitzsimmons acknowledged that he simply could not beat Jeffries, that the only way to do so was to use a sledgehammer. Such was similar to Corbett-Fitzsimmons, with Jim cutting, bloodying, and outboxing Bob, until Fitz's determination, pressure, and body work finally caught up with Corbett.

Visually, the only mark that Fitzsimmons had was a slight abrasion under his right eye. Dr. Cox said one of Bob's ribs had been cracked. He had also sprained his left thumb. He did not mention broken hands.

The *Chronicle* said Jeffries received the hardest punishment of his career, in a wonderful, furious fight in which Fitzsimmons displayed remarkable cleverness. Bob had the clear points lead from the beginning to the end.

Other papers, such as the *Evening Post* and the *Bulletin*, focused on the fact that Jeffries had worn Fitzsimmons down with effective body blows and his relentless non-stop attack. These newspapers gave Jeff more credit in their round-by-round descriptions and analysis. Jeffries had employed his determined hard-punching strategy, and it worked, having stopped Fitzsimmons 3 rounds sooner than he did in their first fight. However, this time, Jeff fought as an attacker and took more punishment, whereas in their first fight, he boxed more cautiously and defensively and suffered less punishment.

In his first autobiography, Jeff said that during the fight, Delaney had urged him to try to rush matters and stop Fitzsimmons as quickly as possible, due to the fact that Jeff's eyes were closing. "The way the old fellow could hit was a wonder. He was hammering my face in. The blows were as heavy as any I ever felt. ... Fitz looked like a winner, for he was almost unmarked, while I must have been a sight." He later said, "Fitz was boxing a clever, cagy bout, and taking few chances. ... Evidently his plan was to cut me up and lick me piece by piece." However, although Fitzsimmons was punching very hard, Jeff's injuries were all on the surface. "Inside I was as sound and fresh as ever. ... I knew I'd win in time. I was all right still inside, not weak or dazed or even tired. And I knew that Fitzsimmons could not keep up such a terrible pace for twenty rounds."

Regarding the end, Jeffries said he could feel that Fitzsimmons was growing weaker, for Bob's blows did not hurt and he seemed to be tiring from the pace and the body punishment. Jeff's left landed just to one side of the pit of the stomach, at the edge of the right ribs, driving them in. Bob straightened up and stood perfectly still for a moment, paralyzed. He gasped, "You've got me, Jeff." At the same moment, Jeffries had started the finishing blow for his jaw.

JAMES J. JEFFRIES, CHAMPION HEAVYWEIGHT BOXER OF THE WORLD, AS HE APPEARED YESTERDAY AFTER THE TREMENDOUS BEATING HE SUSTAINED AT THE HANDS OF ROBERT FITZSIMMONS IN THEIR SENSATIONAL RING CONTEST IN THIS CITY ON FRIDAY NIGHT.

Jeffries had been badly punished by the blows struck with the 5-ounce gloves. His nose was flattened, in line with his cheeks. He required several stitches to sew up the cuts above his left and right eyes, and over his right cheek bone. Given that they wore no mouthpieces back then, "Every tooth in my head was loose. For two days after the fight I couldn't eat. I couldn't move my jaw and I thought it was surely broken. One of my ears was in bad shape." He looked as if he had been run over by a mowing machine. At least that is how Jeff remembered it.[175]

[175] My Life and Battles at 49-50.

One thing to consider is that back then, fights were never stopped on cuts or swellings. In fact, for most of boxing's history, there was no such thing as a doctor stopping a fight. A cut was just a flesh wound, an impediment that a fighter had to deal with, and Jim Jeffries courageously dealt with the sting of the cuts and the blood in his eyes.

The gate receipts were reported to be $31,880. Jeff received a 60% share of 75% of the gross receipts ($14,346), while Fitz received 40% of the same ($9,564). The San Francisco Athletic Club made $7,970. These numbers varied from source to source, but they were all ballpark. The *Bulletin* claimed the fighters split a 70% share of the gross receipts. It said that Jeff was paid $13,389.60 and Fitz received $8,926.40, or a 60/40 split of 70% of the receipts. The club made $9,564.[176]

One of the topics that boxing fans and historians love to discuss and debate is whether Fitzsimmons wore loaded gloves/handwraps in this fight. Oddly enough, this topic was given little discussion at the time. Jeffries did tell the *Chronicle*, "It was the bandages that punished me so much. The blows did not daze me, but every time Fitz landed even a glancing blow it seemed to cut me like a knife." The question is whether he meant that Fitz's regular soft bandages allowed him to have a harder or more protected fist which could generate cutting blows, or whether he meant that Fitz's wraps were hardened by plaster of Paris. After all, hand bandages were a new thing, and Jeffries did not wear them, so there was some natural skepticism regarding their effect, even when soft bandages were used.

Jeffries did not mention anything about loaded bandages in his 1910 autobiography. However, in the much later *Two Fisted Jeffries*, he claimed,

> Just as I was going into the ring someone told me that Fitzsimmons had plaster in his bandages, and while still upset about the ring I turned to Delaney and said: 'Make Fitz take those plaster bandages off his hands.' 'Oh let them go,' said Delaney, 'If he can lick you with them on he can lick you with them off.' ... I did not relish those bandages. Rather than have an argument with Delaney at that stage of the proceedings I allowed Fitz to wear the bandages he had on his hands, and, as a result, I received the worst butchering of my life. ... The plaster of Paris in the bandages had hardened and they had the same effect as if he had brass knuckles on each hand.

Jeff also claimed, "After the fight Fitz admitted he had worn plaster of Paris in his bandages, but I held no hard feelings against him and we became the best of friends and chums later. I blamed myself and Delaney for carelessness."[177]

Other later versions claimed that Delaney discovered the plaster of Paris under the bandages before the bout but Jeff just shrugged and essentially did not care.[178]

[176] *San Francisco Chronicle, San Francisco Call, San Francisco Bulletin*, July 27, 1902.
[177] *Two Fisted Jeffries* at 210-213.
[178] Rex Lardner, *The Legendary Champions* (N.Y.: American Heritage Press, 1972), 140.

It was known before the fight that soft bandages would be allowed. Referee Graney had said so. "By soft bandages is meant the regular linen strips used by surgeons and not heavy bicycle tape. Furthermore the linen must be put on in the ring."

It is clear that both Jeffries and Delaney examined the bandages before the fight and made no objection to them. A local next-day report noted, "Jeffries shook hands with Fitz and then examined the bandages on the Cornishman's hands. He turned away as though satisfied." It later said, "The gloves which were to be used by the fighters were examined by the police officials and pronounced satisfactory. ... Delaney scrutinized the bandages on Fitz's hands and took no exception to them. Jeffries wore no bandages." Thus, both Delaney and Jeffries examined the wraps, made no objection, and there was no debate or controversy before the bout. It could be argued that because hand wraps were somewhat of a novelty at that time, there was much speculation as to their impact. Jeffries might have been looking for an excuse for being cut up so much.

However, the overconfident and/or ignorant Jeff and Delaney might have simply decided to let it go, having been previously forewarned that Fitz wanted some plaster to protect his weakening hands. In June, Fitzsimmons had insisted on such protection for his hands because of their fragility. He then said, "All I want is a little bit of sticking plaster on my hand where it was hurt before." Jeffries responded, "I have no objection to that. It will be subject to the inspection of the referee, of course."[179]

After the fight, Jeffries said, "Fitz should never have cut me up at all. The bandages on his hands did the mischief." Jeffries and Fitzsimmons conversed:

> "Those things on your hands cut me up a lot," said Jeffries, feeling the tape on Fitzsimmons' hands. "You didn't wear them the last time and your blows never cut me up the way they did tonight." "Never mind the bandages, Jim, there were punches behind them. But say, ain't I all right for an old man?" "You are," said Jeffries. "You are the greatest natural fighter that ever was."

It sounded as if Jeffries was not referencing plaster of Paris, but rather the fact that Fitz was wearing wraps at all. Fitz had worn no hand wraps or tape in their first fight, but did so in their second bout, so this, Jeff opined, must explain why he was so cut up. However, Fitz was known for having the hardest punch in boxing, so it should not be surprising that he did damage.

The following year, when negotiating the terms of a fight with Corbett, Jeffries did not want to allow Corbett to wear hand bandages, saying that they made the hands *like* plaster of Paris. Jeff said, "When I fought Fitz last time...he wore bandages which were like a plaster cast. Ordinarily my skin is not easy to open, but when Fitz let go those plaster casts they simply cut me open. The bandages were so hard they even hurt Fitz's hands." Saying wrapping hands tightly made them like a plaster cast isn't exactly saying Bob

[179] *National Police Gazette*, June 14, 21, 1902, August 9, 1902.

was actually wearing a plaster cast. Nevertheless, when Corbett said that Jeff could have a representative observe the wrapping process, Bill Delaney responded, "That's all right, Jim; but you may accidentally 'slip' your hand in a bucket of plaster of Paris while meandering from your dressing room to the ring."[180]

Yet, even as early as 1905, the *Police Gazette* wrote, "It is said that Fitz used to put moistened plaster of Paris on his linen bandages and let the mass grow hard. Then he would have a rocky ridge across his hand that could be felt straight through the glove."[181]

No definitive answer was given at the time of the fight. All that can be said is that Jeffries and Delaney examined the wraps and did not object prior to the fight but later blamed the hand bandages for cutting him up. However, multiple subsequent statements gave the impression that Fitz had indeed dipped his hands into plaster of Paris, but such may have been speculation.

Ironically, if Fitzsimmons had worn loaded wraps, although it might have helped him cut Jeffries and hit harder, the hardened plaster might also have led to Bob's hands being more injured, something which Jeff referenced. Certainly, taking punches from hardened plaster from a known puncher further adds to Jeff's reputation for having an iron chin, if such was the case.

The historically overlooked controversy, the actual controversy that existed at the time, was an allegation that the fight was fixed, although this appears to have been a product of the time's yellow journalism, which sought to generate controversy in order to boost newspaper sales. The *San Francisco Examiner's* lead boxing writer, W. W. Naughton, claimed to have received information that Jeff would win in the 8th round, and he had given the mayor a sealed letter saying so before the fight. The *Examiner*, under the ownership of William Randolph Hearst, was known to be sensational at times.

Naughton said he received "an intimation" that the fight was to be won by Jeff in the 8th round, and that "one of the party who was with Jeffries at Harbin Springs had told my informants to bet that Jeffries would earn the decision in the round named."

Naughton said the way that Fitz was knocked out seemed very strange.

> He was always on the alert and never to be caught napping in the first part of the fight, but when the crisis came his hands were down by his side and two blows were struck by Jeffries that knocked him out. Fitzsimmons was talking all this time, and seemed wholly off his guard, which, to say the least, is a very strange thing. ... No one could quite understand how Jeffries had won. Fitz seemed to be doing the better work except in the seventh round, and the finish was a puzzle to many.

[180] *Philadelphia Public Ledger*, *Press*, *Inquirer*, March 2, 1903; *National Police Gazette*, March 21, 28, 1903.
[181] *Police Gazette*, July 15, 1905.

The suggestion was that Bob allowed Jeff to knock him out.

Mayor Eugene Schmitz confirmed Naughton's allegations. Schmitz said the *Examiner* gave him a sealed letter that was not to be opened until called upon to do so. He opened the letter shortly before midnight on the night of the fight. It said that Jeffries was to win the fight in the 8th round.

The mayor said it looked like a fair fight up until the knockout, but the ending looked odd.

> I am not prepared to say that the fight was a fake, but it certainly looked queer. Both men fought fairly for seven rounds and there was absolutely nothing that happened that might have caused suspicion. Then in the eighth round the unexpected happened. Fitzsimmons had his hands by his side when the blow was struck. Here is the letter left by Mr. Naughton in my possession in which it was stated that the fight would end in the eighth round. It was not to be opened until 11:30 o'clock and I came to my office with witnesses to open it. It is a coincidence that can not be passed with a trivial notice. ... I shall make a careful inquiry and if I find that my suspicions are justified I shall hereafter oppose the granting of permits for prize ring contests in this city.

Naughton and Schmitz questioned why Bob's hands were down. "Perhaps so much stress would not be placed on this fact were it not for the information given to me on the night before the exhibition that the contest would end, and in favor of Jeffries, in the eighth round."

Mayor Eugene Schmitz, Who Declares There Shall Be No More Fakes in San Francisco.

The *Examiner's* Edward Hamilton backed Naughton as well, saying it was too good a fight to end in such a fraud. It had been 7 rounds of "as gloriously brutal sport as a man could wish to see." Fitz cut his man to ribbons and broke his nose before he quit by agreement. Bob said, "Hit me now!" He held up his jaw, Jeff hit him in the wind, and he went down.

It had been 7 rounds of great fighting, "the kind of fighting, with blood in it, which the people thrill over and yell at and talk about for years." Most said it was the greatest fight they ever saw. The crowd yelled with every blow. "There was a frenzy of delight over the power of the blows exchanged." Both men threw blows that had the "force of electric bolts behind them." But it ended in a sham.

> I honestly believe Fitzsimmons could have beaten Jeffries last night had the fight been on the level. He certainly showed himself the big fellow's master in the exchange of blows. Jeffries had not damaged him perceptibly. He had a scratch or abrasion under his right eye, but not a deep cut. Beyond that he was not in trouble. When he went to his corner he sat bolt upright each time, and his breathing was easy and natural. …
>
> As for Jeffries, he was a sight. In the very first round Fitzsimmons started his nose to bleeding. Then, in the third round, the long Cornishman opened the big cut under the champion's right eye. In the sixth both eyes had cuts. As Jeffries is a 'bleeder,' he soon distributed enough gore for a company on a battlefield. …
>
> Now, all this time Fitz had been landing hard and often. He was making Jeffries seem clumsy and inexpert. …
>
> So, everything was going Fitzsimmons' way. He was the idol of the crowd, he was cutting the world's champion to ribbons, and he seemed right in line to get that championship back. Then he carried out his agreement and quit.
>
> But to bring such a fine struggle to such an ignominious end – well, it was a confounded shame!

Hamilton admitted that most who watched the fight "didn't know there was any fraud about it." Yet, they were "mystified" when Bob went down and out. They also wondered how he could have recovered so quickly after being knocked down for the full count. "Still, most of the crowd went away satisfied they had seen a great fight, and a good many of them never will believe the battle was not on the square."

Hamilton did not believe the claims about Bob's weight either. "Then, there's that other yarn about Fitzsimmons weighing 160 pounds. A man could live a long time on the amount of meat he carries over that weight. I weigh 190 myself with my clothes on, and Fitzsimmons certainly must weigh that much stripped; for except in head and feet he'd make me look puny."

Nevertheless, Fitzsimmons' performance was impressive. "Fitzsimmons certainly is a wonderful fighter. I respected his powers last night more than I ever did before, whatever I might think of his honesty." He went through 7 bruising rounds without showing any distress. He was hardly puffing, and his legs were as steady as pillars. He certainly was a wonder in conditioning. He wasn't stale or old, but as sharp as ever.

When Fitzsimmons Stopped Fighting to Talk to Jeffries in the Eighth Round. And a Moment Later the Cornishman Went Out.

Most of the civil servants and others interviewed from the crowd did not believe the fight was a fake. Quite the contrary, they thought it was the best fight they had ever seen. A police judge said, "If that fight was a fake I want to see nothing but fakes. It was one of the fastest and best fights I ever saw. Fitzsimmons had all the best of it for a time, but he unquestionably got the finishing punch. He was put out and all this talk of fake is the most utter rot. The fight was perfectly honest if I ever saw an honest fight." Another man said, "If it was a fake it was the best fake I have ever seen."

Another police judge said there was nothing to be gained by Fitzsimmons taking a dive, given that he was the heavy odds underdog and most thought he would lose. Furthermore, Fitz was such an experienced man at the business that if he really wanted to fake a knockout, he would have done it in a way that no one would have suspected. "He would probably have run into a punch that would have really knocked him down and out, for no one ever pretended that Fitz is afraid of a blow."

Chief of Police Wittman said the fight seemed to be on the level. In fact, according to him, when watching the fight live, the mayor said that it was as fine a fight as he ever saw. Wittman said Fitzsimmons put up a good, hard fight, but "he didn't have much chance."

The captain of detectives echoed that Fitz had no chance. He made a grand showing, and had the speed and strength for a few rounds, but his own exertions finished him. "Each punch he gave left him a little weaker. He made a wonderful showing, but he could not beat Jeffries in a thousand years, but fake, oh, no!" The Oakland chief of police said it was the fairest and squarest fight he ever witnessed. "Jeffries is simply a wonder."

One man gave contradictory statements. On one hand, he saw lips move just before the end of the fight, and thought Bob said, "Hit me now."

However, he also granted that someone at ringside may have said it, as he was very excited. Still, he also said that in his mind, the fight was entirely on the level. "If Fitz did say 'Hit me now,' it was merely that he knew he had received his finish and wanted the fight to end. He was beaten by the terrible body blows he received."

The Alameda County coroner said anyone who called the fight a fake either did not know what they were talking about or had an ulterior motive.

> The fight was one of the squarest I have ever witnessed, only I think Jeffries was foolish in making certain concessions that explained why his face was so badly cut up. ...

> The knockout was as pretty a piece of work as I have ever seen. It is all bosh to say Fitz got right up and took the matter smilingly. It was fully five minutes before he recovered from the blow near the solar plexus, and he had the expression of agony and distress on his face when he stepped up afterward to shake hands with Jeff. I'll bet Fitz's liver will not be right for months to come. Why, sports who lost almost their every cent said they had nothing to complain of.

Bill Delaney said the fake story was ridiculous and absurd.

> I think it is a great injustice to Fitz, taking his age and weight into consideration, and after putting up such a great fight, and after being defeated in one of the greatest and gamest battles in the history of heavyweight pugilism, to be denounced as a faker. As to the letter purported to have been received by Mayor Schmitz, I think he has too much intelligence to notice such an absurdity. Jeff's friends, I myself, have been receiving anonymous letters for some time, saying that the fight would be won in a certain number of rounds. Of course one of them had to come right. I never did like Fitz, but his battle last night won me over.

However, it was noted that atypical of a fight winner, Jeffries seemed anxious to leave the ring. The *Post* noted that Jeff did not seem happy, for he "lost little time in getting out of the ring. In fact, he had to be called back to shake hands." One could speculate that he either was upset and embarrassed by his appearance, or was disgusted by the way matters ended, and wanted to get away from it all. Still, Jeff had left the ring quickly after other fights too. He never was one to linger or engage in repartee. He was a loner and introvert by nature and did not like crowds.

Negotiations to film the fight had broken down, mostly as the result of Fitzsimmons, so we cannot independently determine for ourselves the legitimacy of the knockout. Of course, some could use that to argue that the reason Fitz did not want it filmed was so there would be no evidence. However, the real reason appears to have been financial.

Many of the era's fighters had the habit of speaking to their opponents during a fight, including Fitzsimmons. Fitz had had spoken with Jeff in the 7th round as well. It appeared that Jeffries had capitalized on a brief moment of carelessness. Some claimed that Bob spoke to Jeff before the big blows landed, while other versions said Fitz spoke with Jeff after he had been hit with the big body shot, letting him know that he had enough.[182]

The *Examiner* made various claims regarding what Fitzsimmons said prior to the knockout. The referee was quoted as saying that Fitz said, after receiving a blow to the stomach, "That was a Peach." Another claimed that Fitz said, "Hit me now!" Jeff then hit him in the body and Bob went down. Both Jeff and Fitz vehemently denied that claim.

Fitzsimmons insisted that he was hit with a big body blow that either broke or almost broke his ribs. Although he could hardly breathe, he said as Jeff approached, "I'm gone, Jim."

Referee Ed Graney felt that the fight was honest. He noted that both men clearly were giving it their best, and argued that if Fitz intended to throw the fight, he would not have hit Jeffries as hard or as often as he did and risk defeating him, nor would he have taken the punishing blows that he did throughout. The punishment he absorbed explained why he was worn down. Graney confirmed that a left hook to the body did the trick.

> Fitz was hit in the body two or three times hard enough to knock any man out. There were sixty pounds difference in weight, and the punishing that Fitz took in the body was terrible. He got an awful punching in the round before the last. In the eighth round Fitz turned and said, 'That was a peach.' He referred to the punch he got in the stomach. Then he got a left-hand hook, and then he got a little one on the jaw on top of it, and he went down. During the fight, Fitz hit Jeffries hard enough to knock his head off. In the seventh round he tottered Jeffries with a left-hand punch. He just cut him to pieces. But age was against him. Fitz is a light man. He got hit hard enough to be killed. Fitz was jabbing Jeffries to death. I sat Fitz in his corner myself, and he said, 'I think you broke my rib, Jim.' I thought that Fitz seemed to be as clever as he ever was, and faster than he ever was before..... I think the fight was legitimate.

However, the *Examiner* writers questioned the referee's version of what was said. They also questioned how a man could speak after getting hit with a supposedly devastating body shot. "Now, those who saw Corbett at Carson after he received that solar plexus punch know that he wasn't saying it was a peach, a plum or a piece of mince pie. He wasn't able to say anything. If Fitzsimmons didn't say, 'Now, hit me,' there is nothing in the reading of lips."

The *San Francisco Evening Post*, like the *Examiner*, tried to hype and capitalize on the fix claims, also saying that the fight terminated in a fake. Regarding the end, the *Post* said, "Fitz had been talking to Jeff. What he was saying could not be heard, but a moment or so later Fitz was on all fours on the floor, sent there apparently by a light tap on the jaw." Obviously, this writer missed the body shot that everyone else noticed. Many in the crowd

[182] *National Police Gazette*, August 9, 1902.

were surprised by the suddenness of the ending. They could not understand how Fitz, after having done so well, should so suddenly succumb. "It was the queerest kind of ending to an otherwise exciting fight."

Jeffries laughed at the suggestions that the fight was a fake. "Of course the fight was on the square. It is ridiculous to talk of anything else. Fitz fought a hard fight, the gamest I ever saw."

During the night of the 25th, Fitzsimmons complained about his ribs, some of which he thought were broken. He displayed his swollen hands and said they had been useless since the 2nd round. The day after the fight, Bob had a slight mark under his right eye, and his left wrist, knuckles, and fingers were badly swollen. Bob complained of pains due to the body blows he had received. He also said that he could not lift his left arm and had severe pain under his heart. "I didn't feel that last night. I feel pretty bad today altogether."

The Fitz folks were upset over the fix claims. They asked, "What was there to gain?" A Fitz representative offered $10,000 for any real proof of a fix. Upset and saddened, Fitzsimmons was actually in tears as he denied the story, looking regretfully at his crippled hands.

> It's a damn, malicious lie. ... It's a shame to call it a fake. ... I fought the greatest fight of my life and here I have been branded as a cur. There I was winning all the time, but I couldn't have won anyway. Both hands were gone. I've fought three hundred and twenty-eight battles and have been defeated twice, both times by Jeffries. That shows he is the better man, doesn't it? ... As God is my judge I did my best.

Bob's wife said the 'fake' story was a scheme designed to boom the *Examiner*. She said that her Bob had done his best but had gone down because the other man got in the right punch at the right time. George Dawson, Bob's chief trainer, had sent multiple telegrams to all of his friends advising them to bet on Fitzsimmons. If it was a fake, he would have advised them to bet on Jeffries.

Soldier Tom Wilson, one of Fitz's trainers, stuck up for Bob.

> Fake! Not on your life. If ever a man trained faithfully for a fight it was Bob Fitzsimmons. ... Fitz was determined to win over Jeffries or die in the attempt. No amount of money could have made him lay down or take part in a fake. He was too anxious to win. ... I was with him for weeks at Skagg's Springs and sparred with him daily. ... He left no stone unturned to get in the best possible condition.

Unfortunately, Wilson was unable to see the fight, because the government had ordered him to report to his post of duty and he had to leave two days before the fight. He was back at Fort Myer, Virginia in the service of Uncle Sam.[183]

---

[183] *National Police Gazette*, August 23, 1902.

Many questioned the source of Naughton's information. Apparently, a mysterious woman had written him a letter telling him that Fitz was to go out in the 8th round. However, various fortune tellers had made these types of predictions before many fights, with varying success. Bob was actually aware of the prediction before the fight.

> I knew some woman had written to Naughton that I was to lay down in the eighth. I was told of it yesterday afternoon. … When I got in distress in the eighth last night I thought of the letter and tried to stall off the end, but I couldn't do it. I remember that as I went down I said or tried to say, 'I'm gone,' but I guess it wasn't any more than a gasp. He took all the wind out of my body. I did not say, 'That was a peach,' and if I smiled, as they say I did, that must have been a smile of pain. I tried to last, but I couldn't. I got what I gave many a good man. It was the same blow that I gave Corbett, only it was a little to one side, but it did the business.

> Sometime during the fight Jeff got in one that caught me under the heart. I didn't feel it much then, but this morning about 2 o'clock it caught me good, and I thought I was going to die. I can't raise my left hand now.

Fitzsimmons said he tried as hard as he could, but just got caught.

> It does look funny, but my God! I tried my best. My hands were gone in the second round and I couldn't hurt Jeffries any more. I hit him on the ear with my right and that went. He got me like I got Corbett. … It only takes a punch to knock a man in a fight, and the punch came.

> Why should I go out in this fight? I was offered $750,000 to throw the Corbett fight. … I was offered $1,000,000 to throw the Sharkey fight, but my honor always stood before me. … So help me God, I had nothing to do with a fake. … May God strike me dead if I faked.

If it was a fake, it was a good one, because Bob blasted Jeff with a lot of great punches and busted him up. Certainly, if Fitz was faking, he was risking that he would blow it by knocking out Jeffries first. The punishment to the face nearly closed Jeff's eyes. Fitz was in his best form and was unaffected by Jeff's crouch. Jeffries appeared fast in his training sessions, but seemed slow when compared to Bob, who stabbed and struck him repeatedly in the face, nose, eyes, and chin. Jeff's face was a sight to remember. "And yet the gladiator from the southland had the hardihood to declare that he was not hurt." If one believes that Fitz wore loaded gloves and hit Jeffries very hard, it would be incongruous to do so while simultaneously intending to take a dive.

Fitzsimmons said it seemed contradictory to say he threw the fight when it was obvious that he was doing his best to knock Jeffries out. "I punished Jeff as I never punished a man before. I split his ear, I broke his nose, I cut his face up – and to say that I was faking!" Bob also said, "If anybody thinks Jeff hasn't got a punch in him, he's badly fooled, I tell you; and if anybody tells you he can't stand punishment, don't you believe him."

Bob said he would give up his end of the purse if the mayor could prove that he was connected with a fake. That body shot incapacitated him. "I couldn't speak for some time. The blow simply takes away a man's breath, and he can do nothing."

Fitzsimmons intended to sue W. W. Naughton, the *Examiner*, and the Hearst-owned newspapers on the ground of libel, and ask for punitive damages in the sum of $100,000. Bob said his whole soul was wrapped up in the battle and he badly wanted to win. However, unscrupulous people had tainted his performance. He challenged them to produce evidence other than the letter, which to his mind was simply a lucky guess.

> No man could have fought better than I did; in all my life I never fought better, but after the second round, when my hands began to cave in, I knew that the only chance I had was to keep jabbing. Jeff was too strong and big for me to reach effectively in this way, and when the end came in the eighth that letter, ever in my mind, stirred every bit of gameness in my carcass. I thought, 'If I can only get on my feet.' 'If I can only stall this through to the next round, then that letter will be given the lie.' But nature refused. It was no use. I could not get up. My breath was gone, but my head was clear. The blow that Jeff thought he landed on my jaw went around to my ear, and I knew that Graney was counting me out. I realized it fully, yet, I was helpless to aid myself. I was all in.[184]

Jeffries said he would give Corbett the next chance to fight him. He acknowledged that Jim was a very nimble and exceedingly clever fighter, tough to beat in a short rounds fight because of his fancy displays. However, he had no doubt that he could stop him in a long fight because he would wear Corbett out. "As you know, such fights as those through which I have passed are not to discover who is the better boxer, but to demonstrate who is the better man. They are to show which of the two opponents can stand the exhausting pace the longer and come out the victor in the end irrespective of the amount of punishment inflicted."

Bill Delaney was concerned that all the fake talk would hinder a possible fight with Corbett. Regarding the allegations, Delaney said, "Why, when Jeffries couldn't see for the blood streaming down his face, he was chasing Fitz around the ring, landing blows on him all the time. Does that look as if he was not trying his utmost to put him out? The idea is ridiculous." Delaney said he picked Jeff to win in 8 rounds, but that was just a prediction based on the fact that Fitz lasted 11 rounds the first time, and he felt that Bob could not last as long this time. He believed that Fitz was on the decline after the 5th round and instructed Jeffries to press the action. He said it was a right to the stomach under Bob's left that took his wind, and then a follow-up blow to the chin that finished him.

---

[184] *San Francisco Bulletin*, July 27, 1902.

Delaney realized that Jeffries needed time to heal his face, which was puffed up, blackened and bruised. Jeff had four stitches over his left eye. Under his right eye were two stitches drawing together a deep cut. His eyes were visible through narrow slits in his black-and-blue eyelids, which were swollen. His nose was puffy, and his forehead had a large lump.

The surgeon who was treating Jeffries said the cartilage in his nose being separated from the bridge had caused the excessive bleeding. However, he also said it was not broken. Still, others reported that Jeff had broken cartilage. Clearly though, Jeff's face proved that he had been in with a man who was trying his best to win and beat him up.[185]

Fitz practically was unmarked but actually was more seriously injured. The knuckles of his left hand were knocked back, allegedly in the 4th round. His hand was swollen to double its size, and he could barely move his left arm. A blow over the heart in the 5th round seemed to paralyze the muscles of the shoulder and arm. Fitz went to one of the bathhouses the day after the fight and fainted while there, not recovering for some minutes. Jim Jeffries had punishing blows with long-lasting effects.

The *Bulletin* noted that the gambling results did not support the allegations of a fake. The betting was fairly light, given that most thought Jeff would win, and at Corbett's saloon, where most of the wagering took place, only one bet was made that Jeff would win in the 8th round, and it was for only $10.

An upset Jeffries said he never had taken part in a fake and never would.

> If I were a party to a fake, I would never agree to take the beating I did. This is not the first time I have been marked up, but I always bring home the money. I have fought every man who has had championship aspirations and never received credit for my work. ... I was never guilty of a dishonorable act in my life, and I am not going to commence now.

Jeff said any talk of a fake was ridiculous. "Fitz fought a hard fight, the gamest I ever saw. ... He worked hard all the time and when I got in the double blow on him he was taken off his guard." He angrily said,

> Anyone who says that that fight was a fake is either crazy or a – liar. Look at my face. Does that look like a fake? ... Look at my whole face. Maybe it is painted and is all a fake. Better try and rub some of this color out. Now, let me tell you that I don't have to fight. ... I have money and I can go into many kinds of businesses by which I can make more than I could at my trade. All my life I have tried to be on the square, and I think I have succeeded. ...

> They can all welt me there if they want to, but I'll give it to them in the end. ... [Fitz] walloped me his hardest in the fight we had before in New York. ... He couldn't hurt me there, but I could hurt him where I wanted to, and that was in the wind. ... Not once during the

185 *San Francisco Examiner*, July 26, 27, 1902.

eight rounds was I distressed. With all the blood that was coming from my nose I only had to gargle once, and so that shows how good my wind was and how easily I was going. When a crowd sees blood on a man they think it's all off with him, but I am not one of that kind.

Jeff noted that the money was all wrong for there to be a fake. If anyone was going to take a dive to make a killing in wagers, he should have been the one to do so, because he was the heavy favorite, so betting on Bob would have meant a lot of money if Fitz had won. Instead, because he was such a heavy favorite, his friends were betting thousands on Jeffries in order to win hundreds. Fitz had little to gain by a fix because he was the clear betting underdog. "I think it is a crime to treat Fitz this way, and those who are doing it I don't think much of. He didn't fake."[186]

Local fight promoter J. H. Gibbs brought up the fact that Fitzsimmons years earlier admitted to throwing a fight with Jim Hall early in his career, so he would not put it past him. Fitz wasn't entirely above doing something like that. However, that was when he was a poor nobody and making almost no money in boxing. One writer said Bob's ribs were not cracked.

Jeffries kept insisting that it was a legitimate fight, saying, "I only beat him by the same kind of a blow in the body that I have won most of my battles with." He noted that there were some allegations of fake when Ruhlin quit from his body blows as well. It was his belief that critics were not giving him proper credit for his success against a wonderful fighter.[187]

Responding to its competitor's claims, the *San Francisco Chronicle* reported that most denounced the *Examiner's* cry of fake as ridiculous. There was no doubt that Fitz was trying to take Jeff out. The champion's face was badly battered. His cuts required many stitches, and strips of plaster held together the slit in Jeff's upper lip.

The *Chronicle* said only one person in a crowd of 7,000 could hear Bob say, 'Hit me now.' "This statement is so much at variance with the facts as to make it ridiculous." It noted that the letter handed to the mayor was "not to be opened unless Jeffries did win in the eighth," demonstrating that Naughton was not all that certain of his knowledge. It observed that usually when a fight is fixed, many pick it up like wildfire and it affects the betting. Yet, there was practically no betting on the fight.

A close ringsider said, "The blow that Jeffries struck Fitzsimmons under the heart in the eighth round was of sufficient force to floor an ox. ... It is imbecile to say that he went down on purpose. Up to that moment he had fought the pluckiest fight I ever saw." George Siler insisted it was a legitimate fight and ridiculed the idea of a fake. Another referee said, "No mortal man at his age could stand the body punches Jeff gave him."

Joe Gans, the black world lightweight champion, said,

[186] *San Francisco Bulletin*, July 27, 1902.
[187] *San Francisco Examiner*, July 27, 1902.

No way can you look at that affair and call it a fake. It was simply a great fight and one of the best that I have ever seen. Fitz could have licked anyone else in the world last night. His punch was enough to put anyone away barring the man he met. People don't seem to recognize what a marvel of strength that Jeffries is, and how well he knows how to put the steam behind his blows.

A sporting authority who sat ringside said he saw and heard nothing to make him think it was a fix. "I have seen Fitz in his boxing exhibitions do a fake stunt, as though knocked out, and the worst he ever did could be called crude beside the real article last night."[188]

During the afternoon of the 26th, the day after the fight, the two boxers had a chance meeting. Jeff said, "Do I look like I've been in a fake fight?" Bob replied, "I thought maybe I only dreamed I punched you a little last night." Glancing at his own puffed hand, Fitz said, "You have a hard head. I got this when I landed on your forehead and raised that bump." Jeff replied,

> It's lucky for me most of those lefts you landed on the side of my head were high or it would have been all off with me. I thought you had me in the second round when I got that smash in the nose. I didn't feel any too happy in the fourth, either. I told Delaney I would have to get you quickly, as I was afraid my eyes would close on me.
>
> The ridiculous part of the *Examiner* story is where a writer, who was seated thirty feet from where the fight ended, saw your lips move forming the words 'Now, hit me.' In another place he says: 'Fitz got in a nasty righthander and Jeff ducked from another right which might have settled the fight.' You were certainly careless of consequences if it was fixed for me to win. Those bandages you wore were what cut me up so; they were like knives. I didn't wear bandages, as whenever I do I hurt my hands instead of saving them.

Apparently, Jeff's seconds thought he would win easily, for they only had a small sponge in the corner and had difficulty in getting rid of the blood on him.[189]

The *San Francisco Call*'s headline on the 27th said, "Sportsmen are Enthusiastic over Fight and Ridicule the Lame Story of a Fake." Its writer said there was no foundation in fact for such a silly allegation. Experts were satisfied that the fight was not only legitimate, but the greatest battle in history. It called the *Examiner's* attack on the boxers unjust. "If Jeffries and

---

[188] *San Francisco Chronicle*, July 27, 1902. In May 1902, American black Joe Gans had won the world lightweight championship with a KO1 over Frank Erne, joining Joe Walcott of Barbados, who won the welterweight title in December 1901, as the only black men to own a world title at that point. Fellow black, Canadian George Dixon, had lost the world featherweight crown in early 1900 with a LTKOby8 to Terry McGovern. Prior to winning the lightweight championship, Gans had been stopped by McGovern in 2 rounds. Many believe that Gans threw the fight. Gans would hold his lightweight title until mid-1908. Walcott lost by disqualification in 20 rounds to Dixie Kid in 1904 in a fight that likely was fixed by the referee, who bet on his opponent. As a result, Walcott continued being considered the champion until losing the title in 1906.
[189] *San Francisco Call*, July 27, 1902.

Fitzsimmons did fake – and ninety-nine out of every hundred present at the battle are willing to go broke financially that they did not – then both should enter the vaudeville ranks. They would become famous as the world's great knockout team." The *Call* said only about 15 seconds remained in the 8th round, so Bob certainly was cutting it close if he had intended to throw the fight in that round.

Alex Greggains, on behalf of the San Francisco Athletic Club, offered $1,000 to anyone who could prove the fight was a fake. Fitz said he would give up his share of the purse and his home in Bensonhurst if it could be shown that he was party to any type of improper agreement.

However, both the *Evening Post* and the *Examiner* continued to question the fight's legitimacy. The *Post* held that the strong defense being put up by the fight folks was necessary in order to save pugilism.

> They know that unless some kind of a defense more opaque than the fight is faked up, pugilism is dead in this city. They wish to protect the "sport" and are prepared to do so by originating any kind of a fairy story that will explain why Bob went down and out in the eighth round at a time when he appeared to have Jeffries at his mercy and to be master of the situation.

> Neither Fitzsimmons nor his numerous friends have yet been able to furnish an explanation of the conversation which passed between the two bruisers in Fitzsimmons' corner just before the "knockout" blow was struck. It is very peculiar that men, fighting as they claim, almost for their lives, should hold a chat, at the expiration of which one dropped his arms in a helpless condition and the other administered a blow which sent the faker down and out.[190]

Four days after the fight, despite crediting Jeff's hard blows and the competitive fight Bob put up, Naughton wrote, "The majority of the men who saw that contest think they saw an honest battle. I know I saw a fraudulent knock-out."[191]

When attending a baseball game, Jeff was asked, "What kind of a talk was that you and Fitz had in the ring?" Jeffries replied,

> Talk, talk, all the talk we had was when he started to fight me in the clinch that time. Graney jumped between us and said: 'If you fellows are going to fight that way go ahead.' Fitz replied: 'I don't want to fight that way.' I said, 'Oh, that is all right. That was accidental,' or words to that effect. Now that was every solitary word that passed between us.[192]

On the 30th, Fitzsimmons met with Mayor Schmitz. Bob vehemently denied that he did anything dishonest. He told the mayor how his hands had failed him and how Jeff struck him in an unguarded, careless moment. Bob impressed the mayor as an honest man with an honest face.

[190] *San Francisco Evening Post*, July 28, 1902.
[191] *San Francisco Examiner*, July 29, 1902.
[192] *San Francisco Bulletin*, July 31, 1902.

It was revealed that Mrs. Alfred Hall was the one who had claimed that Jeffries would win in the 8th round. Mrs. Hall was a guest at Harbin Springs while Jeff was training there. She was a fortune teller. She used cards to tell Jeffries his fortune one night, and the cards showed that he would win in the 8th round. This statement became generally known amongst the folks at the springs, and when the *Examiner*'s W. W. Naughton visited there, Mrs. Hall told him that Jeff would win in the 8th. "Mrs. Hall now believes that she brought all the trouble upon Fitzsimmons and bravely comes forward to vindicate him." Naughton's inside source had been a fortune teller.[193]

Two weeks after the fight, on August 8, 1902, exhibiting at Hazard's pavilion in Los Angeles, upon his introduction, 3,000 fans cheered and applauded Fitzsimmons. The crowd called upon him for a speech, and Bob accommodated, saying,

> I am glad to be here tonight, and I feel that you all are my friends. I suppose you wish to know something about that 'fake' fight in 'Frisco. Billy Naughton says it was a fake, but I don't believe Jeffries thinks it was. (Laughter). I am sure I do not think it was. (Laughter). I have fought 328 battles and have lost two of them. They both went to Jeffries. When I went into that ring I was as sure of winning that fight as I was of anything in the world before. I weighed 158 pounds and will state that I do not believe that any other man in the world could make the showing I did against the odds. (Cheers and applause).

Fitzsimmons then sparred Hank Griffin and George Dawson for 3 rounds each, cleverly shifting and bluffing around, bringing forth laughter. Clearly, his hands were not that badly hurt given that he was using them two weeks after the Jeffries contest. When Griffin landed a few, Fitz landed a right to the ribs under Hank's heart, and thereafter Griffin was very careful. Fitz shifted, moved away, then turned and landed two to the head with such speed and skill that it drew applause. "He made the otherwise clever Hank look foolish at times by his superior science and ring tactics."

Fitz showed to even better advantage against Dawson. Bob stepped in and out again, jolting his man and skipping under his swings in a bewildering fashion.[194]

A writer for the *National Police Gazette* said the prediction and claim of a fix was a trick played by Naughton. He sealed it in an envelope and gave it to the mayor, yet reserved the right to request the unopened envelope be returned if he was not correct. This trick had been perpetrated many times, but the prediction was only announced afterwards if it happened to be correct. This *Gazette* author said he had predicted that Jeff would stop Ruhlin in 5 rounds but did not go around claiming a fix when he was correct. "I didn't shoot off any fireworks and pretend to know that the whole thing was a fraud." A guess was not evidence of a fix, or necessarily

[193] *San Francisco Call*, July 31, 1902.
[194] *Los Angeles Express*, August 9, 1902.

of marvelous judgment. He felt that the absence of a motive, together with the splendid battle, disproved the claims. He called Naughton's action a "stunt."

Regarding the fight, Fitzsimmons outclassed Jeffries in science, but Jeff's great strength pulled him through. His face was smashed and cut up, but he never was distressed, and nothing Bob did deterred Jeff's attack. Jeffries landed hard body shots in the 7th round and he kept up a great pace, looking to break his opponent.

> The knockout seemed to come through Fitz's lack of attention for a moment. He made some remark to Jeffries as Jeffries missed with his right. Then came a left hook to the head. Fitz's hands dropped for a moment and he looked as though he would slip under Jeffries' arm again as he had done so often before, but Jeffries brought out his left again and landed a fearful blow just above the solar plexus and Bob fell as though he had been hit by an ax.

This writer did not think it made sense for the men to give and take such punishment if it was a fix. He also believed that given how well Bob was doing, even if it was fixed, he would have double crossed Jeff to win the championship again. Bob could have made big money as champion just as a road attraction. Given the 3 to 1 odds, the big money would have been made by Jeff taking a dive, not Bob. "No, it was no fake. Fitz lost because he was up against a problem that he, with all his cunning, couldn't solve."

It was no surprise to this writer that Jeffries won. Fitzsimmons' wonderful showing made Jeff's victory all the more creditable. He had defeated a very sharp version of Fitzsimmons, who had been well prepared and fought a great fight, but still could not defeat the great champion.[195]

In late August, the *Police Gazette* reported, "The 'fake' story is gradually being forgotten and the originator of it will hardly again enjoy the public confidence which characterized his career as a sporting writer and critic." It said that the whole thing was an attempt to secure advertising for the newspaper. "Not one man in a hundred believes that the fight was anything but on the level." So, the story was "packed away in moth balls."[196]

In August, Fitzsimmons returned to performing in *The Honest Blacksmith*, along with his wife and son Bob, Jr.

In September 1902, Olympic Club amateur heavyweight champion 190-pound Sam Berger accepted an engagement as Fitz's sparring partner in *The Honest Blacksmith*, sparring 3 rounds during each performance.[197] Berger would go on to win a gold medal in the heavyweight division at the 1904 Olympics held in St. Louis, Missouri.

---

[195] *National Police Gazette*, August 16, 1902.
[196] *National Police Gazette*, August 30, 1902.
[197] *San Francisco Call*, September 9, 1902.

CHAPTER 10

A Unique Partnership

In early November 1902, Bob Fitzsimmons and Jim Jeffries were in the process of arranging an exhibition tour of the country together as a sparring combination partnership. Bob said his present theatrical tour would end soon at Woodland, California (which it did on the 22nd).[198] Mrs. Fitzsimmons originated the idea, and both Jeff and Bob agreed that they could make very good money touring together. The combination made sense, given that they were the two biggest names in boxing and therefore could attract large crowds. They would spar each other and sometimes take on local boxers. Their recent fight had increased the respect that Fitz and Jeff felt for one another, and they became friends.[199]

On Tuesday December 9, 1902, at the Exposition building in Portland, Oregon, about 5,000 attended Jeff and Bob's exhibition show, which included several boxing exhibitions, some between black boxers.

When Jeffries and Fitzsimmons appeared, the crowd cheered and waved. Bob was clad in lavender tights with a little belt of American flags knotted around his waist. He was spare in the legs, but above the waist he had the build of a 200-pound man. He was bald, with a fringe of light brown hair on the back of his head. Jeffries, looking like Hercules, was clad in black tights. He was a stocky giant, weighing 235 pounds, "with great layers of muscles standing out from every part of his brawny body." He was hairy, dark, and powerful, like a bear, contrasting him with the much lighter Fitzsimmons, who looked like a thoroughbred racehorse. At first glance, Bob seemed frail and puny compared with the

[198] *San Francisco Chronicle*, November 10, 1902. *San Francisco Call*, November 24, 1902.
[199] *National Police Gazette*, November 15, December 6, 1902.

bulky Jeff. "Upon closer observation his dimensions seem to grow before the eye, and after a time one has a full appreciation of the vitality, strength and energy concealed in the trim and elongated form of the Australian."

The crowd called for a speech. Fitz gave in and said, "Age must give way to youth, and I had to go down before the younger, if not a handier man." Another quoted him as saying,

> Ladies and Gentlemen: I heartily appreciate this spontaneous outburst of enthusiasm with which you have greeted me. I represent a ring career of 15 years in which honest fighting and integrity have been my motto. During this time I met all comers, and my record shows for itself. Jeffries defeated me on his merits. It was simply a case of age making place for youth and strength. I have now surrendered the championship honors to a younger and stronger, but not a handsomer man.

The spectators howled, enjoying his speech.

Clark Ball, the tour's manager, introduced the men, and announced that it was to be a scientific bout, without slugging. Jeff and Bob sparred 3 rounds of two minutes each, displaying the art of boxing. "Both men were quick as cats, and always in the game. Jumping, dodging and ever hitting out with flail-like blows, the two men spent their six minutes in the ring. Both are equipped with arms that shoot out like piston rods or the swoop of a steam hammer, stopping just at the right point..." Another said Jeff crouched and kept his body and jaw well protected. He forced his bulk up against Bob like a bull.

> While fast and scientific, it looked as if sheer force and weight must have been the predominant features which made Jeff the victor over Fitz. The ex-champion impressed one more toward the scientific and technical part of the sport than to ward off the brute force phase. His dexterous ducking and clever sidestepping were a surprise. His blows were delivered with great rapidity, and his blocking and countering were remarkable. He kept an erect position and sparred high. His foot work was fast and effective. He seemed to be able to land with greater frequency and with more assurance than Jeffries. From a scientific standpoint he made a far better showing than his partner, and in boxing for points seemed to be in a position to hand him a bunch whenever he saw fit. Removing the handicap of weight, it seems as if Jeffries would have no chance of doing business with Fitz,...and even with the advantage of superior weight, strength and youth, Jeffries has but little percentage over the warm-haired fighter.

Afterward, Bob said, "I am willing to fight any man in the world, bar nobody. I did intend to quit the ring after my fight with Jeffries, but I am as good a man today as ever I was, and better than any other fighter that I know of excepting the champion."[200]

[200] *Oregonian, Oregon Daily Journal*, December 10, 1902.

Most believed that Bob and Jeff eventually would roughhouse, because both had naturally powerful, punishing blows, even when throwing lightly. "Fitz never had a sparring partner in his life but what had to take a sound beating from him every time something happened to displease the auburn-topped Australian. Fitz is a hard taskmaster." His jolts would jar and wobble, and Bob often excused them by saying they were landed unintentionally.[201]

The *Oregon Daily Journal* said Jeffries stood alone in his division, head and shoulders above the rest. He was so big and strong that he was invincible, and no one had any chance with him. Fitz had the best chance, which was slim, for he lacked the necessary bulk. Corbett was too old, and might sprint around a bit, but eventually would be beaten to a standstill whenever he attempted to fight. "Denver Ed Martin, the long, thin negro, would be annihilated at the first charge of the big champion."[202]

[201] *Oregon Daily Journal*, December 11, 1902.
[202] *Oregon Daily Journal*, December 12, 1902.

It was reported that Jim Jeffries and Jim Corbett were matched to fight a rematch in May or June 1903 before the club offering the best inducements.[203]

In *Two Fisted Jeffries*, Jeff said Fitz weighed 202 pounds, while he weighed 235. Jeff said Bob always was much bigger than folks realized.

Fitz and Jeff exhibited to a sold-out house on December 12, 1902, at the Seattle, Washington theater. Jeffries took little mincing steps, standing erect rather than his usual crouching position. Bob made him "look like a meal ticket fighter." Jeff's face began bleeding in the 1st round. "He is not in anything like as good condition as Fitz, and the latter looked the master mechanic that he is in the ring." The bout was too tame for some, and the rests between rounds as long as the boxing time. They finally did mix it at the very end for about 30 seconds, and the crowd cheered.[204]

Bob Fitzsimmons and Jim Jeffries, Who Box Tomorrow Night.

On Monday December 15, they exhibited in Spokane, Washington at the local theater under the auspices of the Spokane Amateur Athletic club. The sold-out record house was jammed as never before, with about 1,800, two dozen of them women, paying from 50 cents up to two dollars apiece, generating almost $1,700. Many had to be turned away.

After the preliminary bouts, Jeff and Bob sparred. The *Spokane Chronicle*

The Spokane Theater
DAN L. WEAVER, Manager.   TELEPHONE MAIN 84.

Tonight! Tonight!

The World's Greatest Gladiators,

Jas. J. Jeffries and Rob't Fitzsimmons

In a Scientific Boxing Exhibition, Under the Auspices of the Spokane Amateur Athletic Club, Preceded by the Following Exciting Preliminaries:

AL HAMMOND and KID HARRIS
In a three round exhibition.

TOM DOWNEY and V. PAWNELL
In a three round exhibition.

DUDE LEWIS and BILLY ARMSTRONG
In a four round exhibition.

JOE FITZGERALD and CHARLES ELSEY
In a six round exhibition.

Prices—Boxes, logres and divens, $2; parquet, $1.50; last three rows, $1; entire second floor, $1; gallery, 50 cents.

---
[203] Rome Daily Sentinel, December 10, 1902.
[204] *Seattle Post-Intelligencer*, December 13, 1902.

wrote, "No one expected a fight between Jeffries and Fitzsimmons nor did many complain of the work the two men did, but…they might have made their exhibition a little more than four rounds." The bout was good, however, and showed how the two big men could box. "They sidestepped, ducked, guarded and countered with the rapidity of little men. Fitzsimmons looked small beside the mountain of flesh opposite him, while Jeffries showed himself to be active and clever."

The *Spokane Spokesman-Review* observed,

> Fitzsimmons appeared to be in splendid condition. He is heavier than ever before, but has lost none of his speed, and drove into Jeffries' stomach and face as if he meant business. Jeffries is fat and good natured. He looks to weigh about 230 pounds, but the manner in which he darted around the ring, blocked, feinted, jabbed and swung was a revelation to the uninitiated. The big fellows ducked and clinched, swatted each other on the mouthpiece, landed resounding blows on each other's ribs and were coltish in their actions. They were applauded vigorously….

The *Spokane Press* said,

> Their four-round bout was decidedly good. They way they punched, swung, ducked and feinted was marvelous, and many of the blows delivered were anything but love taps. Fitz was expected to be speedy, but the remarkable agility of the big champion was a surprise to everyone. This tour in company with Lanky Bob will do him a world of good, as he is adding daily to his science.[205]

They were scheduled to appear that week in Coeur d' Alene, Idaho, Missoula, Montana, and at week's end, Butte, Montana.[206]

On Friday December 19, 1902, they exhibited to a crowded Union Opera House in Missoula, Montana. The local *Daily Missoulian* called it a first-class fake, and successful only if a person felt that the mere sight of the famous pugs was worth the price of admission. Their 3 rounds of boxing was a farce. Yet, a non-local report claimed they gave an "intensely

[205] *Spokane Chronicle, Spokane Spokesman-Review, Spokane Press,* December 16, 1902.
[206] *Butte Miner,* December 18, 1902.

realistic" 3-round exhibition, perhaps a bit of marketing.[207]

One report claimed that they went at it pretty hard in a 4-round San Francisco exhibition in which 240-pound Jeff tried to stop him early, but Bob came back and cut him up.

Another alleged that in a Seattle exhibition, their boxing was stopped after 2 rounds when they really mixed it up and Jeff was badly bleeding.[208]

Of course, such reports likely were just hype to stimulate patronage at what probably were generally tame exhibitions. Jeff and Bob likely just worked with each other, although with two greats in the ring, they might have gotten heated up here and there. Two great punchers could not help but land some good ones. One report said, "They do say that when Jeffries and Fitzsimmons get together in their boxing bout, on their present tour, that they put up a smart contest."[209]

Years later, Fitz said of one of their numerous exhibitions,

> While we were giving an exhibition out West one night Jeffries landed a swing on my temple. The effect of the blow glued my feet to the ground. I was stunned, unable to move as I stared at Jeffries. I heard him say, 'the old man is faking again.' He thought I was playing a joke on him, when as a matter of fact I was helpless and he could have come to me with all kinds of wallops and I would have been powerless to resist them.[210]

Although Jeffries was intending to give Corbett a rematch in the near future, he thought more of Fitzsimmons, who "gave me the hardest fight of my career, and is still the best of them, next to myself. I would rather take 50 punches from Jim Corbett than to run into one of the pokes that Fitz can hand out. He hits harder than a mule can kick."

[207] *Daily Missoulian, Anaconda Standard,* December 20, 1902.
[208] *Two Fisted Jeffries* at 220; *Anaconda Standard,* December 19, 20, 1902; *Butte Inter Mountain,* December 20, 1902.
[209] *Butte Miner,* December 17, 1902.
[210] *National Police Gazette,* February 18, 1905.

Jeffries also said, "I am now entitled to a rest. I am doing pretty well as it is. We are copping off about $10,000 a week, and that is a good deal better than fighting for a purse."

Colored champion "Denver" Ed Martin via his manager Billy Madden (who also managed Ruhlin) had challenged Fitzsimmons, but Bob rebuked his challenge as not being sufficiently financially lucrative. "Yes, I saw that Madden had posted a forfeit…and has given it out that I can make $2,500 by meeting his coon for six rounds in Philadelphia. I dare say that Jeff and I will make that much apiece tonight. Indeed, we can make it any old night. I wouldn't consider such a cheap offer. … As for that nigger, Martin, he has not claims to fight me. … Let him whip Corbett first." Martin needed to establish himself as a bigger draw.[211]

Broadway Theater

GRAND ATHLETIC EXHIBITION.
The Pugilistic Wonders,

James J. Jeffries
Champion Heavyweight of the World.

Robert Fitzsimmons
Champion Middleweight of the World.
Three great local contests.

Admission, $5, $3, $2 and $1

Saturday, December 20.

On December 20, 1902 in Butte, Montana, Jeffries was scheduled to box a 4-round exhibition bout against Jack Munroe, alleged amateur heavyweight champion of the Pacific coast, who learned to box at the San Francisco Olympic Club, while Fitz was to box Jack Stewart. If either man was to stay the 4 rounds with Jeff or Bob, they would be paid $250, but if they were knocked out, they would receive $100. "Monroe is powerful and looks as though he might have a chance" to last the distance. Another said, "Munro is built along the same lines as the champion, and although not as large, is shiftier and more clever." In 1900, Munroe had lost a 20-round decision to Hank Griffin.

Fitzsimmons quickly knocked out local heavyweight Jack Stewart in the 1st round, with ease. "Fitzsimmons made a monkey of Jack Stewart. He only hit the 'shadow' three times – once in the breast, once in the jaw and a third in the jaw with his right and Stewart took the count."

Munroe lasted the full 4 rounds with Jeffries. Several false reports were circulated nationally, claiming that Munroe had beaten Jeff and even knocked him down in the process. Actually, Munroe "won" the monetary bonus because Jeff had contracted to knock him out within 4 rounds and failed to do so. Munroe had not beaten Jeff on the merits. In reality, it was Munroe who went down

JACK STEWART

[211] *Butte Inter Mountain*, December 20, 1902; *Butte Miner*, December 21, 1902.

187

several times, not Jeffries. Still, Munroe had been competitive.

Even after Jeff had boxed Munroe, "Jeffries and Fitzsimmons wound up the program with a lively four-round exhibition." Jeff still had enough in the tank to box another 4 rounds with Fitzsimmons.

Afterwards, Fitz posted a forfeit of $500 to knock out Munroe within 4 rounds, but Munroe did not accept.[212]

Jeffries laughed at the national fight reports. In an interview with the *Anaconda Standard*, he claimed that he carried Munroe and let him stay the 4 rounds because he wanted the crowd to have some entertainment, given that Fitzsimmons had stopped his man so quickly in the 1st round. He even told Fitz in the corner that he was carrying him. Bob confirmed that Jeff told him that he was going to let Munroe stay.

Another local paper, the *Butte Intermountain*, confirmed that because the Fitz-Stewart match had been a farce, the management approached Jeffries and asked him to allow Munroe to last the 4 rounds and make a good exhibition.

However, the *Butte Miner* disagreed. It said that Jeffries did his best to stop "Monroe" but failed.

> It is conceded that Monroe would not stand as much show with Fitz as he did with Jeffries, for the reason that Fitz is in the better condition. Jeffries has not done any sparring since he last fought Fitz until they started out two weeks ago on this tour.

However, Fitzsimmons confirmed that he had told Jeff to take him out, but Jeffries refused.[213]

The *Butte Intermountain* subsequently confirmed that the nationwide stories had been false.

> It's too bad that an enthusiastic newspaper man allowed himself to be carried away to the extent that he sent an Associated Press report East to the effect that Jack Munroe had knocked Jeffries down. The New York and Chicago papers played the fact up in big type and the papers there sold like hot peanuts. As a matter-of-fact there is not a word of truth in the report. Jeffries has never been knocked down in his life…. As before stated in these columns Munroe put up a great showing and displayed superb grit and generalship, but that "he had Jeff going," is false. He went into the ring to stay four rounds and he succeeded in doing it…. It was in the nature of an exhibition and not a fight. The referee gave Munroe the decision because the miner had entered the ring to stay four rounds and had done it; not because he had the best of the boxing.[214]

On December 22, 1902, at the Margaret theater in Anaconda, Montana, Jeff and Bob exhibited 3 rounds. "Naturally no one for a moment thought

212 *Anaconda Standard*, Butte *Inter Mountain*, December 19, 1902; *Billings Gazette*, December 23, 1902. *Butte Miner*, December 21, 1902.
213 *Anaconda Standard*, Butte *Inter Mountain*, *Butte Miner*, December 22, 1902; *Anaconda Standard*, *Seattle Post-Intelligencer*, December 23, 1902.
214 *Butte Inter Mountain*, December 24, 1902.

that the heavy hitters would attempt to do damage, and on the whole the exhibition between the heavy-weights was creditable."[215]

On December 25 at the Grand opera house in Great Falls, Montana, before one of the largest crowds that ever gathered there, Jeff and Fitz primarily engaging in a "mild slapping bout" of 3 rounds wearing 8-ounce gloves.[216]

On December 26, 1902, in Bozeman, Montana, at the local opera house, Bob Fitzsimmons knocked out 180- or 190-pound Mike Ranke 15 seconds into the 2nd round with a heavy blow to the jaw. Bob injured and possibly broke his right hand. However, not wanting to disappoint the fans, he only used his left while sparring against Jeffries. It was said that Jeff wanted to train for a while before undertaking to stop someone again.[217]

One writer opined that Jeffries never was a quick knockout artist as Sullivan had been, and therefore he should avoid these types of short bouts in which he undertook to stop someone quickly. Fitzsimmons was much better suited to such short exhibitions.[218]

Fitzsimmons spoke about the Munroe exhibition, calling the report that Jeffries was dropped a malicious falsehood.

> Munroe was never in the game during the four rounds. I told Jeff to put him out after the first round. Jeff said no; that he would let him stay and give the people the worth of their money. They have done Jeff a great injustice. I was surprised at the press doing such an injustice to an American champion. To prove that Jeff let him stay four rounds he offered Munroe $1,000 if he would stay four rounds again. Munroe refused, which goes to show that Munroe knows himself that Jeff can put him out in four rounds if he wished to.[219]

However, Fitz admitted that Jeff tried to stop Munroe after the 2nd round. So, Jeffries carried him for 2 rounds and then went after him in the 3rd and 4th, but he had waited too long, because Munroe was clever and tough. By not punching very often, Munroe left Jeffries with few openings or counterpunching opportunities. Still, Munroe was saved by the bell in the 3rd round. Munroe also was able to clinch and/or go down and take his time in rising in order to kill the clock. Back in Sullivan's day, these were known as Tug Wilson tactics.[220]

How such a skewed view of the Jeffries-Munroe bout got generated and disseminated may be explained by what transpired after the bout. Clark Ball, Fitz's manager and brother-in-law, who had been managing the Fitz-Jeffries tour, severed relations with the combination and signed a contract with Munroe. Ball intended to make Munroe the star attraction of an athletic show managed by him.

---

[215] *Anaconda Standard*, December 23, 1902.
[216] *Great Falls Daily Tribune*, December 26, 1902; *Great Falls Leader*, December 27, 1902.
[217] *Butte Miner*, December 25-27, 1902; *Great Falls Daily Tribune*, December 27, 1902; *Gallatin County Republican, Missoulian*, December 23, 30, 1902.
[218] *Seattle Post-Intelligencer*, December 28, 1902.
[219] *Butte Miner*, December 29, 1902.
[220] *Butte Miner*, December 29, 1902.

After Ball separated from them, when Fitzsimmons met Ball in the lobby of the Thornton hotel in Butte at 1 a.m., there was some wrangling between the two men. Ball was leaving the combination for Munroe and asked for the money that he was owed. Fitz said they owed him nothing. Ball called Fitzsimmons a liar, and Bob floored his former manager with a left hook to the jaw. On the way down, Ball's head struck the corner of the counter, and it was lacerated. "Lie there, you cur, until you come to. I'll teach you to talk that way to me. I'll knock your bloody block off even if you are my brother-in-law. Why, I made the man." Ball was the husband of a sister of Mrs. Fitzsimmons. The cut required five stitches. The question not overtly raised at the time was whether Ball was the one who put forth the tainted reports in order to boost Munroe. This appears to have been the case.[221]

ROBERT FITZSIMMONS.

In his first autobiography, Jeff said that the night of the Munroe exhibition, Fitz had a falling out with Ball. Therefore, Ball rushed over and signed Munroe and began wiring all over the country that Munroe had defeated Jeff and knocked him down.

In *Two Fisted Jeffries,* Jeff said, "The Monroe myth was built on the plot of a press agent who saw a chance to advance himself and get some money for Monroe and himself at my expense." Jeff said Ball had sent out the story. The only time Jeffries had been down in the bout was when he missed a punch and slipped down when trying to get at Munroe. Fitzsimmons actually was angrier than Jeff was, because Ball was his brother-in-law, so he felt responsible. Therefore, when they met in a hotel lobby, Bob knocked Ball out.[222]

Speaking about his career, former champion John L. Sullivan said, "I never met a man who really hurt me. Men like Kilrain, Mitchell and Ryan landed on me, but their blows never did me any damage." Sullivan said the present-day fighters were a good lot. Jeffries was "in a class all by himself" and was a "great fighter." "Because he is big he does not seem clever, but he is faster than people imagine." He was too big for Fitzsimmons, who was the next best man in the world. "I think he can defeat any man in the world at his weight."

Sullivan said the fighters of his era were not quite as clever as the boxers today, in part because they fought to win by knockout, not for points.

[221] *Butte Inter Mountain,* Anaconda Standard, December 29, 1902; *Seattle Post-Intelligencer,* December 30, 1902.
[222] *My Life and Battles* at 51.; *Two Fisted Jeffries* at 214, 218.

We went in the ring for business, not to dance around. We all had enough science to get out of a pinch when it came our way, but in those days men did not care for decisions on points. A man wanted to win as quickly as possible, and the sooner his man was put out the better.

Corbett is the cleverest man I ever boxed. He is the fastest big man in the ring. His only trouble is he has not got the punch. That's what tells in the fighting game.[223]

The Jeff-Fitz combination performed in Pocatello, Idaho on December 29. When Jeff and Fitz sparred, Bob did all of his work with his left, given his right-hand injury. Some said he actually had hurt his hand on Clark Ball's teeth.[224]

The world champions at year end 1902 were: heavyweight – Jeffries, (colored) – Ed Martin, light heavyweight – George Gardner, middleweight – Tommy Ryan, welterweight – Joe Walcott, lightweight – Joe Gans, featherweight – Young Corbett, bantamweight – Harry Forbes.

On January 1, 1903, Jeff and Fitz were in Salt Lake City, Utah. The crowd hooted them for what was called a farcical 4-round exhibition of tapping. It was far too tame. Bob was still nursing his hand.

Some said that Jeff would not attempt to put a man out in 4 rounds again unless he was in top condition. Local Mexican Pete Everett (whom Jeff had stopped in 3 rounds in 1898, and who in 1901 had fought Jack Johnson to a 20-round draw) had offered to go with Jeffries, but the offer was declined.[225]

On January 6, 1903, Jack Munroe fought Jack Sullivan, and although he did not put him out in 4 rounds, he had Sullivan on the floor 26 times. A fighter named Mose Lafontise stayed 4 rounds with Munroe on January 7, but Munroe was said to be a clever boxer. On January 9, Munroe beat up a black fighter named Ike Hayes over 4 rounds. "Although the negro stayed he was given an awful beating and only his continual clinching enabled him to last the bout out." Ball was building Munroe.[226]

It was reported that Clark Ball intended to place Munroe under Tommy Ryan's tutelage. When they heard about this, both Fitz and Jeff laughed and said Munroe could earn $1,000 any time he desired to try to stay 4 rounds with either one of them. Fitz said Munroe could train with Ryan for a year and it would not matter.[227]

Jeff and Fitz continued touring the country with their money-making exhibitions. In January, they toured throughout Colorado, as well as St. Joseph and Kansas City, Missouri. In early February, they were scheduled to

[223] *Butte Inter Mountain*, December 29, 1902.
[224] *Idaho Daily Statesman*, December 30, 1902.
[225] *Salt Lake Telegram*, January 2, 1903; *Butte Miner*, December 30, 1902, January 2, 3, 1903; *National Police Gazette*, January 31, 1903. In March 1903, Gus Ruhlin would stop Mexican Pete Everett in the 2nd round.
[226] *Butte Miner*, January 3, 7, 8, 10, 1903; *National Police Gazette*, January 31, February 14, 1903. The *Police Gazette* later revealed that Peter Maher had knocked out Ike Hayes in 2 minutes.
[227] *National Police Gazette*, January 31, 1903.

exhibit in Springfield and St. Louis, Missouri; Indianapolis, Indiana; Louisville, Kentucky, and other places on their way east.

Fitz and Jeff gave a scientific 3-round sparring exhibition in Cripple Creek, Colorado on January 17. In the 2nd round, Bob slipped and fell backwards onto his hips. This seemed to give him the old fire, and he waded in thick and fast, and the big boilermaker got winded at the high altitude.

That night, at the National hotel, Fitz was asked to give his response to Munroe's claims that Fitz and Jeff attempted to suppress the news of his good performance against Jeff by offering a $1,000 bribe to the news correspondent. Fitz responded to the purported statement:

> I do not believe it was made by Monroe. It was made by Clark Ball, my brother-in-law, who proved traitor to me in Montana. After the fight at Helena he made a secret arrangement to manage Monroe. Afterward he tried secretly to get all of our boxers to go with him. When I learned of these things I discharged him and he whined to be allowed to be with me and Jeff.

> As he had neglected our business and repeatedly had been in such condition that he could not do any business and had acted like an ungrateful traitor after I had helped him, I refused to keep him. Then he abused me in the vilest language and I gave him a short arm jolt that sat him on the floor.

> Immediately after the Helena fight both Jeff and I offered $1,000 if Monroe would stand for either of us for four rounds. I will now agree to make it $5,000 and will have one of my hands tied and lie on my back on the floor.[228]

In St. Louis, Jeff told a reporter, "Bob Fitz put his man out in 15 seconds and one of the other contests ended in two minutes. It was up to me to give the house a run for its money. I decided that the proper thing would be to let Munroe stay four rounds, and fought with the idea of sacrificing the $250 forfeit."

Jeff said he was earning about $2,000 a night with Fitz. Therefore, he could make more money by touring and exhibiting for a couple weeks than he likely would earn with one fight, and without all the worry, trouble, hassle, training, or training camp expenses. Hence, Jeff was not eager to end his tour any time soon unless sufficient financial inducements were offered.

Jeff assured the press that although his nightly bout with Bob was a mere exhibition, it was far from tame, for occasionally, when they got warmed up, they would really go at it.[229]

[228] *Grand Junction Daily Sentinel*, January 19, 1903.
[229] *St. Louis Post-Dispatch*, February 5, 1903.

Despite his representations and the advertising hyping their exciting exhibitions, their bout on February 5, 1903, at the St. Louis West End Club was exceedingly tame. In fact, it was said to be even tamer than typical exhibition bouts. Each of the 3 rounds only lasted about a minute or so, and they took a few minutes of rest between each round. "Despite press agents' tales, no one really expected to see anything like a fight."

However, the fans at least expected something approaching a fair exhibition. The local paper said the preliminary handshake proved to be the hardest blow struck. It was a farce, as the men clowned around, smiled, and moved about, only using slow and light taps. Some laughed, some hissed, and others left before it was over. "For the most part the crowd accepted, with good-natured acquiescence, that they had been done again." Jeff said they were not being paid enough to fight and show the real thing. Nevertheless, the locals felt a bit swindled. "The majority of spectators went away from the club convinced that Jack Munroe stayed four rounds with him on his merits." Jeff looked fat and slow and was breathing heavily despite little exertion.[230]

It was obvious to the St. Louis newsmen why Jeff was not eager to fight again any time soon. "Not only is he too busy making money, but it would take him at least three months to get into anything like shape." Both Jeff and Fitz ate and drank a fair amount while in the city, contradicting the illusion that they were abstemious.[231]

On February 5, 1903 in Los Angeles, Jack Johnson won a 20-round decision over "Denver" Ed Martin to win the undisputed colored heavyweight championship. Johnson previously had obtained a claim to the

[230] *St. Louis Post-Dispatch, St. Louis Daily Globe Democrat, St. Louis Republic,* February 6, 1903.
[231] *St. Louis Post-Dispatch, St. Louis Republic,* February 7, 1903.

colored championship on October 21, 1902, when he stopped Frank Childs in the 12th round.

Jeff and Bob sparred another tame 3 rounds in Paducah, Kentucky on February 6. Earlier on that card, Fitzsimmons refereed a 5-round bout between colored boxers Charles Shannon and Al Blanch, which he declared a draw. Bob also refereed an 8-round bout between Hurley Randall and colored Alabama Kid, won by the Kid in the 5th round.

Perhaps just press agent's hype, the dispatch regarding their exhibition in Paducah reported, "Fitz had his nose slightly skinned and a few drops of blood were brought from Jeffries' cheek."

They were also set to travel to places like Evansville and Indianapolis, Indiana; Cincinnati, Ohio; and Louisville and Lexington, Kentucky (the latter on February 11).[232]

On February 7, 1903 at the Grand Opera House in Evansville, Indiana, before about 1,500 men and 3 women, in addition to sparring with Jeffries, Fitz boxed local 180-pound George Weikel, who wanted to attempt to last 4 rounds with Jeffries for $250, but the offer was declined. Instead, Fitzsimmons boxed 3 rounds with Weikel in clever fashion. "It showed Fitzsimmons to be clearly entitled to his reputation as one of the greatest ring generals of the present day. The work of the middleweight champion was as pretty and gratifying an exhibition as any lover of the sport could wish to see." The aggressive Weikel put up a spirited fight and made it fascinating from start to finish.

FITZSIMMONS.

In the 1st round, Weikel rushed, hit Fitz a few times and left numerous openings, but Bob did not take advantage of them.

In the 2nd round, Fitz picked it up and there were rapid exchanges. Weikel slipped and fell to his right knee. There was much fast work. Bob hit his face at will but also took some hard blows. In the last part of the round, Fitz gave Weikel several stiff jolts on the jaw just to remind him that he was in fast company.

In the 3rd round, Fitz hit Weikel in the face frequently. Bob's footwork and dodging was "perfect." He ducked about 15 vicious left lunges, and each time, Weikel's breastbone ran into Bob's shoulder. Weikel clinched a fair amount as well. Weikel grew tired, and Bob forced him around the ring, until the gong sounded.

[232] *Paducah Sun*, February 7, 1903; *St. Louis Daily Globe Democrat*, February 8, 1903.

Weikel had made a creditable showing. Afterwards, Fitz told Weikel that he had been hit hard enough on three different occasions such that had he been an everyday dub, he would have been on the floor.

Bob then boxed Jeffries for 3 rounds which were called half earnest, half fun. Bill Delaney introduced them and refereed. Jeffries was introduced as the champion of all champions. One said he appeared to be a massive man of muscle and iron flesh. Another said he was fat. "While not overly clever, the champion has acquired genuine skill in boxing." During a mix-up, Jeff was cut over the left eye. In return, he brushed some flesh from the bridge of Fitz's nose. In the last round, Jeff lost his temper and went after him in earnest. There was some genuine hard fighting for a minute or so. Nevertheless, the exhibition overall was "rather disappointing, taken as a whole."

Another observer said,

> The exhibition was pretty from the start, both men going in for good, fast and clean work, and the old Cornishman had all the best of it from the start. Both men showed much science in their work, were earnest, and conscientious about delivering telling blows and at times went at one another pell mell.
>
> In the second round blood began to flow down over the big face of the champion. The crowd saw it and cheered the former king of the ring. The blood flowed from an old sore, however. ... It is broken open almost every night the men show and for this reason the blood flowed freely.[233]

Angered at the false stories that Jack Munroe and/or Clark Ball on his behalf were continuing to circulate, Fitzsimmons said,

> I am tired of talking about that dub. I will give him $1,000 if Jeffries or myself cannot stop him in three rounds. I am tired of allowing him to go about this country advertising himself at our expense. I want to go on record as stating that he is a third-rate dub and that if anyone thinks he is not a dub just get him to face me for three rounds and let him earn $1,000 if I fail to knock him out.[234]

On February 9, 1903, at the Auditorium in Louisville, Kentucky, 1,500 people saw Jeff and Fitz box 3 lively but friendly rounds. They were active at all times and did more than the usual love-tap match. They wore big gloves and boxed as they might in a training bout. Major Hughes said, "Nobody will be able to lick that big bear during the next ten years." 99 out of 100 agreed. Jeff was a rugged giant with big muscles, but quick as a cat. He was not muscle-bound. He was the "foremost fighter of the century with his fists." "Last night he appeared unusually active, and even clever against clever Fitzsimmons. ... Fitz also showed up well. He is just as clever as he ever was and still has that deadly shift with its right swing to the solar

---

233 *Evansville Courier, Evansville Journal,* February 7, 8, 1903.
234 *National Police Gazette,* February 7, 1903.

plexus as well as his famous short left hook, which has many times produced sleep." Of course, they weren't fighting, and no one expected that. It was a high-quality hippodrome.

Local fighter Marvin Hart was introduced at the show, and he issued a challenge to fight any man in the world, except for Jeffries and Fitzsimmons. The announcement of his challenge was largely cheered.[235]

On February 20, Jeffries and Fitzsimmons were in Richmond, Indiana at the Phillips, boxing 4 rounds. "It was hard to tell what fighter had the better of the exhibition, since both landed at will and seemed to hit wherever they wished."[236]

On February 26, 1903, in Los Angeles, Jack Johnson won a 20-round decision over Sam McVey to defend his colored heavyweight title. Johnson, "the colored heavyweight, who has been trimming them all at Los Angeles," challenged Jeffries.

The *Police Gazette* said engaging in 4-round all-comers exhibitions was a dangerous proposition, because it was not that easy to stop everyone in 4 rounds. Jeff had been weighing 240 or 245 pounds and was not at his best. Munroe was in good physical condition and had boxing experience. It remembered when Jeff contracted to put out 195-pound Bob Armstrong but failed to do so in 10 rounds, in part owing to a broken hand and the fact that Bob fought warily. Stopping a man was not always that easy.[237]

Jeffries was willing to fight Corbett next, but also said that he was making such good money with Fitzsimmons on their exhibition tour that he wanted to put the fight off. He also wanted a fight to the finish, or at least one of many rounds, concerned that Corbett would run around and try to extend the bout with his fast footwork.

After boxing with Fitzsimmons in Terre Haute, Indiana in late February, on March 1, 1903, Jeffries and Fitzsimmons traveled to New York to negotiate with Corbett.

Jeffries and Corbett agreed to a 20-round bout using five-ounce gloves, with either man able to wear soft bandages, but the wraps were to be put on in the ring in full view of the audience and to the satisfaction of the referee. The rematch was tentatively scheduled to take place in California in June or July 1903.

As they were leaving, Fitzsimmons said to Corbett, "I'm going to train Jeffries for this fight, Jim." Fitz would take a position as a Jeffries trainer and sparring partner.[238]

In the meantime, Jeffries and Fitzsimmons continued their money-making exhibitions. On March 2, 1903, in Philadelphia, they sparred 3 fast 2-minute rounds in pleasing style. There was much excitement amongst the crowd, although there were a number of empty seats, demonstrating that exhibitions were not the draw that the real thing was. One said, "Both men were in surprisingly good physical condition, although Jeffries was, of

[235] *Louisville Courier-Journal*, February 10, 1903.
[236] *Richmond Evening Item*, February 21, 1903.
[237] *National Police Gazette*, February 14, March 28, 1903.
[238] *National Police Gazette*, February 28, April 4, 1903.

course, a trifle corpulent, but the speed they exhibited in their six minutes of give and take work electrified the crowd." Jeff was looking quicker with his hands and feet, and more skillful, but not quite as powerful. Of course, he always held back his power in sparring and exhibitions. Another said, "There is no denying the fact that Jeffries and Fitzsimmons are the greatest fighters of this age."

2,000 people crowded into the armory at Chester, Pennsylvania on March 3 to watch Jeff and Fitz in their 3-round exhibition. Unfortunately, some of the rear seats fell with a crash, carrying many men to the floor. One suffered a broken leg.

Jeff and Fitz again exhibited in Philadelphia on March 4 as part of a larger charity show that included boxers Philadelphia Jack O'Brien, Peter Maher, Tom Sharkey, and Kid McCoy.[239]

On March 6, the Jeffries-Corbett fight was pushed back to August, interestingly enough, at the behest of Corbett. Jim wanted sufficient time to train, and he also wanted to finish out his own theatrical contracts, which probably had become more lucrative now that he was matched to fight for the title again.

In *Two Fisted Jeffries*, Jeff said that while in Philly, they received a telegram saying that Bob's wife Rose Julian Fitzsimmons had come down with pneumonia and was seriously ill. They closed their show and Bob returned to their Coney Island home.

Rose Fitzsimmons eventually died of pneumonia on April 17, 1903.[240]

Two months after Rose Fitzsimmons' death, in June, the papers announced that Bob Fitzsimmons was engaged to actress Julia Gifford. She was wearing a diamond solitaire ring. Bob admitted it was a case of love at first sight. "She's a dear little thing. I love her and she loves me. I know it, so what could I do?"[241]

[239] *Philadelphia Public Ledger, Philadelphia Press, Philadelphia Inquirer*, March 2-4, 1903; *National Police Gazette*, March 21, 28, 1903.
[240] *Police Gazette*, June 13, July 4, 1903; *Two Fisted Jeffries* at 221.
[241] *Chicago Daily Inter Ocean*, June 19, 1903.

CHAPTER 11

Championship Trainer

Bob Fitzsimmons was convinced that Jim Jeffries would defeat Jim Corbett, again calling Jeff the greatest fighter ever. Jeffries-Corbett II was set for August 14, 1903, in San Francisco.

In June, Jeffries began preliminary training work under Bill Delaney's direction at Harbin Springs, California. He would continue to do so until Fitzsimmons arrived. However, reports were that Jeff was not doing much and refused to do more until Bob arrived. Fitz was in Chicago, apparently courting his new lady, actress Julia Gifford.[242]

Fitzsimmons said Jeffries was much faster with his footwork than he was when last seen on the east coast. He said Corbett would find a much-improved man, one who would quickly catch up with him. He predicted that Jeff would win inside of 10 rounds.[243]

On July 25, 1903, at the Palace Hotel in San Francisco, the recently widowed 40-year-old Bob Fitzsimmons got married again, to 23-year-old Julia Gifford. His best man was George Dawson.[244]

Fitzsimmons and His Bride at the Wedding Dinner.

A couple days later, Bob and his new wife left for Harbin Springs, where he would help train Jeffries.

In late July, a bear badly bit Jeffries. One of the boys kept a bear named Brownie chained up near the hotel. One day, Jeff boxed with the bear for fun, but he must have hit it a little too hard, because the bear then attacked,

[242] *Police Gazette*, June 6, 20, 27, July 4, 1903.
[243] *Police Gazette*, July 11, 18, 1903.
[244] *San Francisco Chronicle, Muncie Morning Star*, July 26, 1903.

biting his wrist and then left calf. The bear chewed holes in Jeff's leg before the pugilist got away.

Fitz attempted to sew up the wound with needle and thread but found the skin so tough that the needle failed to puncture it. Therefore, according to one source, he used a hammer to drive it through. Another said Fitz used a knife to cut holes for the needle.[245]

Unfortunately, soon thereafter, Jeff became feverish and broke out in inflamed sores. His leg swelled and was black up to the knee.[246]

However, the leg soon began healing.

Jeffries was out of training only for a short while. He was back training again on July 31. Fitzsimmons teased Jeff about his thinning hairline, saying that soon he would look like he and Delaney did.

Jeff wrestled with the 203-pound Fitzsimmons, tugging, pushing, pulling, and leaning on him for seven minutes straight, until Bob asked for time to be called. Afterwards, Jeff laughingly said to Bob, "You're pretty strong for a little fellow." Bob told Jeff that if he tried leaning on Corbett, Jim would rub his hand over his face. Jeff replied that he would bet that Jim never would put his hand in his face, fearing the consequences.[247]

Fitzsimmons said Jeffries would have no trouble in disposing of Corbett because Jeff was the world's greatest fighter, could hit a tremendous blow, and "there is no doubt that his blows will gradually knock Corbett into a state of helplessness." He spoke from experience. Jeffries was a 2 to 1 and even 3 to 1 betting favorite.[248]

On August 1, Jeffries went on a short run, and boxed for the first time in camp with Bob Fitzsimmons, as well as Joe Kennedy and brother Jack Jeffries, 2 rounds with each man. Fitz sparred in a lively fashion, attempting

---

[245] *San Francisco Call*, August 2, 1903.
[246] *Police Gazette*, August 8, 1903; *My Life and Battles* at 51-52.
[247] *San Francisco Call*, *San Francisco Bulletin*, August 1, 1903.
[248] *Police Gazette*, August 15, 1903.

to mimic Corbett's tactics, quickly moving away and then stopping suddenly to slip in a left swing or jab.[249]

With his leg healed, Jeffries was doing the work of three men. On the 2nd, after exercising for a couple of hours with the pulleys, light dumbbells, punching bag, and skipping rope, he boxed 2 rounds each with Fitz, Joe Kennedy, and Jack Jeffries. Fitzsimmons was not a believer in love taps, and he and Jeffries mixed things in a lively fashion. Bob kept Jeff chasing him constantly, emulating Corbett's style.[250]

On August 3, Jeff and Fitz sparred 3 fast rounds.

> He continued to hustle the big Cornishman about without a let up. At the end of the third round Fitzsimmons came reeling from the ring and, exhausted, sank into a chair while flecks of crimson showed on his lips and dropping to the pink tights that he wore, bespattered them for the first time in many a day. Jeffries, though not even breathing to excess, also received a slight cut in his mouth. The go was a very fast one.

---

[249] *San Francisco Evening Post*, August 1, 1903; *San Francisco Call*, August 2, 1903.
[250] *San Francisco Call*, August 4, 1903.

After that bout, Jeff sparred 6 more rounds, alternating rounds between his brother Jack and Joe Kennedy. Jeffries "is undoubtedly faster at the present time than at any in his career."

One man who observed their sparring that day said Jeffries fought like a demon, tearing into Fitzsimmons like a cyclone. They went at it, and Fitz was panting for wind after 3 rounds. Jeff was tireless and strong. This observer predicted that Jeffries was certain to sap Corbett's vitality and reduce his agility to a point where he could get at him and put him out. If hard hitters like Sharkey, Ruhlin, and Fitz could not damage Jeffries, then Corbett could not do so either.

Another report said all three sparring partners were winded, while Jeff was fresh and strong. Fitz was Jeff's most ardent admirer. He slapped him on the back and announced that he was unbeatable. "What surprises me more than anything is that I made so good a fight against you as I put up. Your strength is overpowering and your stamina so great that I do not understand how any man can hope to cope with you."[251]

On August 4, Jeffries took a short walk and run, worked the gymnasium apparatus for an hour, and skipped rope 1,200 times. He then went 3 corking rounds with Fitzsimmons. Jeff's footwork was rapid and had improved so much that Fitz found it almost impossible to escape his rushes, even in a 25-foot training ring. They exchanged hard blows. In the 2nd round, Fitz landed a left uppercut which caused Jeff to bite his tongue slightly. At the close, Bob's mouth was bleeding. Jeff then boxed 3 rounds each with Joe Kennedy and Jack Jeffries, going at them hard, yet still finishing up fresh.[252]

On the 5th, Jeff worked 4 rounds with Fitz and 3 each with Jack and Joe. The pace was not mild, but the intensity was less than it had been.[253]

On August 6, in the evening at the Harbin Springs Music Hall, for a charity benefit performance, before a standing-room-only crowd, Jeff sparred in a lively fashion with Fitz, Kennedy, and brother Jack, 3 rounds each, for 9 total rounds. First Jeff sparred with Fitz, engaging in fast and fierce exchanges that left Bob well winded at the finish. Jeffries was so fast with both hands and feet that Fitzsimmons found it difficult to either sidestep or duck his rushes.

> Jeff was fast and forced Fitz to break ground continually. Using at times his low crouch and again standing erect, he frequently got home a punch that left its mark. Fitz stabbed back hard, but his piston-like drives that found lodgment had only the effect of stimulating the champion to greater speed. In the second round a ripping left uppercut from Jeff took Fitz in the ribs and his eyes rolled for a moment. The final round was the fastest yet put up here between the

[251] *San Francisco Evening Post*, August 3-5, 7, 1903; *San Francisco Evening Post*, August 4, 1903; *San Francisco Examiner*, August 4, 5, 1903.
[252] *San Francisco Call*, August 5, 1903; *San Francisco Evening Post*, August 4, 1903.
[253] *San Francisco Call*, August 6, 7, 1903.

two men, and Jeff on his feet and with his arms acquitted himself somewhat after the fashion of a lightweight.[254]

Speaking of their sparring, Fitzsimmons said that he tried to hustle Jeff, "but it was like punching at a mountain. You can't hurt the concentrated mass of energy and muscle, no matter how you attempt to take him on." Bob said Corbett could not keep away from Jeffries.

He did the dancing master's act at Coney Island, but it did not avail him. Jeffries now knows his style, and will wade into the slaughter conscious of the fact that he will not be hurt. He knows he can beat down Corbett's guard, and will then follow with a punch to the jaw. … You know I know what I am talking about. Jeffries' wallops hurt.

[254] *San Francisco Examiner*, August 8, 1903.

Bob also said Jeff was much improved and even better than when he last fought him.

> I have found that he has developed speed and is clever. Mark what I tell you, Corbett will have some trouble in getting to Jeff. ... You might as well talk of a rabbit crushing a grizzly. You can't hurt that monster. Corbett may cut him up a bit like a mosquito, but his punches will not go beneath the skin.

Delaney said that at between 225 and 230 pounds, Jeffries was as hard as iron, clever and fast, and his condition perfect. [255]

After working with Jeffries for only a week, Fitzsimmons left with his wife on the 7th. Some speculated that his departure was a sign that he was not too happy with Jeff buffeting him about so much in their bout at the benefit the night before. Jeff looked speedy and strong as an ox. "Crafty and cunning as is Bob Fitzsimmons, he was only a boy in the hands of Jeff."

However, the rumors were groundless, for there was no friction. Fitz actually wanted to do more boxing, but Jeffries said he was satisfied with his condition and had sparred enough. Fitz said, "Just think! I came 3,000 miles to box ten light rounds with Jeffries. ... I thought he ought to have boxed more, and so did Delaney, but Jeffries had a different opinion, and he had his way. Jeffries is very stubborn in his views, and when he gets his mind made up there is no changing it."

Contradicting Fitzsimmons, Delaney said he was happy with Jeff's condition and did not want him to risk injury either to his hands or from one of Bob's powerful blows. Fitz was well compensated for his time. He was paid $55 per round of sparring. Apparently, they boxed six times, 3 rounds each time, for a total of 18 rounds, which cost Jeff $1,000. Bob still was set to be the champion's second for the fight.[256]

Fitzsimmons called Jeffries the greatest fighter in the world and predicted that he would knock out Corbett.[257]

On the day of the championship fight, Fitzsimmons said,

> It will be a repetition of the Jeffries-Jackson affair. Old Peter looked just as good as Corbett does now, he was just as scientific, just as graceful in the ring and could deliver a much harder wallop than Corbett ever could and you remember what a chance he had with the champion. ... You can say that I will be behind Jeff in his corner tonight and if I ever coached in a winning corner, I have scheduled this evening to be that time.

Jack Jeffries said his brother James was stronger, faster, and harder than ever and would win by knockout. Joe Kennedy said Jeff could give him,

[255] *San Francisco Evening Post*, August 7, 1903.
[256] *San Francisco Call, San Francisco Bulletin*, August 9, 1903.
[257] *San Francisco Examiner*, August 12, 1903; *Police Gazette*, August 15, 1903.

Jack Jeffries and Bob Fitzsimmons all they could handle in 3-round doses, and there was no chance for Corbett alone to handle him for 20 rounds.[258]

Just over one year after his last title defense against Bob Fitzsimmons, on August 14, 1903 in San Francisco, the 28-year-old 225-230-pound James J. Jeffries again took on then 36-year-old (almost 37) 186-190-pound former champion James J. Corbett. 10,669 people, who generated $62,340 in gate receipts, breaking all attendance and gate records in the state of California, attended the fight. The receipts were even greater than Jeff-Fitz II, which allegedly amounted to $40,000. Only Corbett-McCoy and Jeffries-Fitzsimmons I in New York had generated more.

Fitzsimmons was one of Jeff's cornermen. The bandaging of Corbett's hands took place in the ring, which Delaney and Fitzsimmons carefully watched. Ironically, both Fitzsimmons and Delaney protested Corbett's bandages. Delaney went over and consulted Jeffries. Jeff walked over to inspect, made an examination of the wraps by feeling them, and then nodded his approval and made no objection. Jeffries did not wear hand bandages.

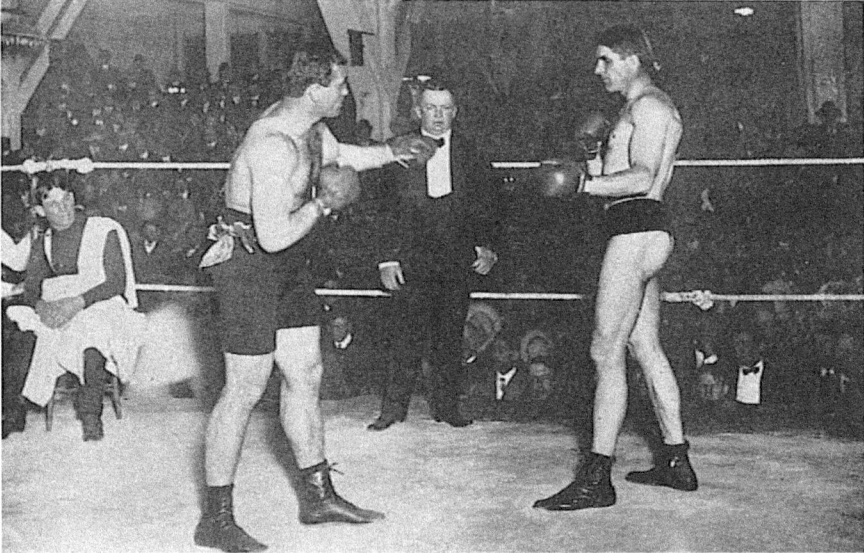

As for the fight, Jeffries relentlessly attacked from the start. He hurt Corbett with a body blow in the 2nd round, decked him in the 4th with a left hook to the body, and again in the 6th round with head and body blows. Corbett struggled valiantly, holding his ground more than usual and attempting to punch hard, and clinching more rather than using up energy with a lot of footwork. When he did move, Jeff was on top of him so quickly that Jim would punch and grab. Corbett landed several good blows in the 8th and 9th rounds, exciting the crowd, but Jeff's punches were harder and more effective. At the end of the 9th round, Fitzsimmons was begging Jeff to go out and end the fight. He was upset because Corbett had lasted 9 rounds, when Jeff had put Bob out in 8 rounds. The end came in the 10th

---

[258] *San Francisco Bulletin, San Francisco Evening Post*, August 14, 1903.

round, when Jeffries dropped Corbett with a left to the stomach. He rose, but a right to the body put him down and out for good.

Afterwards, Corbett said to Jeff, "I thought I could whip you, but I realize now my mistake. The man who can take your measure has not yet been created." He also said, "Now I want to be counted one of your admirers. You are a great fighter."

Bob Fitzsimmons told Harry Corbett, "Take him out of the ring, Harry." Jim, who was speaking with Jeffries, caught the remark, turned and said, "You mind your business or I'll punch you in the nose."

In his dressing room, Corbett said,

> Jeffries surprised me. He has made wonderful improvement. I never saw him so fast. I am certain that he was not that quick when he fought Fitzsimmons. His footwork has improved and his hitting is cleaner. He did not employ his crouch in the manner that he did in our previous contest. ...
>
> It's fifteen months gone out of my life, but I don't feel bad.... I was in perfect condition. Science cuts no figure when you are against a man of Jeffries' bulk. ... I tried to give Jeff a hard fight, and I think I did. But he's too big and powerful. No man can put him out. He's abnormal – a giant of strength. It isn't science that counts with him, because no matter how many times you land you can't put him out.... There's not a living man in the ring to-day who can put him out. He's too big and powerful – that's it, that's the whole thing. ... No man living today, nor was there ever one, has any business with Jeffries. He is in a class by himself. He is just as strong as he ever was, much cleverer and...his speed was a revelation to me. It was my ill fortune to find him at his best and I have paid the penalty.

Tommy Ryan gave Bob Fitzsimmons credit for helping to improve Jeffries' skill, which added to his already big power. "In the year since he beat Bob Fitzsimmons down and out he has added wonderful science to his enormous bulk and unbeatable strength. He could have acquired his knowledge in but one way – from Bob Fitzsimmons, with whom he toured the country and boxed almost nightly."

In the days following the fight, Corbett was complimented for his gameness. He was outclassed in weight and hitting powers, but he did not break ground as much as he had in the past. Jeffries went at him with utter disregard for his punches, confident that Corbett could not knock him out. Jeff's lack of fear made him appear even cleverer.

Even Bob Fitzsimmons, no friend of Corbett's, gave Jim credit for the game fight that he put up. "I know full well how Jeffries can hit and I think Corbett, as I have said before, made a great showing."

Jeff said that his favorite punch was the left hook to the body, for he had defeated Ruhlin, Fitzsimmons, and Corbett with that punch.[259]

[259] *San Francisco Call, San Francisco Evening Post*, August 17, 1903; *Police Gazette*, September 12, 1903; *San Francisco Bulletin*, August 23, 24, 1903.

CHAPTER 12

Three-Division Champion

Although George Gardner had been claiming the world light-heavyweight championship crown, most believed that the highly respected, skilled, and hard-punching Jack Root had won that title with an April 1903 decisive 10-round decision over Kid McCoy, decking him multiple times.[260] However, Gardner already had knocked out Root in the 17th round in August 1902, Root's only loss, so he may have had the superior claim. No matter, because on July 4, 1903, in Fort Erie, Ontario, Canada, just outside Buffalo, 25-year-old 165-pound Gardner, (37-4-3), went on to win or solidify his claim to the world light-heavyweight title with a KO12 over 165-pound Jack Root (44-1-1). In a fierce fight, Gardner hit harder, was more aggressive, and had speed. Gardner's body attack was impressive. In the 12th round, when Root attempted a left, Gardner's right went inside it and dropped him. He rose but was too weak to proceed and the referee stopped it. Jim Corbett held Gardner "in great esteem and he thinks the Lowell man is one of the cleverest fighters in the business at his weight."[261]

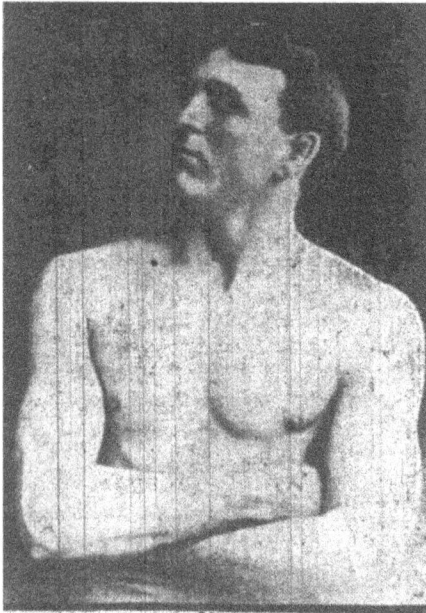

GEORGE GARDNER

GEORGE GARDNER,
Winner of yesterday's battle at Fort
Erie, for light heavyweight
championship.

---

[260] Root easily handled McCoy, dropping him in almost every round. *Police Gazette*, May 9, 1903.
[261] *Police Gazette*, July 18, 25, 1903, August 8, 1903. The Root-Gardner fight was successfully filmed by polyscope.

Having stopped Root twice, via KO17 and KO12, Gardner was the only man to have beaten Root. Footage exists of one of their bouts, although it is not entirely clear which one it is. The footage reveals that Gardner was taller, with longer arms. Gardner threw sharp, quick punches, and utilized his height and reach well, both when moving back and when attacking. Root was a tough fighter also, throwing hard combinations, looking his best when advancing, putting up a competitive fight. However, eventually, Gardner came over with two consecutive rights that dropped Root. Gardner dropped him again with a right off a double jab. George again attacked with a series of quick rights and lefts to drop him a third time. Root just missed beating the count.[262]

Bob Fitzsimmons scheduled a world light-heavyweight title challenge against champion Gardner to take place in late 1903. If he won, he would be the first man to win championships in three different weight classes.

When Fitzsimmons tipped the scales at 203 pounds in late July, Gardner insisted that Bob make 168 pounds for their fight, and Bob agreed. Some thought that losing so much weight might weaken Fitzsimmons.

In September 1903, the legendary John L. Sullivan said, "There is a great boxer in Bob Fitzsimmons, and people may call him an old man, but, in my opinion, he can defeat any one in the world, bar Jeffries." Sullivan said his opinion included George Gardner.[263]

GEORGE GARDNER

ROBERT FITZSIMMONS

On Wednesday September 30, 1903 at Philadelphia's Washington Club, in a scheduled 6-round tune-up bout, before a crowd of a couple thousand, Bob Fitzsimmons took on "giant" Irish heavyweight Con Coughlin. Heralded as the Irish champion, Coughlin had fought in an amateur heavyweight tournament in Philadelphia. He won a decision over Jack McCormick on a foul but lost in the finals. Joe Butler subsequently knocked him out, quite some time ago.

---

[262] Contrasting the footage, the *Police Gazette* said only one knockdown took place in their second bout. It is possible that the footage was actually of their previous bout, when the *Gazette* said three knockdowns took place in the 12th, although if true, it erroneously reported that body shots led to the knockdowns and that Root's corner stopped the bout.
[263] *Buffalo Commercial*, September 23, 1903; *Detroit Free Press*, September 27, 1903.

1st round

As was often the case with a Fitzsimmons fight, the bout did not last very long. For 30 seconds, Fitz feinted, trying to draw a lead, but Con was wary. Fitz feinted him back into a corner, and in a sharp exchange that followed, Fitzsimmons dropped Coughlin with a vicious left flush on the jaw. Con barely beat Referee William Rocap's count.

A right to the body dropped Coughlin the second time, but he got up quickly at three. Bob landed some lefts to the body which hurt. Fitz again backed him to the ropes, and after landing another pair of left-handed wallops, Con looked like he had enough.

Bob held his hands high above his head to call attention to the fact that he thought it should be stopped, but Con would not quit.

Fitz landed a left to the body and Coughlin went down again. Bob had him at his mercy, and since it was apparent to all that another blow would put Con into dreamland, his manager humanely gave up the contest on behalf of his man, throwing up the sponge. It was over at 2 minutes into the 1st round.[264]

Joe Grim, the Marvel of the Ring.

Two weeks later, in another 6-round no decision tune-up bout, on Wednesday October 14, 1903 at Philadelphia's Southern Athletic Club, before a crowd of 5,000, Bob Fitzsimmons fought Italian Joe Grim (32-40-15) (whose real name was Saverio Giannone). Grim was a trial horse known for his durability. Although he usually lost to top fighters, he almost always lasted the distance. Grim's record included newspaper decision losses to Philadelphia Jack O'Brien, Bob Thompson, George Cole, Kid Carter, and Joe Walcott, and a LDQ3 to Peter Maher (low blow).

---

[264] *San Francisco Evening Post*, July 25, 1903; *Philadelphia Inquirer, Philadelphia Public Ledger, New York World*, October 1, 1903; *Police Gazette*, October 17, 1903. Some reported it was stopped at 2:52 of the round.

The *Police Gazette* reported that Fitz made a good showing, and although Grim was badly punished and floored at least nine times, he lasted the 6 rounds. Bob dropped him in the 2nd round with a left to the wind. In the 3rd, Fitz dropped him with a right to the chin. Joe arose bleeding from the nose. In the 4th, Bob rained blows upon him and had Grim groggy. A solid punch to the face dropped him. Twice more Fitz decked him but could not finish him. In the 5th, Bob knocked Grim down twice in succession, and again at the bell Fitz floored Grim with a right under the heart. The final round was exciting, with Grim landing a hard right that almost dropped Bob. A second later though, Fitz landed a right that dropped Grim again. He made it to the final bell.

Some reported that Grim had been down over 20 times, one saying 24 times.

According to the *Philadelphia Record*, before the fight, Grim made a speech in the ring, saying that Fitz was trying to scare him by keeping him waiting, but declared that he would not be frightened and Bob would have to knock him out to make him quit. He kept his word, for there was plenty of opportunity to quit had he been so inclined.

Fitz earned $1,000 and Grim $600. Both had demanded and received their money before the bout, which may have caused the long delay before Bob appeared.

When they faced one another, the size disparity was marked. Fitz towered a head above the Italian. Yet, Grim was as agile as a cat. He had a shiftiness that had fooled all of the big men he had met, including Jack O'Brien, Peter Maher, Joe Walcott, and Kid Carter.

For 3 rounds, Fitz chased him around the ring with strong feints, and now and then landed, mostly lightly. Bob wore a puzzled smile. Grim adopted evasive tactics from the start and merely tried to stay. He was not a hitter, mostly using open hands. Bob allowed himself to be cuffed a number of times in order to draw him on, but the wily Grim could not be drawn out. Still, Grim went down twice in the 2nd and once in the 3rd.

In the 4th round, Fitz began to warm up and really got down to business. He often landed a straight left, bloodying Grim's nose and mouth, but found great difficulty in opening Joe up for a right on the jaw. When Grim found that Fitz's long left could land in spite of everything, he tried covering up and crouching. Grim carried himself low, and Bob often missed over the top. Still, Bob succeeded in reaching his face a few times.

JOE GRIMM.

Fitz eventually broke him of his crouching habit with a few hard right swings into the kidneys. Bob seemed afraid to hit hard to the head, fearful of breaking his hands. One of the body blows dropped Grim. Twice more, Grim went down.

When Grim found that things were getting too hot, he began going down without a blow, about half a dozen times in the last two rounds, as Fitzsimmons was now doing his best to stop him. Grim received some hard ones to the face and the jaw, which dropped him as well. The local lad did all he could to prevent Fitz from stopping him.

In total, Grim went down 20 times, often to avoid punishment. Grim was down twice in the 2nd, once in the 3rd, three times in the 4th, six times in the 5th, and eight times in the 6th. To his credit, few others could have taken such blows and shown so little effect from them.

The *Philadelphia Inquirer* said Grim "took a terrific drubbing – enough to have killed most men, but the sledge-hammer blows of the old champion seemed to have no lasting effect." Bob dropped him often, but the Italian wonder arose quickly and never was close to being counted out. Grim went down 8 times in the last round alone.[265]

BOB FITZSIMMONS

In late October, Fitzsimmons said he was weighing 176 pounds and would make the 168-pound limit for the late-November title fight against Gardner without any trouble.[266]

The big fight of late 1903 was the world light heavyweight title fight between Bob Fitzsimmons and George Gardner, set to be held in San Francisco. Fitz was going for his third world title in three different weight divisions at a time when there were only a small handful of weight classes recognized: no super or junior divisions like today. The fight garnered a great deal of interest, discussion, and debate because it was considered to be a very good match-up. The bout certainly had a big-fight atmosphere surrounding it.

The 5'11 ½" middleweight Gardner had suffered an 1899 LKOby18 to Jimmy Handler,[267] but scored a 1900 KO3 win over Handler to avenge the loss. Gardner sandwiched a 1900 14th round disqualification win over black George Byers between two 15-round draws with him fought in 1899 and 1900. He knocked out Bill Hanrahan in the 9th round.

---

[265] *Philadelphia Record, Philadelphia Inquirer, New York World*, October 15, 1903; *Police Gazette*, October 31, 1903.
[266] *Chicago Tribune*, October 23, 1903.
[267] *National Police Gazette*, November 4, 1899.

Gardner defeated the well-respected, exciting, and hard-punching Kid Carter four times, including 1900 WDQ19; 1901 KO18[268] and KO8; and 1902 W6.[269]

In 1900, Gardner won the middleweight championship of England with a WDQ4 over black Frank Craig, who clinched throughout and threw Gardner down.[270] Gardner lost a 1901 20-round decision to Joe Walcott,[271] but avenged the loss with a 1902 20-round decision victory over Walcott.

Gardner had a 1902 LDQby7 to Jack Root, but avenged the loss that year with a KO17 over Root. However, Gardner then suffered a 20-round decision loss to the larger heavyweight, 182-pound Jack Johnson.

Gardner also had a 1902 W6 Billy Stift; and 1903 4-round tame no-contest with black heavyweight Bob Armstrong, KO7 Al Weinig, and KO1 Peter Maher.[272]

On May 13, 1903, in Louisville, Kentucky, 164-168-pound George Gardner and 176-178-pound Marvin Hart fought an action-packed, exciting contest, but after the 12th round, Hart retired with a broken hand.

Gardner followed the Hart victory with his KO12 over Root to win undisputed recognition as the world light-heavyweight champion.[273]

Although initially the legendary Fitzsimmons was the 10 to 6 betting favorite with the public, most of the boxing experts were picking the much younger and friskier, prime Gardner to win. Fitzsimmons was 40 years old, and many thought he was even older. They figured that no man, no matter how great, can defeat father time. Bob seemed a bit lackluster in his sparring with 220-pound Joe Kennedy and 180-pound Sam Berger, showing the wear and tear of many years of boxing. He was "anything but the Fitzsimmons of old." Bob would have a good day and a bad one. Some wondered whether the beating he endured in the last Jeffries fight had affected him. Furthermore, for the first time in nine years, he was compelled to make weight, 168 pounds at 3 p.m. on the day of the fight. This time he would have to prove his weight. He had been weighing 190 pounds just a few months earlier, and some wondered whether the removal of all that weight might have drained him and would affect him in a 20-round bout. Bob had been doing a great deal of running to lose weight, and his feet were badly blistered and sore. He had been suffering from colds.

---

[268] "Gardiner showed that he is a cleverer, a cleaner, harder puncher, and by far the better ring general." Gardiner dropped Carter 8 times over 18 rounds. Both weighed less than 165 pounds. *National Police Gazette*, September 21, 1901.

[269] The Carter fight was rough and fierce, but Gardner had the advantage in each round. Gardner cut him up, staggered him with uppercuts, and almost had him out in the final round. *Anaconda Standard*, December 30, 1902.

[270] *National Police Gazette*, October 6, 1900.

[271] Gardner weighed 158 pounds to Walcott's 146. One report said it was a close fight all the way and many felt it should have been a draw. *Los Angeles Express*, September 28, 1901. Another report gave the impression that Walcott was the aggressor, dropped Gardner once early, and finished more strongly. *National Police Gazette*, October 19, 1901.

[272] Boxrec.com; Cyberboxingzone.com.

[273] Root's prior bouts included: 1900 D6 Tommy Ryan, KO1 Dan Creedon, and KO9 George Byers; 1902 WDQ7 George Gardner, KO2 Billy Stift, LKOby17 Gardner, W6 Kid Carter, W6 Marvin Hart, and W10 Kid McCoy.

His legs were noticeably lean, and even his wondrous shoulders did not look as formidable as they did a few years ago.[274]

On the other hand, Gardner was just as tall and allegedly had a one-inch reach advantage at 76 inches. The young but fairly experienced Gardner (with 45 bouts) looked bigger and better than at any time in his career. He had speed, power, skill, footwork, and condition. He was on a 6-fight win streak, including victories over Billy Stift, Kid Carter, Al Weinig, Peter Maher, Marvin Hart, and Jack Root, and held a victory over the highly respected Joe Walcott.

A native of Ireland, but living in Lowell, Massachusetts, the 26-year-old Gardner was described as "cool, crafty, a two-handed fighter, carrying a wicked punch in either fist, clever enough to engage in long range boxing with the best of them, and rugged, strong and willing to mix it up at any stage of the game." Another report said,

> Anyone who has never seen Gardner box has no idea what a wonderfully clever boxer he really is. He is without doubt the best man of his weight in the world when it comes down to science and strength combined....
>
> Gardner is a magnificent two handed fighter, moves free and easy without displaying any great effort. His coolness in delivering a blow and his alertness in blocking a return compares favorably with the wonderful work of Young Griffo when he was in his prime.[275]

TRAINING FACE OF FITZSIMMONS, WHO WILL FIGHT GEORGE GARDNER FOR THE LIGHT HEAVY WEIGHT CHAMPIONSHIP OF THE WORLD.

[274] *San Francisco Examiner*, November 17, 1903.
[275] *Louisville Courier-Journal*, May 10, 1903, May 11, 1903, May 12, 1903, May 13, 1903; *Louisville Times*, May 12, 1903.

LIGHT HEAVYWEIGHT CHAMPION GEORGE GARDNER BOXING WITH LIGHTWEIGHT CHAMPION JIMMY BRITT.

FITZSIMMONS GETTING AWAY FROM A DAN-GEROUS SWING.

Spider Kelly was certain that Gardner would beat Fitzsimmons. Tim McGrath said Gardner could beat clever men as well as sluggers. DeWitt Van Court said Fitz had met his match in a young, clever, dashing man. Eddie Hanlon said Gardner looked too big and strong, and he was a man who could take an awful punch and still keep going strong. Aurelia Herrera said George would wear Bob out. Toby Irwin said Gardner had speed, condition, and good hands, and Fitz would not be able to keep up the pace. There was a general feeling that the young and frisky Gardner would wear Fitz down. Bob McArthur said Gardner was the coming wonder for sure.

Sandy Ferguson had once been a Fitzsimmons sparring partner for 14 weeks. He recently had sparred with Gardner, so he was well equipped to assess the match-up. Ferguson said, "This fellow Gardner is the fastest fellow I ever sparred. I look to see him knock Fitz out inside of ten rounds."

Alex Greggains, who was training and sparring with George, said Gardner would be the only man in the fight, for he was very fast, trained to the minute, very confident, and with every reason to be. He had improved wonderfully during the past year and had grown 10 pounds bigger. Greggains had sparred with Fitz many years before, when Bob was preparing for the Maher fight in New Orleans (in 1892), so he knew how to coach Gardner on the pitfalls he needed to avoid. Alex said Fitz was only human and was past his best. "I believe that Gardner, in his present shape, would have been a match for Fitzsimmons the best day the Cornishman ever saw and I think Gardner will put Fitzsimmons away in a few rounds, because Fitzsimmons is only an imitation of the Fitzsimmons that was fighting a few years ago."

George Gardner had seen Fitzsimmons box and was not afraid. "Now don't you think that Fitzsimmons is going to walk up and bang me the way he did Jeffries the last time. He is not going to do it, for I won't let him." George had a great coach, and had the advantage of having seen Fitz fight, whereas Fitzsimmons had never seen him box. "I have seen Bob fight and made a study of his style, but he has never seen me box."

Regardless, age never had been a detriment to Fitzsimmons. In the past, he could look so-so in training, not feel well, or be dealing with injuries or ailments, but perform at a high level in the actual fights and still find a way to win. Fitz rose to the occasion. Bob said, "I have something the matter with me every time I fight. I really think if I went in the ring feeling right once I might kill some one." Some said that only heavyweight champion Jeffries could beat him.

> The rules which apply to other pugilists and other athletes do not seem to apply in his case. ... Fitzsimmons is a creature of surprises. ... His opponent may appear to be having all the best of the argument and Fitz may be staggering around and seemingly ready to fall when he will turn the tables completely with one little shift or jolt that may be sent in so covertly and from such short range that two-thirds of the crowd will fail to see it.

There were some who said that although Gardner was a very good, well-rounded fighter, Fitz was special, the best of his weight alive. Bob's sparring partner Sam Berger said Gardner had never met a man like Fitz and would not touch him at all. Further, "You may think him old but watch Gardner when Fitz lands either hand. It's the worst wallop in the ring still."

James Jeffries picked Fitzsimmons. "I have fought him and know that he is a great fighter. In fact, I think he is the hardest proposition I have ever encountered. He is a wonderful hitter, and is on to all the tricks of the game. He is an excellent ring general." That said, even Jeff admitted that like other professions, a fighter cannot always last. Fitz's hands were not what they once were, and he had endured many hard fights. Still, Jeff said, "I know of no other fighter who can hit a harder blow than Fitzsimmons."

A couple days before the fight, Gardner money was pouring in, bringing Fitz down to just a 10 to 9 favorite. James Corbett said he was betting at least $500 on Gardner.

TRAINING QUARTER "SNAPS" OF GEORGE GARDNER AND ROBERT FITZSIMMONS, BOXERS WHO ARE TO BATTLE FOR THE LIGHT-HEAVYWEIGHT CHAMPIONSHIP.

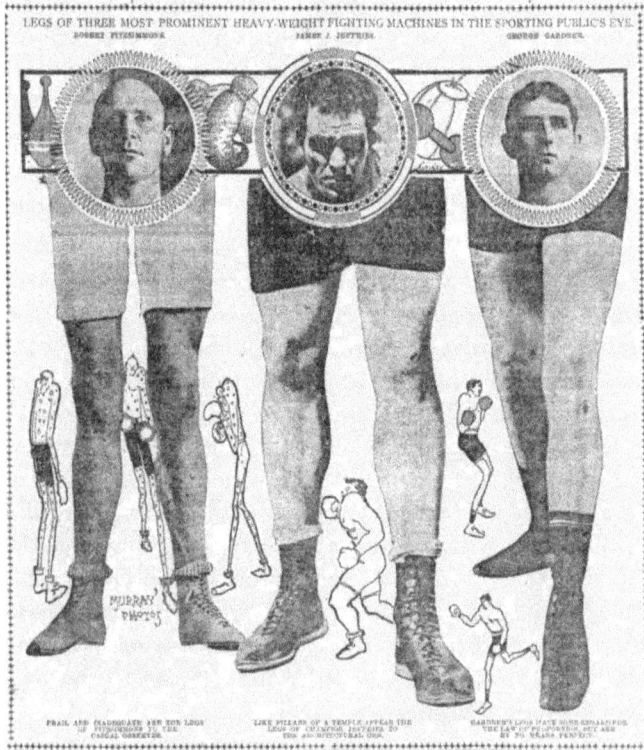

LEGS OF THREE MOST PROMINENT HEAVY-WEIGHT FIGHTING MACHINES IN THE SPORTING PUBLIC'S EYE.
ROBERT FITZSIMMONS.   JAMES J. JEFFRIES.   GEORGE GARDNER.

FRAIL AND INADEQUATE ARE THE LEGS OF FITZSIMMONS TO THE CASUAL OBSERVER.   LIKE PILLARS OF A TEMPLE APPEAR THE LEGS OF CHAMPION JEFFRIES TO THE ARCHITECTURAL EYE.   GARDNER'S LEGS HAVE SOME REGARD FOR THE LAW OF PROPORTION, BUT ARE BY NO MEANS PERFECT.

216

Gardner predicted that his strength would wear Bob down. He had bet several hundred dollars on himself. The day of the fight, he said he was in perfect condition and confident that he would stop Fitz within the limit. "I know that Fitzsimmons is a crafty ring general, but I am sure that I know his style and his favorite punches, and that I can cover up for his attacks, and give him some punches that will be new to him." He also said, "If I am successful in winning from the old man, as I know I will, I will issue a challenge to Champion Jeffries."

On the other hand, Fitzsimmons said the odds were about right. His body was stiff, but he would do his best regardless. He was not predicting victory, but would give anyone who bet on him a run for their money. "I can't say how long the fight will last, but as long as I am on my feet those present will admit that they saw a fight."

Gardner insisted on soft surgical bandages, not hard bandages, fearful that he would be cut-up the way Jeffries was in his last bout with Fitzsimmons. He was going to have a man with Bob when he put the bandages on, and he would examine them in the ring as well to make sure they were all right. "Bandages sometimes harden up when they are on too long." Gardner also wanted to make sure Fitz did not use any surgical plaster the way he did with Jeffries.

Referee Eddie Graney said Fitz liked to use surgical tape, and Gardner had agreed to it. The men agreed to break when ordered to do so, but would protect themselves at all times, including while breaking. The contest was set to begin at 9:20 p.m.[276]

On Wednesday November 25, 1903 at San Francisco's Mechanics' Pavilion, under the auspices of the Yosemite Club, 40-year-old former world middleweight and heavyweight champion Bob Fitzsimmons, 64-5-14, took on 26-year-old world light heavyweight champion George Gardner, 38-4-3. Both weighed in at 168 pounds at 3 p.m. on the day of the fight, neither causing the scale's balance bar to move. They agreed to ordinary surgical tape, without the application of collodion or any liquid which would have a hardening effect.

It was anticipated that before the men were introduced in the ring that Philadelphia Jack O'Brien would climb through the ropes to challenge the winner. However, his actual challenge was to fight any man at 158 pounds. He did not want to go out of his weight class, at least not at that point.

A crowd of about 6,000 was on hand. Fitzsimmons approached the ring at 9:05 p.m. He entered first, wearing purple trunks with a belt of American flag colors, and lavender socks. He put on green gloves. Bill Delaney, Sam Berger, Joe Kennedy, and Johnny Croll, Jr. assisted him. He was the crowd favorite, receiving an ovation.

Gardner came on after Bob. He wore emerald trunks, green belt and socks, with a bathrobe over his shoulders. Alex Greggains, Billy Pierce, Harry Foley, and Dave Barry advised him. Jack Johnson was in attendance.

They agreed to fight straight Queensberry rules. Announcer Billy Jordan let the crowd know that the men would break at the referee's order and protect themselves in the breakaway. He then howled out his well-known "Let 'er go," and the gong sounded.

1st round

Each tried to feint the other into leading. They sparred cautiously. Gardner danced and ducked in lively fashion. The pace was slow, with both men exercising great care. Gardner seemed very nervous, while Bob was cool. George was a bit more aggressive, though, and slightly opened Bob's eye with a left jab. Fitz appeared to be bothered by a lingering cold. However, Fitzsimmons landed a stinging jab to the jaw, another left to the jaw and right to the stomach and then sent Gardner's head back with a left hook to the jaw. One opined that honors were even. Another said the advantage was slightly with Fitzsimmons.

2nd round

Both were cautious again, with little vim. Gardner rushed Bob to the ropes with a series of body blows. Bob puffed, and his motions were slow. Gardner was rushing Bob around the ring, but there was not much force to the majority of the blows he landed. Bob was content to defend, elude, and

[276] *San Francisco Bulletin*, November 10, 11, 20, 24, 25, 1903; *San Francisco Examiner*, November 17, 20, 23-25, 1903; *San Francisco Chronicle*, November 24, 25, 1903; *San Francisco Call*, November 25, 1903.

counter. The *Call* said it was a comparatively even round, with the advantage, if any, being with Gardner.

3rd round

Fitz did not appear to be trying hard. However, near the end of the round, Fitzsimmons suddenly woke up to the fact he was in a fight and stopped Gardner's rush with a fierce left to the face and a terrific smashing right to the jaw. Bob finally had decided to let Gardner taste his power. After a clinch, they exchanged some hard blows, and Bob rushed him to the ropes with a series of short-arm smashes. Bob was no longer sparring but firing in hooking blows. He landed a left to the face and a right to the body. Fitz had given a flash of his old fire. He drew George on, and Gardner fought back hard. It was Fitz's round.

The *Examiner* and *Bulletin* said the contest was even through the first 3 rounds. Bob's right to the jaw in the 3rd round was the fiercest punch of the fight thus far.

4th round

Gardner worked Fitzsimmons to the ropes, forcing matters. A right to the body seemed to hurt Bob, for he clinched to save himself.

However, Fitz finally acted like himself and suddenly rushed at George and showered in hard blows. Fitzsimmons landed a left hook and right to the jaw that dropped Gardner like a log.

George took an 8-count as the crowd cheered.

Bob pounced on him with right and left short-arm swings to the body and head, rocking Gardner's head from side to side with his savage hooks, beating him back to the ropes. Gardner reeled about the ring like a badly beaten fighter. The audience was in an uproar. Gardner saved himself by clinching.

While in a clinch, Fitz half wrestled and half punched him to the floor with a vicious right. After Gardner rose, Bob doubled him up with a left to the body and continued battering him along the ropes with frightful blows. Gardner was all but out on the ropes but was saved by the bell. The audience tumult for Fitz was tremendous.

Afterwards, one reported that Bob said he badly hurt his left hand in this round. Another said Bob claimed he broke his right.

5th round

Bob kept a good pace for the first minute. Gardner was still dazed from the previous round. Fitzsimmons floored Gardner with a short but powerful left hook on the jaw. Bob landed the punch with so much force and forward momentum that he fell forward, and Gardner, in attempting to grab, in part pulled Bob down over himself as George went down in a heap onto his back. Fitz jumped up at once.

Gardner was down for 8 or 9 seconds. He rose, appearing hurt and weary. After Gardner rose, Fitzsimmons mauled him with left jabs and rights that had steam. Fitz did all the hitting, doubling him up with savage digs in the stomach and beating his head from side to side with short snappy hooks. Gardner was hurt but moved around the ring and clinched repeatedly in order to survive. He held on until he recovered. Gardner's nose was badly bleeding.

Fitzsimmons grew tired from his own exertions in attempting to finish Gardner, and his blows became taps. Some thought that Fitz appeared to be playing with Gardner as a cat does a mouse and allowed him to recover. They could not understand why Bob began waiting. He even let George hit him and did not try to hit back. Fitz was laughing and stalling, and some thought he was trying to create the impression of being tired. Others thought he actually was fatigued.

Gardner rallied and began roughing it in the clinches and hitting Bob's body and kidneys. George took the offensive, but his blows had little force and did no damage. Bob had the crowd guessing as to whether he was shamming or actually tired.

The *Bulletin* said Bob had broken one of the knuckles in his right hand in the previous round. He did not reveal this until after the fight.

6th round

Both seemed tired. Gardner slowly and steadily walked towards Fitzsimmons, throwing leads. Fitz contented himself with moving or walking away, or covering up, clinching, and grinning over his shoulder, as if to show how easy it was to get away from Gardner's leads. Fitz was inclined to rest, reserving himself. Still, every time Bob feinted, George would duck and clinch, obviously concerned about Bob's blows. The crowd hissed the tameness of the fighting.

With a left shift, Fitzsimmons cut Gardner's right eye. George clinched. His eye began to swell and it became discolored. Gardner was following Fitz around but was cautious while doing so. Most of his blows were directed at the body. Bob's lips began to puff up a bit. The bout had become slow.

7th round

Fitz was fiddling and feinting, moving around and then moving away, stalling. Gardner stood away, landing body punches and the occasional clip on the face, but there was no punishment in his blows, although Bob's lips began bleeding. Both looked tired. The crowd jeered and urged them on. Fitz appeared to be losing his speed, and he seemed content with acting on the defensive more often.

8th round

Bob backed away, allowing George to do the leading. However, Fitz would occasionally spurt with hard punches. Bob's rallies would jar Gardner. Bob landed a left and right to the jaw and then left to the jaw and right to the body. When Bob bothered to punch, he put Gardner on the defensive, and George would clinch to save himself. However, the round was mostly slow, with Fitz dancing away.

One paper said Fitzsimmons improved in this round and the advantage was his.

9th round

They sparred cautiously, Fitz backing away, bent on resting. Gardner half-heartedly advanced and led. The crowd grew angry at the bout's tameness and hissed and called on the men to fight. Gardner's straight lefts puffed Bob's lips and caused the blood to well from his mouth, but his blue eyes showed no distress. The pace was very slow. Bob landed a left hook to the jaw and danced away. Gardner chased but did not land. Fitz suddenly waded in and forced George back. But then he slowed up considerably, evidently waiting for a choice moment to land his famous knockout punch. He would rest for a while, then suddenly lash out and test Gardner.

10th round

Bob backed away and contented himself with blocking leads. He took some blows with a view of getting in a good return. Bob occasionally landed a good jolt. He landed a left hook on the mouth that caused Gardner to spit blood. Gardner's nose began bleeding as a result of the rights and lefts that Fitz occasionally landed. When Bob wanted, he could work his shifts at will, but he picked his spots. Blood came from Fitz's lips and Gardner's nose.

In a rush, Gardner slipped down to the floor, partly from a right cross to the jaw and partly from clumsiness. Some, like Young Corbett, called it a knockdown. This round had a trifle more ginger.

11th round

Fitz quickened up, but his spurts were short, and between them, there was a lot of inactivity. Gardner blocked several blows. His own punches lacked force. Bob jolted him with a straight left to the stomach. Fitz took most of the light blows but blocked the harder ones. Gardner sent in a right to the face, but Bob sailed in with a left hook to the jaw, staggering Gardner. The gong rang. Bob had the advantage in the round.

12th round

Fitz was winded, breathing heavily. As usual, he backed away but landed a nice right uppercut to the chin. The pace again slowed up and the crowd yelled at them. Gardner's punches were very light. He had yet to land a telling blow.

Fitz was stalling a great deal. He would occasionally let out and mix it for a few seconds, but he spent most of the time gliding around and keeping out of encounters. Gardner pressed, but not hard enough to do anything effective. This pattern continued.

13th round

Although Gardner was less afraid to punch, infusing more ginger into his work, landing some lefts to the face, he still was not doing much effective work. Halfway through the round not a solid blow had landed. Gardner kept pegging away but could not land. What did land had little force.

At the end of the round, when Gardner rushed, Fitz suddenly held his ground and landed another mule-kick overhand right to the jaw below the ear that sent Gardner down to his knees, just as the bell rang.

Gardner rose in a couple of seconds, though, and seemed okay physically, although he had a look of distress on his face.

The *Chronicle* said there was little to choose from the 9th to the 13th rounds. The rounds were poor. Fitz's shifts were the only redeeming features. However, he was not leading at all. Yet, when he did throw and land on rare occasion, his punches were more powerful and effective.

14th round

Fitz feinted with a right and sent in two lefts to the jaw. He followed with a hard left hook to the jaw and a hard right to the body.

Fitzsimmons landed a stiff right to the chin that sent Gardner down for 5 to 7 seconds. He got up groggy. Fitz tried to finish him, but the Lowell man moved, covered up and held. Bob's blows were a bit wild. Bob was blowing hard, but he was punishing Gardner. Fitz's hard right cross and right uppercut to the chin staggered Gardner. Blood streamed from George's nose.

However, Bob slowed up again and allowed Gardner to make the pace. George began rushing again but could not land. He was the aggressor but in a half-hearted way. Gardner seemed to have been weakened by a combination of the tension and excitement of the big contest, the fear of the dreaded Fitzsimmons wallop, as well as the big blows he had endured. Fitz's manner left the impression that he had no fear of Gardner's punches. The balance of the round was uninteresting. Both were tired and did little effective work. Gardner went to his corner appearing groggy, while Fitz coolly smiled at his friends.

15th round

Bob kept away from George's rushes and jabbed him with the left. Fitz fought carefully and made his blows count. Bob jarred him with a hard right to the jaw and left hook to the body. Gardner again stalled with movement and clinching. In the clinches, Bob hit George with right uppercuts that distressed him. Gardner's face was covered with blood. It was Fitz's round.

16th round

Fitz nursed his strength carefully and made no unnecessary moves. Gardner's fight had been disappointing, with no strength.

17th round

The round was mostly desultory sparring. Bob did some clever blocking. Gardner landed a hard right at the end, but not hard enough to bother Bob, who went to his corner smiling.

18th round

Fitz acted as though he was mighty tired. He clinched frequently. Gardner hit his body. George forced Fitz about the ring, missing swings. Both finally landed some good blows.

19ᵗʰ round

Gardner went after Fitz, ripping in a number of body shots that hurt and troubled him. Bob wrestled George to the mat. Fitz complained that Gardner was hitting low. The claim was not allowed, though the referee cautioned George. Gardner landed a good left to the stomach that brought a look of pain on Bob's face. Fitz kept covering and grabbing tightly. He occasionally let out and drove George off. Bob was too clever to allow Gardner to land anything like a knockout punch. The round ended in a lively mix. George landed several short lefts to the stomach, but they had little power.

One said honors were even, while another said Gardner won this round.

One summarized that rounds 16 through 19 were tame, and neither scored heavily. Gardner did most of the leading, while Bob moved about the ring. Fitz did not seem to be trying. Gardner was short with his blows to the face but landed several good punches to the body.

20ᵗʰ round

Gardner feinted while Fitzsimmons danced around. Fitz acted almost entirely on the defensive, defending Gardner's blows. Fitz blocked and took body shots, and though tired, did not seem worried. Still, near the end of the round, Bob had enough strength left to send his left to the head and body, staggering Gardner, who clinched. Gardner held on, and the referee could not separate them. The bell rang ending the bout. One said Gardiner won the 20ᵗʰ, but winning the last two rounds came too late to do him any good.

When Referee Ed Graney pointed to Fitzsimmons as the winner of his decision, the crowd stood and cheered the new world light heavyweight champion, Bob's third world championship crown. They wanted a speech, but all Fitz would say was, "Haven't I done enough for one night?" He was tired, but happy. Bob had a puffed lip. Gardner's face was badly swollen, and he had a cut over his right eye.

Fitzsimmons had dropped Gardner in the 4ᵗʰ, 5ᵗʰ, 10ᵗʰ, 13ᵗʰ, and 14ᵗʰ rounds. Bob alternated between boxing cautiously from a distance and keeping the pace slow, using his jab, doing very little, playing defense and allowing Gardner to work, and then occasionally suddenly exploding with hard punches. Fearful of Bob's power, Gardner was loath to take too many chances and fought cautiously despite being the aggressor.

Referee Ed Graney said although it was a slow affair, this was wise strategy on Fitz and Delaney's part. If Bob had mixed it too much or for too long, he might have worn himself out or left himself open to Gardner, who at all times was dangerous. Gardner was in better condition and was strong, but he failed to take enough chances until the last few rounds. He seemed afraid of Fitz's heavy punch. Graney said Bob was tired at the end but held his own in all but very few rounds. His knockdowns counted a long way in his favor. All of his punches carried sting, whereas "Gardner could not hit hard enough to break a pane of glass." Although Bob rested and moved away a lot, stalling for time, Gardner did nothing worthy of mention, despite being more active. He forgot to bring his punch. Fitz was too strong for him. However, Bob was out of shape. "Had he been the old-time Fitz he would have won in three rounds."

Fitzsimmons said if his hands had not gone out on him, he would have stopped Gardner in 5 rounds. He said he broke his right early, dislocated a knuckle on his left hand the first time he knocked Gardner down, and further disabled his left in the 13th round. Still, he admitted that he grew tired, and he gave Gardner credit. "There is a great deal of praise due to Gardner, for he fought a game, hard fight. He was always ready to come back into the fray after he had been hit hard, and he mixed it when the opportunity was afforded."

Bob's hands really were injured. It was necessary to cut the gloves from his hands. In the dressing room afterwards, a physician examined Bob's right hand and confirmed that the knuckles of the thumb and first finger were fractured. Bob's left hand was swollen to twice its natural size. Later, he could not handle a knife or fork to eat.

Still, although agreeing that hurt hands might have affected his ability to put Gardner away, most felt that the predominant reason was that Bob no longer was what he once was. Even Fitzsimmons recognized that he was past it. "I did well for an old man, but my ring days are over."

> Tonight's battle ends my career in the prize ring. I will never fight again. I am getting old … Why a week ago I wrote George Dawson that I would be lucky if I won, and I tell you now that I am a lucky fellow. I was a sick man, I tell you, and I can easily feel the effects of Gardner's punches, even though they were not very hard ones. …

In another interview, Bob said,

> It was simply an old man against a good young man. Gardner is a tough nut to crack. … I got tired and hurt my hands, and it dawned on me I would have to fight for a decision. … His punches never bothered me. The blows he sent in were usually caught on my arms. His jabs were easy and never worried me. My hands hurt me more than Gardner's punches. They were knocked out on Jeffries and they got bad before many rounds. Pretty good showing for an old man, eh?

Bill Delaney said Fitz showed that he was getting old, but Gardner never stepped close enough to land a big punch. Bob mostly bluffed his way through the bout, save for the flashes of his old-time form. He gave Gardner credit for taking the punching he did, getting up off the floor and coming back again. Gardner was aggressive, but not confident. When he finally showed some confidence at the end, his strength was gone. Still, taking those big punches showed that he was gritty and game.

Gardner said he did all the leading and forcing, hence he felt that he was entitled to the decision or a draw. Bob's heavy blows staggered him early and took a lot of the fight out of him. Still, he noted that his condition was good, while Fitz weakened in the second half, and during the last part of the fight Bob did nothing but stall. He admitted that Fitz was the hardest proposition he ever went up against, very tricky, strong and dangerous. Defensively, Bob was able to make George's most powerful blows land on arms and shoulders, or he took well the ones that did land.

His coach and trainer, Alex Greggains, said Gardner should have won the decision. He was the aggressor from the 13th round on, following his opponent about and forcing the fighting. Still, he admitted that George did not fight up to his standard. He was slow and his blows lacked force.

Robert Edgren said Fitz seemed slow throughout, but at times showed amazing bursts of speed. Gardner used left jabs to the face and body to hold Bob off.

All of the local newspapers agreed with the decision.

However, all of the reporters also agreed that Fitz's best days were past, for Gardner would have been an easy mark for Fitz back when Bob had been at his best. The reporters felt that it had been a relatively poor fight, the poorest of Fitz's career. It was slow and spiritless. Some said the fight was pathetic, while others said the bout was good and bad in streaks. Fitz's statement during training that he was not in his old-time form was proven correct. Age and a lengthy career clearly were telling on the war-worn veteran. Some said Fitz could no longer punch like he once could, while others said he still had a punch, but fatigued quickly and could not keep it up like he once could. Many thought Bob should retire. The *Chronicle* opined that this version of Fitzsimmons would never land on Jack Johnson.

Observers said Bob was tricky and clever as ever, but he "does not work his fists so rapidly and the sting is gone out of his shifts and swings." A short time ago, the same punches would have meant a knockout. At present, he "tires very easily," "cannot lash out in the rapid style of the old days," and "there is not half the poundage in his punches." One said Fitz was slow and weak compared to what he once was.

Fitzsimmons fought well in spots, but he would alternate flashes of power with fatigue. He knew when and where to hit, and was not slow in starting to punch, but he was quick in stopping, looking to kill the clock after striking hard blows. His wind was not good. When he had Gardner groggy and going, Bob was too weak to take the chance of rushing in to finish, but instead would fiddle and stall for the balance of the round. Fitz no longer had the same vim, and it was inability and not unwillingness that held him back.

Fitzsimmons had Gardner down on the floor twice in the 4th round and once in the 5th round. After failing to knock out Gardner, Bob seemed to realize that his steam was lacking, and he paced himself. He was content to outpoint Gardner. Bob rested up frequently. Although his hands were hurt, it also appeared to be the case that sheer weariness affected Fitz and not just crippled fists. Still, Bob's flashes of hard punches won him the fight. Gardner was down again in the 13th and 14th rounds. Some thought that Bob was just toying with Gardner. For round after round, it seemed that Fitz could have ended matters whenever he wanted to, but he allowed Gardner to recover.

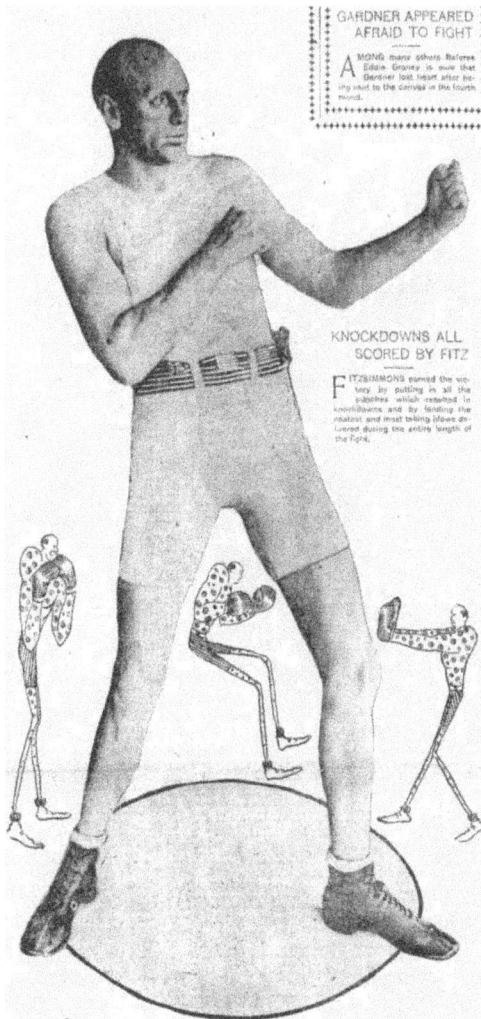

GARDNER APPEARED AFRAID TO FIGHT

AMONG many others, Referee Eddie Graney is sure that Gardner lost heart after being sent to the canvas in the fourth round.

KNOCKDOWNS ALL SCORED BY FITZ

FITZSIMMONS earned the victory by putting in all the punches which resulted in knockdowns and by landing the cleanest and most telling blows delivered during the entire length of the fight.

Bob won because he scored all of the knockdowns and his hitting was much cleaner and more forceful, and he generally handled Gardner, who could not hurt him. Even with two hurt hands, Bob managed to stall off the younger and faster man. Bob was too experienced, crafty, and powerful for him. Fitz had the class, some saying he outclassed Gardner and had used his veteran generalship with flashes of power to win, despite his age, poor condition, injured hands, and fact that he had been suffering from a cold. "Fitz showed the most consummate ring generalship. His every move seemed to have been studied out and he hardly wasted a blow."

Gardner was a disappointment. He was too nervous and overly cautious. He seemed to be a victim of stage fright. He did not show the form he had in training or in his fights with Walcott, Carter, Hart, and Root. Gardner mostly fought at long range, and ineffectively. His blows, when they landed at infrequent intervals, had little sting to them, and had no impact on Fitz, who mostly just warded them off on his arms and elbows.

After making a flowery showing at the start, despite the fact that Fitz had broken hands and had grown fatigued, Gardner had a wholesome respect for Fitz's wallops. He seemed unable or unwilling to get in close enough to be effective. The spectators were amazed at Gardner's poor showing, given his previous performances.

Gardner lost his courage after he was knocked down in the 4th round, and he never really regained it. "It was rarely after that that he made anything like a determined effort to beat the Cornishman down." Gardner rarely took real chances, perhaps too worried about running into a big blow.

From the 5th to the 18th rounds, although Gardner carried the fight to Bob, he did it in a half-hearted and ineffective way. George's condition was first class, but when Fitz worked in his shifts and right and left blows, Gardner seemed to go to pieces. "Toward the close of the fight he kept tapping tired Mr. Fitzsimmons on the midsection with his left. He caused the impression that he was trying to create an opening which never came." Gardner's battling spirit was low. He did not make a showing until the end, doing some good work in the last two rounds when his courage revived and he stung Fitz with some good body blows. It was too little, too late.

ROBERT FITZSIMMONS, THE GRAND OLD MAN OF THE RING, WHO CLEARLY OUTCLASSED GEORGE GARDNER LAST NIGHT IN THEIR TWENTY-ROUND FIGHT IN MECHANICS' PAVILION, UNDER THE AUSPICES OF THE YOSEMITE CLUB.

World featherweight champion Young Corbett said Fitz no longer had the same punch, but barring the loss of his "death-dealing punch," he still was the same great fighter, with ring generalship, blocking, stalling, backing, and foxy tactics. The decision was the only one possible.

> Once could not picture a more heady fighter than Fitzsimmons. He fought as if in a boxing school. He had Gardner going in the fourth round, and again and again had him on Uneasy Street, and yet never for a moment did he lose his cunning or the wonderful coolness that has marked his great ring career.

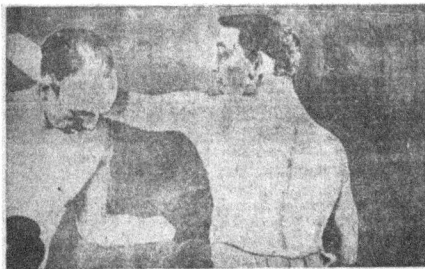

FITZ'S LEFT TO THE PIT OF THE STOMACH.
Gardner Felt This Punch on Three Different Occasions Last Night, but at No Time Did It Put Him Down, Only Seeing to Chiefe His Aggressiveness.

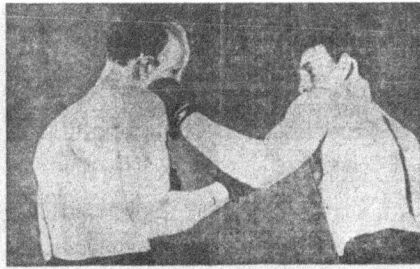

GARDNER'S LEFT TO FITZ'S JAW.
Gardner Tried to Settle the Fight with the Punch, but Never Could Get It Exactly on "The Point"—It Always Glanced Off, and Fitz Only Smiled at Its Effort.

The total gate receipts were $16,435, which was split between the fighters and the club. The fighters split their purse 75% winner, 25% loser. Hence, Fitz earned $6,163 and Gardner $2,054. Apparently, though, Bob also had an understanding with the club wherein he received 10% of the gross receipts as a bonus. That brought his earnings to $7,500.[277]

The fact that even at age 40, Bob Fitzsimmons could beat a much younger, talented and experienced champion to win his third world championship, scoring several knockdowns despite bad hands, and going the 20-round distance after making 168 pounds on the afternoon of the fight, despite having lost over 30 pounds to make weight, further stamps Fitzsimmons as one of the all-time greatest pound-for-pound fighters ever, and certainly one of the greatest if not the greatest middleweights and/or light-heavyweights of all time. Just think of what he had done over the course of his lengthy career from 150 ½ pounds at ringside on the day of the 1891 middleweight championship fight, all the way up into the 170- or 180-pound range as a heavyweight, including against far bigger men, back down to 168 in 1903 the day of the light-heavyweight championship fight. He usually had not just won, but he knocked them out. The mere fact that he had scored several knockdowns but had been unable to finish champion Gardner actually was used as an indication that he was slipping. If that was slipping, just imagine how good he was in the 1890s. The feeling was that in days past, Fitz's punches would have knocked Gardner out cold.

However, some credit has to be given to Gardner for being really tough and able to get himself out of trouble. After all, he had successfully taken the blows of Kid Carter, Joe Walcott, Jack Root, Marvin Hart, a much heavier Jack Johnson, and now Bob Fitzsimmons.

In December 1903, Fitzsimmons said the solar plexus blow was his favorite punch. "Give me the solar plexus every time. I prefer it to any other punch. Once you land it properly there is no fear that your man will ever recover within the time limit. The effect is more lasting than a blow on the jaw."[278]

Sometimes Bob said he was retired, primarily owing to his bad hands, and at other times he said he would fight again if or once his hands healed. Some newsmen reported negotiations for potential bouts with James J. Corbett, Marvin Hart, Philadelphia Jack O'Brien, and others.

[277] *San Francisco Chronicle, Examiner, Bulletin, Call, New York Evening World*, November 26, 27, 1903.
[278] *Winnipeg Daily Tribune*, December 30, 1903.

PARK MATINEE EVERY DAY

COM. TO-MORROW (MONDAY) MATINEE.
EXTRA CHRISTMAS ATTRACTION.

BOB THE GRAND OLD MAN OF THE ART OF SELF DEFENSE.

AND

JULIA LATE STAR OF THE WHITNEY OPERA CO.

FITZSIMMONS

Starring in the Big Musical Comedy,

Peck and His Mother-in-Law

A Genuine Novelty.
"OUR BOB" IN COMEDY.
Dec. 25—THE HEART OF A HERO.

(MRS. BOB FITZSIMMONS)
WITH "PECK AND HIS MOTHER-IN-LAW"
(AT THE PARK.)

Fitzsimmons returned to vaudeville with his wife Julia Gifford, which was his pattern between fights.

In December 1903, the *Buffalo Commercial* wrote, "Fitzsimmons' career may be considered as good as over. He has served his time in the ring, and served it gloriously. Pound for pound, when all is said, the ancient antipodean must go down in ring history as the greatest fighter that ever drew on a boxing glove – a fistic star without a peer."[279]

CHARACTERISTIC POSE OF THE CORNISHMAN

ROBERT FITZSIMMONS OLD MAN OF THE RING

---

[279] *Buffalo Commercial*, December 7, 1903.

CHAPTER 13

Philadelphia Jack O'Brien

In early January 1904, Bob Fitzsimmons said his hands were feeling good again, and he was willing to fight any man in the world except James J. Jeffries, who was in a class by himself and unbeatable. He most wanted to fight Corbett again. Nevertheless, "I'll meet Marvin Hart, Sandy Ferguson, or any white man, provided there is enough money in it."[280]

In late January 1904 in Philadelphia, Anthony J. Drexel-Biddle entered a lawsuit against his insurance company. Bob Fitzsimmons had given him the gloves that he wore against James J. Corbett in 1897. However, the gloves were stolen last fall when Drexel-Biddle's gymnasium was robbed. Drexel-Biddle alleged the gloves were worth $3,000, but the insurance company disputed that amount.[281]

On January 27, 1904, in Philadelphia, Tommy Ryan and Philadelphia Jack O'Brien, both claimants to the world middleweight championship, fought a very close 6-round no decision. Some said Ryan won, some said O'Brien, while others said it was a draw. Bob Fitzsimmons still claimed to be the middleweight champion, but he had not officially weighed in as a middleweight since 1894.

On February 27, 1904, Jim Jeffries was in attendance at Philadelphia's Second Regiment Armory to witness 27-year-old 196-pound Jack Munroe unofficially "win" a 6-round no-decision bout against 30-year-old 182-pound Tom Sharkey, showing that he could beat an elite man.

As a result of the victory, and Jeff's desire to set the record straight, he made a championship match with Munroe. San Francisco's Yosemite Athletic Club guaranteed a $25,000 purse for a 20-round Jeffries-Munroe fight. On February 29, the parties signed articles of agreement for a fight, originally set to be held at the end of May 1904, although eventually it was delayed until late August.

Also on February 27, 1904, in Chicago, Illinois, before a packed house, the largest crowd that ever attended a boxing show at the Chicago Athletic Association, Bob Fitzsimmons boxed a 4-round exhibition with George Dawson. According to George Siler, who wrote for the *Chicago Tribune*, Fitz kidded around and made a comedic hit, with both fighters intentionally going down and out at the final gong.[282]

There was talk about Fitz fighting Kid McCoy. The Kid wanted a bout at 165 pounds, but Bob said he would not get down that low in weight

---

[280] *New York Sun*, January 12, 1904. On January 5, 1904, Marvin Hart had fought a 15-round draw with George Gardner, but most thought Hart had won.
[281] *Finger Lakes Times*, January 28, 1904.
[282] *Chicago Tribune*, February 28, 1904.

unless it was for a 20-round contest. The only places to fight were either California, Philadelphia, or Chicago, but the latter two only allowed 6-round contests. Bob said, "I only weigh 180 pounds stripped now, and I am far from being in trim. I can get to 158 pounds if need be, but what's the use in a six-round bout?"[283]

San Francisco matchmakers were against utilizing Fitzsimmons again, calling him an old has-been who was all-in, whom younger men were seeking to use to obtain a reputation. Naturally, Bob took exception to such comments, vehemently disagreeing.[284]

On March 31 in Boston, 40-year-old Bob Fitzsimmons, "one of the most remarkable pugilists in the history of fistiana," visited 45-year-old John L. Sulivan, "Boston's greatest fistic idol," who was ill, penniless, and residing at his sister Mrs. Anne Lennon's home at 87 Brook avenue, Roxbury. Only four and a half years difference in age separated them, but their life and career

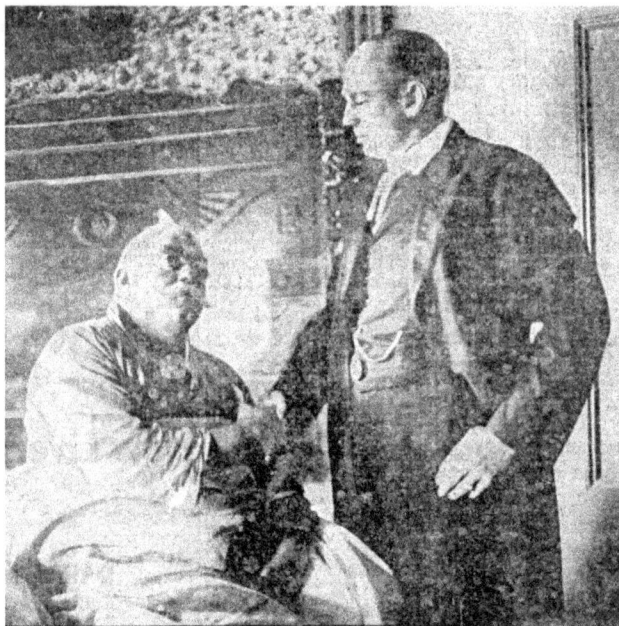

FITZ AND JOHN L. SAYING GOOD-BY.

trajectories had been vastly different. John L. was very fat with gray/white hair and a mustache. Bob did not have a wrinkle and appeared to be in perfect health, having lived a quiet, careful life. "One would have said that Fitz was about 35, while Sullivan was at least 50." Sullivan, "perhaps the most picturesque character that ever graced the prize ring," was battered and wrecked from disease and the excesses of high living. "The once mighty gladiator had lost all of his old-time vim and vigor."

Sullivan and Fitzsimmons spoke for more than an hour, discussing boxing, philosophy, and religion. John L. said, "I tell you, Bob, a fellow can't play with the kind of water I've been up against and still hope to be there. ... I've gained some weight.... Then I smoke a good deal, and d—d if the pipe ain't as good as eating and drinking to me." The ex-champ said he would be all right soon. He was going to quit taking the medicine he had been given. "I never did believe much in medicine. This world is all a 'con'

[283] *Buffalo Enquirer*, March 8, 1904.
[284] *Brooklyn Times*, March 19, 1904.

anyway. Why, they talk about religion, and heaven and hell. What do they know about heaven and hell? They never were there, and no one ever came back and told us what they were like. I think when a guy croaks he just dies, and that's all there is to him." John L. wanted to be cremated.

Fitz and Sully discussed the 1892 Sullivan vs. Corbett fight. "Well, Bob, he licked me and beat me on the level." "Yes, John, but you were not yourself then. Why, I remember, I sat at the ringside, and if you remember, you nearly nailed him in the very first round. I don't think I will ever forget it. It was with a right swing and just missed him by an eighth of an inch. Lord, but it was a wallop, and if it ever landed, there would have been no more of Corbett." Corbett barely pulled his head back from it, and if he had not, the fight would have been over.

Bob volunteered his services at Sully's benefit that was being planned. Bob later forged a steel horseshoe which was to be auctioned off and the money donated to Sullivan at and for his benefit. "Fitzsimmons is as good a blacksmith as he ever was a fighter."[285]

Ex-Champion Makes an Emblem of Good Luck For John L.'s Benefit.

AT THE ANVIL   FITZ AND HIS HORSE SHOE

On the afternoon of April 28, 1904, at the Boston Theatre, 3,500 or 4,000 men appeared at John L. Sullivan's benefit. Former Sullivan foe

[285] *Boston Post, Boston Globe*, April 1-3, 1904; *Buffalo Evening Times*, April 2, 4, 1904.

Charley Mitchell attended. "It was when Bob Fitzsimmons was announced, however, that the storm of cheers broke loose in full volume." Speaking with a pronounced Cornish accent, "dropping some of his h's and putting in a few unnecessary ones," Bob said it was a pleasure to do anything for a worthy cause, particularly to attest respect for "the greatest fighter that ever stepped into a ring under any sky." John L. was broke in part because of his big heart and generous impulses.

"John L.," the world's most famous fighter, as he looked yesterday, and some of the noted sporting men who assembled yesterday to do him honor.

Fitzsimmons, clad in white and pink, and Tom Sharkey, wearing green, sparred 3 exhibition rounds that were a "ludicrous" "sham battle." Nevertheless, some of the spectators actually believed that the knockdowns and knockouts were genuine. Both Bob and Tom went down in the 2nd round. In the 3rd, Tom was groggy but sent Bob down again. Then they both went down together, and at the end, in an exchange, both went down to the floor again, and they were counted out. "If it had been in earnest, it would have marked an epoch in pugilism." But they were faking and having fun, though it still looked semi-real to some.

The *Boston Evening Transcript's* writer concluded that the large crowd that appeared proved that Sullivan "reigns like a god," and the world was mainly composed of 12-year-old boys of all ages. It was the "most beautiful state occasion that Boston has ever seen."[286]

Bob Fitzsimmons, Kid McCoy, and Jack O'Brien were all discussing potential fights with one another. McCoy said,

> Fitzsimmons is the foxiest man in the ring. Why, the old man has us young fellows all beaten a mile when it comes to tricks. We have to watch him all the time and duck whenever we see anything coming over. He always has something up his sleeve. I lived with him and boxed with him for a couple of years, and I've often thought that I knew everything he could teach me. But just about that time he would unlimber some stunt that he had been figuring on, and that I hadn't thought of. ... Oh, he's the wisest of them all. I'd rather fight six rounds with all the Jeffs and Ruhlins and Corbetts in the business than with Fitz.[287]

On May 14, 1904, in Philadelphia, Charles 'Kid' McCoy and Philadelphia Jack O'Brien fought a 6-round no decision that most called a very scientific but relatively tame draw.

Fitz, who was living and training in Bensonhurst, New York, said he would not fight anyone unless he received a $3,500 guarantee. He was in discussions to fight famous and very experienced middleweight Philadelphia Jack O'Brien. Eventually, on June 13, O'Brien and Fitzsimmons agreed to fight at a 165-pound catchweight for a 6-round no decision bout in Philadelphia at the National League Baseball Park, originally scheduled for July 8. They were to weigh-in at 165 pounds at 8 p.m. on fight night.[288]

O'Brien was known as the world's best 6-round fighter. Being from Philadelphia, he was used to that distance, the maximum allowed there. His record included victories (including newspaper decisions) over the likes of George Cole, Jack Bonner, Tommy West, Jimmy Handler, George Chrisp, Jack Scales (O'Brien 157, Scales 186), Frank Craig, Yank Kenny, Joe Walcott, Young Peter Jackson, Charlie McKeever, Jack Beauscholte, Billy Stift, Joe Choynski, Peter Maher, Jim Jeffords, Marvin Hart, Al Weinig, Joe Grim, George Byers, Kid Carter, Jack 'Twin' Sullivan, Mike Schreck, and Hugo Kelly. He had fought on relatively even terms with Kid McCoy and Tommy Ryan.[289]

---

[286] *Boston Evening Transcript, Boston Post,* April 29, 1904.
[287] *Elmira Daily Gazette And Free Press,* April 21, 1904. Fitz sparred and trained with Kid McCoy around 1894.
[288] *New York Evening World,* June 11, 1904; *Brooklyn Times,* June 13, 14, 1904.
[289] Jack O'Brien's career included: 1899 WND6 and W20 George Cole; 1900 LKOby13 Young Peter Jackson, WND6 Jack Bonner, WND6 Tommy West, WND6 and WTKO6 Jimmy Handler; 1901 KO11 George Chrisp, W6 and KO1 Jack Scales, WDQ6 Frank Craig, and TKO4 Yank Kenny; 1902 WND6 Charlie McKeever, WND6 Joe Walcott, WND6 Young Peter Jackson, TKO4 and WND6 George Cole, WND6 Jack Bonner, KO1 Charlie McKeever, KO3 Yank Kenny, W6 Jack Beauscholte, W6 Billy Stift, W6 Joe Choynski, WND6 Peter Maher, WND6 Jim Jeffords, and WND6 Marvin Hart; 1903 KO12 and TKO4 Al Weinig, WND6 Joe Grim, W10 Jim Jeffords, WND6 Joe Choynski, D10 Joe Walcott, LND6 Marvin Hart, WND6 George Byers, WND10 Jack Bonner, WND6 Kid Carter, WND6 and W15 Jack 'Twin' Sullivan, W6 Mike Schreck, and D10 Hugo Kelly; 1904 DND6 Tommy Ryan, W15 Mike Schreck, W6 Hugo Kelly, KO3 Jack 'Twin' Sullivan, TKO3 Kid Carter, DND6 Kid McCoy, and WND6 George Cole.

Robert Edgren said the light-heavyweight championship essentially was on the line. "Jumping Jack" had a rapid-fire style. "O'Brien is a faster and more clever fighter than Gardner, and less nervous in the ring. He is a showy boxer and is inclined to waste his strength in unnecessary footwork. Fitzsimmons never moves an inch without some definite purpose."

On June 19 at Bensonhurst, Brooklyn, New York, near Bath Beach, Edgren watched Fitzsimmons spar 6 rounds with black heavyweight Bob Armstrong, his chief sparring partner, who once had gone the full 10 rounds with Jeffries and later became the champ's (and Fitz's) sparring partner. Afterwards, Bob kiddingly complained about having to make 165 pounds ringside. "It's awful hard for me to make the weight. I don't seem to be able to lose anything. I am afraid I may have to call the fight off." Yet, he stepped on the scale for Edgren with a grin, and it said 165 ½ pounds.[290]

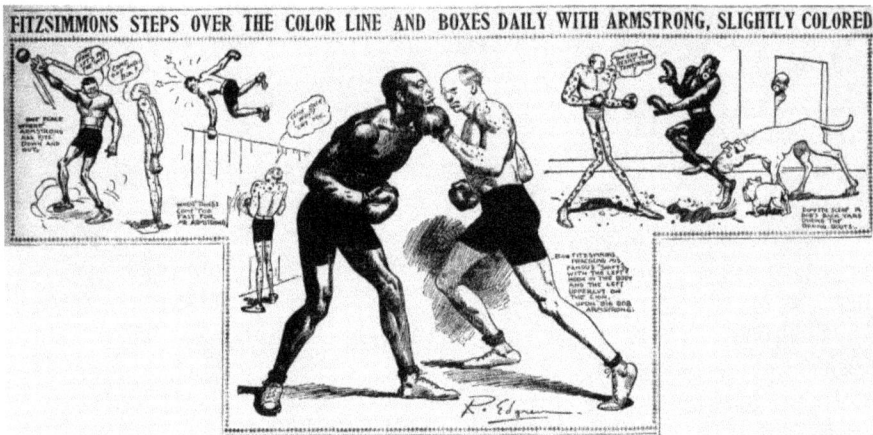

FITZSIMMONS STEPS OVER THE COLOR LINE AND BOXES DAILY WITH ARMSTRONG, SLIGHTLY COLORED

John Considine said, "Fitzsimmons is a great fighter, and he should have no trouble in winning. He has the wallop… Fitz is a knocker out, and it is even money that he will stop O'Brien before the limit."[291]

On June 25, 1904, at the American League Park, Manhattan, New York, Bob Fitzsimmons and Tom Sharkey sparred in a 3-round exhibition for charity under the auspices of St. Matthew's Athletic Association. Bob appeared to be in the pink of condition, while Sharkey appeared fat. They boxed in a 24-foot ring pitched in the middle of the diamond.

In the 1st round, Sharkey was the aggressor and landed a few telling blows to the face and ribs. In the 2nd, Fitz sailed in to get even and floored Sharkey with a stiff right to the jaw. Sharkey came up a little groggy and used the remainder of the round in keeping out of danger. In the 3rd, Tom floored Fitz twice. Bob got even. He slammed Sharkey to the turf with terrific rights. Then, by prearrangement, both tapped each other on the head and laid down for the count at the end of the round. The whole performance had been a hippodrome, both shamming for entertainment purposes, the same as they had done at John L. Sullivan's benefit.[292]

[290] *New York Evening World*, June 20, 1904; *Freeman*, July 23, 1904.
[291] *Brooklyn Times*, June 23, 1904.
[292] *Brooklyn Daily Standard Union*, *Brooklyn Citizen*, June 26, 1904.

Jack O'Brien admitted that Fitz was a fighter but felt that this time he would go into the ring once too often. Jack said,

> Freckled Bob's time has come. The 'Grand Old Man' has done some great fighting, but he has been winning long enough. Some one will beat him sooner or later, and I think I have him right. I sat at the ringside when he took the light-heavyweight championship from Gardner, and I watched every move Fitz made. I made up my mind that I could have beaten him if I had been in Gardner's place. …

> I think that I have a better chance to beat Fitzsimmons than any one of the big fellows. They are all too slow for him, while I will be twice as fast in the ring as he will. He could land on Jeffries as often as he pleased, but he will find it a different matter with me. … As I figure it, I am just the right sort of a fighter to get away with him. I am faster than he is, and I can hit him. It will be a question of agility, and I am counting on my superior agility to win the fight for me.

O'Brien was weighing 161 pounds, sparring a husky 195-pound Jim Brady, middleweight Joe Hagan, and featherweight Bob Kerns.[293]

JACK O'BRIEN DISPLAYS HIS AGILITY AND CANNOT SEE WHERE FITZ HAS A LOOK-IN IN FIGHT

As the fight approached, Fitzsimmons said, "I will knock O'Brien out Friday night. I never saw him box, but no matter how fast he is he will find me faster, and he will be easy game beside the men I have been fighting." Bob said he would knock out O'Brien with the old shift and solar plexus

punch that had stopped Corbett, Ruhlin, Sharkey, and others. "I don't mind telling O'Brien that before the fight. I told Corbett the same thing in Carson, but he couldn't prevent my turning the trick. I'm the only man who

---

can use the 'shift,' and there's no man living who can get away from it."
Bob said his hands were just fine, having tested them on Armstrong.[294]

Assessing the contest, the *Philadelphia Inquirer* wrote, "With the possible exception of Tommy Ryan, Fitzsimmons is the greatest general that ever stepped into the ring. His capacity to give and to take punishment has been the wonder of ring followers for the past thirteen years. In mental alertness and quickness to take advantage of openings he never had an equal in the ring."

However, O'Brien was said to be the cleverest matchmaker in the business. He knew that Fitz had gone back, and it was doubtful if Jack would have matched himself with Bob unless he knew that his hands were weak. He saw Bob box Gardner, and felt convinced that he had a good chance with him. In fact,

BOB FITZSIMMONS.   JACK O'BRIEN.

O'Brien had then said that Gardner allowed Bob to bluff and stall, using his foxiness to keep a comfortable pace, and that a faster pace would have worn out the elder Fitzsimmons. He noted that Fitz was slower and no longer able to finish a man. "Poor old Bob. He fought a brainy fight, but he is not the man of old." Jack thought Bob should retire.

With over 140 bouts, the very experienced but still young 26-year-old O'Brien was somewhat of a Jim Corbett type – a clever, fast, quick-footed, scientific boxer. Hence, he would have the advantage of youth and speed, particularly against a boxer who had been sapped of some of his vigor by Father Time. Fitz had not fought since his late November 1903 victory over Gardner. O'Brien fought 6-round bouts all the time, in his hometown of Philadelphia, where the fight was taking place.[295]

Robert Edgren said Fitz was looking good, knocking out two of Armstrong's teeth in their sparring. O'Brien was working on speed, hoping to outfoot Fitz, jabbing and getting away. "O'Brien can hit when the circumstances are favorable."[296]

Unfortunately, as often happened when it came to popular fighters, politics got in the way. Clergymen/ministers appealed to the mayor to stop the bout. Talk and advertisements used to hype the fight said Fitz was going to attempt to knock out O'Brien, and the bout was for the light-heavyweight championship. Arguments were propounded that it would not be a boxing exhibition but a brutal prizefight. Although the mayor initially

[294] *Buffalo Commercial*, July 5, 1904.
[295] *Philadelphia Inquirer*, July 8, 1904; *San Francisco Bulletin*, November 26, 1903.
[296] *New York Evening World*, July 7, 1904.

declined to do anything, holding that 6-round exhibitions without a decision were legal, on the day of the fight, July 8, the mayor eventually gave in to political pressure and decided that the bout could not proceed, threatening to arrest the fighters if they stepped into the ring. Many thousands who were in town to see the contest were disappointed.[297]

In November 1903, it was reported that since 1758, over the course of 145 years, only 124 pugilists had died from injuries sustained as a result of boxing. Yet, legal impediments and political and police interference continually hovered over the sport.[298]

The Fitzsimmons-O'Brien promoters, backed by former Mayor Warwick acting on their behalf, took the matter to court to seek an injunction against the mayor, restraining him from interfering with the contest. On July 15, the promoters convinced a judge that the exhibition was to be a scientific affair, with no violence or brutality. The judge said the police could be present and could stop the bout as soon as it developed into a prize fight. Hence, the contest was on again, though with a new date, two weeks later, on July 23. All of this was a joke, of course, because there had been scores of brutal 6-round no-decision matches held in Philadelphia, but famous fighters and fights often had a way of causing politics and the law to inject themselves into these bouts.

The promoters were criticized to a certain degree for hyping the contest too much, mentioning that Fitz was seeking a knockout. (Wasn't that what he always did?) Giving the contest too much publicity, as well as the type of publicity they used, got the attention of the anti-boxing folks. "They killed the bout by the character of publicity which they gave it. … They wanted to thrill the public. With that end in view they caused to be printed statements which they admitted were only figments of a press agent's robust imagination." Softer talk got the bout to be rescheduled with legal approval, although under the watchful eye of the police. The question was, to what extent and degree would they really fight, or have their contest be limited or affected in some way by the police.[299]

On the afternoon of Saturday July 23, 1904 in Philadelphia, eight months after winning the world light-heavyweight championship, 41-year-old Bob Fitzsimmons (65-5-14) fought "Philadelphia" Jack O'Brien (115-7-19) in a 6-round no-decision bout. The ring was pitched over home plate at

[297] *New York Evening World*, July 8, 1904; *Philadelphia Inquirer*, July 9, 1904.
[298] *San Francisco Bulletin*, November 4, 1903.
[299] *Brooklyn Times*, July 14, 1904; *Wilkes-Barre Leader*, July 15, 1904; *Philadelphia Inquirer*, July 16, 1904.

the Philadelphia Ball Park, located at Broad and Huntingdon Streets. Tickets were $1 up to $10. The bleachers were nearly filled. Some watched from the lower and upper decks of the cantilever. Some paid $5 for seats placed between the ring and the cantilever. Those were nearly filled. It was the first big affair in Philly held in the daylight. There were over 6,500 men and 83 women present. Another said there were over 7,000 men with 50 women present. 150 police officers were on scene.

At 5:05 p.m., Fitz entered first. He wore a pair of sky-blue tights held up by an American flag belt. About 10 minutes later, O'Brien entered the ring. He wore green tights and a light bathrobe.

Fitz's hands were bandaged with white tape. Jack examined Bob's hand bandages and objected to them. Upon close inspection, O'Brien discovered something under the tape. Fitz declared that it merely was a bit of soft plaster to keep the bandages and tape in position. O'Brien was not convinced and maintained that they were or would become as hard as iron. He wanted Bob to remove the wrapping and to re-wrap his hands. This Bob and his seconds tried to do, but the wraps had been put on to stay and would not yield. O'Brien offered to permit Fitz to keep the bandages on if he would cover them up with more tape. O'Brien had no bandages, but tape, which he offered to lend to Fitzsimmons. Bob agreed to this. The Associated Press reported that there was a pre-fight wrangle in which O'Brien protested Bob's hand wraps, and Fitz removed the plaster from his bandages. Perhaps the plaster was removed but he added more tape.

Fitz's seconds were Benny Murphy, Joe Edmonson, Jim Savage, and Whitey Lester. O'Brien had Billy McCarney, Joe Hagan, Joe Riley, Billy Reynolds, and Lew Bailey.

Referee Ernest Crowhurst called the men to ring center and instructed them that they were to box with no hitting on the breakaway. Technically, Philadelphia rules required the principals to box until ordered to break, and then to break clean. This fact was announced to the crowd. Fitz then said, "We can hit with one hand free." The announcer said, "Oh, yes." Fitz replied, "Then tell the people so." However, the announcer did not comply.

Fitz wanted the crowd to understand that hitting in the clinches would be allowed, so that they would not turn against him if he did so, which in some instances was considered foul.

Two sets of gloves were thrown into the ring – one pair green, and one yellow. O'Brien selected the yellow gloves. Fitz took the green, which went well with the red hair surrounding his bald head.

One said O'Brien appeared to be the heavier man. Another said the opposite, estimating that Fitz weighed 174 pounds to O'Brien's 159. There was no public weigh-in, so no one knew for sure. Another said Bob appeared to be a bit taller and heavier, but old enough to be his father. Their previous contract called for both men to weigh 165 pounds. Both were on weight as of July 8, the original date, but it is uncertain whether this term applied to July 23. Likely not. The fight began at 5:30 p.m.

1st round

O'Brien circled all around the ring, demonstrating his elusiveness. He landed his left jab flush on Fitz's mouth. Bob landed his right on Jack's body as the latter was retreating, but in getting out of harm's way, O'Brien slipped down to the canvas floor on his knees.

O'Brien was up in an instant and again landed his jab. Jack jabbed Fitzsimmons incessantly. Blood began flowing from Bob's lips, and his mouth bled freely. O'Brien landed his right and left to Bob's nose, cutting it, and a little stream of blood flowed. O'Brien's outside stick-and-move boxing left Fitz's face smeared with blood, but he was not disconcerted. Bob knew that he was in front of a young, agile opponent and would have to take a few to land one. Fitzsimmons went to his corner with his nose and mouth bleeding. The round was all in O'Brien's favor.

2nd round

Fitz rushed but O'Brien jabbed his nose. Jack coolly stepped in and landed his right and left three times on Bob's nose and mouth. Fitz tried, but could not land with leads or counters. O'Brien's footwork was nearly perfect. The crowd marveled at his side-stepping and circling. O'Brien's left jabs landed with monotonous regularity. Bloody Bob presented an unpleasant sight. He did not seem to mind the jabbing though, and in the clinches, he grinned over Jack's shoulder, just as he did with Corbett. In fact, the bout resembled Bob's heavyweight championship bout with Jim. Finally, Fitz rushed hard, and they pummeled each other viciously to the body with both hands when the gong sounded. According to the local reports, this round also was decidedly in O'Brien's favor.

O'Brien lands on Fitz's body.

3rd round

An O'Brien right to Fitz's left cheek bone opened a nasty cut, causing the blood to flow from it. Fitz rushed and landed his right hard over Jack's heart and he also shot his left to the face. Bob tried to follow up, but Jack danced around. When O'Brien skipped away from a swing he laughed tauntingly. Jack sent Bob back with three left jabs to the face.

The determined Fitz rushed and rallied. In some exchanges, Bob landed his famous hard left shift to the stomach that was loud enough to be heard a considerable distance from the ring. The blow landed under the local man's heart, and there was a look of distress on Jack's face.

Fitzsimmons gave him no rest for the duration of the round. However, Jack fought back and landed his blows in return, almost at will. They mixed it up furiously. Fitz appeared bewildered by the storm of blows. Although Bob did much better work in this round than he had in the prior rounds, the locals said O'Brien still had the advantage. Fitz was again bleeding freely, while O'Brien did not have a mark. But Bob was making him fight more, and despite being hit a lot, was landing a few of his own at this point, particularly some hard rights to the body which caused O'Brien to clinch more. Although outpointed, Fitz finally was getting going.

FITZ AND O'BRIEN IN THE RING AT THE PHILADELPHIA BALL PARK YESTERDAY AFTERNOON

4th round

In this round, the tide of battle turned Fitz's way. The effect of his body punches began to show on O'Brien's footwork, which was not quite as fast as it had been.

Fitzsimmons came out of his corner with his left eye black and rapidly closing. He savagely rushed but Jack either moved away from or inside of his blows. O'Brien was forced to be evasive, and in that role, he was not dangerous. Fitz never permitted him to get set.

They spoke with each other in the clinches, repeatedly engaging in conversation. Bob landed both right and left to the body. He ignored O'Brien's jabs and continually pressed him. Bob's body blows in the clinches, although not as flashy as Jack's jabs to the face, were "more far-reaching in their result." Fitzsimmons was about effectiveness, not showiness. O'Brien tried to block as many as he could, but many of his efforts were futile. Bob landed a left uppercut to the jaw and a hard left to the body. When O'Brien jumped away from a repeat dose, Bob laughed. He landed a left jab that caused O'Brien's mouth to bleed a little.

The *Philadelphia Press* reported that Fitzsimmons dropped O'Brien in this round. It said Fitz rushed again and landed a right squarely on the jaw, dropping O'Brien to the floor. When he rose, blood was coming from Jack's mouth, and the bell rang. The *Philadelphia Record* version said, "Just before the round ended Fitz dropped Jack to his knees with a right hook on the mouth, and Jack rested with a stream of blood on his chin. At the count of '5' the bell sounded." The other locals failed to mention this knockdown.

5th round

Fitzsimmons looked more revived after the minute's rest than did O'Brien. He walked right in and landed with both hands to the body. Bob received the usual jabs in return. Jack rushed and forced Bob to the ropes, but Bob shot a terrific right to the body and Jack broke ground in a hurry. Fitz missed a right but quickly landed his left to the nose, drawing blood. Bob landed several body shots. He was after Jack wherever he went and would not take no for an answer.

O'Brien was unable to stall Fitz's rushes. In one of the mixes, Fitzsimmons rushed and drove O'Brien across the ring, sending him almost through the ropes, in part as the result of a slip, in part because of punches. He fell with both feet out of the ring. Some dispatches said it was a left to the jaw and right on the wind.

O'Brien rose and tried to fight back. Fitz, with blood streaming from his nose and mouth, would not be denied, and kept up the attack. The bell was a welcome sound to O'Brien, who retired to his corner with badly damaged lips and blood trickling from a cut over his left eye. The round was decidedly in Fitz's favor. O'Brien's seconds worked on him furiously during the minute's rest.

6th round

Fitzsimmons took the aggressive. He landed his left twice to the nose, drawing blood. A Fitz right over the left eye sent blood in a stream down Jack's face. O'Brien's footwork showed that he was rapidly tiring. Both fought hard, though. O'Brien landed a couple jabs to the mouth, but Bob retaliated with a terrific right to the body. He repeated the blow. Fitz was quite willing to take one to give one, and he succeeded.

After 1 minute, 22 seconds had elapsed, as Jack was coming in and led, Fitz perfectly judged his distance and caught the advancing O'Brien with a well-timed hard left hook to the jaw. Jack tottered backwards and tried to hold his feet but then sat down on the floor. Another said Bob landed a right to the ribs and clean left on the chin that caused Jack to stagger back and sit down hard.

O'Brien got up quickly, and Fitz went right after him. However, Police Captain James Hamm ordered that the bout be stopped, and the timekeeper rang the gong more than a minute before the round should have ended.

Both had bleeding cuts on their faces, as well as bleeding mouths and noses. They were a sight when the bout was stopped.

O'Brien had outboxed him for the first few rounds, but Fitzsimmons owned the last three, dropping O'Brien in 4th and 5th, and obviously in the 6th round with a clean left hook, causing the police to step in and terminate the bout early, not wanting to allow Fitz to finish him.

Captain Hamm told the reporters, "I had orders to stop the contest if it became brutal. In the last round O'Brien was bleeding and pretty nearly done for. Then I jumped up and called to the referee to stop it." Politics had once again injected themselves into the sport of boxing. Fitz was denied over a minute of time to attempt to stop or drop him again.

The *Philadelphia Inquirer* opined that had the bout gone to a finish, Fitzsimmons would have won. It was fast from start to finish. O'Brien clearly had the better of the first 3 rounds, landing frequently, but Fitz had the better of the last 3 rounds. He was aggressive all through, and his punches had much greater effectiveness than O'Brien's did, particularly in the 5th and 6th rounds. It opined that a draw would not have been an unjust decision to either man, had a decision been allowed.

The *Philadelphia Public Ledger* said Fitzsimmons, as old as he was, proved that he was Jack O'Brien's master. Captain Hamm's advancing to ringside and waving his hands for hostilities to cease was made necessary by Fitzsimmons' catching O'Brien with a straight left to the chin, sending O'Brien staggering back to the ropes and down to the floor. The captain wanted no rough work and told referee Ernest Crowhurst to stop the bout to prevent O'Brien from being knocked out. 1 minute 32 seconds remained in the round. "Analyzed, O'Brien had clearly the best of the first two rounds. The third was in favor of Fitzsimmons, while honors were even in the fourth. Fitzsimmons had all the best of the last two rounds." Hence, 3 Fitz, 2 O'Brien, 1 even. It felt that the police captain's stopping the bout when he did was further evidence that Fitzsimmons had won, although the referee reportedly said that he would have ruled the fight a draw if decisions were allowed.

Few spectators realized the bout had been cut short, unaware of the fact that the police had interfered. The women present enjoyed the contest. One said, "It was better than a football game."

The *Philadelphia Press* said it was a fast, clean, and bitterly contested bout. O'Brien, with his speed and youth, had the best of the first 3 rounds, frequently landing jabs, while Bob evened matters up in the last 3 with his powerful body and head blows. In the opinion of good ring judges, the no-decision bout was a draw. Many were surprised that O'Brien carried the battle to his opponent, though Fitz was always eager to mix it up. Both were badly marked up with cuts. Bob left the ring with a black eye as well. O'Brien would be bruised for many days from the body blows.

O'Brien offered to fight Fitzsimmons again for any number of rounds at catch weights.

The *Philadelphia Record* offered a different view than the other locals. It said O'Brien was down four times total, once each in the 1st, 4th, 5th, and 6th rounds, although he was dazed only once, the last time, in the 6th. O'Brien landed more often and had Bob's face bleeding from the 1st round on, but he never was able to shake the old-timer, who stood very firmly on his feet. Fitz gave O'Brien a few soaks in the ribs that would be remembered for weeks to come. He once landed his famous solar plexus shift, but it landed lightly. At the end, Bob had a mouse under his left eye and was bleeding from numerous scratches and bruises about the mouth. O'Brien was bleeding from a cut near his left eye and about his mouth, where Bob's dangerous right had landed with telling effect.

Robert Edgren noted that O'Brien was the only middleweight ever to last the full limit against Fitzsimmons, although it was a mere 6-round bout. Edgren said O'Brien showed himself to be a first-class fighting man.

At the start of the fight, O'Brien showed better than ever before. Before the 1st round ended, he had Fitz's left eye closing and blood streaming from mouth and nostrils. Jack was as quick as a panther. Near the end of the round, he landed a right hook on the chin that sent Bob reeling.

For two more rounds, the 2nd and 3rd, the lightning-fast Philadelphian outpunched the veteran. He used a peculiar jab, crouching low as he came in, striking like a rattler and springing back in time to elude any return. Whenever there was an opening, O'Brien came in with a dash. When distressed by a blow, O'Brien knew how to keep out of range. He often used a short sidestep with a turn of his body that enabled him to slip and avoid Fitz's savage hooks.

However, Fitz never fought well during the early rounds against fast boxers. Corbett jabbed away at him for 6 rounds. Ruhlin and Sharkey beat him in the 1st round of their contests, with Sharkey knocking him down.

In the 4th round, Fitz suddenly took the lead, and thereafter O'Brien had to use all of his skill and cunning to last. He took a fearful beating in the body and over the heart. He would have gone out had he not pulled his body away as each one landed, lessening the force.

In the 5th round, a hard blow to the pit of the stomach took away half of O'Brien's speed. "It was only after that Fitz knocked him down twice with smashes on the jaw."

O'Brien was so fast on his feet that he seldom gave Fitz a chance to get set for a punch. Toward the end, O'Brien did little hitting, for he stalled and jabbed as he danced about. Jack asked, "Have you broken your hands yet?" Fitz replied, "Not yet." O'Brien countered, "Well, I wish you'd hurry up and break them." Bob laughed so hard that foxy O'Brien was able to jab him three times.

Upon orders from the Philadelphia police captain, the last round was shortened by 35 seconds in order to save Jack O'Brien from a knockout, for he believed that O'Brien was tottering on his last legs.

Edgren opined that although O'Brien was one of the greatest 6-round fighters in existence, he would not beat Fitz in a 20-round bout, for Bob had wonderful recuperative powers and was a great distance fighter who became stronger and fresher the longer the fight went. Conversely, O'Brien "fights so fast that he is pumped out after a few rounds," and thereafter would be easy plucking for Fitzsimmons.

Others said there was 1 minute 38 seconds to go in the round when it was stopped.

The *Brooklyn Daily Eagle* said the bell saved O'Brien from being knocked out. Bob again proved himself a wonder. "Fitzsimmons had the best of the go from the third round to the end. He caused O'Brien to stagger time and again with his short arm jolts in the stomach." When the gong rang to end the bout,

> O'Brien was sprawling on the floor, the result of a hard swing on the cheek from Fitz's right. Two or three teeth were missing and both eyes were badly cut. Bob's face was puffed up considerably, but he was ready to put his man out when the gong intervened. Thirty full seconds were chopped off the final round, in order to save the Philadelphian.

They wanted to prevent a knockout blow to future boxing events. The mayor had sent word that he would stop all fighting should any man go down for the full count.

The fighting was fast at all times. O'Brien won the 1st round with ease, landing left jabs at will. Fitz rallied and came back with some body punches, but his work was not enough. The 2nd was fierce. O'Brien attempted to finish Fitz, but the latter came back at the end and made the round even. From that time on, Fitz waded in, and O'Brien, despite his footwork, could not elude some wicked swings. Bob started the 3rd with two solid left jolts that made O'Brien groan. In the exchanges, Fitz landed two to one.

Near the end of the 5th round, Fitz sent O'Brien to the floor for 7 seconds. O'Brien half slid down when the punch landed. When he rose, he was minus some teeth and covered with blood. He kept hugging. Fitz landed hard uppercuts, while Jack's blows lacked steam. Fitz sent him down again with a hard right on the back of the head. He took 8 seconds to rise. Yet, O'Brien landed a hard straight left to the nose, his best of the fight.

In the 6th round, O'Brien landed some blows, but Fitz landed a swinging right on the jaw that sent him down in a heap. "There was no doubt that the gong then saved him from defeat. He was carried bodily to his corner, a pitiable sight."

In summary, "It was plainly a case of a clever, shifty man being beaten with the punch. O'Brien put up a plucky fight and took the awful body punches with a stout heart." Afterwards, Fitz laughingly remarked that he was old, but still young enough for any of them.

The Associated Press said O'Brien landed the greater number of blows, but Fitz's punches counted for more, being much more damaging, and he was the fresher one at the end. It was a very fast bout. Bob's lips were twice their normal size, and his left eye was almost closed, while O'Brien's left eye was cut and swollen. This version said there were no clean knockdowns, but O'Brien was on the floor three times, twice when he was endeavoring to get away, and the third time partly from a right to the neck and partly through their feet getting tangled.

Mrs. Fitzsimmons saw the bout, and afterwards, she rushed to Bob's corner, climbed the steps, and planted a kiss on his badly swollen lips.[300]

[300] *Philadelphia Inquirer, Philadelphia Public Ledger, Philadelphia Press, Philadelphia Record, New York Times, Brooklyn Daily Eagle, Buffalo News,* July 24, 1904; *New York World,* July 25, 1904.

A couple days later, the *Lancaster Daily Intelligencer* said the result was not satisfactory to either of the principals or their friends.

> One thing is certain, each man did all he was able, and the result was a stand-off. O'Brien, as usual, was very aggressive at the start, and had far the best of the match for at least three rounds. He seemed to hit Bob when and where he pleased, while Fitz was both wild and slow. Along about the fourth round Fitz grew better, and from that out he hit O'Brien quite hard at times and had him distressed. ... O'Brien told Fitz that he would like to meet him in a long contest, which Bob was perfectly willing to do.[301]

Starting in August 1904, Bob Fitzsimmons and his wife Julia Gifford started touring the country, acting in a play called, "A Fight For Love." Once again, Bob seemingly was semi-retired from boxing and thereafter would act with his wife. Of course, he always left open the possibility of a fight if sufficient inducements were offered.

On Friday August 26, 1904, in San Francisco, 224 ½-pound James J. Jeffries made what wound up being his final title defense, taking on 208-215-pound Jack Munroe. Jeffries won with ease, decking Munroe three times in the 1st round with brutal hooks and uppercuts to the jaw and body, and twice more in the 2nd with left hooks to the jaw, until the referee mercifully stopped the contest to prevent further pounding.[302]

Bob Fitzsimmons told reporters, "I told you so. ... Munroe 'as been travelin on a bloomin fake reputation for years." Bob had told Jeff not to carry Munroe at all, to remember Butte, and to "cop im at the start." Jeff did just that.[303]

Meanwhile, Fitz and his wife Julia continued touring with their play, doing so for nearly a year, all the way until May 1905. It was easy money, kept his wife happy, and Bob didn't have to train or endure punishment.

[301] *Lancaster Daily Intelligencer*, July 25, 1904.
[302] *San Francisco Call, San Francisco Evening Post, San Francisco Bulletin, San Francisco Examiner,* and *San Francisco Chronicle,* all August 27, 1904; and *National Police Gazette,* September 3, 1904.
[303] *San Francisco Bulletin,* August 28, 1904.

THE PUGILIST AND THE LADY.
Latest Photographs of Robert Fitzsimmons, Ex-Champion of the World, and His Handsome Wife—They Play Buffalo Next Week.

Fitzsimmons wanted to fight again, against either Jack O'Brien or Jim Corbett, but nothing had come to fruition. Bob told Robert Edgren,

> Jeff and I 'ave a 'ard time getting any one to fight us. Jeff is so bloomin' big that they are all afraid of 'im, and they seem to think that I 'ave a mean disposition. I 'aven't, at all. I can't 'elp knocking 'em out. I don't like to 'urt 'em, but accidents seem to 'appen when they get in the ring with me. That's why James J. Corbett won't fight me again.
>
> Corbett calls me an old man. He's been waiting ever since I licked him in Carson, 'oping I'll get so old he can whip me. The only way I could get 'im to fight me again would be to wear whiskers and walk with crutches. If I got a certificate saying I was fifty years old, instead of only forty-two, maybe James would take a chance.
>
> Jack O'Brien? He wouldn't put on the gloves with me again. Didn't they stop the sixth round 'alf a minute before the end to save 'im from being knocked out? ...
>
> It's 'ard on me and Jeff, the way these fighters sidestep us.[304]

Fitzsimmons called Jeffries the greatest fighter in the world and the best man he ever fought. He called Corbett the cleverest fighter he ever met, and Sharkey the best slugger, depending entirely on his strength. He said Choynski had hit him the single hardest blow he ever received. The body shot with which Jeffries hit him in their rematch was the next wallop he most remembered.[305]

---

[304] *New York World*, January 4, 1905.
[305] *National Police Gazette*, February 5, 1905.

Alec Greggains, matchmaker for the San Francisco Athletic Club, made an offer for a Fitzsimmons vs. O'Brien fight. Fitzsimmons said he would not be able to fight until June 1905 or later, given his theatrical obligations. O'Brien accepted and said he was willing to do a $5,000 side wager.[306]

Fitz declared that the accuracy of the landed blow mattered most. A long blow that lands with a loud thud often does less damage than a short blow of a few inches that makes little or no sound and which few notice.

> Many times I have had to laugh to hear the expressions of surprise from fight followers when I slammed in a clout on an opponent's head that sounded like the report of a cannon. Well, I knew that the blow did little damage, but to hear the ouches that ripped through the audience one would think that I had shattered a couple of bones.
>
> Then again, I have sent over knockout punches at a distance of a few inches, and when my opponent rolled over on the canvas, the audience seemed spellbound.

Bob said he knocked out Peter Maher at Langtry with a short, sharp right cross to the jaw just after Peter had missed his own right. It was a four-inch punch, but the blow almost tore his head off. "It was one of the most powerful blows I ever landed. Maher went down as though he had been hit by a sledge-hammer, and he stayed down until someone dragged him from the ring. The blow raised a lump on his jaw bigger than a hen's egg. Very few of those present knew the real power of that blow..."

Likewise, it was a shift and short left to Corbett's solar plexus, the pit of the stomach, which ended him. "His face turned ashen white, his eyes seemed to protrude from their sockets and his limbs seemed paralyzed." Bob could strike a blow that carried the force of a mule's kick from any position.

Fitzsimmons had been in the ring for 25 years. He said his first ring appearance was at Timaru, New Zealand, in 1880. He won the world middleweight championship in 1891, world heavyweight championship in 1897, and world light-heavyweight championship in 1903.[307]

Regarding their prior contest, Fitzsimmons said of O'Brien,

> [H]e was so scared that the best he could do was to peck at me like a bird and then jump away. In the sixth and last round I had him on the ropes and was about to deliver the final punch when his seconds appealed to the police and the fight was stopped. In the previous round I had knocked him over the ropes, and that's where he would have gone again had not the police stopped the fight.[308]

On March 28, 1905, in San Francisco, Marvin Hart was awarded a controversial 20-round decision over Jack Johnson.

Shortly thereafter, when asked about what he thought of Hart, Fitzsimmons said, "It looks like Johnson received a bad deal, but I'm

[306] *Syracuse Herald*, February 7, 1905, March 2, 1905.
[307] *Buffalo Enquirer*, March 3, 1903.
[308] *Buffalo Express*, March 14, 1905.

willing to fight him if he wants to make the match. I do not know much about him, but from what I have heard I guess he is a 'comer.' If Jeffries does not take him on, and I understand he is not likely to, I will meet him."

In late April 1905, there was talk of Bob meeting Mike Schreck (who had victories over Tommy Burns and George Gardner, but a loss to Jack O'Brien), and the fight was made, but then later called off in mid-June when the promoters were unable to furnish the bond/forfeit money.[309]

In May 1905, James J. Jeffries announced his retirement as the undefeated world heavyweight champion.[310]

There was discussion regarding who should fight for Jeff's vacant crown. Fitzsimmons was considered to be too old and inactive.

Marvin Hart had won a debatable late March 1905 20-round decision over colored champion Jack Johnson. Still, the victory over the world's best black heavyweight catapulted Hart to the top contender status.

Jack Root had won a 1902 6-round decision over Hart, decking Marvin in the process. Although he previously had losses to Gardner, Root was coming off a 1904 6-round decision victory over Gardner in a fight in which Root dropped Gardner in two of the 6 rounds and clearly had the better of the bout. Root also had a W10 over Kid McCoy. Root's skill and style were well respected, having won about 47 fights, and having lost only twice, both times to Gardner, whom he had recently defeated in an impressive performance. He was a skilled boxer and a hard puncher whom the fans appreciated. Hence, promoters arranged a championship battle between Hart and Root, and paid Jeffries to referee and announce the winner as the new champion.

On July 3, 1905, in Reno, Nevada, 28-year-old 190-pound Marvin Hart fought 29-year-old 171-pound Jack Root for the vacant world's heavyweight championship, refereed by retired champion James Jeffries. Although Root brutally decked Hart in the 7th round with a right to the chin, the durable and tough Hart recovered and eventually knocked out Root in the 12th round with a right uppercut to the body.

New York writer Tad Dorgan said Hart was the world champion, and no one was better, except for Jeffries. "Fitzsimmons hasn't shown any form... Fitz has about blown.... In the last two years he hasn't put up a first-class fight." Bob generally was considered to be past-it, but he still was a big name.[311]

There was some discussion of a Hart-Fitzsimmons bout, but Bob went to Paris in July to fetch his wife, who was rumored to have left him. "Why the red-topped hurricane should start on a European trip just at a time when he could have fought Hart has puzzled the fight fans. At last the truth has come out. Fitz went after his wife." He eventually came back with her and said he was willing to fight anyone, including Marvin Hart.[312]

[309] Buffalo Evening Times, April 6, 1905; Buffalo Courier, April 24, 1905; Brooklyn Citizen, June 14, 1905.
[310] Seattle Post-Intelligencer, May 3, 1902; Chicago Tribune, May 14, 1905; Philadelphia Inquirer, May 15, 1905.
[311] Louisville Courier-Journal, July 7, 1905, quoting "Tad" of the New York Journal.
[312] Louisville Courier-Journal, Buffalo Evening News, July 10, 1905; Buffalo Evening Times, August 1, 1905; Buffalo Evening News, August 3, 1905.

CHAPTER 14

A Final Title Fight

Bob Fitzsimmons previously had proposed to fight Jack O'Brien in a 25-round battle "to determine who is best fitted to hold the heavyweight championship title." In truth though, both men were large middleweights or light heavyweights, so any fight between them really would be for Bob's world light heavyweight championship.[313]

Fitz also said he wanted to fight Marvin Hart. Some said Bob was too old and past-it, but others said the only one yet to beat him was Jeffries, who outweighed him by nearly 50 pounds, so he deserved a chance. In the meantime, while awaiting offers, Bob remained in show business.[314]

Eventually, seeing that promoters did not seem interested in matching him with Hart, or that Hart was not interested in fighting him, in late October 1905, Bob issued a challenge to Jack O'Brien. "Hart does not mean to tackle me and will do anything he can to get out. I am done with him. O'Brien is out for the money, and I would like to get the [heavyweight] championship title back again, and he seems to be the next in line." 165-pound O'Brien recently defeated 190-200-pound Al Kaufman via KO17 on October 27, 1905 in San Francisco, and that impressive victory made him a good drawing card there.[315]

San Francisco promoter James Coffroth was in negotiations to make a Fitzsimmons vs. O'Brien contest. Coffroth had pulled off most of the great battles of the past 5 years.

W. W. Naughton opined that although most thought he was too old and inactive, there always was the suspicion that Bob Fitzsimmons had one battle left in him, and such would cause fans to take the fight seriously.[316]

Jimmy Britt said, "It ought to be a great contest. I believe O'Brien is too speedy and scientific to be beaten by Fitz. ... Fitz was a ring marvel in his day. For a dozen years O'Brien, and nothing like him, would have had no chance with the Cornishman, but this is 1905 and near to 1906."[317]

---

[313] *Louisville Courier-Journal*, July 11, 1905.
[314] *New York Sun*, September 26, 1905; *Buffalo Evening Times*, October 19, 1905.
[315] *Buffalo Evening Times*, October 30, 1905.
[316] *Brooklyn Citizen*, October 31, 1905; *San Francisco Examiner*, November 2, 1905; *New York Evening World*, November 4, 1905.
[317] *Buffalo Illustrated Times*, November 5, 1905.

As of November 7, 1905, it was announced that Fitz and O'Brien had been matched to fight before the Yosemite A.C. in San Francisco to fight on or about December 20. The fight was for 20 rounds or more, and according to the articles, was "for the world's heavy-weight championship."

Bob subsequently gave W. W. Naughton a copy of the articles of agreement. The fight was scheduled for 20 rounds under straight Queensberry rules at Mechanics' Pavilion. Coffroth had until December 1 to name the date, which could be between December 20 and 31. The fighters would receive 60% of the gross receipts, with the winner taking 75% of that, and the loser the remaining 25%. The club and the boxers each were required to post $2,500 cash as a guarantee of good faith. Eddie Graney would referee for a fee up to $500. The club and principals would share equally in any profits from the motion picture enterprise.

Fitzsimmons said, "I can beat O'Brien, but at that I'm not belittling him. He's a shifty boxer and is in good condition. Furthermore, he has been fighting right along and is keyed up to the proper pitch. After I fight him I'll take on any of the others who will draw a house. I'll fight Hart if he shows he means business, but he's got to show me before I sign articles with him."

Fitzsimmons also said O'Brien had wanted to split the purse evenly, but Bob was the one who insisted on a division based on winner/loser, showing who had the true confidence. "O'Brien thinks he has a chance. But he don't think he's got any chance. He wrote me and asked me to split the money even. Huh! He's a business man. All he thinks of is the money. He don't want to take a chance. He'd rather have a sure thing."

"BOB" FITZSIMMONS AND HIS PET LIONS   BOB FITZSIMMONS.

However, "Many are of the opinion that Fitzsimmons has seen his best day and that it is about time he left ring doings to the younger generation."

Experts believed that this time, in a longer match, O'Brien would pace himself, fight cautiously, and win because of his youth. Others said Fitz had the punch and O'Brien did not, so Bob would be dangerous at all times, while O'Brien most likely would focus on winning a points decision with his speed and footwork.

Most considered Marvin Hart the heavyweight champion and the O'Brien-Fitzsimmons bout to be for the light heavyweight championship.[318]

Fitzsimmons had not fought since his July 1904 6-round bout with O'Brien. He had grown older by more than one year since then and had been inactive during that time.

"PHILADELPHIA JACK" O'BRIEN

Conversely, O'Brien had remained very active, having 18 bouts since he had boxed Fitzsimmons, losing only once. His record included: 1904 WND6 Hugo Kelly, KO2 Billy Stift, KO1 Joe Butler, WND6 Tommy Burns, KO3 Jim Jeffords, WND6 John Willie, WND6 Dixie Kid, WND6 Black Bill, WND6 Larry Temple, and WND6 Morris Harris; 1905 WND6 Willie, WDQ2 and W10 Young Peter Jackson (avenging prior loss; O'Brien claims world middleweight title), L10 Hugo Kelly, and D20 Jack "Twin" Sullivan. In late October 1905, O'Brien scored a KO17 over then highly touted up-and-comer Al Kaufman. The 19-year-old 196-pound Kaufman had just turned pro, but already had scored a KO1 over Jack "Twin" Sullivan, who in turn had a 1904 10-round decision win over Mike Schreck and 20-round draw with O'Brien. The *Police Gazette* had given Kaufman a great deal of coverage despite his relative inexperience.[319]

Fitz arrived in San Francisco from New York on November 14. He claimed to be the heavyweight champion. "Jeffries won the title from me, and now that he has retired, it should go back to me."[320]

Bob would spar with middleweight Harry Foley, Billy Bates, and Harry Chester at Croll's Gardens in Alameda, where he trained for Gardner.

O'Brien was at Sheehan's Tavern on Ocean Boulevard, in Ocean Beach, San Francisco, where he trained for Kaufman.

Naughton noted that O'Brien was in great shape, as the pace he sustained throughout the Kaufman fight plainly showed.

---

[318] *Buffalo Evening Times, Buffalo Commercial, Binghamton Press, Brooklyn Times*, November 7, 1905; *Binghamton Press*, November 8, 1905; *Elmira Gazette and Free Press*, November 9, 1905; *Buffalo Illustrated Times*, November 12, 1905; *San Francisco Examiner*, November 16, 1905.
[319] *Police Gazette*, October 14, 1905, October 28, 1905, November 4, 1905, November 11, 1905.
[320] *San Francisco Chronicle*, November 15, 1905; *San Francisco Call*, November 16, 1905.

Rumors were that Fitz was not in great shape, seeming exhausted after his roadwork. Others said he looked good in sparring, though with far inferior men. Training and a real fight could be two different matters.[321]

On December 10 at Croll's Gardens, Alameda, nearly 400 people paid 50 cents apiece to watch Fitz go through 16 rounds of training. He hit the bag for 8 rounds and sparred 8 rounds with Billy Bates and Harry Chester.

The highest priced seats for the upcoming contest were $10 for ringside.[322]

W. W. Naughton said the fight would be the man with the knockout punch against the man of sidestep, duck, block, stab, and peck away to wear out a foe. By this method, O'Brien was able to knock out a much stronger and heavier man in Kaufman. However, the Cornishman was up to all the tricks of the trade. Many only saw O'Brien in it because of Bob's age.[323]

In training, O'Brien looked very fast with his feet. Jack said he would use speed to peck away at Fitz's face, blind him if possible, and when he was helpless, try to knock him out. O'Brien insisted on a large 24-foot ring. It was obvious that he wanted a big ring so that he could utilize his fast footwork. Jack said the pace he set would be too much for Bob. It clearly was a matter of activity, youth, speed, and footwork, against Fitz's power and brand of cleverness and timing, handicapped by age and inactivity.

Fitzsimmons claimed to be in very good shape, and looked fit, but he also oscillated between saying it likely would be his last fight and/or that he might consider a fight with Hart if he won. The question was how much he had left at his age. O'Brien was 28 years old, while Fitz was at least 42 years old, and had only boxed one 6-round bout, that with O'Brien in July 1904, in the two years since winning the world light heavyweight championship in November 1903. Even in late 1903, after defeating Gardner, writers were saying that Bob was past it and should consider retiring. Still, some said Bob had been sick going into that fight, and suffering hand and foot problems, but did not want to call off the contest. He had decked O'Brien.

Although they claimed to be fighting for the world's heavyweight championship, really they were contesting for light heavyweight honors, as neither would weigh over 175 pounds. W. W. Naughton wrote,

> O'Brien owns up to 164 pounds at present, and while Fitzsimmons is inclined to be reticent about his weight, the chances are he weighs several pounds more than his prospective opponent.
>
> The light-heavy championship is certainly involved…. As to the heavyweight championship, Fitzsimmons and O'Brien have as much right as anybody to battle for it under existing circumstances, but other contests will be required before the question of superiority among heavyweights is settled definitely. Marvin Hart will demand recognition, of course, and as he has already figured in an event

[321] *San Francisco Chronicle*, December 10, 1905.
[322] *San Francisco Call*, December 11, 1905.
[323] *San Francisco Examiner*, December 12, 1905.

which was winked at as a world's championship, he is entitled to consideration.[324]

FITZ SPINNING ALONG A ROAD IN ALAMEDA WITH THE GARDNER BROTHERS

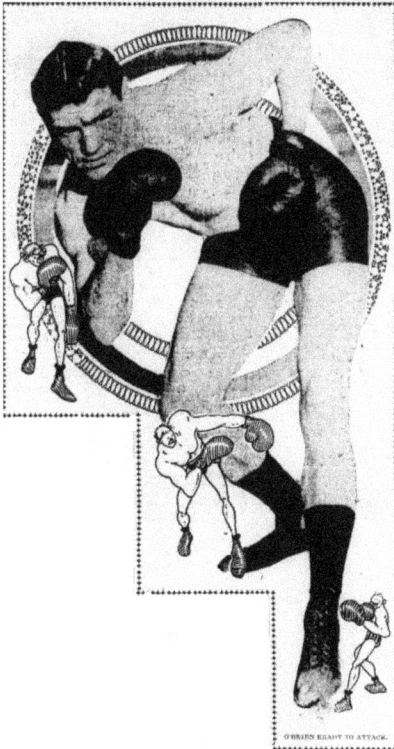

O'BRIEN READY TO ATTACK.

[324] *San Francisco Examiner, San Francisco Bulletin*, December 13, 1905.

HERE IS A PICTURE OF BOB FITZSIMMONS AT PLAY WITH HIS DOGS. "RUDDY ROBERT" PUTS IN HIS SPARE TIME TEACHING HIS PETS CIRCUS TRICKS

THE GLADIATORS WHO ARE TO FIGHT TWENTY ROUNDS TO-NIGHT. THE WINNER WILL BE HAILED BY THOUSANDS AS THE CHAMPION OF THE WORLD

O'BRIEN IN AN ATTITUDE OF DEFENSE, HIS LEFT PROTECTING HIS JAW AND HIS RIGHT THE BODY.

O'Brien said his performance on the 20th would be his reply to Fitz's stories about how the officials prevented Bob from knocking him out in their prior contest. Eventually, O'Brien said Fitz had tried to cross him. Jack had been told that their 6-round bout was to be a mere exhibition. Hence, he stopped training. "Fitzsimmons came into the ring wearing hand bandages three-quarters of an inch thick. I immediately realized that I had been 'jobbed' and that Fitz was going to try and hurt me. I made objections to the manner in which Fitz's hands were bandaged and he was compelled to remove the layers of adhesive tape he had put on his knuckles." Jack asked Bob what sort of contest they were to have, and Bob told him that he would have to look out for himself, for he intended to get him if he could. "For four rounds he did not land an effective blow, while I kept hitting him at ease. After four rounds I began to tire and I admit that I was all in at the finish." O'Brien would be in better shape this time around.

O'Brien further said, "I am in better shape now than I was when I defeated Kaufman." Regarding his plan, Jack said, "I will fight Fitzsimmons after the same style I employed in all my fights. My plan will be to peck away at his face, blind him if possible and when he is helplessly groping in the dark, try to put home a sleep producer."

Bob said he was in shape and had no injuries or ailments. "He's not the first clever boxer I have faced in the ring, and some of the fanciest of them had to take the count when I got through with them. Maybe O'Brien is so fast that I can't hit him, but I want to see it proved before I acknowledge that I can't hit any more."

O'Brien was a 7 to 10 odds favorite. He was just an inch shorter in height at 5'10 ½" to 5'11 ¾", and at 28, much younger than the 42-year-old, though some said Bob was 43 or 44.[325]

On the 17th, after running 5 miles and doing his gym work, including sparring with lightweight Willie Fitzgerald and "Terrible Swede" Swanson for 4 rounds, O'Brien weighed 162 pounds.

That same day, Fitz sparred Harry Chester and Billy Bates 4 rounds each, for 8 rounds total, mostly playing defense and using footwork.[326]

O'Brien's insistence upon a 24-foot ring made it clear that he intended to move a lot. Nevertheless, Jack said, "I found out in my last affair with Fitzsimmons that there is a good deal of exaggeration about the weight of his blows. He claims to have knocked me out of the ring, but nothing of the kind happened. He didn't even knock me down. I fell twice through slipping on wet spots in the corner that I fought from." Jack said he was going to show Bob that he could punch too. "I profited more than the average person would suspect by my former bout with Fitzsimmons. I had little or no confidence when I faced him then, whereas I have every confidence in the world now. I feel that Wednesday night's battle will terminate with a knockout, and the face on the floor will not be Jack O'Brien's either."

---

325 *San Francisco Examiner, San Francisco Call,* December 16, 1905.
326 *San Francisco Examiner,* December 18, 1905.

So much wagering on Fitzsimmons had come in that the odds shifted from O'Brien the favorite to Fitz the favorite at 10 to 9.[327]

On the cusp of the contest, Bob said he had trained faithfully since November 16 and was in top shape. He even worked 21 rounds total the previous week to test himself, hitting the bag for 14 rounds and sparring for 6. "I realize that O'Brien is a very clever fellow. No doubt he will bother me for a while. But once let the old left shift land, and then you may be on the watch for the end." Bob was positive that he would win, but, "If I lose I will never go into the ring for a purse again. This is final."

O'Brien said,

> Of course my great forte is in my rapid footwork. I think that I can set so fast a pace that 'Sir Bob' will be bewildered, and will not be able to set himself for his knockout punch. I will peck away until I have him blinded and helpless and unable to protect himself. ... I will weigh about 165 in the ring. Fitz, I think, will weigh a good deal more. But I will upset that advantage in a jiffy.

Battling Nelson said Fitzsimmons no longer could stand a long fight and his strength had diminished with time. O'Brien was much younger and in better condition and hence had a much better chance of winning.

Referee Eddie Graney said they would box with clean breaks. "Each man must loosen his hold and stand back the instant I give the word."

In his day-of-the-fight analysis, W. W. Naughton said O'Brien was much younger, a grand boxer, with knowledge of the finer points of the game. In his day, Fitz had just as many of the fanciful touches, a graduate of the Jem Mace style of sparring. "As Fitzsimmons worked upward in his calling he discarded much that he had learned." Fighting much bigger men, he worked more on winning with his wallop. Sparring partners often said landing on him did not mean anything, for he often allowed such in order to counter or time them with his own blows. In summation, "O'Brien, it might be said, has cleverness that dazzles; Fitzsimmons possesses cleverness that counts."

Naughton said that years prior, a match between the two would have been looked upon as a mismatch. But time had changed that. Bob looked good in training, but only the fight itself would make plain whether the passing of years had dulled the Cornishman's dash.[328]

On Wednesday December 20, 1905 at Mechanics' Pavilion in San Francisco, in the winter's biggest fight, before a crowd of 8,000, 28-year-old Philadelphia Jack O'Brien, 131-9-20, fought 42-year-old Bob Fitzsimmons for the world light heavyweight championship; although some claimed and advertised that the bout was for the heavyweight championship.

O'Brien entered the ring at 9:10 p.m. He wore a big brown bathrobe. With him were Spider Kelly, Young Gorman, Battling Swanson, Willie Fitzgerald, Chappie de Wolf, and Billy Springfield.

[327] *San Francisco Examiner*, December 19, 1905.
[328] *San Francisco Examiner*, December 20, 1905.

Fitzsimmons soon followed, stripped to his light blue fighting trunks. The cheering he received for several minutes far exceeded that which was given to O'Brien. Bob's seconds were Billy Bates, Harry Chester, and Young Croll. Bob had left his toupee in the dressing room.

O'Brien threw off his robe and disclosed green trunks. Both men wore red, white, and blue belts.

Billy Jordan introduced O'Brien as the "Beau Brummel" of the prize ring. Fitz was presented as the middleweight and light heavyweight champion of the world. He received great cheers. It was announced that Marvin Hart and Jack 'Twin' Sullivan challenged the winner.

Referee Eddie Graney sported a new tuxedo suit for the occasion. He met with the fighters at ring center to discuss the rules. They had agreed to break at the referee's order and not to hit in the clinches or breakaways.

Fitz wore olive green gloves. O'Brien's gloves were dun colored (slightly brownish, dark gray, or dusty gray-brown). Billy Jordan announced, "Let 'er go!" The bell rang and the fight began at 9:25 p.m.

1st round

The round was marked by O'Brien's marvelous footwork. Both feinted and danced, with O'Brien being quicker to retreat. Jack threw some lefts and either moved away or clinched. He landed a left to the mouth and right to the ribs. Fitz tried to corner him, but Jack ducked under a right and got away. He dodged all around the ropes. Fitz missed repeatedly. O'Brien landed a left to the stomach and clinched. Fitz landed a right on the ribs, the only blow he scored. Overall, he seemed puzzled and unable to land.

C. E. Van Loan's summary said O'Brien gave a great exhibition of jumping around the ring, hopping in and out like an acrobatic dancer. Whenever he saw Bob about to punch, Jack would go running about like a sprinter. The crowd howled at his tactics.

2nd round

O'Brien continued hitting and moving, although more peppering blows were thrown in this round. Fitz landed some grazing but hard blows. O'Brien landed some lefts and a hard right. His left began to sting like a wasp.

Van Loan said Fitz chased and threw while O'Brien ducked like a flash. Jack feinted quickly, which kept Fitz cautious. Bob did land a hard right to the jaw, and the crowd cheered him.

3rd round

O'Brien blocked, feinted, and made Bob miss. O'Brien's heavy left jab to the nose made Bob stagger back. Fitz came back and pressed O'Brien to the ropes, scraping skin from his forehead with a left hook. He also landed a right. O'Brien's seconds yelled, "Be careful, Jack!" Fitz threw a hard left into the body. O'Brien stood close and jolted Fitz's head with lefts and rights.

Just at the close of the round, O'Brien suddenly stopped moving and leapt in with a plunging, snappy straight left. It landed between the eyes, on the nose, and sent Fitzsimmons crashing to the floor on his backside with a thud that could be heard all over. Bob grinned and quickly rose as the bell rang. Jack had opened Bob's nose.

Van Loan said that at the end of the round, O'Brien was running around the ropes with his hands down, with Fitz slowly circling after him. Suddenly O'Brien stopped and leaped forward with his left flush in Fitz's face and took him off his feet with a crash. The old man rolled over on his back and kicked his legs in the air, jumping up with a laugh on his face. The bell rang just as he got to his feet. It was a most peculiar knockdown. Bob seemed surprised.

4th round

Fitz forced matters but missed so badly that the impetus of his punches caused Bob to throw himself down to his knees. O'Brien danced around, with Fitz chasing. Jack also stopped and landed lefts and rights. Bob's nose bled. O'Brien also used rights to the body to wear him down.

Later in the round, O'Brien rushed and hustled Fitz to the ropes and Bob fell down. He was up quickly. It was not a true knockdown. Bob attacked, but Jack blocked and clinched. O'Brien landed a left and right on the face, punishing blows. Fitz's face was covered with blood. One said his left eye was badly cut.

Van Loan said Fitz tried to even up matters, rushing and swinging, with O'Brien ducking and getting away. His own rush caused Bob to go to his knees. The clever O'Brien was fighting carefully, using lightning left jabs to the face, starting the blood which never stopped flowing.

O'Brien hustled him to the ropes and Fitzsimmons went down with a bang. His legs were unsteady and his footing unsure.

5th round

O'Brien jabbed away, pumping them into Bob's face. Blood ran from Bob's nose and mouth, and his face was badly cut up. He kept trying wicked swings to no avail. He could not land with any force. O'Brien landed hard rights to the wind and easily escaped counters. He received a warning from the referee about his use of the elbow.

Van Loan said there was a little slugging in this round. O'Brien landed a very hard body blow. Fitz grunted but replied with the same kind. They made three exchanges to the body. Spider Kelly called to O'Brien, "Steady, Jack! Feint him out! Feint him! That's the stuff!" Jack had Bob guessing badly. Fitz was covered with blood but seemed as strong as ever and full of fight.

6th round

O'Brien again used extreme speed to get out of danger. He was very cautious, skipping around as Fitz tried in vain to reach him. Jack generally landed his left and clinched or ran away again. Bob kept missing his right. Some of the crowd hissed O'Brien's sprinting tactics. Fitz did land one left flush on the mouth, starting the blood from Jack, who held onto Bob's neck for a time.

Van Loan said Fitz missed another terrific hook and swung himself to his knees. The gong found them clinched. Jack slapped Bob on the back.

7th round

O'Brien danced around but further marked up Bob. Fitz landed a right to the body and left on the side of the head to roars of satisfaction from the crowd. Jack kept jumping away and landing lefts. Fitz landed a stiff right under the heart and followed with a left to the stomach. Spider Kelly yelled to O'Brien to steady himself. Fitz's right eye was puffed. One said there was a cut over his eye. Another said his right eye was nearly closed.

8th round

O'Brien used his left jab until Fitz caught him with a right to the stomach, which made Jack cautious. O'Brien ripped in a nasty left over the eye.

When they both swung rights, O'Brien landed first with his short right to the jaw that dropped Fitz down onto his back. Bob quickly scrambled to his feet at once, but he staggered a bit.

O'Brien tried to finish him. A right to the jaw forced Bob to the ropes, and a series of left jabs and rights almost put him out. Jack also struck him with several body blows. Bob was groggy and in a bad way.

Van Loan said the round nearly saw a knockout. They both swung short rights to the jaw. Fitz went down on his back, but he immediately rose. Yet, his legs were bending under him and there was a dazed look on his face. He staggered back against the ropes. The house was in an uproar, half of them yelling at O'Brien to finish him, and the other half yelling at Fitz to clinch and stall. Bob was badly hurt and swung wildly. But O'Brien was cautious, for he heard that Fitz was very dangerous when hurt. Hence, instead of trying to finish, he allowed Fitz to bluff his way to the gong, very badly hurt and all but out. He nearly missed his chair.

9th round

Fitzsimmons showed his gameness and recuperative powers, coming on strong. O'Brien did all he could to avoid the vicious blows. O'Brien swung a left on the eye, cutting a gash. Jack kept landing and ducking or clinching. Bob landed a right to the stomach, but there was no force. O'Brien looked confident as he skipped around. He landed a right to the body, straight left, and two hard rights on the jaw. Fitz's face was badly marked, and his legs dragged.

Van Loan said Bob was very tired but saved himself well.

10th round

O'Brien caught Fitz with a straight left, and after avoiding a Fitz swing, Jack swung a left on the cheek. As Jack advanced, Fitz rammed his right into his ribs, but it didn't seem to have the usual weight behind it. O'Brien kept jumping in the air and shooting straight lefts into Bob's face, meanwhile drawing back from Bob's left hooks and jolts. Fitz landed another right to the ribs, hard this time. Jack clinched and held on, clearly affected.

One said the round was all in Fitz's favor until just before the bell, when O'Brien landed a right to the head that hurt.

Van Loan said Fitzsimmons landed a terrific body blow which made O'Brien's eyes stick out.

11th round

O'Brien came forward crouching but landed a straight left. Fitz caught him with two lefts to the face and a right on the stomach. O'Brien hung on in a clinch, and some of Bob's admirers stood up to encourage him with yells. Between clinches, O'Brien sent in lefts to the face and ran around the ring, with the crowd hooting him. Fitz landed one punishing right in the stomach and Jack held on all the harder. But when they broke, O'Brien rushed him to the ropes. The crowd was yelling for Fitz as they went to their corners, appreciating his work, but O'Brien did not appear to be hurt.

Another observer of the round said Fitz landed often with both hands to the body, which had O'Brien backing away. Jack butted him badly and was jeered. O'Brien ran away a lot.

12th round

As usual, O'Brien landed his left jab, and they clinched. Jack forced Fitz to the ropes with lefts to the face. Bob landed his own clean left to the face, which sent Jack back staggering. The crowd hooted O'Brien for running, but when Jack stood and fought, he did great damage with his left jab. Bob again reached the ribs with his right but was repaid with two jabs. When Fitz tried to corner him, Jack sidestepped and got away cleverly, which drew more hoots. O'Brien then stood in close and tilted Fitz's head a number of times with lefts. Bob was unable to land on the nimble Philadelphian.

One summarized that the 10th through 12th rounds were marked by Bob's futile efforts to land, and constant jabbing and uppercutting on the part of O'Brien, which served to wear down Fitzsimmons gradually.

Van Loan said that in the 11th and 12th rounds, O'Brien was running around the ring, holding in the clinches, and doing all he could to wear out the old man.

13th round

O'Brien danced from side to side and landed lefts to the face. Fitz swung on the jaw, and they clinched. O'Brien feinted and punched him twice in the face with the left. Bob tried hard to catch him with left hooks, but Jack either ducked or blocked. He stopped a right body blow with his elbow and clinched. A Fitz left to the head could be heard all over the house. The crowd cheered Bob and hooted Jack for holding on. Fitz scored a solid right to the body.

O'Brien mixed it, landing a vicious left hook to the body and a fierce left on Bob's swollen lips. Some said a right to the jaw landed as well. The bell rang. The blows did not immediately show their effects. However, as he went to his corner, Fitz bent over.

Another said the round was more of the same, with O'Brien outboxing Fitzsimmons. Just before the round ended, Jack landed a wicked short left into Fitz's stomach.

Bob went to his chair, and while there, he unexpectedly pitched forward and would have fallen had his seconds not caught him. He vomited considerable blood and was in a state of collapse. Another claimed he collapsed and slid to the floor, sinking as if he had feinted. Spider Kelly called attention to it. When Referee Ed Graney went over and saw Bob's condition, he immediately waived the contest off.

W. W. Naughton said that after about 30 seconds in his corner, an exhausted Bob sank to his knees. His eyes were nearly closed, his nose spread, and his lips swollen. Bob began vomiting, and the blood ran from his mouth. Naughton claimed that Bob said, "Eddie, I'm all gone."

Another paper said Bob tried to say something about being hit with a body shot, but then collapsed while seated, the blood flowing from his nose and mouth, leading to the stoppage.[329]

It was a bloody battle, but O'Brien had been in control throughout, outboxing Fitzsimmons with his fast footwork and quick punches,

---

[329] *San Francisco Bulletin, Examiner, Call, Evening Post, Chronicle,* December 21, 1905.

dropping him in the 3rd round with a straight left between the eyes, and in the 8th round with a right. The left hook to the body just before the end of the 13th round took the rest of the fight out of Fitz, who essentially had to retire after the 13th round.[330]

TWO "EXAMINER" FLASHLIGHTS, SHOWING FITZSIMMONS SPRAWLED ON THE FLOOR OF THE RING AS THE RESULT OF O'BRIEN'S KNOCKDOWN BLOWS

O'Brien gave a speech, saying, "Gentlemen and ladies...I ask for no glory for defeating Mr. Fitzsimmons to-night. I regard him as the grandest fighter that ever donned a glove!" Continuing, "I was too fast for the old man and set a pace I was at all times sure would win in the end." He just had to watch out for the one punch that might turn the tide of battle. He allegedly took no credit for the victory, but also said, "I am prepared to defend the title of heavyweight champion of the world, which I now claim belongs to me. Marvin Hart and all the pugs the public think are entitled to a meeting will be accommodated." O'Brien also said, "I am now ready to fight any man in the world for the middle-weight or heavy-weight championship, provided he is white."

Another quoted O'Brien as saying afterwards,

> I am sorry for old Fitz. He fought the gamest sort of a fight and did the best that was in him. Now I am going after the middle and heavyweight championship. First I want to take on Tommy Ryan at 158, and then I'll meet Hart or any one else in line. ... I am not damaged in the least ... and I was working under wraps all the way. I never extended myself because I felt confident of winning every second of the time. It was a sorry ending and the public cannot regret it more than I, for Fitz is a grand old man and everybody in the game likes him.

The crowd paid $16,407. 60% went to the fighters, with the winner receiving 75% ($7,383.15) and the loser 25% ($2,461.05) of that 60% share.

[330] *Police Gazette*, December 30, 1905.

It was the largest crowd that had attended any fight in San Francisco that year. The club earned over $6,000 after expenses.

The *San Francisco Evening Post* said Fitz fought hard, but was no match for O'Brien, who was too fast, too active with hands and feet, and too elusive and cautious. The game Fitz took a fearful beating. He had to fight both O'Brien and father time. His age was too much of a handicap.

The *San Francisco Examiner's* W. W. Naughton said Fitzsimmons was thoroughly beaten. Fitz was too slow for him. O'Brien was as nimble as a rubber ball, and he punished Bob throughout. The bulk of the damage was done with stiff straight lefts as Jack danced about. Fitz wanted to get close enough to land one of his numbing blows. O'Brien was intent on avoiding returns while pecking and stinging as fast as he could. He fought him as he did Kaufman, jabbing and skipping about, swooping under stiff blows. Fitz could not get through to the defensive-minded O'Brien. He was too elusive. Fitz was too slow, his footwork was not there, and his wallop had lost its force. Fitzsimmons simply no longer was what he once was.

C. E. Van Loan said, "The old man was a pitiful sight. His right eye was all but closed and tiny streams of blood trickled from a dozen cuts on his face. His lips were puffed and crimson and from forehead to chin he was one red smear." The crowd rooted for Fitz and encouraged him throughout, and hooted O'Brien for running away. But it was O'Brien who did the execution. He won, but, "It was only the old man's ghost which came back into the ring last night." And the ghost did not have his legs. "Bob Fitzsimmons has fought his last fight; the next time he issues a challenge they should send the wagon after him."

The *San Francisco Chronicle* said game old Fitz was outdone by O'Brien's speed and cleverness. O'Brien severely beat Fitz's face and body until exhaustion caused him to collapse in his corner after the 13th round. Bob made a fight that no other man his age could make. He always tried, fighting hard and furiously, but youth was served. At intervals Fitz showed flashes of his awkward cleverness, but age was not to be denied. O'Brien was abnormally clever, in and out with the ease of a dancing master. He fought carefully, willing to bide his time. The left hook to the stomach at the end of the 13th caused the final collapse. In his corner, Bob said, "Eddie, he got me – a punch – in the – stomach," and he fell forward on the floor. Referee Eddie Graney then awarded the fight to O'Brien.

Ultimately, old age is what got Fitzsimmons, who had been a "wonderful fighter," "the greatest fighter of his weight the world ever saw."

O'Brien was as fast as a lightweight with great cleverness, willing to wait, but passing up no opportunity to strike.

Referee Eddie Graney said the force and vitality that made Fitzsimmons one of the world's best fighters simply was not there. O'Brien was too shifty for him. If Fitzsimmons still had the power in his legs that he had retained in his arms it would have been a different fight. O'Brien was too shifty, and Bob's legs were too slow.

One writer said Fitzsimmons was not his former self but instead was a pitiful spectacle.

Fitz admitted that O'Brien was too young and lively for him. Jack had Corbett's footwork, although he was not as big as Jim. Bob also complimented Jack's ability to duck and get out of tight places. He did not fault O'Brien for doing so much running away. Corbett did the same. It was a stomach blow just before the end of the 13th that took all the wind out of his sails. He could hardly breathe and was unable to continue. "My bloody 'eart's broken; that's all." Some thought he was sad that his career appeared to be over and his world title gone. Others later said he was talking about his wife, who had left him, allegedly for another man. Another quoted him as saying,

> That clip in the stomach did me. I have seen the day that I could lick six of them fellows. Jack fought a good fight. I was beaten and with a punch that won many a battle for me. My friends say that I fought fast during the last three rounds. That is wrong. O'Brien was getting slower. I am not what I used to be by a long shot. I guess my fighting days are over. I've fought my last fight. I will never get into the ring again. I doubt if ever I will put another glove on. If I do, it will only be in exhibitions. My bloody, bleeding 'eart is broken.

The *San Francisco Call* said Fitzsimmons carried the fight to O'Brien, but the strain on his vitality proved too great. His ultimate collapse had been expected for several rounds. The cumulative force of O'Brien's blows seemed to be telling on the veteran. Bob had been down in the 3rd, 4th, and 8th rounds, and seemed to have lost his vitality in the 9th. He improved over the course of the next three rounds, but eventually nature gave out.

O'Brien fought in streaks. "He did considerable running away, but when he stood up and fought his work was quite effective. His footwork and ducking were marvelous to behold, carrying him out of many dangerous places." It was a pitiable sight to see Fitz attempt to hit the moving target. O'Brien flitted about the ring with a smile. Fitzsimmons kept trying throughout to change the tide of events and took many hard knocks in an effort to send home one punishing blow. His judgment of distance had been defective, and he could not land on his will-o'-the-wisp foe. O'Brien's left jab did a lot of damage to Bob's face, causing a bumpy, puffy, cut visage.

O'Brien at times butted and used his elbow. Eventually, in retaliation, Bob used the heel of his glove on O'Brien's face, and his elbow as well. A number of times, O'Brien had a wrestler's hold on Fitz's neck and tried to shut off his breath.

Afterward, Bob sobbed in his corner, mumbling over and over again, "My heart is broken." He shook hands with O'Brien to show no hard feelings.

The next day, Fitzsimmons again said he was done with the ring. He saw the openings, but he could not punch when he wanted. His old-time speed was not there, and his feet dragged. He felt slow. "When I started to fight I found my brain and my muscles did not work in accord. I would see an opening, but before I could take advantage of it the chance was gone. I think men in all the professions find age dulls their faculties." Bob asked, "Could you picture O'Brien doing this to me when I was younger?"[331]

MRS. FITZSIMMONS, WHO HAS LEFT BOB "FOREVER"

JULIA MAY GIFFORD.
She Notifies the Lately Defeated Fighter, Who Is Now in San Francisco, That She Is Going to Europe.

Explaining his reference to a broken heart, Bob revealed that just before the fight, his wife Julia, who was not in town, sent letters indicating that she was divorcing him. She was running away with another man. Such a thing had to have a big psychological impact on Bob, who said as much after the bout. He initially thought of calling off the contest, but his manager prevailed upon him to honor his contract and fight as best he could. Her doing that right before his fight was quite cruel, if that was the case.[332]

In subsequent days, Fitz said,

I cannot realize that Julia would treat me in such a manner after what I have done for her. She has eloped with, or will meet a man of Franklin, Pa., with whom she has been in love for years. She told Leon Friedman, my manager, that she intended marrying him, and she wanted to leave me last Summer, but Friedman talked her out of it.

She has taken my jewelry, and, I believe, my money, and left me heartbroken, and I am helpless to know how to turn.

Bob's manager Leon Friedman revealed a telegraph sent to him by Julia which said, "I am leaving New York forever. Took step week ago, long contemplated; am determined. My attorney's letter should reach Bob to-day. Julia." Friedman said Julia had access to Fitz's bank account in New York which had about $32,000 in it. He claimed Bob earned $3,000 from the O'Brien contest. He said Julia had long been planning to leave Fitz. She failed to write or wire him for days before the fight, and as a result, Fitz was in a bad way with worry when he entered the ring with O'Brien.[333]

Bob claimed that Julia had eloped with Charles Miller, head of the Franklin Manufacturing Company in Franklin, Pennsylvania. Miller strongly denied the claim. He threatened to kill the pugilist if he molested him. Miller said he had not eloped with Bob's wife and had no intention of doing so. He claimed that he had not seen Julia for quite a long time.

---

[331] *San Francisco Call, San Francisco Chronicle*, December 22, 1905.
[332] *San Francisco Examiner*, December 24, 1905.
[333] *New York Telegraph*, December 24, 1905.

I have known Mrs. Fitzsimmons for about eight years. I knew her before Fitzsimmons did. ... The last time I saw Mrs. Fitzsimmons was in June of this year, when she was going abroad to Paris to study vocal music. I accompanied her to the steamer in New York and saw her off. She had no one else to go with her, and I went to the dock, the same as I would with any other friend. Fitzsimmons knew that I accompanied his wife to the dock. He was mad about it, and has never got over that. He goes mad every time he thinks of it.

Fitzsimmons is insanely jealous, and when word came from her that she was leaving him for all time he evidently jumped to the conclusion that I was going with her. ... If he comes bothering around with any of his talk about me eloping with his wife I'll let daylight through him. I mean what I say and will not tolerate his circulating such scandalous reports about me.

Friedman said Fitzsimmons would institute a $100,000 lawsuit against Miller for alienating the affections of his wife. Upon reading what Miller said, Friedman responded,

[I]f he wants to do any shooting, let him try it on me. I am the one who brought Miller's name into this affair. I know all about him. Mrs. Fitzsimmons confessed everything to me, and I have other sources of information. This shooting threat of his is the rawest kind of a bluff. If Fitz was in the same city with him Miller would shake himself to death. He is in a nasty position and the best thing he can do is to remain very quiet. He took Mrs. Fitzsimmons away from her first husband and now he has taken her away from Bob.

I would have Major Miller know that I have got a pretty extensive line of 'dope' on him. I know about him at the Auditorium Hotel in Chicago and the Bartholdi Hotel in New York. Just now I can't explain what I mean by this, but Miller will know.

Fitz received the information that Miller would shoot him on sight with unusual calmness.

I am not in the business of making threats. I am satisfied to let the law take its course. Miller's threat is laughable. He hasn't the nerve to do anything of the sort. However, if he wants to make good on the proposition, let him tell me where to meet him after the first of January. ...

After all I guess I'm lucky to get rid of a woman like my wife. But I don't think I deserve the treatment she has given me. I did everything I could for her. I sent her to Paris. That cost me $5,000, and I have bought her lots of jewels.[334]

Another paper said actress Gifford had cleaned out Bob's bank account and ran away with his money. Bob had paid for her musical education in

[334] *Oakland Tribune*, December 25, 1905.

Paris, had lavished diamonds upon her, and given her everything that her heart desired, all to no avail. Bob's second wife had died on April 17, 1903, and Bob had surprised his friends by marrying Julia less than four months later. When his second wife died, it was discovered that all his money, some $28,000, was in her name, and it was held in trust for his three children, who were attending a convent in New Jersey. Now, Fitz only had the few thousand he made from the recent O'Brien fight.[335]

JULIA GIFFORD FITZSIMMONS

Left Her Husband to Go to Paris and Study For Operatic Stage.

MRS ROBERT FITZSIMMONS. (Julia May Gifford.)

THE THIRD MRS. ROBERT FITZSIMMONS, FORMERLY PRIMA DONNA OF "WHEN JOHNNY COMES MARCHING HOME," WHO DESERTED THE PUGILIST IN THE DARKEST HOUR OF HIS PUBLIC CAREER, AND HER HEART-BROKEN HUSBAND.

---

[335] *Utica Globe*, December 30, 1905.

Although the bout had been at light-heavyweight, Philadelphia Jack O'Brien began claiming the heavyweight championship. He believed that when Jeffries retired, the championship reverted back to the previous title holder, Fitzsimmons. "That makes me champion." The victory certainly made O'Brien an even bigger name on the boxing scene, although he already had been quite prominent. He was the first man to defeat Fitzsimmons on American soil other than Jeffries. Initially, the *Police Gazette* agreed that O'Brien had a clearer claim on the title than Hart. Jack claimed that he wanted to fight Hart for the undisputed title.[336]

O'Brien was cut from the cloth of James Corbett. He was handsome, well dressed, intelligent, well-spoken, had a sharp tongue, and could play hardball in negotiations. Even their styles were similar. O'Brien was fast with his hands and feet. The press loved him.[337]

However, despite O'Brien's talk, when Alex Greggains offered a February date to Marvin Hart and Jack O'Brien, Jack declined, saying that he wanted to rest until March, and was more inclined to take on Tommy Ryan at middleweight first. Such reluctance to fight Hart, and the desire to fight at middleweight, took O'Brien out of the running for consideration or recognition as a true heavyweight champion. Furthermore, "Like all the champions, O'Brien has drawn the color line and will never fight a negro. The manager of Jack Johnson, the colored heavy-weight, has offered to bet O'Brien $2,500 that the black man can take his measure, but O'Brien has refused to take the matter under consideration."[338]

Tommy Ryan, another claimant to the world middleweight championship, said O'Brien's victory over Fitzsimmons meant little, because Bob actually was defeated by old age.[339]

Nearly a year later, W. W. Naughton said of O'Brien's victory over Bob, "He defeated Fitzsimmons, yes, but was it the Fitzsimmons that used to be? No sir! There was as much difference as there is between a living breathing man and one of your ancient Egyptian mummies."[340]

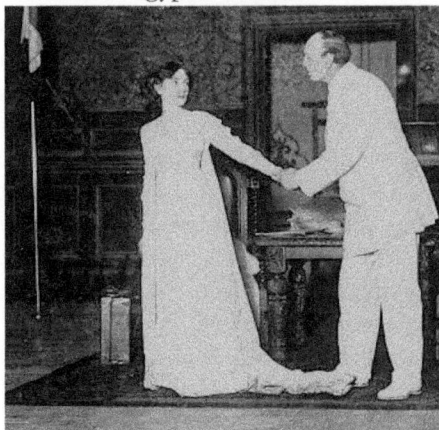

[336] *Police Gazette*, January 13, 1906.
[337] *Police Gazette*, January 13, 1906.
[338] *San Francisco Evening Post*, December 21, 1905; *Utica Globe*, December 30, 1905.
[339] *Los Angeles Express*, February 16, 1906.
[340] *Los Angeles Examiner*, November 28, 1906.

CHAPTER 15

Derailed

Bob Fitzsimmons had an interesting history with women. His first wife was an Australian woman, with whom he had three children in Australia, two of whom died as infants (Ellen 'Nellie', 1886-87; Robert W., '88) and the third who survived, Charles Robert Fitzsimmons (b. 1889). Soon after Bob attained fame in America, they were divorced and she married Martin Julian, Fitz's manager. Fitz married Rose Julian, his manager's sister. The marriage was a happy one, and they had three children, Bob Jr. (age 10, b. 1895), Martin Carson (in honor of Martin Julian and Carson City) (age 8), and Rosalie Julia (age 7). When Rose Julian died, a couple months later Bob married Julia Gifford, who was half his age. He had met her in McVicker's Theatre in Chicago and fell in love at first sight. She eventually left him for another man. Bob said, "I treated that woman like an angel. She bought hats that cost 65 dollars and 50 dollars, and I didn't say a word. She had my cheque book, and could draw all the money she wanted. Nobody could have treated a woman better. You see what I got for it."[341]

Yet, in early January 1906, it was announced that Bob Fitzsimmons and his wife Julia were making up and reconciling their relationship.[342]

Shortly thereafter, Bob and his wife Julia would return to stage work, performing in the play, "A Fight For Love," which interestingly mirrored his own personal life. Bob was an actor, no longer boxing, or so it seemed. Bob had a habit of coming out of retirement every so often.

The man who allegedly had been involved with Gifford, "Major" Charles Miller, was upset by the adultery allegations, calling it all a fraudulent scheme.

> Well, they got what they started after – a lot of free advertising – and now they kiss and make up, go to New York with the announcement

341 *Sydney Sportsman*, January 31, 1906; *Anaconda Standard*, January 2, 1906.
342 *San Francisco Examiner*, *Philadelphia Inquirer*, January 7, 1906.

274

that they are having a new play written for them… And who is it that has to suffer for all this free advertising? Why me. I think it is an outrage that a man's character should be attacked in such a manner. I am more convinced now than ever that the affair was a prearranged scheme. Fitzsimmons lost his fight and could not go around the country posing on his reputation any longer. He had to have something new. The old divorce proceedings story was pretty well played out, and they had to have something to liven it up. So they picked on the idea of bringing some one of prominence into it, and I was selected, simply because I happened to be acquainted with Julia Gifford, and had, on several occasions, befriended her when she needed a friend. And this is the thanks I get.[343]

On February 23, 1906, in Los Angeles, former middleweight but now 175-pound Tommy Burns won a 20-round decision over 195-pound Marvin Hart to win the world heavyweight championship.

In early April, Fitz agreed with promoter Tom O'Rourke to fight either Jack O'Brien, Tommy Burns, or Gus Ruhlin on Memorial Day/Decoration Day. He did not care who he fought, as long as he was paid well.[344]

On April 18, 1906, a huge earthquake and resulting fires devastated San Francisco. Over 3,000 died and more than 80% of the city was destroyed.

In late April, it was reported that Fitzsimmons and Tommy Burns had agreed to a 20-round bout in North Essington, 10 miles from Philadelphia, on May 29 or 30 for Tom O'Rourke's Tuxedo Athletic Club. They were guaranteed a $5,000 purse, plus the privilege of 50% of the gross receipts. O'Rourke believed the fight would draw at least $30,000. Fitz trained at Dunellen, New Jersey.

The *Los Angeles Herald* opined, "Of course Burns will win, and win easily. It is no trouble to whip Ruby Robert now…but, really and truly, it appears on the order of the ridiculous." Burns was much younger, strong as a bull, and clever, as proven by his local bout against Hart.[345]

Supposedly, on May 6, 1906, Bob's 88- or 89-year-old mother Jane Fitzsimmons (nee Strongman) died at her home in Timaru, New Zealand. (However, her gravestone says she died on April 3.) She had 12 children, of whom Bob was the youngest. She left five daughters and one son in Timaru, and two sons in the U.S. She was born in England.[346]

On May 12, 1906, at Madison Square Garden, about 8,000 people attended a boxing and wrestling exhibition show, the proceeds going to a California relief fund for the San Francisco earthquake sufferers. Amongst them, James J. Corbett refereed a 3-round exhibition bout between Bob Fitzsimmons and Kid McCoy, who lightly tapped one another in clever sparring. It ended with a comedic burlesque wrangle, with Corbett throwing McCoy to the floor, then Fitz grabbing Corbett around the waist, throwing

[343] *Philadelphia Inquirer*, January 8, 1906.
[344] *Minneapolis Journal*, April 7, 1906.
[345] *Montreal Daily Star*, April 27, 1906; *Topeka Daily Herald*, April 28, 1906; *Los Angeles Herald*, April 29, 1906; *Pittsburg Press*, May 7, 1906.
[346] *Chicago Tribune*, May 8, 1906; *Philadelphia Inquirer*, May 9, 1906.

him down and falling on top of him, and then all three rising and shaking hands. The spectators enjoyed it and shouted for more.[347]

Tommy Burns said he expected to knock out Fitzsimmons. "O'Brien stopped Fitz in 13 rounds. Every one who has seen O'Brien and myself in action knows I can hit harder than Jack. He is clever, undoubtedly, but I have the punch. If he could stop Fitz with his punching in 13 rounds, I think I shall be able to do it in 10."[348]

However, the day before the Burns vs. Fitzsimmons fight (then scheduled for May 29), on May 28, Pennsylvania Governor Pennypacker directed the police to prevent the bout. He sent several state police officers to make sure it didn't happen. However, the local sheriff wasn't sure why the governor was doing so, given that he believed the contest would be legal. Nevertheless, the governor believed the contest would violate the law, and said he wasn't going to allow New Yorkers to pull off a contest in his state that they could not pull off in their own state.[349] There was a general feeling that the powers-that-be did not want to see Fitz get used up and pounded upon at his advanced age.

BOB FITZSIMMONS PROVED HIMSELF A TRUE SPORTSMAN

Burns claimed the $500 forfeit money from the promoter. So far as Burns was concerned, the fight was off. Fitz, the "Grand Old Man" of the ring, declined to take the forfeit money. One said he wired back, "Don't send me forfeit money; I want to fight and not to travel around the country claiming forfeits." Another quoted him as saying, "I do not want to make it a business traveling over the country claiming club forfeits because the promoters strike a bit of misfortune. My business is boxing. Let the club hunt up another competitor for me, since Burns is so eager to crawl out of the match. ... When Burns quibbled over the size of the ring I was satisfied that he was convinced that I could outgeneral and outbox him."[350]

In early June, Bob's pet lion, "Senator," nearly broke his chain at the carnival and almost got loose. Bob's lion now and then tended to scare the daylights out of folks.[351]

[347] *Brooklyn Standard Union, New York Sun, Pittsburgh Post*, May 13, 1906. Philadelphia Jack O'Brien sparred Prof. Murray for 3 rounds as well.
[348] *Pittsburg Press*, May 26, 1906.
[349] *New York Daily Tribune, New York Times, Altoona Tribune, Philadelphia Inquirer, Pittsburgh Post*, May 29, 1906.
[350] *Topeka Daily State Journal*, June 15, 1906; *Buffalo Illustrated Times*, June 17, 1906; *Harrisburg Courier*, June 26, 1906.
[351] *Plainfield Courier-News*, June 4, 1906.

On November 28, 1906 in Los Angeles, in a fight for the world heavyweight championship, Tommy Burns fought Philadelphia Jack O'Brien to a controversial 20-round draw, as ruled by the referee, former champion James J. Jeffries. However, most thought Burns had won. The films show O'Brien doing a tremendous amount of moving and clinching.

In January 1907, reports were that Fitzsimmons and Burns had been matched for a 6-round bout on March 16, 1907 in Philadelphia. However, the next day it was said that the promoters did not want to take a chance of stirring up latent opposition to boxing by making such a fight.[352]

There had been and occasionally were some discussions of Fitzsimmons potentially fighting again, but nothing ever seemed to materialize.

On Thursday March 7, 1907, at the Opera House in New Castle, Pennsylvania, at the close of his stage performance, "A Fight For Love," which was touring the country, "Robert the Red" Fitzsimmons sparred 3 rounds with local young up-and-coming Italian Tony Ross, who was preparing for an upcoming bout the following week. After the play and bout, Bob said to Ross, "You are a great one, lad. Keep at the game and you will make something out of yourself." The local *New Castle Daily Herald* said Ross was a trifle stage struck but nevertheless got in two or three beautiful punches. "Fitz played to a large audience. He still has freckles on his legs."

Opera House

THURSDAY, MARCH 7.
Look! Who's Coming.
Mr. J. C. Matthews presents
America's Natural Actor
ROBERT
FITZSIMMONS
In his successful Comedy Drama
A FIGHT FOR LOVE
Supported by an Excellent
Company and Presented Exactly as
in the Big Cities.

SEE FITZSIMMONS
In a Three-Round Glove Contest, in
a Marvelous Bag Punching Ex-
hibition, Make Horseshoes and
Shoe "Ben Ali," the Arabian
Pony in Full View of the Aud-
ience.
PRICES..........25, 50, 75c, $1.00.
Seats on Sale.

TONY ROSS.

In subsequent days, Bob said, "That man Ross has the speed and the punch, but he needs a trifle more science. He is a comer and I would not be at all surprised to find him at the head of the heavyweight class." Another reported, "After the bout Bob said Ross had the punch of a champion, but lacked skill."[353]

In April 1907, Fitz wrote, "Statements that I have retired from the ring are untrue. I am still in the game and will fight any white man living. Will undertake to stop O'Brien in 10 rounds."[354]

352 *Buffalo Enquirer, Geneva Daily Times*, January 15, 1907; *Buffalo Commercial*, January 16, 1907.
353 *New Castle Daily Herald*, March 2, 7 - 9, 1907; *Pittsburg Press*, March 10, 1907. In 1909, then heavyweight champion Jack Johnson would win a 6-round no decision over Tony Ross.
354 *Cincinnati Enquirer*, April 10, 1907; *Topeka Daily State Journal*, April 12, 1907; *Leavenworth Post*, April 13, 1907.

Still, Fitzsimmons had not fought for more than a year, since his late 1905 O'Brien bout. Bob primarily had been an actor. Although he said he was willing to fight, for various reasons, either nothing materialized, or agreed-upon bouts were thwarted. Many thought he was too old and should no longer enter the ring, for his own sake and for the sake of the sport.

On May 8, 1907, in Los Angeles, world heavyweight champion Tommy Burns won a 20-round decision over Philadelphia Jack O'Brien, who primarily fought to survive, running like a gazelle.

The fight was controversial, because before the contest started, Referee Charlie Eyton called off all bets. Burns subsequently revealed that O'Brien had refused to fight again unless Burns agreed to throw the fight, which he did, but then double-crossed him and fought to win. O'Brien not only admitted that the fight had been fixed but went one step further by claiming that their first fight was an agreed-upon pre-arranged draw. He claimed that Burns was the one who approached him to induce the fraud. Most believed Burns, especially after James J. Jeffries revealed that O'Brien once had offered him $80,000 to lie down to him. O'Brien's integrity had taken a major blow.

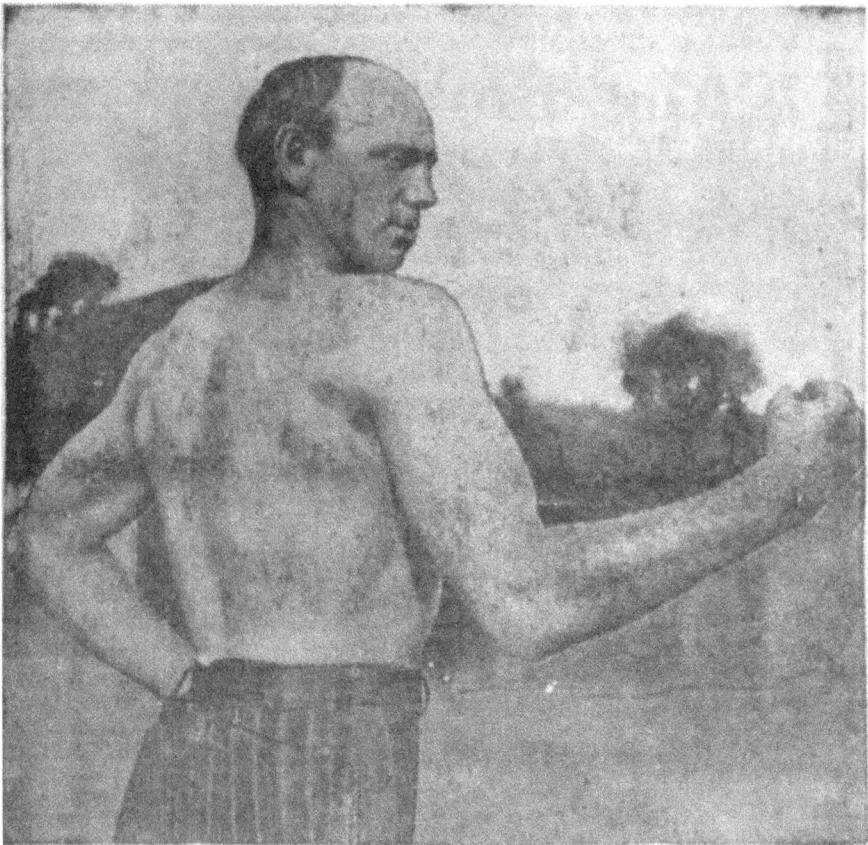

ROBERT FITZSIMMONS.

CHAPTER 16

Crossing the Color Line

On May 17, 1907, old and inactive Bob Fitzsimmons agreed to cross the color line and take on colored heavyweight champion Jack Johnson. "Now that Fitzsimmons' theatrical tour has come to an end he has decided to get back into the ring and will take on the negro, of whom it is said all other white fighters are afraid." Most white fighters had drawn the color line on Johnson. The fight likely would be held within the next two months. Bob claimed to have been training on and off for a while.[355]

Back in September 1905, Fitzsimmons had written an article regarding his current views on the color line:

> You'll hear a lot of men tell you that drawing the color line won't affect a record. That's all foolishness. It will and it must, because for a man to be champion in any class he must meet all the men who think they have a chance to get the championship away from him, and if one or two of those chaps are negroes, there will always exist a doubt as long as he refuses to meet them. ... No colored man has yet come running up to tell me who thought he could wallop my head off and take it away from me, but if he did I'm inclined to think I'd have to give him a battle for it. ...
>
> I've met negroes and I've always found them so and so. I don't mean that they're easy, for they're not; but I never saw one yet that could get away with me anyway, and maybe that's why I'm not refusing any of them that have a legitimate claim, a chance to get what's coming to them.
>
> Jeffries drew the color line and I think he made a mistake.[356]

Jack Johnson started boxing after Fitzsimmons already had won the world heavyweight championship in 1897. His record included 1901 LKOby3 Joe Choynski, D20 Mexican Pete Everett, L20 and D15 Hank Griffin; 1902 KO4 Joe Kennedy, D20 Hank Griffin, TKO12 Frank Childs (colored championship), and W20 George Gardner; 1903 W20 Denver Ed Martin (undisputed colored championship), W20 (twice) Sam McVey, W10 and W20 Sandy Ferguson; 1904 KO20 Sam McVey and KO2 Denver Ed Martin; 1905 L20 Marvin Hart, TKO4 Black Bill, WND6 Jack Munroe, WND6 Joe Grim, WND3, LDQby2, and WND6 Joe Jeannette, and WND12 Young Peter Jackson; 1906 WND3, W15, WND6, and W/DND10 Joe Jeannette, and W15 Sam Langford; and 1907 KO1 Peter

[355] *Cleveland Plain Dealer*, May 18, 1907; *Butte Evening News*, May 22, 1907.
[356] *Nashville Banner*, September 9, 1905. However, Fitzsimmons at times had drawn the color line.

Felix and KO9 Bill Lang. The 6'1" 190+-pound Johnson was known as one of the world's fastest and cleverest fighters. The color line, fear, and economics had prevented him from obtaining a title fight thus far.

44-year-old Bob Fitzsimmons had been boxing longer than the 29-year-old Johnson had been alive. His amateur career dated back to the 1870s, and his professional career spanned over 27 years, since the early- to mid-1880s. He won his first world championship way back in 1891, 16 years prior. Although Fitz was old and coming off a long year-and-a-half layoff, not having fought since December 1905, he was a big-name fighter, one of the biggest in boxing, and a former three-division world champion who still was highly respected. His reputation preceded him. Bob had that special aura and charisma that made fans want to see him no matter what; and suspend their disbelief about his age and inactivity. After all, only Jeffries and O'Brien had truly defeated Bob.

Bob Fitzsimmons. Jack Johnson.

San Francisco said the East was crazy over the bout. When the match was first made, some made light of it "on the ground that Fitz was too old and physically unfit" to engage a young man like Johnson. However, as the bout grew closer, despite his advanced age and fact that he was well past his best days, many conceded the legendary Fitz a chance against Johnson. Several writers boosted the bout. Fitz was full of confidence and said he believed that he could defeat Johnson. Bob Edgren said,

Robert Fitzsimmons

> Fitzsimmons surely has the courage of his convictions. His fight with Jack Johnson will squelch those howlers who claim white men fear the big smoke. Bob Fitzsimmons never feared any man. … And when Jack sees the icy glint in Bob's blue eyes it's a good bet that he will feel less like fighting than like running a hundred yards in 9 3/5 seconds.

After all, Fitz was crazy enough to keep lions as pets. He feared no man.

Dick Kain said many criticized the match on account of Fitz's advanced age, inactivity, lack of fitness, and bad hands. However, there was nothing weak about Bob's heart. True, Johnson was clever and much younger. "But that lets the colored man out. If there is anything yellow about him Fitz will not be long in finding it out and then the way things will come to Johnson will be sure to surprise him."

After his rematch with Fitzsimmons, Jeffries said,

> I never believed a man could hit so hard. I had eight stitches taken under my right eye after the fight and eight over it. My left eye had to be sewed up. My nose was pushed flat on my face and my teeth were loosened. Fitz was the greatest fighter I ever saw. These little fellows fighting now wouldn't have classed with him for a minute.

Kain asked, "The question now is, how much steam and strength does Fitz still possess?" Fans were willing to pay to find out.[357]

Fitzsimmons said he was just as good as young men, for he had taken care of himself and lived a temperate life.

> I figure that Johnson, who has gained a lot of prominence in the ring because the white men have refused to meet him, will be so busy blocking that he won't be able to hit me. I may step in with a shift and land one of my 57 varieties. One, I think will be enough. I expect to win with a knockout.[358]

"JACK" JOHNSON.   ROBERT FITZSIMMONS.

Regardless of any hype or excitement, Fitzsimmons had barely boxed, averaging only one fight in each of the past three years, although occasionally he sparred in some exhibition bouts. He still was tricky, clever, and powerful, but did not hit quite as hard, as rapidly, or as often, and grew tired much more quickly. Most writers were calling upon him to retire after he defeated Gardner at age 40 in late 1903, feeling that he most certainly was near the end. Fitz had agreed, saying, "I did well for an old man, but my ring days are over." Two years later, when stopped by O'Brien in late 1905, many said that Fitz was shot and done-for as a fighter and that only father time had beaten him. Fitz again agreed, saying that he was slow of hand and foot, and no longer could respond to the openings. At that point, Fitz once again retired. Yet, like many retired fighters, he came back again and again. He was a year and a half older, and age does not improve an already aging fighter. Still, even today, fans love to watch old fighters go at it yet again.

---

[357] *San Francisco Bulletin*, July 8, 1907.
[358] *San Francisco Call*, July 8, 1907.

Bob was very proud of his naturalized American citizenship status. He was born in Cornwall, England, of parents with Irish heritage.[359]

On July 4, 1907, in Colma, California, Tommy Burns knocked out Australian heavyweight champion Bill Squires in the 1st round. The fight was filmed, and showed Burns to be very smooth and well-balanced with his footwork, and an effective puncher, with excellent timing and sense of range, particularly with his powerful right.

Tad Dorgan said the pressure was on Johnson to win by knockout, and if he did not, he would be about as dead as Jack Munroe. "For years the sports have waited for a white heavy-weight to down the dark gent, and one by one they drew the color line, until there was not a man left who would fight." Johnson was training in Atlantic City. He said he was after Burns and wanted a beating in the worst way. Jack always did have a comedic touch.

Fitzsimmons felt he had nothing to lose and everything to gain. "If he is defeated, he is no deader than he is at present." If he won, he might get a go with Burns. "Not long ago we were told that Fitz knocked out big Al Kaufman in private. If that is on the level and the go was on the square, Fitz has just as good a chance today as he ever had." Yet, Tad also said losing by knockout to O'Brien showed that Bob was pretty far gone, even though he was loaded with trouble at the time.[360]

Fitzsimmons trained at Dunellen, New Jersey. Bob had been sparring with Joe Rodgers and Kid Cutler, but the Kid left, for he "did not relish the walloping he was getting."

On July 14, just three days before the fight, Bob trained with Joe Rodgers and black Joe Jeannette, who was added to the camp as a substitute for Kid Cutler. Jeannette had fought Johnson competitively 7 times, and Johnson never stopped him.

Present to see Bob train were Tex Rickard, Bat Masterson, Tom O'Rourke, Bob Edgren, George Considine, Tom Sharkey, and Kid McCoy, who would second Bob. Many came by automobile.

Fitz boxed 4 fast rounds with Joe Rodgers, putting him to his knees in the 2nd round. He then boxed 4 more rounds with Joe Jeannette (who likely weighed around 185 pounds). "They slugged hard all the way, but neither let out his best."[361]

[359] *New York Evening World*, July 3, 1907.
[360] *Buffalo Enquirer*, July 12, 1907.
[361] *Philadelphia Record*, July 15, 1907.

Robert Edgren said Johnson had the advantages of youth, swift cleverness, and greater size and physical strength, while old Bob had prestige, craft, and the wallop that years ago was dangerous at all times and the best in the world, but now was of an uncertain quality. Bob also was courageous, absolutely fearless and game. "In a losing fight he is the gamest and the most dangerous man the ring ever saw." Taking a fight with Johnson, the most avoided man, further proved Bob's courage. In his day, at close range, Fitz was the greatest fighter the world ever knew, with terrific power. His blows were so powerful that he often broke his own hands. But it was unclear how much power he had left.

Edgren said Johnson usually was too clever and strong for his foes. "Add gameness to Johnson's strength and skill and he'd be a champion." Fitz would be a big middleweight fighting a full-fledged heavyweight, but he was used to it. "This Johnson has all of the qualities for a great fighter except courage." He was as tall as Jeffries, with a tremendous reach, wide shoulders, and sinewy strength. He was remarkably clever, as clever as a lightweight. Like Corbett, Jack could send in lightning-like jabs at long range and shoot in snappy hooks that damage. He certainly would use all of his cleverness to avoid Bob's body blows. "Johnson has been unable to get matches with Burns, O'Brien, Schreck and other claimants of heavy-weight championship honors. Their claim that there is no money in fighting negroes may be true, but it surely looks as if they were side-stepping the black giant for some more potent reason." They knew he was no easy mark. Given Fitz's advanced age, if Johnson failed to win impressively, he would be looked upon as a joke.[362]

FITZ HAS COURAGE AND A RECORD, JOHNSON HAS EVERYTHING ELSE.

Barratt O'Hara said at 44 or 45 years of age, Fitz's tackling of Johnson, who was "perchance the best heavyweight in the world at this time," certainly showed Bob's courage. Fitz had not fought for nearly two years, when against O'Brien he was beaten by Father Time. Still, in only a 6-

[362] *New York Evening World*, July 15, 1907.

rounder, he had a chance to put up a creditable performance. Yet, "Johnson's friends expect to see him stop Bob in a round or two."[363]

Jack Johnson said,

> I'll have him down for the count a whole lot of times before the bell rings for the end of this battle, and I'll show a few people what I can really do. I think I can lick any heavy-weight in the world, and…I'm going to keep in the ring until I prove myself the real champion. … That fight ain't going no six rounds if I can help it, and if he licks me he's going to travel a whole lot faster than he ever dreamed of.[364]

The *Philadelphia Record* said the upcoming bout had the fight critics guessing. Some took it as a joke and declared that it was nothing but a frame-up, believing that Johnson would carry Fitz. Others took it seriously and declared that the old man was due to get an awful lambasting unless he landed one of his famous solar plexus blows early in the contest.

> Bob's hands have been broken too many times to allow him to think of trying to knock Johnson's head off, even were Jack less clever than he is, for a negro's skull is harder than a white man's broken hands, and Bob would surely get the worst of it.

> Johnson is a fast boxer, and it is likely that he will pepper Fitzsimmons pretty much at will unless he gets a smash that slows him up.

Some speculated that Johnson had agreed not to stop Fitz, but he denied it. The gate receipts would be divided based on an agreed-upon percentage, regardless of result. Still, both were motivated to do well.

> A decided victory for either man will do him a lot of good. It would be a great feather in Fitzsimmons' cap to knock out the man whom all the other white heavies have been dodging. … Johnson, by putting Fitz away in a decisive manner, can strengthen his claim for a fight with Burns or any other white heavyweight who claims the championship.[365]

Jim Corbett picked Fitzsimmons to win. He knew how Bob could punch, and "he also knows that the big negro heavyweight dislikes body blows. The bout has excited unusual interest, and it is likely that all attendance records will be broken at the clubhouse."[366]

Tad Dorgan said many were picking Fitz to win, including those who came to see him train, such as Tom O'Rourke, George Considine, and Kid McCoy.

Harry Harris said, "I saw Fitz box Jeanette in the training quarters, and honestly, if he ever lets out, Jeanette would never go four rounds. As it was Fitz just fooled with Joe and at that held him safe every second [of the]

[363] *Buffalo Evening Times*, July 15, 1907.
[364] *Brooklyn Times*, July 15, 1907.
[365] *Philadelphia Record*, July 16, 1907.
[366] *Philadelphia Public Ledger*, July 16, 1907.

bout. I hear that Jeanette has fought Johnson five or six times and once or twice held his own."

Kid McCoy said, "I am surprised to see the old man look so well. I figure that Johnson is a lot cleverer than Fitz but then the cleverest men in the world get it, you know. Fitz is as hard a hitter right now as any man in the world."[367]

FITZ WILL MAKE JOHNSON SHOW WHAT HE IS MADE OF TO-NIGHT.

Bob Edgren said Fitzsimmons would earn 35% of the receipts, while Johnson would earn 30%. Everyone wanted to know whether or not the "Big Smoke" was genuine or spurious. "The fight will probably go the full six rounds. Johnson is a big, clever fighter – a hard one to put away in such a short time." No one had stopped Bob in a mere 6 rounds. Even Jeffries and O'Brien required longer than that. (Still, they fought younger versions than the one Johnson was fighting.) Bob usually fought poorly early but then got going as the fight progressed. He likely would take some early punishment before loosening up and tearing in harder than ever. He was an expert at anatomy. He knew where to place his blows.

> Johnson is a different sort of fighter. He is forty pounds heavier than Fitzsimmons. He is taller and longer of reach. He is much younger. He is tough and wiry. He is a clever boxer. In all, he seems to have a tremendous advantage in everything but punching power. And the only reason that he has lacked that in his former fights is that he is afraid. He naturally jabs or chops, and then slips back out of range. He is going away before his blow fairly lands, and so he doesn't put the power behind it that he really could put there if he were more courageous.

> Johnson is this kind of a fighter. Let him be in the ring with a dangerous man and he is clever and swift in getting away. He is very cautious. He develops a wide yellow streak. But let him once think

[367] *Buffalo Enquirer*, July 16, 1907.

that he is winning easily and he becomes a raging slasher. If he finds Fitz weak he'll jump in and try to butcher him. He'll be as bold and dangerous as a lion. In that case there will be plenty of vim behind Johnson's blows.[368]

When asked if he ever fought colored fighters before, Bob said, "Yes, I licked Black Griffo and George Godfrey and they were never heard of again." These fights, if they occurred, do not appear on Fitz's record. Bob did fight black fighters in Australia, such as Pablo Fanque (1886 KO2), Jack Bonnar (1887 WND4)(possible aborigine), Edward "Starlight" Rollins (1890 KO9), and in the U.S., Harris "Black Pearl" Martin (1891 WND4).[369]

Johnson was the 10 to 7 favorite because he had too many advantages.[370]

BOXING TONIGHT Washington Sporting Club. 15th and Wood.
BOB FITZSIMMONS
vs. JACK JOHNSON
THREE HEAVYWEIGHT PRELIMINARIES.

On Wednesday night, July 17, 1907, at the Washington Sporting Club at 15th and Wood streets in Philadelphia, 29-year-old Jack Johnson, 41-5-8, who was announced as weighing 185 (but could have been 195), fought 44-year-old former three-division world champion Bob Fitzsimmons in a scheduled 6-round bout, the longest allowed there. They wore 5-ounce gloves. Tommy Keenan was scheduled to referee.

The day of the fight, the local *Record* called Fitzsimmons "the daddy of them all at mixing it up," and Johnson "the big black, whom they all have passed up as too hard a game." Both were in good condition, having trained for the past four weeks.[371]

Among the 2,500 men and one woman present, most were Fitz fans and friends. The spectators paid from $1 to $5 each for tickets. The house generated $8,000. The fans, which completely filled the building, sweltered in the heat for two hours, first watching some preliminary bouts.

JACK JOHNSON.

Although Johnson was the odds favorite, the old warrior's backers' almost inexplicable confidence made some wary and refuse to bet.

Yet, before they entered the ring, it was rumored that Fitz had a very sore arm from a blow received in training.

[368]368 *New York Evening World*, July 17, 1907.
[369] *Buffalo Enquirer*, July 17, 1907.
[370] *Brooklyn Times*, July 17, 1907.
[371] *Philadelphia Record*, July 17, 1907.

It was 10:30 p.m. when Johnson skipped over the ropes. There was feeble and scarce applause. Deputy Sheriff Billy Leedom served a writ upon him. Obviously, someone was claiming that Jack owed them money. Johnson was seconded by Sam Fitzpatrick, Barney Furey, and Black Bill. Spectators amused themselves by throwing money/coins at Bill, who was holding Johnson's chair. Earlier that evening, fellow black fighter Morris Harris had knocked out Bill in the 3rd round.

Two minutes later, Fitzsimmons came down the aisle. Bob received deafening cheers from nearly every man in the house, which continued for several minutes. Fitz had Tom O'Rourke, Young Corbett, and heavyweight Joe Rodgers in his corner.

Joe Jeannette and Sandy Ferguson were both on hand to challenge the winner or any man in the world. They were introduced, as were Jack Blackburn, Dick Hyland, and Frankie Neil.

Johnson wore blue trunks. Fitz wore a long pair of trunks and a belt made of an American flag. Upon his introduction, when he stood up, Bob received another rousing cheer. Johnson was almost ignored.

The first shock of the evening came when Referee Tommy Keenan announced to the crowd, "Gentlemen: The majority of you don't know, but I have a little reputation to sustain. I hear from a very reliable source that Fitzsimmons has broken his right arm. Now unless Fitz will stand for a physical examination, I am done." Keenan then left the ring.

Fitz, Johnson, and their seconds were in the ring at the time, with their gloves on, ready for the bout.

Fitzsimmons raised his hand to ask for quiet, and said,

> I did meet with a little accident. On Monday last when sparring with Joe Jeannette he hit this arm (holding up his right), forcing it a little farther than it ought to go, and since that time the doctor has taken out three ounces of blood and pus from the elbow. But at that it is in pretty good shape now and, since I am willing to take a chance, I don't see why any one else should worry over it.

Another quoted him as saying,

> Gentlemen and friends: In sparring with Joe Jeannette last Monday he hit my old bum right arm and forced it back. I have had two operations performed on it, and a doctor in Paterson took the blood and pus out. If I am willing to take a chance I don't see why the public isn't.

This seemed to satisfy the spectators. There was a yell of "good for you, Bob, go on." The crowd wanted to see them fight, regardless.

Another paper reported that Fitz had torn the ligaments of his right elbow on Monday afternoon (the 15th), two days before the fight, sparring with Joe Jeannette.

Apparently, Fitz was having financial difficulties and was not about to pull out of a payday. The same day as the fight, George Considine obtained a $4,200 judgment against him on a note dated July 1. Considine executed an attachment summoning the Washington Athletic Club as garnishee. So, injured or not, Fitz needed the money to pay his debts.

Club manager and matchmaker Billy McCarney settled matters by jumping through the ropes and announcing that he would referee. McCarney called the men to the ring center. Shortly thereafter, he signaled to Timekeeper Lew Derlacher and the bout began.

1st round

The round was slow and tame, with little to it, for both men appeared very cautious. There were numerous clinches and some pretty left-hand work by both. Fitzsimmons boxed entirely with his left, keeping his right over his chest in close. Bob only used his right for defense, moving it up and down whenever he saw a blow coming. Bob ducked a number of blows and repeatedly made Johnson jump away by a strong feint.

No one looked for anything resembling a fight. However, Johnson was the faster man and occasionally landed a left or right. Fitz landed two or three times, once bringing cries of "that's the place" from the crowd when he reached for the stomach. Fitz kept dancing away, and when Johnson got close, Bob made passes with his left. There was feeble applause at the end of the round. Neither man had landed an effective blow.

More specific descriptions of the round said they sparred for several seconds. Fitz missed a left hook and they clinched. Johnson jabbed and jumped away. He landed a light left to the body and they clinched. Johnson hooked a left to the face and swung a hard left to the body. There was a lot of fiddling, with Fitz dancing away. Johnson twice landed his left to the body. They sparred again. Fitz landed a left hook on the ear and the crowd yelled. Jack jabbed the face with his left and uppercut him on the cheek with his left. Bob ducked and danced away. Fitz hooked a left to the ear, and Johnson jabbed the face and threw the left to the wind at the bell.

2nd round

Johnson was more determined and rushed in, endeavoring to make short work of Fitz. Each local Philadelphia newspaper had its own version of what happened:

Record: Upon the first clinch, Johnson sent Fitz down hard with a left hook followed by a twist that made Bob fall very heavily.

Inquirer: Johnson swung a right to the face and then threw Fitz to the floor, an act for which the referee warned him.

Public Ledger: Fitz ducked two vicious left swings and ran into a clinch. Johnson picked him up and threw him to the floor.

Press: Fitz started to shift but stopped. Johnson swung his right to the face and threw him down hard. Fitz took a five-count and rose.

Fitzsimmons seemed to be jarred and unnerved considerably, and he took his time in rising. He still was full of fight, though, and went after

Johnson hard. Bob landed a short left hook to the body, which Johnson returned in kind. Each local paper had its version of the end:

Record: A Johnson left and right sent Fitz down again. "Bob rolled about on the mat as though doing a circus stunt, and some thought he rather overdid the matter, for he was on his feet, apparently strong, two seconds after McCarney had counted him out."

Inquirer: Johnson jolted him with a right. Fitz went down, and tried to rise at nine, but fell over sideways and the referee stopped the fight.

Public Ledger: Johnson fired off two right uppercuts, one landing under the heart, and the other opening a gash on Bob's left cheek bone, sending Fitz down. He rolled over onto his back. At the count of five he got up onto one knee, but then his head went down onto the mat, and he fell over gracefully as the referee counted him out.

Press: Johnson swung his right to the body, and when they came together with a hard collision, Fitz fell to the floor without being struck by a blow. He rolled over and over on the floor, and, being in such a helpless state, Referee McCarney put his arms around him and led him to his corner.

The *Philadelphia Record* reported that Fitz was counted out in the 2nd round after making a weak showing against the burly negro. The fight was "only a farce," and the fans were "handed a lemon." Johnson was "in his prime" and in perfect condition. "The fight, if such it could be called, did not amount to much. Fitzsimmons, who is only a poor imitation of his former self, was no match for the big black, who could probably have stopped Bob in the first round had he gone at it with a little more determination."

Afterwards, Johnson said the crowd wanted him to allow Fitz to last the 6 rounds, but he was taking no chances with Bob, treating him with as much consideration as he dared in justice to himself. He was not about to allow Fitz to land a devastating blow on him and figured that getting him out as soon as possible was the best course of action.

The *Philadelphia Inquirer* said Referee McCarney stopped the bout in order to save Fitzsimmons. The blow that dropped him in the 2nd round did not appear hard enough to have done much damage, but the crowd made no fuss. It was evident that Fitz was too old to have a chance. Most of the spectators were glad that he was not completely knocked out cold.

The *Philadelphia Public Ledger* said Johnson's victory was clean-cut, but there was little credit attached to it, for Bob's right arm was practically useless. Fitz put up no competition, and the crowd received little action for their money. However, Bob's addressing the spectators as "fellow Elks" before the fight had "acted as a balm, and they were apparently willing to stand for anything." They liked him.

The *Philadelphia Press* said Fitz attempted to box with a useless, crippled right arm, but practically collapsed after a round and a half of boxing. The pitiful spectacle was a farce and nearly a fake. During the four and a half minutes of fighting there were not three hard blows struck.

The crowd saw two big men wander around the ring. In the 1st round, it was apparent that Johnson was inclined to be merciful. Typically, when the crowd has paid good money to see men box, it would urge the fighters on, but this time, the spectators fell into the colored man's whim and were happy that he was merciful. They wanted to see Fitz survive. However, in the 2nd round, Johnson threw him down and then bumped him down, and the referee, seeing that feeble Fitz was helpless, stopped the bout.

The fight was called a lemon and a big barney, with Fitz to blame for handing it to his followers. He had no excuse to enter the ring when he knew that physically he was unable to defend himself. He should have called off the affair. He permitted the public to pay the exorbitant prices of $1 to $5 to see him with the expectation that he would put up a good contest. That he did not and could not do.

Johnson escaped censure because of his apparent effort to be merciful. Tom Keenan proved his honesty and willingness to protect the public. His reputation was sustained.

There was some censure for the club, but as it had gone to big expense to bring the men together, it was understandable why it still supported the bout in spite of Bob's injury.

For the *New York Evening World*, Robert Edgren said Fitzsimmons was knocked down and counted out in the 2nd, but prior to that, Johnson fouled him. "It was anything but an unclouded victory for Johnson. He won his victory through a foul which if committed in any ring outside of Philadelphia, would have immediately cost him the decision." Despite the fact that a cloud hung over the battle, the result proved that the veteran's fighting days were over. When Referee McCarney tolled off the fatal 10-count, thousands stood up and watched silently. "There was not a cheer for the dusky victor." Not one man rejoiced the end of the "greatest fighting career in ring history." When he left the ring, a roar of cheers followed the veteran to his dressing room.

At the start of the 2nd round, there was a moment of sparring, with Johnson in awe of Bob's once-mighty wallops. Jack tapped lightly and stepped back from returns. There was a clinch and break. Fitz gave ground. Johnson followed. As they came to close quarters, Johnson stepped in with his left foot, swung his left hand, and, catching Fitz around the neck, threw him heavily to the floor.

> The throw was given with what wrestlers call a hiplock. Fitzsimmons, lifted over Johnson's left thigh, was raised from the ground and thrown violently down from a height of three feet. He struck flat on his back, with his right arm, a crippled right arm, doubled under him. From the crowd rose a bedlam of groans and hisses. Johnson stepped back. Fitz rolled over and came to his knees. For a moment he stayed there. Then, dazed from the effects of the fall, he got up, looked around for his enemy and rushed gamely into a mixup. Johnson was

waiting for him. As Fitz closed in the black giant's thick right arm moved in a swishing upper cut, a short little blow with the weight of his great body behind it. His fist struck squarely over Fitzsimmons's heart. And then came the end.

It had all happened so suddenly that the crowd could hardly understand that it was all over. The foul throw was fresh in its mind. It hissed and hooted.

Three days prior, in training, "Joe Jeannette caught his right arm and gave it a severe wrench that tore the ligaments of the elbow." The elbow swelled out of shape. A needle was injected, and matter was drawn out to reduce the swelling. Still, Bob came to fight. In the dressing room, the bandages were removed from his injured arm.

Edgren said Fitz was competitive and aggressive in the 1st round. "He was forcing the fight already and Johnson, wary of these ancient wallops, was moving back before him." Johnson landed a hard right to the body, and Fitz grinned. Fitz landed a vicious left hook to the mouth that drew a wide smile from Johnson, and another that made him get more serious. "A buzz of comment went through the crowd. 'The old man is still there,' said the ringside spectators. But then came the second round, the hard throw, the knockout blow delivered under the heart."

Edgren still gave Johnson some credit, saying he was a clever boxer and a giant in strength. He may not have intended to give Fitzsimmons the foul throw that dazed him. "He may have intended to rough in a clinch, and when he lifted Fitz clear off the floor and threw him it may have been only an accidental application of his strength, not a deliberate foul." Johnson knew how to use his tremendous advantages in strength and weight. Fitz, with two working arms, might have made a good fight. Still, the crippled arm was an illustration of the truth of what Joe Gans said: "Age has grabbed Fitz." "And as for Johnson, it is up to Tommy Burns."

FITZ SHOWED HIS OLD FORM IN FIRST ROUND WITH JOHNSON.

On the opposite spectrum, Thomas Rice was very hard on Fitzsimmons, calling the fight a horrible fizzle. From the start, there was a feeling that it was simply a stall to get easy money from the liberal-spending Elks who were in Philadelphia that week by the tens of thousands. Fitz got himself in bad because he not able to give even a good sparring exhibition, let alone put up a competitive fight. He deliberately deceived the public about his condition until fight-night, allowing them to pay high prices, and then springing the sympathy gag. Also, he likely cost gamblers their wagers.

> It was a shameless action on the part of a man who spends nine months of the year traveling around the country with a cheap melodrama soliciting the patronage of the public because he was once a great fighter and in some ways a credit to the game.

> Fitzsimmons' star has set not only in pugilism, but in popular estimation. O'Brien, with his faked fights in which there was at least plenty of action, was little, if any, worse than Fitzsimmons, who, in his craving for gate money, fooled his friends into paying to see something not worth seeing and into betting on a sure-thing loser.

Biddy Bishop said Fitz's career was over for all time. He only lasted the 1st round owing to Johnson's leniency. In the 2nd, Johnson whipped one to the point and it was over. "It was pretty generally expected that Bob Fitzsimmons would be made an awful sucker out of by Johnson. The old warrior has seen his day in the ring and he has been up among the 'also rans' for a long time." Bishop said he was at ringside more than a year ago when he watched O'Brien make a monkey of him in one of the poorest exhibitions he ever saw. "Little Jimmy Quinn, who had conditioned Fitz for the battle told me before the contest that his legs and feet was in such poor shape that it was impossible for him to take road work."

Nevertheless, Bishop called Johnson one of the best men in the ring. "Johnson is a great fighter and barring a little timidity, which is a lack of grit in a mild form, I think he can clean almost anything we have in the ring at this time."[372]

A few days after the fight, Barratt O'Hara said the 45-year-old Cornishman's last stand against Father Time was heroic, dramatic, and pathetic all at the same time. He had dauntless heart to go up against Johnson, who was as strong as a lion.

Fitz had injured his right arm on Monday while boxing Joe Jeannette and had undergone two operations. He had kept the whole matter secret. But there was a two-inch cut where the surgeon's knife had penetrated. In the dressing room before the fight, Tom O'Rourke touched the cut and Bob screamed with pain. O'Rourke advised, "Call it off." Fitz retorted, "I won't. I'll not be called a quitter. Besides, I can whip him with one hand." Fitz's great ego gave him fighting spirit, confidence, and courage. "Contrast that for a moment with Tommy Burns' reputed assertion. 'I'm the

[372] *Philadelphia Record, Philadelphia Inquirer, Philadelphia Public Ledger, Philadelphia Press, New York Evening World, Washington Times, Tacoma Daily News,* July 18, 1907.

champion now and I must get the money and take no chances.'" O'Rourke notified the club management about the injury, and the news reached referee Tommy Keenan, who informed the crowd and recused himself.

In the 1st round, Fitz carried his right arm over his chest as though in a sling and threw few blows. Bob landed one to the face and another to the ear. Johnson played for the body.

In the 2nd round, Johnson rushed in, swung his right to the face, and then, coming in to a clinch, threw Fitz heavily to the floor. The fall jarred Fitz and brought forth hisses. Bob rose and landed a left to the stomach. A Johnson right to the chin put Fitz down. He rose at nine, only to fall down again, and the referee stopped the fight. O'Rourke carried him to his corner. Bob's wife hurried to the dressing room to tender solace to her husband.

On one hand, O'Hara said it was not to Johnson's credit to whip an old man with a crippled right arm in less than 2 rounds, for Tommy Burns or even Bill Squires might have done the same. And yet, he also said, "Johnson of course has gained prestige by his victory. It adds another name, and a great one, to the list of his knockout victims."[373]

The black-owned *Freeman* reported that the 1st round was tame. It was apparent that Johnson would at least win on points, but the knockout was not looked for, at least not so early. Fitz was not in the same class as Johnson but showed flashes of his old form.

Fitzsimmons claimed that Johnson deliberately fouled him by wrestling and throwing him to the floor in the 2nd round. That dazed him and left him vulnerable to the subsequent punches. "He wrestled me to the floor. I fell flat on my back and the blow hurt me." Some said there was a right or a left hook that landed before he was wrestled down, which might have had something to do with Bob being dazed.

After rising, a quick, snappy right hook to the chin sent Fitz down like a sinking ship, lifeless, hopelessly beaten and outclassed. Johnson, the man whom every other top white fighter had avoided for over a year, seemed as surprised as the crowd. Bob tried to rise at nine but fell over sideways. The packed crowd sat in a numbed and pitying silence.

Even Johnson gave no signs of exultation. "He seemed to feel as the crowd did - that he was viewing the wreck of the greatest fighter that the game ever saw." There were no cheers. It had the feel of a funeral for a great fighter.

Many said it would have been a totally different fight if the Fitz of ten years ago had been present. Some said Johnson would not have lasted 6 rounds. Tom Sharkey said Bob had seen his day and was a fighter no more. He still had cleverness, but the speed and snappiness were no longer there. "He was willing, but the colored fighter, young and active, as quick as a cat, was too good." Tom O'Rourke said Bob's age told. "He was a kingpin in his day, but his days are over." Young Corbett, who seconded Bob, said, "The old man tried once too often." His age caused his strength to give out

---

[373] *Kansas City Journal*, July 21, 1907.

early on. It might have been a slightly better fight if Bob had not been injured coming into the bout.[374]

Initially, Fitzsimmons did not give Johnson much credit as a puncher, even though he had stopped Bob in only 2 rounds, when the fastest Jeffries had managed to stop him was 8 rounds. Of course, they had met two totally different versions of Fitzsimmons. Bob said Choynski was the hardest puncher he ever met. He ranked Jeffries second, but with the #1 chin.[375]

It was the first time that a black man had defeated a former world heavyweight champion. Although Fitzsimmons was a shell of himself, as has proven to be the case in boxing, names sell tickets, and putting names with reputations on one's record helps build a fighter's reputation. Ironically, although in a competitive boxing sense, it meant very little, this victory actually helped boost Johnson's reputation much further.

Years later, Johnson said he realized that Fitz was only a shadow of his former self. He normally allowed fighters to last rounds in order to give the crowd their money's worth, but he could not afford to compromise his reputation, given that Bob was so old. Therefore, he decided to take him out quickly. Johnson took little credit for beating a man so far past-it. However,

> The oddest thing about the entire affair was that this knockout earned me a huge leap in everyone's esteem. He knocked out Bob Fitzsimmons! This Johnson must be a real boxer! … This goes to show how reputations are made. For years I had been fighting the best men who ever put on the gloves and all of those bouts put together did less for my reputation than knocking out poor old Bob Fitzsimmons!

The fact was that Fitzsimmons was a very big name to have on the resume, and history has proven that fight fans often foolishly care more about name and reputation than anything else.

In his later autobiography, Johnson said, "I do not take much credit to myself for this bout, but it seemed necessary at the time in clearing the course that was before me."[376]

The year after Fitzsimmons vs. Johnson, in March 1908, just before Sam Langford was going to fight Joe Jeannette, Tom O'Rourke said Langford would have to be a wonder to win, for Jeannette had developed into a great boxer, with an effective left and a wicked right. He also was very shifty on his feet. "When Fitzsimmons was training for his last bout, O'Rourke had Jeannette box the old warhorse, and the set-to had to be stopped to save Fitzsimmons, as Jeannette completely outboxed him."[377]

On March 3, 1908, in Boston, Sam Langford and Joe Jeannette fought to a 12-round draw.

[374] *Freeman*, July 27, 1907.
[375] *Freeman*, August 3, 1907.
[376] *My Life and Battles* at 60-61; *In the Ring and Out* at 55.
[377] *Boston Globe*, March 2, 1908.

CHAPTER 17

Semi-Retired Actor-Pugilist Again

HYDE & BEHMAN'S OLYMPIC — **CRACKERJACKS** — Mr. and Mrs. Bob Fitzsimmons — Smoking Permitted. — Mat. Daily.

As usual, Bob Fitzsimmons returned to stage work with his wife, including in "Cracker Jacks," a vaudeville show, starting in late September 1907 in New York.[378]

On December 2, 1907, in London, England, Tommy Burns knocked out British champion Gunner Moir in the 10th round. The fight was filmed.

In late December 1907, Fitzsimmons, who was at the Hamilton theater in Buffalo that week, spoke about the current heavyweight champion:

> Tommy Burns is a game little fighter, but he is pretty soft just now. He has had nobody of class to defeat, and until he meets a good man, the heavyweight championship will be looked upon as a joke. If Burns ever meets Jack Johnson the negro will lick him to a standstill. I have given up the fighting game, but any time that Burns wants a fall out of me I will post a substantial bet that I can defeat him inside of ten rounds.[379]

Typical of Bob, he often claimed to be retired and at the same time said he was willing to fight again.

The *Syracuse Herald* said that occasional fakes were part of the sport of boxing. Joe Gans, Jack O'Brien, and Bob Fitzsimmons all had confessed to taking part in pre-arranged fakes.

> So far as the records go it appears that Bob Fitzsimmons is the original confessor, and his confession was followed by clean breasts on the part of Gans and O'Brien. But Fitzsimmons acknowledged only one fake and says that it was a small one, as he received only $75 for feigning defeat in a bout with Jim Hall in Australia in 1890, at which time Fitz had barely got into the fighting game and he really did not understand what he was doing when he consented to take $75 and permit Hall to have all the glory. There is a suspicion, however, that Fitz is not entirely frank in the matter, and that he has taken part in at least two bouts in this country that had a fishy look.

This writer suspected that Fitz's knockout of Hall in the U.S. was also a fake. "Of course turn about was fair play, and it was no more than clubby for Hall, to whom Fitz had 'laid down' in Australia, to himself 'lay down' to Fitz in America." Of course, such was pure speculation, but one fake tends to lead to speculation regarding other fights.

---

378 *Brooklyn Citizen*, September 29, 1907.
379 *Buffalo Evening Times*, December 27, 1907.

Marvin Hart once had to agree, owing to his weight advantage, to not knock out Jack O'Brien, or if he did, forfeit his entire share of the purse.

Joe Walcott had beaten Tommy West before, but for one of their matches, at Madison Square Garden, Walcott agreed to lose. Joe beat Tommy up for a while but always refrained from finishing him. Then Joe quit, claiming that his arm was broken. "There was no doubt among those who saw the bout that it was one of the rawest fakes ever perpetrated."[380]

On February 10, 1908, in London, England, Tommy Burns knocked out Jack Palmer in the 4th round.

In late February, the *Buffalo Commercial* wrote,

> The only middle-weight of history who will always stand head and shoulders over any we may raise is Bob Fitzsimmons, the greatest fighting freak that ever stepped into a ring. Lanky Bob in his day would have been able to whip all the other middle-weight champions that ever drew on a glove, one after another. Even foxy Tommy Ryan wouldn't have classed with him for a moment.[381]

Bob entered his dogs into a kennel club show held in Buffalo from March 4 - 7. One of the dogs was "Bob," who cost him $5,000, but had won many first prizes in Europe. The other was named Othello. Lanky Bob also was in Buffalo for his theatrical engagement with his wife Julia Gifford, doing some bag punching during the show, "A Man's a Man for a' That." "Their act is the highest priced act in burlesque." Naturally, "Bob" won the dog show. "Bob Fitzsimmons must feel some disappointment, as his dogs won on points."[382]

BOB FITZSIMMONS AND HIS PRIZE WINNER

The dog in the picture is Bob, the $5,000 French poodle, which won every first in his class and took the special for the best poodle in the show.

On March 17, 1908, in Dublin, Ireland, Tommy Burns knocked out Irish champion Jem Roche in the 1st round.

On April 18, 1908, in Paris, France, Tommy Burns knocked out Jewey Smith in the 5th round.

In May 1908, Fitzsimmons again picked Jack Johnson to defeat heavyweight champion Tommy Burns if they ever met:

[380] *Syracuse Herald*, February 8, 1908.
[381] *Buffalo Commercial*, February 26, 1908.
[382] *Buffalo Evening Times*, March 3, 6, 7, 1908; *Buffalo Commercial*, March 9, 1908.

I did not take much stock in Johnson as a fighter until he beat me at Philadelphia. I thought I could beat him easily. ... Before we had been at it a minute I saw I was up against a big, strong, clever fighter, and really was not surprised when he knocked me out. I must admit Burns is a good little man but Johnson is a good big man and therefore should beat him.[383]

On June 13, 1908, in Paris, France, Tommy Burns knocked out Bill Squires in the 8th round.

That day, famous referee and writer George Siler died of a heart attack.

In July, Fitz and his wife were performing in Spokane, Washington.

Bob had issued a challenge to fight current world middleweight champion Stanley Ketchel, but his challenge was not taken seriously.

While in Spokane, on July 18, 1908, Bob got into a fight. Fitz accused Pantages manager E. Clarke Walker of giving a story to a local paper, classing him as a "has-been" and ridiculing his aspirations to meet Ketchel. Bob claimed that Walker did this because Fitz had signed with the local Natatorium Park to give daily sparring exhibitions, but an upset Walker contended that his contract with Bob prevented him from giving any exhibitions inside of three months after his vaudeville engagement. Hence, he had the derogatory articles published.

There was an argument with Walker's wife, who had approached Bob to deny his claims. Mr. Walker snuck up and smashed a glass bottle into the back of Fitz's head, cutting his scalp, which would require several stitches. Bob then swung on Walker, landing the manager in a heap. Telling his version, Bob said, "An' then, Zing! He swing on me with a baby's bottle, an' I just hit him with a little punch on the side of the neck. Not a real hard punch, just a shove...and he went over." Manager Walker said, "I may have hit Fitz first, I don't know." "He hit me twice, once on each side of the head, but I was only dazed for a short time, and it didn't mark me any." Both were arrested for disorderly conduct and posted $15 bonds. Neither defendant appeared in court, and their $15 bonds were forfeited. They had mutually agreed to let the matter drop.[384]

On August 24, 1908, in Sydney, Australia, Tommy Burns knocked out Bill Squires in the 13th round.

Ten days later, on September 3, 1908, in Melbourne, Australia, 174-pound Tommy Burns knocked out 186-pound Bill Lang in the 6th round.

In mid-September, Fitz and his wife were in Watertown, New York, doing a turn at the Orpheum. Bob owned a farm in New Jersey. He still believed that he could beat the present-day fighters.[385]

On September 21, 1908, in Benson Mines, New York, Bob Fitzsimmons took on Jim Paul, "who for years has been the terror of the North Woods lumber camps," and beat him to a pulp in 1 round. The lumber jack started in viciously with his famous rushing tactics, but a Fitz right to the jaw

[383] *Freeman*, May 9, 1908.
[384] *Spokane Spokesman-Review, Spokane Daily Chronicle*, July 19, 20, 21, 1908.
[385] *Syracuse Post-Standard*, September 15, 1908.

dropped him like a log. Recovering, Paul landed a swing to the face, and in return got a shower of blows which almost put him to sleep. The gong saved him from a knockout. Paul decided not to try a 2nd round.[386]

Bob and his wife continued with their vaudeville performances.

On November 21, 1908, Fitzsimmons and his wife set sail for England to perform in vaudeville there and in France for 25 weeks. His wife also planned to study music and singing in France. As usual, Bob left open the possibility of fighting while overseas.[387]

Shortly before heavyweight champion Tommy Burns fought Jack Johnson in Australia in December 1908, Bob Fitzsimmons said,

> My humble opinion is that Johnson will win easily, and if he doesn't I will be the most surprised man in the world. Johnson is a terrific hitter. I can vouch for that myself. He knocked me out in two rounds in Philadelphia some time ago with a right hand uppercut. One punch, mind you, and it was as hard as any that was ever landed on me.
>
> When you look at the fight you must figure it the way you do everything else. Johnson is a bigger man than Burns. Johnson is cleverer and has a harder punch and he will weigh more than Tommy, and that's the way I have it on my cards.
>
> You know a good big man will invariably beat a good little man, and no matter how good the Canadian may be, Johnson is the winner, according to all sorts of figuring.[388]

On December 26, 1908, in Sydney, New South Wales, Australia, 192-pound Jack Johnson dominated and clearly won the world's heavyweight championship from 168 ½-pound Tommy Burns, scoring several knockdowns throughout, causing the police to stop the bout in the 14th round of a scheduled 20 in order to prevent Johnson from knocking him out. Upon earning the referee's decision, Johnson became the first black man to win the world heavyweight championship.

---

[386] *Brooklyn Citizen*, September 22, 1908. This previously unknown fight should be added to Fitz's record.
[387] *Brooklyn Daily Eagle, New York Sun*, November 22, 1908.
[388] *Buffalo Evening Times*, December 17, 1908.

When Fitzsimmons sailed to Europe, he had visions of making money fighting their champions as Burns did, but no substantial offers were forthcoming. Fitz declared that the fighting game was dead over there, and the highest price they would offer was $500. "I'm through with the fight game, and next summer I expect to devote all my time to farming. I expect to reap some profit on the 800 berry bushes I had planted last year..." Bob said he was willing and interested in fighting Jack Johnson again, but "I think there is little show of me getting back in the ring again. They all think I'm getting too old to fight, and while I feel as young as I ever did, the opinion of the experts may be correct, so I guess it will be the farm for me."

Bob said their theatrical tour of England, Ireland, and France had been a huge success, particularly in his native country, in the Cornwall district.[389]

Jim Jeffries was considering a comeback by popular demand. In March 1909, one observer of his exhibition with Sam Berger said,

> Jeffries is simply making a bluff to get the money. $2,500 a week is too much for him to turn down... I don't believe that Jeff has an idea of fighting Johnson or anybody else. ... His training stunts on the stage amount to nothing. He doesn't exercise more than ten minutes all told, and he doesn't do enough hard work to get up a sweat. ... I'll bet that the way Jeffries is doing things now he'll be no better physically at the end of twenty weeks. ... Jeff today isn't as fast or as fit as when he made a failure of his ten round bout with Bob Armstrong here ten years ago. He weighs about the same, but he's gone back. He is forty pounds heavier than when he won the heavyweight title from Fitzsimmons.[390]

In late April 1909, Jim Jeffries said Jim Corbett was the cleverest boxer he ever met. "Bob Fitzsimmons was the hardest hitter and the greatest ring general I ever faced." Tom Sharkey was a glutton for punishment.[391]

While in London, on May 15, 1909, Bob Fitzsimmons met Sam Langford at Sam's training camp at Willesden, at the Coach and Horses. Also present were Jem Mace and bantam Jimmy Walsh. "When 'Fitz' and Langford were introduced, they behaved like two good-natured boys who neither feared nor envied each other." They talked, and Bob told Sam about his fights and his pet lion.

Famous Fighters Caught in One Group at Langford's English Training Camp

REMARKABLE FLASHLIGHT TAKEN RECENTLY, SHOWING RING HEROES OF PAST AND PRESENT

Jimmy Walsh.   Jem Mace.   Bob Fitzsimmons   Sam Langford.

[389] *Buffalo Evening Times*, February 3, 1909.
[390] *Elmira Star-Gazette*, March 11, 1909.
[391] *Buffalo Evening News*, April 28, 1909.

Although only 5'6 ½" in height, the 160-pound Langford had broad shoulders, long, powerful, muscular arms, and a thick neck. Sam was scheduled to fight England's 196-pound Ian 'Iron' Hague. After watching Langford spar, Fitzsimmons said, "Without picking a winner, Hague is a big, strong fellow, built of the best English beef. You never can tell. Langford's sidestepping and slipping are very fine, and the man who can take his punch without feeling it must be made of cast-iron." Also, "There are heavyweights I'd fight to-morrow without an hour's training, but Langford is not one of them."[392]

On May 19, 1909, in Philadelphia, Jack Johnson defeated or drew with Philadelphia Jack O'Brien in a 6-round no decision contest. O'Brien was much busier, active with quick blows. However, O'Brien's performance was not sufficiently strong enough to warrant any promoters trying to make a match between them for a longer duration. Johnson's punches were much harder and more effective, with O'Brien knocked down cleanly at least once, and down several other times from a combination of factors.

On May 24, 1909, at the National Sporting Club, Covent Garden, in London, Sam Langford knocked out Iron Hague in the 4th round. Bob Fitzsimmons was in attendance. He said,

> Both Langford and Hague lacked agility and cleverness…. It seemed to me that Hague held his own with Langford up to the time of the knockout blow. He did most of the forcing, while Langford let go time and again and missed. Tip-top fighters don't miss – at least, they don't keep on missing, because a blow that misses generally throws the man who delivers it into an exposed attitude. Langford's judgment of distance was very bad…

Bob said he had sparred Hague at the end of the previous year and noticed that he slowed up a lot after the 2nd round. He wasn't much fitter against Langford and missed many opportunities to counter Sam's misses.

[392] *Hull Daily News*, May 17, 1909; *London Weekly Dispatch*, May 23, 30, 1909.

On May 25, 1909, at the Arena, Villiers-street, Strand, Charing Cross, London, England, a benefit took place for former bareknuckle champion Jem Mace. At the benefit, Bob Fitzsimmons consented to spar with Joe Jeannette (who on April 17 stopped Sam McVey after 49 rounds). Former English champion Charlie Mitchell refereed, wearing formal attire. The go, "although an exhibition, was fast enough to awaken the big crowd to an enthusiastic pitch." Next, Fitz forged a horseshoe on the stage, and at auction it realized 12 pounds for Mace.[393]

On June 9, 1909, in Philadelphia, Stanley Ketchel knocked out Philadelphia Jack O'Brien in the 3rd round.

On June 21, Bob Fitzsimmons returned to the U.S. from Europe, where he had been giving theatrical exhibitions.

Bob said if Jeffries trained properly and hard he could beat Johnson, but if he did not, he would suffer a terrible beating.[394]

On June 30, 1909, in Pittsburgh, Jack Johnson dominated Tony Ross in a 6-round no decision bout, dropping him in the 1st round.

Fitzsimmons said Stanley Ketchel could not whip Jack Johnson.

> Now, listen. Don't fool yourself. Ketchel is a little fellow, for all that. He's not tall and never will be. I am five feet eleven and three-quarters in my socks. With my fighting shoes on I stand six feet. Don't overlook that. Though I weighed a little over 150, I had broader shoulders than a man weighing 280 in perfect trim. No one denies that I hit the hardest punch of any man who ever entered the ring. I hit harder than Jeff, and Jim will admit that himself. Besides that, I was foxier than any of them, if I do say so myself. I may not have been the prettiest thing that ever danced about a ring, but the noodle was always there, and when I hit them they went down. ... Johnson is a great boxer and a crafty one. He's probably forgot more about the fine points of the game since he was champion than the

---

[393] *Evening Standard and St. James's Gazette*, May 25, 1909; *Daily Mirror*, May 26, 1909; *Brooklyn Citizen*, June 29, 1909. Bob's wife attended.
[394] *Buffalo Evening Times*, June 22, 1909.

impulsive Ketchel will ever take the time or the pride to learn. ... A fast puncher will get that boy [Ketchel]. ... I'd like to see him beat Johnson, but he can't. He can't jump up and batter that black hulk down.[395]

On September 9, 1909, in San Francisco, Jack Johnson clearly won in dominant fashion a 10-round no decision over Al Kaufman, who held victories over Sam Berger, George Gardner, Mike Schreck, Jack 'Twin' Sullivan, 'Fireman' Jim Flynn, Jim Barry, and Tony Ross.

In mid-September, reports were that Fitzsimmons was going to sail to London again, to join Hugh McIntosh. They would proceed to Australia with Bob's wife, for a vaudeville tour arranged by McIntosh. Bob would engage in sparring exhibitions with Tommy Burns, who had remained there after his loss to Johnson. Bob might fight Bill Squires or Bill Lang. It would be Fitz's first visit to Australia in two decades.[396]

On October 16, 1909, in Colma, California, Jack Johnson knocked out Stanley Ketchel in the 12th round with a blazing-fast powerful right in a combination, just mere seconds after Ketchel had put him down with an overhand right. Johnson had decked Ketchel in the 2nd round, and appeared to back off and carry him, even holding him up at one point in the fight when Ketchel seemed to be going down. Many debated whether Johnson had taken a dive for the motion pictures or if he really had been caught by one of Ketchel's famous powerful blows, and then, only momentarily stunned, decided to stop playing and take matters seriously.

Johnson showed off his torn, blood-stained right glove from the Ketchel fight. The blow that knocked out Ketchel was so hard that it dislodged several teeth, one of which broke off and was embedded in the padding. Jack said, "At that I hit harder than I intended. I was so certain of victory that I did not care to risk injury to my hands, and would have been content to wear him down in easy stages if he hadn't banged me upon the head and knocked the caution out of me. I am saving that glove to offset arguments that I cannot hit hard."[397]

Bob Fitzsimmons had been fighting for nearly 30 years, which seemed impossible. Many called him the "greatest fighter who ever lived." He was hoping to fight in Australia for Hugh McIntosh.[398]

34-year-old Jim Jeffries said,

> I think my first fight with Sharkey was about the roughest passage I ever had. Sharkey was the roughest 'tough' that ever drew breath, and when we clashed he started in to play his little games with me. Well, I don't want to brag, but when Tom tried to 'rough' me I just bore him off like a rat. ...
>
> The hardest puncher I ever ran up against was Bob Fitzsimmons. My goodness! How that man could punch. I caught one wallop in our

[395] *Buffalo Commercial*, July 27, 1909.
[396] *Buffalo Commercial*, September 18, 1909; *Brooklyn Times*, September 20, 1909.
[397] *Arrow*, December 25, 1909.
[398] *Syracuse Post-Standard*, October 19, 1909.

second match that made me think of home and mother! If Fitz had only been a little bit bigger he would have achieved even greater fame than he has already won. But at that I don't think he would even have beaten me, for to tell you the truth it was practically impossible to really hurt me when I was in my prime.[399]

Although Jeffries had not fought since 1904, at the public's demand, plus a boatload of money, he was coming back to fight Jack Johnson.

Bob Fitzsimmons said if Jeffries was half as good as he was when they met, "e'll 'ave no trouble in beating the black." Bob said no man had any chance against Jeff at his best. Fitz hit Jeff hard and cut him to the cheekbone, but never even rocked his head. "Johnson never saw the day 'e could 'it like I could."[400]

Dr. Latson, the eminent physician, picked Johnson to beat Jeffries. He said Johnson did not have any tells, so foes did not know what he was going to throw or when. Johnson likely would wage a waiting battle, jabbing away and allowing Jeff to exhaust himself by rushing and missing. "It will be subtlety against strength, the getaway against the punch."

However, "Ringsider" countered, "Jim Corbett was a better boxer than Johnson ever will be. He was one of the best generals that ever climbed into a ring. Fitzsimmons was a fighter, cunning as they could make them, and could land a harder punch than Johnson." Fitz had subtlety, strength, speed, and science, and was "the coolest strategist that ever pulled on a pair of five-ounce gloves." Yet, despite his wonderful cunning, Jeff beat Bob. Jeffries could take it and dish it relentlessly, for a long time. He had a long reach and could crouch, and he was harder to jab or hit cleanly than most thought. Jeff was not muscle-bound, and he had great stamina. He had never grown tired in a fight. Hence, Ringsider picked Jeffries to beat Johnson, who was "only a negro with a good frame and a pair of fast hands."[401]

Sam Berger could not understand why so many doubted Jeff's ability to come back. He was only 34 years old. Fitzsimmons still was in his prime at 40. Of course, everyone ages differently. Fitz never had a 5-6-year layoff.[402]

In another interview, Fitzsimmons opined that unless Jeffries beat Johnson within 12 rounds, the latter would win, because after such a lengthy period of inactivity, Jeff likely had lost a lot of what he once had.

> The Cornishman does not think much of Johnson at that and declares that ten years ago he could have stopped the colored champion in a couple of rounds. In Fitz's opinion Jeffries, in his prime, was a phenomenal heavyweight, the best the world ever saw, but he expresses some doubt as to whether the boilermaker can recover the old stamina.[403]

[399] Brooklyn Daily Standard Union, October 19, 1909.
[400] Goulburn Evening Penny Post, November 4, 1909.
[401] Brooklyn Citizen, November 5, 1909.
[402] Buffalo Evening Times, November 15, 1909.
[403] Buffalo Evening News, December 11, 1909.

CHAPTER 18

Bill Lang and Australia

On November 4, 1909, Bob Fitzsimmons and his wife arrived in Freemantle, Perth, Australia. He planned to fight for Hugh McIntosh (who was traveling with them), potentially against Bill Lang and Bill Squires in 20-round fights.[404] It was Bob's first return to Australia in nearly 20 years, having left in 1890.

On November 9 at a reception in Melbourne, Fitzsimmons met former champion Tommy Burns for the first time. Tommy and his wife enjoyed living in Australia.

BOXING   BOXING

Next Wednesday Night
NOVEMBER 10.
AT THE STADIUM, RUSHCUTTERS BAY
Rudolph Unholz
The Hurricane from America, Conqueror of Battling Nelson, known to his intimates as the "Fighting Machine,"
TO BOX 20 ROUNDS, or a DECISION, with
Arthur Cripps
The Wariest, Cleverest, and Coolest Exponent of the Art of Boxing in Australia.
A clean, well-fought, and interesting Contest is assured. Both boxers are diametrically opposed in their methods of attack and defence.
BOOK YOUR SEATS NOW at McMillan, Decey, and Co., Ltd., Sports Depot, Pitt-st., near King-st., City. PRICES: 10/, 5/, 3/, and 2/.
Mr. Bob Fitzsimmons
who returns to Australia next Wednesday with Mr. Hugh D. McIntosh, will referee this Contest.
Gates open at 7 o'clock. Men in the Ring at HALF-PAST EIGHT SHARP.
SCIENTIFIC BOXING and SELF-DEFENCE, LIMITED.   E. COVELL, Governing Director.

On November 10, 1909, at the Stadium at Rushcutter's Bay in Sydney, NSW, Australia, before a crowd of an estimated 15,000 - 20,000, Bob Fitzsimmons refereed and decided the 20-round Arthur Cripps vs. Rudolph Unholz bout, won by Cripps on points. 960 pounds was generated.

Bob said he had won over 100,000 pounds in America and had two big homes there.

"When I met Mr. M'Intosh in London I was showing with my wife in 'A Man's a Man for A' That,' and was getting 250 pounds a week."

When asked what effect the result of the Johnson-Burns contest had on the coloured population in America, Bob said the greatest jubilation was shown. "It would not in my opinion give the coloured people in America feeling of superiority over the white, because of the fact that J. J. Jeffries hitherto undefeated has challenged Johnson, but if Jeffries be defeated, then there is no doubt whatever that the result will lead to racial unrest." Fitz thought Johnson would be afraid of Jeffries at the start, then he would punish Jeff for a while, but the latter ultimately would win, if he was himself. Jeff had the superior punch, which he maintained throughout with his great condition, plus underrated skill and a tremendous ability to take it.

Bob said he stood 6'1" in his fighting shoes but was 5'11 ¾" without them. He said he tipped the beam at 12 stone 2 pounds (170) in his clothes and claimed that he never fought at over 11 stone 4 pounds (158) in his life. (Obviously untrue, given his refusal to step on the scales for reporters.)[405]

---

[404] *Barrier Miner*, November 5, 1909.
[405] *Mount Alexander Mail*, November 10, 1909; *Sydney Morning Herald, Gympie Times, Barrier Miner, Maitland Daily Mercury, National Advocate, Sydney Sun*, November 11, 1909.

Fitzsimmons was matched to fight Bill Lang, 19-5-1, on Boxing Day, for Lang's Australian heavyweight championship.[406] Fitz had not fought a world-class man for over 2 years, since Jack Johnson stopped him in July 1907. Bob was said to be 47 years old (though actually 46), quite ancient for a boxer.

Bill Lang's record included: 1907 LTKOby9 Jack Johnson, KO10 Peter Kling, KO12 Peter Felix, and TKO8 Arthur Cripps; 1908 TKO7 Peter Felix, LKOby6 Tommy Burns (world heavyweight championship; Lang decked Burns in the 2nd), and TKO5 Jim Griffin; and 1909 KO17 and KO20 Bill Squires to win and retain the Australian heavyweight championship.

When someone called Fitzsimmons the greatest boxer who ever lived, Bob responded, "Stop! Peter Jackson was the greatest boxer the world has seen, and if Peter had only used a few of the hooks now so much the vogue in America no man of his day would have stayed half-a-dozen rounds with him!" But Peter never believed in hooks – he was exclusively a straight puncher.

Fitz also said, "In a way, I became a man in Sydney, and, encouraged by you people, I crossed the seas and won fame and fortune." He left Sydney when he was 26 years old. He had since "qualified for a position in the list of the greatest athletes this old world has ever known."

Bob's latest pet, which he carried around with him, was a mongoose. He fed and cared for it as if it were a child.[407]

On November 13, 1909, at a boxing show at Boyle's-hall in Sutherland, New South Wales, Australia, Jack O'Brien (of the Royal Artillery) knocked out Harry McLeod in the 10th round. Bob Fitzsimmons acted as referee and Promoter Hugh McIntosh as timekeeper. After the contest, McIntosh and Fitzsimmons gave an interesting 4-round exhibition of boxing.[408]

On Wednesday afternoon, November 17, 1909, at National Park, where he was training, Fitzsimmons sparred with Tasmanian champion Bill Turner and set him guessing until Turner's ankle went back on him in the 2nd round. Bob also sparred with Australian ex-amateur heavyweight champion Dave Smith (who recently defeated Jack Blackmore). Smith "had a lively rough up with Fitzsimmons. The bout lasted five rounds, and while Fitzsimmons did not let himself go as freely as it was plain he could have

BILL LANG,
CHAMPION OF AUSTRALIA.

---

[406] *Evening Mail*, November 4, 1909; *Kyabram Free Press*, November 12, 1909; *Yonkers Statesman*, November 19, 1909.
[407] *Referee*, November 17, 1909.
[408] *Daily Telegraph*, November 17, 1909; *South Coast Times*, November 20, 1909. Another paper said the knockout came in the 9th round. *St. George Call*, November 20, 1909.

done, enough was seen to indicate that there's considerable vigor in the man yet, and he has not forgotten his skill." (Another said it was 6 2-min. rds.)

THE STADIUM,

RUSHCUTTERS' BAY (take King-street tram).

SATURDAY AFTERNOON, 27th NOVEMBER, AT 2.30 P.M.

ROBERT FITZSIMMONS,

EX-HEAVYWEIGHT AND MIDDLEWEIGHT CHAMPION OF THE WORLD,
will give his Famous PHYSICAL CULTURE AND TRAINING EXHIBITION, opening
at THE STADIUM on SATURDAY AFTERNOON, NOVEMBER 27th, at 2.30 p.m.
LADIES SPECIALLY INVITED.   FULL BAND IN ATTENDANCE.
AFTERNOON TEA PROVIDED.
MRS. FITZSIMMONS WILL ACT AS HOSTESS.
A LUCKY HORSESHOE, MADE BY MR. FITZSIMMONS, WILL BE GIVEN
AWAY TO THE HOLDER OF THE LUCKY NUMBERED ADMISSION TICKET.

THE CHAMPION WILL BOX WITH:

PETER FELIX, ex-Australian Champion.
DAVE SMITH, ex-Amateur Champion of Australasia.
BILL TURNER, Champion of Tasmania.
A. McLAGLEN, Heavyweight Champion of British Columbia.
ADMISSION: 2/ & 1/.   LADIES FREE.
Scientific Boxing & Self-Defence, Ltd.,
E. COVELL, Governing Director.

THE STADIUM.

WEDNESDAY, NOVEMBER 24th,

AT 8.30 P.M.

MIDDLEWEIGHT CHAMPIONSHIP OF AUSTRALIA.

ARTHUR CRIPPS V. DAVE SMITH.

(HOLDER),   (CHALLENGER),

BOB FITZSIMMONS WILL REFEREE.

PRICES: 10/, £/, 3/, 2/.

E. COVELL, Governing Director,
Scientific Boxing and Self-Defence, Ltd.

Smith said Fitz was not the decrepit old man most believed him to be. Bob said Smith was one of the best and cleverest middleweights he had met.

This was interesting, in part, because Fitzsimmons was scheduled to referee Smith's upcoming fight with Arthur Cripps the following week.[409]

Fitzsimmons and Dave Smith continued sparring with one another in preparation for their upcoming bouts. Smith said,

> We have been boxing six three-minute rounds since Wednesday, and, let me tell you, Fitzsimmons is a wonder. He boxed me to a standstill every day, and is, I am certain, able to go for forty rounds. There is no doubt about his stamina, and he is certainly the freak he has been heralded by the newspaper writers for the past 20 years. He has a wonderful punch, and is tricky and clever. That famous left shift of his is a wonderful effort, and he executes it with remarkable quickness.[410]

On Friday afternoon, November 19, 1909, Fitzsimmons boxed 4 fast rounds with young London heavyweight Arthur McLaglen, and 4 more with Mark Higgins, and he had each man in trouble all the time. Bob still was very clever, with a good stock of vitality. Bob encouraged McLaglen to do his best and not hold back. Arthur swung away with heavy wallops, but Bob was shifty and clever. Bob rocked him but then stood back until he recovered. Melbourne's Higgins was persistent, but he was badly baffled and beaten back.

When interviewed, Bob said, "In my spare moments I read a great deal. I once waded through Homer's Iliad, and the deeds of his heroes made my hair stand on end, particularly was I taken with that chap Ajax …"[411]

On Wednesday November 24, 1909, at the Stadium at Rushcutters Bay in Sydney, before a crowd of 10,000, Bob Fitzsimmons refereed the

[409] *Daily Telegraph*, November 19, 1909; *Newcastle Morning Herald and Miners Advocate*, November 20, 1909; *Sunday Times*, November 21, 1909; *Referee*, November 24, 1909.
[410] *Sydney Sunday Sun*, November 21, 1909.
[411] *Daily Telegraph*, November 22, 1909; *Referee*, November 24, 1909.

scheduled 20-round Arthur Cripps vs. Dave Smith fight. At the bout's conclusion, Fitz declared it to be a draw, which was considered popular and just. Fitzsimmons said, "It was the best fight I have ever seen, and I've seen just a few, you know. Cripps is a steady, cool, scientific fighter; and Smith, with whom I have been sparring during the past few days, is, I am sure, going to develop into a champion."[412]

Fitz typically took a 5-mile morning run. In the afternoon, he usually sparred Dave Smith, Arthur McLaglen, and Mark Higgins, handling them with ease and cleverness.

On the afternoon of Saturday November 27, 1909 at the Stadium, Rushcutters Bay, a crowd of 8,000 saw Fitzsimmons spar 8 rounds, 2 rounds of 2-minute duration apiece with black Peter Felix, Tasmanian heavyweight champion Bill Turner, who defeated McLaglen in Sydney recently, "Soldier" Bill Thompson, and Arthur McLaglen (or M'Laglen). Upon both his appearance and introduction as the "grand old man of the ring," the crowd gave Fitz a prolonged outburst of cheering.

Bill Turner

During the four 2-round bouts, Fitz took matters very cooly and did not endeavor to inflict punishment. He landed a very accurate right cross and straight left, varied occasionally by a left hook.

BOB FITZSIMMONS HAS A "BREAVHER" WITH FELIX AT THE STADIUM.

FITZSIMMONS KEEPS BILL TURNER MOVING.

Nevertheless, McLaglen, who went last, in his 1st round was caught with a nicely timed right to the jaw which dropped him. The same thing happened in the 2nd round.

> The difference in the old and the new style of boxing was made clear by the ex-champion during the spars which he indulged in. Instead of the usual dancing tactics that are indulged in by the majority of present-day fighters, Fitzsimmons, when eluding a punch, simply made a head or body move, or stepped back an inch or two, so that

[412] *Gympie Times, Bathurst Times,* November 25, 1909; *Sydney Sun,* November 28, 1909.

at any time he was in a position to resume the attack. Another noticeable thing about his work was the amount of straight punches he employed, rather than swinging. Fitzsimmons stands up to an opponent something after the style of Johnson, though he does not spread his feet as wide as the colored boxer, and his punches are sent in with a great deal more power behind them.

Bob also exhibited ball-punching. Then he forged two horseshoes, which, together with photos of himself, were presented to the holders of numbered tickets (who won a raffle). Rudie Unholz was training Bob.[413]

On the afternoon of Tuesday November 30, 1909, in Sydney, for the benefit of metropolitan firemen, Fitz boxed exhibition rounds with firemen Fred Baker (Snowy Baker's brother) and George Cox.[414]

THE STADIUM, RUSHCUTTERS BAY, TRAINING EXHIBITIONS
BY
ROBERT FITZSIMMONS
(Light-heavyweight and Middleweight Champion of the World), and
BILL LANG
(Champion of Australia),
COMMENCING TO-MORROW (WEDNESDAY) AFTERNOON, DEC. 1st, AT 2.30.
And EVERY MONDAY, WEDNESDAY, THURSDAY, and SATURDAY AFTER.
BOB FITZSIMMONS WILL APPEAR TO-MORROW (WEDNESDAY),
And EVERY WEDNESDAY and SATURDAY in Boxing Bouts, and will give Exhibitions of Famous Punches he has used in all his big fights in America. He will box six rounds each with
SNOWY BAKER   PAT O'KEEFE   BILL TURNER   A. M'LAGLEN
(Amateur Champion of the World), ("The Irish Lad"), (Champion of Tasmania), (Champion of British Columbia),
BILL LANG
(Champion of Australia) will Commence Training at the Stadium NEXT MONDAY and EVERY MONDAY and THURSDAY after, and will box Four Rounds with all-comers.
ADMISSION: 2s AND 1s.   E. COVELL, Governing Director.

Fitz and Lang were so popular that folks paid just to watch them train. Starting on December 1, 1909, at the Stadium, Bob would box with amateur champion Snowy Baker, well-known middleweight Pat O'Keefe (who often sparred Tommy Burns), Tasmanian champion Bill Turner, and British Columbia champion Arthur M'Laglen. He also would go through his bag punching, rope skipping, and dumb-bell exercises. Ladies would be admitted for free.[415]

On the 1st, "young giant" McLaglen got too confident and commenced roughing Fitz a bit, until Bob reminded him who he was by landing a solid blow to the jaw that dropped him to the boards. Thereafter, McLaglen was careful not to get too close.[416]

In various training exhibitions, Bob also sparred with welter George Johnson, Soldier Bill Thompson, Rudolph Unholz, and Peter Felix.[417]

On December 4 at the Stadium, Fitz had a most interesting and decidedly clever sparring bout with Snowy Baker, and he also boxed with Bill Turner and Soldier Bill Thompson. To the ladies whose tickets bore lucky numbers, Bob gave out two more horseshoes with his photograph attached.[418]

---

[413] *Sydney Sunday Sun, Sunday Times*, November 28, 1909; *Daily Telegraph*, November 26, 1909.
[414] *Sydney Star*, November 30, 1909.
[415] *Sydney Star*, November 30, 1909.
[416] *Newsletter*, December 4, 1909.
[417] *Queensland Times*, December 6, 1909.
[418] *Sydney Sunday Times*, December 6, 1909.

On Tuesday December 7, 1909, at the Victoria Barracks, Paddington, for a crowd of about 200, Bob sparred with soldiers named Bill Thompson, Jack Thompson, Coghill (runner-up for the New South Wales amateur heavyweight championship), and O'Grady.[419]

Prior to coming to Australia, Bob and his wife had been touring the U.S. and England in a sketch called "A Man's a Man for a' That."[420]

Offering advice to youngsters, Bob said, "Don't smoke, don't drink, don't chew."

Dr. Herbert Maitland, the well-known Sydney doctor, said, "Fitzsimmons is not old; he's the youngest man in Sydney to-day. He does more work in his training than any three pugilists I have seen train, and his heart is as sound as a bull." His measurements were: height 5 11 ¾, neck 16, chest 44, waist 28, hips 40, thigh 21, calf 14, ankle 8, biceps 14, forearm 12, wrist 8.[421]

On December 8, 1909, at the Sydney Stadium, "Irish Lad" Pat O'Keefe fought Bill Turner. Tommy Burns seconded O'Keefe, while Bob Fitzsimmons worked with Turner. Snowy Baker refereed. For the first 10 rounds it was Turner, but thereafter O'Keefe took over, decking Turner twice in the 19th round. At the start of the 20th round, after Turner went down once more, the police stopped the contest, and O'Keefe was declared the winner.[422]

On Saturday the 11th at the Stadium, Fitz sparred 2 2-minute rounds each with Jack O'Brien, Soldier Bill Thompson, who was shaken up a couple times, and Snowy Baker.

---

[419] *Daily Telegraph, Star*, December 7, 8, 1909.
[420] *Newcastle Morning Herald and Miners' Advocate*, December 9, 1909.
[421] *Cobargo Chronicle, River Express & Kyogle Advertiser*, December 10, 1909. Bob's measurements were listed in feet and inches.
[422] *Bendigo Independent, Barrier Miner, Sydney Morning Herald*, December 9, 1909.

Tickets for Fitzsimmons vs. Lang were selling, in pounds, for 5, 3, 2, and 1, and 10 and 5 shillings.

The general impression from Australian newspapers was that Lang was an improving fighter who was strong and would be a tough nut for an old Fitz to crack.[423]

On Monday the 12th, at the Tivoli charity entertainment, Fitz, along with his wife, appeared in the sketch, "A Man's a Man for a' That."[424]

THE BOX PLAN
FOR THE CONTEST,
FITZSIMMONS V. LANG,
(The finest glove fighter the world has ever seen).   (The Champion Heavy-weight of Australia).
THE STADIUM, AT 10.30 BOXING DAY.
OPENS TO-DAY (WEDNESDAY) AT
HUGH D. M'INTOSH'S BOX PLAN OFFICE,
100 KING-STREET, Close to Corner of Pitt-street.
BOOK EARLY TO SECURE YOUR SEAT.   PRICES: £5, £3, £2, £1, 10/, and 5/.

THE STADIUM, TO-NIGHT, WEDNESDAY, AT 8.
GEORGE UNHOLZ v MARK HIGGINS, Preceded by SECOND ROUND OF NOVICE TOURNAMENT.
ADMISSION: 10/, 5/, 3/, 2/.

FITZSIMMONS v TOMMY BURNS.—At the STADIUM, NEXT SATURDAY, AT 3, ROBERT FITZSIM-
MONS meets TOMMY BURNS in a Four-round Spar.   Ladies invited.   Tea.   Band.
ADMISSION: 2/ and 1/.   E. COVELL, Governing Director.

Fitzsimmons was training at Hugh McIntosh's residence, "The Rest," National Park. He appeared to be in fine condition, having worked hard, harder than most, nearly four hours total each day. Rudie Unholz, the American lightweight, was in charge of the camp, assisted by brother George Unholz. The sparring partners were Bill Turner, A. McLaglen (British Columbia champ), and Victorian boxer Mark Higgins. Bob ran 5 to 10 miles a day and was a fast runner. He also swam. He was massaged. He chopped wood. In sparring, he glided lightly around the ring, with cat-like movements.

Larry Foley said, "There is no doubt that Fitz is the greatest boxer the world has ever produced, and he proved it by conquering such men as Jas. J. Corbett, Tom Sharkey, Gus Ruhlin, Joe Choinsky [sic – Choynski], P. Maher, Dan Creedon, and Jim Hall. He'll beat any heavy-weight in Australia."

In training, Bob didn't try to knock out his sparring partners, but instead carried them, yet still dropped them now and then. He boxed every day for about an hour. In the evening, he and his wife sang ragtime songs.

Fitz's solar plexus blow was a "remarkable and clever movement," performed so quickly and deceptively that it was almost impossible for foes to avoid being struck. He also punched the ribs and then shifted the same hand up to the jaw in clever fashion as well. He ducked smartly, and just as he got out of the way of a punch, he would step in and deliver his own blows.[425]

Bob often wrote about and gave physical culture lectures in conjunction with his sparring, offering fitness and training advice.

[423] *Star*, December 11, 1909; *Sunday Times*, December 12, 1909; *Daily Telegraph*, December 13, 1909.
[424] *Referee*, December 15, 1909.
[425] *Cobargo Chronicle*, December 17, 1909.

On Tuesday December 14, Fitz sparred 3 rounds each with Firemen Fred Baker and George Cox, as well as promoter Hugh McIntosh.[426]

On December 18, 1909, before a crowd of 7,000 or 8,000 at the Sydney Stadium, Rushcutters Bay, Bob Fitzsimmons sparred in a 4-round exhibition with former world heavyweight champion Tommy Burns, who had lost his championship one year ago at the same location.

The *Sydney Sun* said any doubt regarding Fitz's ability to give and take punishment and last a distance was dispelled. For two rounds, neither did anything startling, but in the remaining two rounds, there was sufficient excitement for the "veriest glutton." Burns was a bit heavy, but as active as ever. He was persistent, boring in all the time. The grand man of the ring never was troubled. He stood off, punched often, and never wasted a blow. He timed admirably, and there was plenty of sting to his blows. Although a number of hard punches were exchanged, none affected Fitz. A punch opened the skin between his eyes, but it did not inconvenience him at all. Many believed that Fitz would prove to be too clever and cunning for Lang.

Afterwards, Burns said,

> I have boxed both Fitzsimmons and Lang. Of course, Lang is youthful, and as a result people are making him favorite for the fight. I don't think there are any odds in it. I think it is an even chance. Fitzsimmons is punching as hard as ever, and anyone receiving a blow from him will remember it. He moves like lightning, and I look for one of the greatest fights ever seen in the country.

---

[426] *Bega Budget*, December 18, 1909.

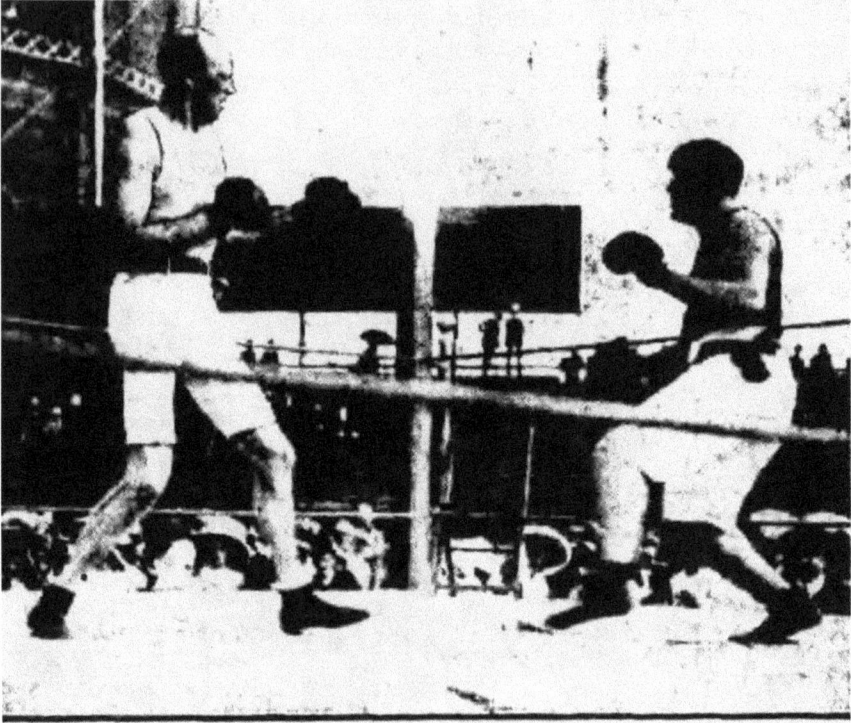

BOB FITZSIMMONS v. TOMMY BURNS.

The *Sydney Times* said that throughout the 4 rounds the pace was fast and some of the blows were quite forceful. There were several vimful rallies. Burns got in close and Fitz stood his ground. They traded punches as if they enjoyed them. Tommy danced around, while Fitz was content to wait. During one rally, Burns's head came into contact with Bob's eye, and it was cut. But it was small and should heal quickly.

Burns told this newspaper,

> Bob Fitzsimmons is a better fighter to-day than a good many people give him credit for being. Bob certainly went well with me, and is undoubtedly in good fix. ... I feel satisfied that he and Lang are going to put up a good, even battle. You know, I fought Lang twelve months ago, and I have a clear recollection of what he can do. It would only be guessing were I to attempt to tell the public which of the pair is most likely to succeed.[427]

Not everyone was impressed with Fitz's performance. One paper said Burns moved around with the lightness of a bantamweight and was very clever. "Fitzsimmons' movements were rather slow and stiff, and left the impression on the minds of many that unless there is a knock-out early he will not stand up long against Lang."[428]

---

[427] *Sydney Sun, Sydney Times*, December 19, 1909.
[428] *Newcastle Morning Herald and Miners' Advocate*, December 20, 1909.

The *Daily Telegraph* said Burns and Fitzsimmons supplied a most attractive display of science. Neither spared the other when he saw a chance to land. There was plenty of steam in the set-to. Rallies brought great joy to the spectators, who frequently applauded. Tom's head bumped Bob hard over his eyes, cutting him, but not badly. Fitz's work was impressive, landing some telling body jolts, which apparently escaped the attention of many, but he demonstrated that he was capable of doing considerable damage.[429]

The *Referee* said one had to have some misgivings about the contest, given that Fitz was in his 47th year of life, extremely old for a fighter. He had made his reputation before Lang was even born. Lang was a powerful young fellow. Conversely, Bob had practically finished his career four years ago when he lost to O'Brien. True, no athlete ever took better care of himself, but age did not improve an old fighter. Still, he was in great shape, having done a great deal of work to prepare, running many miles and sparring all-comers.[430]

Bob Fitzsimmons.

Bill Lang.
Champion Heavyweight Boxer of Australia.

On Tuesday December 21, Fitzsimmons was at the Victoria Barracks gym, where he sparred 2 rounds each with Soldier Bill, Jack Thomson or Thompson, and Gunner Coghill. That day, he also hit the punching ball for a full hour without stopping.[431]

[429] *Daily Telegraph, Barrier Miner*, December 20, 1909.
[430] *Referee*, December 22, 1909.
[431] *Daily Telegraph*, December 22, 1909.

On Wednesday, December 22, Fitz boxed 2 rounds with welterweight George Johns and A. McLaglen (British Columbia champ).

Fitz and Lang were fighting for a £3,000 purse.[432]

THE GREATEST GLOVE FIGHTER THE
WORLD HAS EVER SEEN.

ROBERT FITZSIMMONS

(Who has Conquered the Best and Most Scientific
Boxers of the Day),
MEETS

BILL LANG

(Champion of Australia),
For the Light Heavy-weight Championship of the
World and a £3000 purse.

ON BOXING DAY AT 10.30
AT
THE STADIUM
(Rushcutter Bay).

BOX PLAN OPEN at
Mr. HUGH D. McINTOSH'S BOX PLAN OFFICE,
100 KING ST., near Pitt St.

SEATS : £5, £3, £2, £1 10/, and 5/.

BOOK EARLY AND SECURE YOUR SEAT.

SPECIAL TRAM SERVICE.
ALL KING STREET CARS GO TO THE STADIUM
Telegrams and Letters promptly attended to.
E. COVELL,
Governing Director.

BILL LANG,

46-year-old Bob Fitzsimmons had been born in 1862 or 1863 and started fighting in about 1880. 28-year-old Bill Lang stood 6-feet tall, weighed about 189 pounds, and started his pro boxing career in 1906, but already had 25 fights.[433]

On Monday December 27, 1909, in Sydney, on Boxing Day, an Australian holiday (in which Christmas boxes were exchanged), in a scheduled 20-round bout, Commonwealth heavyweight champion Bill Lang fought Bob Fitzsimmons.

The *Sydney Star* had a same-day report. It was science and generalship in Fitzsimmons against youthful, rugged fighting power in Lang, who was 1.5-stone (21 pounds) heavier.

Thousands had watched them train. For weeks, up to the fight date, Lang had been the pronounced 5 to 2 favorite. Fitzsimmons in his training had not greatly impressed the crowd, but his ungainliness was merely a veil over a wonderful boxing frame. Fitz was a fighter of the Mace school, while Lang was "of the more attractive if less effective present-day style."

Special trams ran from the city to Rushcutters Bay. The crowd numbered at least 10,000. One said 11,000, while another said 12,000 were present. Hugh McIntosh said fully 12,000 were present. Over 7,000 had paid for admission to the 5/ seats alone.

[432] *Cobargo Chronicle, Western Champion*, December 24, 1909.
[433] *Brisbane Courier*, December 27, 1909.

The 20-round main bout was scheduled to start at 10:30 a.m. The fighters appeared at 10:45 a.m.

Both combatants received cheering and applause upon their appearances.

Fitz's seconds were former champion Tommy Burns, the Unholz brothers – Rudie/Rudolf and George, Pat O'Keefe, and Patsy Burke.

Lang's seconds were his brother Ernie or Eddie Lang, Bob Bryant, Dutch Hielman or Hickman, Jack Blackmore, trainer Harry Nathan, and Mick Dunn.

Lang weighed 13 stone, 5 ½ pounds, or 187.5; Fitz 11 stone, 2 pounds, or 156, or so he claimed and was reported and announced. Hence, a possible difference of over two stone, or 28 pounds, if those weights were accurate.

Lang wore green trunks.

Fitzsimmons wore white trunks with a red, white, and blue belt with two miniature Union Jacks, the colors of the United Kingdom.

The hot sun already was overhead when they met at ring center for the handshake, for it was Australia's summer. Both men were perspiring freely already. They shook hands and posed for the cinematograph moving pictures.

Arthur Scott, a local boxing instructor, refereed the contest. They agreed to fight with clean breaks.

About 16,000 people witnessed the boxing contest between Lang and Fitzsimmons for the Heavyweight Championship of Australia. Lang retained the Championship, having defeated Fitzsimmons in the twelfth round.

1st round

The *Sydney Star* said they sparred and boxed. Lang fired leads, but Fitz played defense and was measuring his man. Lang landed a left jab. Fitz landed a nice right to the ribs. Lang kept playing for the body with his left but found little success. Bob mostly brushed the blows aside.

Fitz handled a couple mild rushes, but in another, he slipped down, but was on his feet again in two seconds. Lang hooked a nice left to the jaw. Fitz got going at close quarters and sent his left to the body. Lang was catching him with his left, and Fitz rushed, but as he came in, Lang landed a steadying left hook. Fitz landed a couple rights to the body and blocked a hook. "The round ended slightly in Lang's favor."

The *Sydney Morning Herald* version said initially there was a fair amount of jousting, sparring, and clinching, neither landing. Bob eluded a left and landed a right to the body. Fitz was good at stepping inside blows.

Lang's oncoming body met him with such force that Bob was pushed down. He was up instantly. Bob sent into the body both a left and right. Lang scored a few short jolts in close but had no advantage.

The *Referee's* version said that after some sparring, Fitz landed a hard right to the ribs. There were frequent clinches. Bob ducked several blows. Bob's left to the ribs provoked a bull-like rush from Lang, and Fitz, evading, slipped to his knees.

Fitz rose instantly and fought back but caught a left hook to the head. Another inevitable clinch followed. Bob's right rattled the ribs, and Lang came on with two quick lefts to the face, one after another. Lang stopped a right with a left to the throat. Bob landed left and right to the head, and they were clinched at the bell.

2nd round

The *Star* said Lang fired his left to the face. Fitz played for the ribs. Lang was aggressive, but Fitz was showing too much generalship. As Bill was advancing, Bob landed a stiff left hook to the jaw which nearly lifted Lang off his feet. Lang kept at him though, landing only occasionally. Bob landed two left hooks. Lang caught Fitz with a powerful left to the face.

Bob was boxing very coolly, and occasionally landed a hard right to the ribs. He then landed a left hook to the chin. The punishment finally deterred Lang a bit. Bob hooked his jaw again.

The *Morning Herald* version said Lang missed a heavy left and Fitz landed a short left jolt to the jaw that caused Bill to break ground. Bob neatly stepped away from a vicious right. Lang landed a short drive that brought a trickle of blood from Bob's lips. Bill let himself go, and, keeping in close, sent a number of short swings for the head. Fitz's wonderful evasion skills stood him in good stead, very few landing.

The *Referee* version said Lang was first to get going, but he missed. Bob's right rattled the ribs. Fitz ducked too adroitly, and Lang could not land. Bob's right to the head and left to the ribs were effective, but Lang kept attacking. Lang landed a right, left to the stomach, and, while being held, another left to the body.

After an exchange of lefts, Fitz got busier. Lang was eager to fight and punch whenever he could. Fitz ducked and dodged and banged a right to the ribs. His left to the head caused Lang to clinch again. Lang came in like a catapult and caused Bob to be wary, ducking splendidly, which thousands noted and applauded.

3rd round

The *Star* said Fitzsimmons got to work early and swung a terrific left to the face that dropped Lang to his knees. He rose and attacked, missing.

Fitz rushed in. At close range, Lang landed a left on the jaw, but Bob forced matters, landing a couple nice rights to the chin. Lang waited, and swung on the jaw, but with little force. Bob waited, and Bill drove to the ribs and left to the jaw. Lang also swung a right to the jaw. Bob cleverly dodged blows to cheers but received a left to the jaw and powerful right to the side of the head. Bob did not flinch, and he cleverly evaded the attack. The round ended with Lang using his left and right to the head.

The *Morning Herald* version said Bob immediately landed a heavy left square on the nose. Bob tripped over Bill's leg. Lang scored with a left jolt to the face, which Bob repaid with a straight left to the body. Bob pivoted and swung around on his left foot and landed a short right jolt. Lang livened up and bore in, swinging rights. Fitz's head movement was a treat to witness. His timing was perfect. Time and again his left stopped Lang's onward rush. Lang would not be denied, though, and kept working in close all the time. Lang fought hard, while Bob was defensive.

The *Referee* version said Fitz hooked a left to the jaw and fell but rose and clinched. Lang landed some lefts and a right to the jaw. Fitz stalled a bit. He was an artist at such tactics. Lang hooked the face while Fitz hit the body with his left. Lang hit the jaw with a right on the break while Fitz landed a right to the ribs. Lang tore in and landed an excellent right uppercut. His left and right to the face scored. Fitz ducked and clinched. Bob skillfully stalled and blocked a right with his glove.

4th round

The *Star* said Lang was the aggressor but missed many left leads. Fitz got him with a left hook to the jaw and hard right to the ribs. Bob avoided a left swing. Lang's lefts fell short.

Bob was resting, punching only occasionally. He twice landed his left to the jaw, and while in close landed a stiff right uppercut to the same place. Lang came back strongly but Fitz got away and hooked another left to the jaw, followed quickly by a right, shaking Lang considerably. Fitz fought very cleverly, and the round ended slightly in his favor.

The *Morning Herald* said they started carefully, but Lang began fighting more confidently. Bill was attacking but met with a number of left hooks and a right uppercut that made some think that Bob was just playing with him. Fitz landed a straight left to the face and also a right jolt. "This round put Fitzsimmons well in the lead."

The *Referee* said Fitz still seemed strong but also was feeling the heat. Lang rushed him to the ropes, but Bob was too alert to allow a right to land. Bob landed a right uppercut to the chin. They tussled at close quarters. Fitz's generalship stood him well, making Lang miss or only land grazing blows. Bob landed a couple lefts and a fine right uppercut to the jaw. Lang moved in but ran into a left. Bob again used stalling tactics. He eluded blows and then landed a left to the head and right to the jaw. Fitzsimmons won the round with ease.

5th round

The *Star* said Lang kept trying to get close, but his left hooks went over the top of the ducking Fitzsimmons. The crowd cheered Bob's pleasing evasive work. Bob landed a stiff left on the advancing Lang, but Bill bustled Bob badly. Still, the veteran always had him safe. None of Lang's blows landed squarely. Lang kept swinging his left for the jaw, but Bob's head never was where he expected it to be. Fitz was taking matters easily. Lang swung a left that landed on the neck. Bob landed his right to the ribs. Once again Bob was dodging lefts and landed a snappy right to Lang's jaw. Lang fired left and right but only grazed.

The *Morning Herald* said Lang nailed Fitz with a right to the jaw and then attacked vigorously. Fitz evaded. Lang landed a left hook high on the head. He missed a right. Bob jabbed his left twice in the face. Lang attacked up to the end of the round.

The *Referee* said Fitzsimmons clinched and played defense, while Lang expended energy without results. Bill attacked but ran into a right to the head. Bill used his elbow in the clinch, which brought boos. Fitz jabbed the mouth and socked his left into the ribs. Lang landed a right to the jaw and left to the head. Fitz's right found the jaw. Lang's blows were fended off by forearms. Lang landed a left to the head and right to the other side. Overall, Fitz was fighting "wonderfully cleverly for one so placed in years."

6th round

The *Star* said Lang kept forcing the fight, but his swings missed over the top of the ducking Fitz. Bob was fighting quietly and watching for his opportunity to send in a powerful blow. He was wasting no energy, allowing Lang to do the leading. Bill hustled in again, but to no avail, though he landed a powerful right to the ribs and then fought in the clinches, which brought hoots. Lang kept punching vigorously but did no damage. He only occasionally landed. One powerful left to the head seemed to stagger Fitz, but Bob stood up well. Fitz subsequently received a left and right on the head, and seemed to be in a bad way, but kept his feet when Lang landed a stiff left into the face at the gong.

The *Morning Herald* said Fitz landed a left jab. Lang missed with both hands. In a clinch, Lang butted Fitz on the chin. Bob was piling up points with his left. Lang was inclined to hang on and hit with his disengaged hand. He kept working in close. Fitz's defense was too good. However, just before the bell, Lang scored a solid left hook that rattled Bob.

The *Referee* said Lang swung away, while Fitz won applause through his manner of eluding. Lang landed some blows, including in the clinches. Both men fired some good punches. A Fitz right cross near the left eye seemed to daze Lang a little, but after that, Bill had the better of matters. A Lang right swing to Bob's temple did much harm. Fitz ended the round seeming a bit worse for wear and tear.

7th round

The *Star* said Lang kept leading, and Fitz got in very few punches, spending most of the time dodging the heavy blows. In close, Lang landed a right across the jaw. Fitz landed a pretty left hook to the jaw. They exchanged. Bob landed a right to the ribs. He was cautious, but swung his left to the body a couple of times. Lang landed a right to the chest.

The *Morning Herald* said Lang set the pace. He drove a straight left to the chin. A rally ensued in which Fitz more than held his own, owing to his better timing. Lang landed a short left to the body in the breakaway. Fitz landed his famous left shift, but there wasn't sufficient power behind it. Fitz's cleverness in evading blows brought a smile from Lang, who was not bothered by his foe's trickiness.

The *Referee* said Fitz clinched to avoid blows, and Lang used his head. Fitz landed a hard right to the ribs and the crowd cheered. Lang landed a couple of rights to the ear and neck. Bob received plaudits for his fine head movement and footwork, and he dug a left into the body. Lang came back with interest, for his right to the stomach rattled Bob. Another right grazed Bob's chin. Fitz landed a blow to the jaw and laughed and smiled. Bob blocked nicely. He landed rights to the ribs and head as Bill bore in, but the former champion did not have his old-time power.

8th round

The *Star* said Fitz landed a left, but it had no power. He ducked some blows. They clinched, and Bob pushed him off. He was showing cleverness but no power in his blows. However, when Lang came in, Bob knocked him with a jolt to the jaw which rattled Bill badly. Lang rushed in and landed a right to the jaw. Bob was visibly weakening, but Lang was too anxious to take proper advantage of it. There was a lot of clinching. A vigorous rally by both at the end finished the round with honors even. The crowd cheered.

The *Morning Herald* said Lang rushed in wildly. Fitz's timing stopped him with a left jab. Undaunted, Lang advanced and landed a left to the face and short right to the ribs. He missed a long left hook but followed with a right that landed. At the end, they were standing toe to toe, exchanging, with Fitz doing the better work.

The *Referee* said Bob landed a left jab. Lang landed a short left hook to the head. Lang blocked a body blow, while Fitz dodged a left. His cleverness served him well. Lang was badly flummoxed for a while, for Bob knew how to be where the punch was not. Bob jolted either side of his head. Lang butted the chin. Fitz landed left and right, and also a left in the stomach, and he again bothered Bill with his evasive ability. However, Lang's heavy left to the chin caused Fitz to sway and sag. He recovered quickly though. Bill's left and right to the head were good punches. Bob landed on the body. The crowd cheered and exhorted Fitz on. No blood thus far.

9th round

The *Star* said Fitz stabbed his left to the face, but there was no weight in it. Lang swung but Bob clinched. Bill drove his left home and blood showed on Fitz, but only a trickle. Lang was fighting close. While trying to land a left to the body, Bill caught a jolt with his chin. Lang kept swinging his right. Fitz was getting very weak, stopping two lefts with his jaw. Then he made a wonderful rally and landed two lefts to Lang's jaw, followed by a hard drive to the side of the head. It was a grand recovery, and the old man was cheered loudly as he returned to his corner. "Still, under ordinary circumstances, the end was in sight."

The *Morning Herald* said they sparred a bit. Fitz landed a couple light lefts to the nose and escaped the returns. Lang whipped a left to the jaw. He lowered his head and charged. Bob straightened him up with uppercuts, then followed with two left hooks in quick succession. Lang was trying to mix. "Fitzsimmons ahead on points, and scoring all the clean punches. So far, his exposition of boxing had been scientific and masterly, Lang's methods in comparison appearing laboured and awkward."

The *Referee* said Lang was eager to clinch. Fitz landed a left to the forehead and right to the jaw. Lang's left encircled the neck. Bob came away bleeding from the mouth or nose. Lang's left and right struck Bob's head, and his follow-up body blows with both hands told. Lang's unlawful use of his head was in evidence again. Bob was plainly tiring but dodged a great number of blows very skillfully. Fitz landed three successive left hooks to the jaw, and another. The crowd roared and encouraged Bob.

10th round

The *Star* said they clinched and threw. Fitz landed a left to the body, but it had no ginger in it. After sparring, Lang scored with his left. The crowd cheered Fitz for avoiding a series of swings, but Lang kept working away despite his heavy blows missing or being blocked. Overall, it was a tame round. Fitzsimmons seemed stronger than he was at the conclusion of the prior round.

The *Morning Herald* said Lang started off by backing away. Fitz pursued but took a left to the throat. They countered one another with lefts. Lang attempted to hit the body hard with his left, but Bob's elbow blocked it.

The *Referee* said Lang got in close to butt a bit and miss with his punches. However, his left struck the throat hard, and a right just grazed the nose. Again, Bob's cleverness in stalling was cheered. Tommy Burns remarked, "You've got him tired now, Bob." Not much happened for some time. Near the end, after Lang missed a right, he landed a left hook on the jaw.

11th round

The *Star* said Lang rushed and showered away with blows, doing damage, but he could not land a telling blow. Fitz landed a left to the body, but it was ineffective. Throughout, Bob weathered a very strong storm all in Lang's favor.

The *Morning Herald* said that after some misses, Lang landed a left to the face. Fitz, working his left in characteristic fashion, opened the flesh over Lang's eye with a left hook. He followed up with several left jabs. He feinted his left then worked his famous left shift, doubling up Lang. A left to the face and short right to the body rattled Lang. Bill landed a couple of good body blows, and just before the end of the round landed a right jolt to the jaw.

The *Referee* said that during the minute's rest, Bob was munching on a piece of lemon or an orange. Both came up apparently as strong and alert as ever. Fitz poked his left into the face, and Lang's left hooked the chin. Fitz did better with a jab to the nose, which brought blood. Lang missed a right but landed left to the head, skimmed a right to the jaw and hung on in a clinch. Bob landed successive lefts to the jaw, stomach, and chest. Lang landed left and right to the head, and another right. Fitz was stalling beautifully again. Bill jabbed the throat, and Bob struck a right to the body. Close in, Lang's left and right hit the head. Bob shoved him off with the left and swung a right to the head, then right to the stomach, which hurt.

As he sat in his corner, the appearance of Lang's right eye and nose showed there was considerable steam behind some of Bob's blows. Fitz showed no marks beyond a cut and slight swelling under one eye.

12th round

The *Star* said that when the bell rang, it could be seen that Lang had a mouse over his right eye. He rushed in and almost forced Fitz through the ropes with his momentum and weight but not punches. Lang ran into a forceful left but swung his right in reply and missed, but a second later landed his right on the side of the jaw, driving Fitz back. In the rally, Lang caught him again and sent Fitz down for five seconds.

Upon rising, it looked as if only one punch would be necessary to finish Fitzsimmons. The old man was very groggy on the ropes, but Lang failed to land the finisher. They got to mid-ring, where Lang landed a right uppercut that sent Fitzsimmons down and out. The superintendent of police interposed and put an end to the proceedings.

The *Morning Herald* said Fitz ripped a left to the ribs. Lang rushed him into a neutral corner, where both tripped and Fitz fell through the ropes with Lang on top of him. Bill helped Bob up.

At ring center, Bob landed a light left. Lang rushed in close and Bob backed away. As he did so, Lang landed with a right swing on the point of the chin. Fitz staggered and fell.

Fitzsimmons rose at 7. Lang, seeing him in a bad state, rushed in to finish, raining a perfect hail of blows upon his tottering form. Fitz took a lot of punishment. With his back to the ropes, his head hanging loose and arms by his sides, Lang sent a smashing right on the jaw. Bob fell, and as he did, a police officer raised his baton to stop the contest. No notice was taken, and Bob was counted out.

The *Referee* version said Lang rushed with ginger and vim, crowding his man, making Bob back before the onslaught. Fitz hit the ropes in a neutral corner and flopped down to a sitting posture on the lower strand before the vigor of a left and right to the neck. Bill extended a helping hand to raise him up, and the crowd cheered the apparent magnanimity. However, Bob would have been better served if allowed to take his full measure of rest.

Once up again, a left dashed hard to his face, and the right found the body. A left to the chest drove Bob back. Lang socked the left under the heart and right to the chin, sending Fitzsimmons down on his back for an eight-count.

Upon rising, the excited Lang bore upon him. Bob faced the rush with grit, but Nature went back on him. Badly dazed and weak, Bob took left and right to the chin and leaned on the ropes. Fitz staggered to the center, then tottered back to his own corner. Now that he had his man at his mercy, Lang charged in stronger than ever. Bang went left and right to the jaw, and a heavy right uppercut to the chin a la Jack Johnson sent Fitz down headlong to the floor, beyond all possibility of recovering.

Superintendent Mitchell leaped to the ringside to interfere, and the timekeeper counted away until Arthur Scott declared Lang the winner. The fight had been "good all through, and very exciting."

As soon as he stood up, heartfelt sympathy and cheering greeted Fitzsimmons. They hooted Lang. Bob smiled as he left the ring, being cheered and patted on the back by everyone who could do so.

Although the fight was filmed in its entirety, very little remains (or has been found, located, or revealed). Lang looked strong and full of vim, while 46-year-old Fitzsimmons appeared relatively slow, with little snap on his blows.

In the 10th round, Lang was the aggressor, throwing first and more often. Bill sometimes retreated in order to bait Fitz into advancing, but it was Lang who threw as Bob got into his range. Bill swung away with hard rights and hooks, but usually Bob ducked, blocked, or clinched. Bob only snuck in the occasional blow.

During the 12th round, Fitzsimmons jabbed and clinched as Lang fired a right. Bob then moved away warily and slowly and clinched a couple times to avoid the aggressive Lang's attempted right. Bill bulled in and then landed a short but powerful left hook that sent Fitzsimmons down into a helpless heap, laying on the bottom rope, but it was not ruled a knockdown. Bob was allowed to rise with Lang's assistance, and they continued.

The strong and ferocious Lang kept stepping in with blows, as Bob seemed very slow and fatigued, hands down, primarily clinching, but sometimes sneaking in a jab or straight right. Lang attacked and landed a barrage of nonstop blows, right and left hooks, until the final right sent Fitz down.

Bob rose and tried to clinch as the ferocious Lang belted away, landing heavy rights and left hooks. Bob was tough, took it, and either moved away or bulled in and clinched. The onslaught continued. However, Fitz was too weak, and Lang too strong and relentless, and a series of rights and left hooks to the head followed by a coup de gras right uppercut sent Fitz down and out cold, flat on his back.

The referee counted him out. Bob's cornermen partially lifted his seemingly unconscious body and dragged him back to his corner to place him on his stool to revive him.

In conclusion, the *Sydney Star* said given that Fitz gave away over two stone in weight and nearly 20 years in age, the fight he put up was surprising. His cleverness badly troubled the Victorian. Fitz had a left which jolted Lang's head back time after time. When Lang rushed, Bob cleverly side-stepped. Bill's swings missed. Bob was under them every time. The crowd yelled itself hoarse with delight at Bob's skill. There was no dancing about. Fitz merely moved a few inches forwards, backwards, or sideways. "It was a contest between skill on one side, and weight, strength and youth on the other." Had the decision been given at the end of the 11th round, Fitzsimmons would have been the winner. Nature finally gave out. Bob had been fighting for 33 years, five more than his opponent had been alive.

The *Sydney Morning Herald* said Lang successfully defended his Australian heavyweight championship. "But it was not a great athletic or boxing achievement. Lang won because of his superior strength and his youth. Fitzsimmons lost because of his age – because he no longer possesses the vim and vigour which are necessary for championship standard, and which have but a limited duration in the life of an athlete." Fitz was encouraged to retire. Nevertheless, he showed in every round that he had a wonderful knowledge of every point of the game, and still was the cleverest boxer in Australia. But it was all in vain. Lang gave his weight at 13 stone 5 ½ pounds. Fitz was 11 stone 2 pounds, or 2 stone 4 pounds smaller.

Fitz stood erect, his head even thrown backward, with no crouch, and his leads came straight from the shoulders. Lang used a slight crouch.

From the start, their methods did not vary. Fitz's hitting was clean and his footwork extremely clever. Bob displayed magnificent scientific boxing, but he did not have the strength. Lang was a bull who had no straight clean punches, but rather dashed in with repeated swings, which Bob invariably avoided or blocked. But at close quarters, when clinched, Lang got in the only effective blows of the first 11 rounds. Although Fitzsimmons scrupulously honored the agreement to fight with clean breaks, Lang frequently was guilty of fighting in clinches. If he had a hand free, he would use it. The crowd hooted Lang, believing that he had transgressed the rules of a clean-break fight and also had accidentally butted a couple of times.

In the 1st round, Lang led nervously. Fitz met him with short body jolts. When they closed in, Lang wildly and fiercely swung for the jaw, but the old veteran produced a storm of applause by the dexterity of his rapid head movement, avoiding danger.

In the 2nd, again Fiz avoided nearly all of the younger man's swings, and received an infinitesimal portion of the intended punishment, giving more than he received. Still, Bob was weak, his strength already gone.

In the 3rd round, Fitz again was weak. Lang landed several times to the head. He received many times the number of hits, but they had little effect on his strong and muscular frame. Lang's seconds evidently had advised him to rush the fighting. Bill fought with tremendous vigor but little skill. He bored in repeatedly and fired with never-tiring rapidity. But Bob's head movements roused the crowd's enthusiasm.

Round after round, Fitz gave a masterly exhibition of defensive tactics. He landed a sufficient number of blows in the right place to settle the fight a dozen times if his blows had the necessary driving power behind them, but his force was sadly missing.

Most of the rounds, purely on points, were pronouncedly in Fitz's favor. However, as the rounds passed, he was perceptibly tiring and growing weaker, while Lang remained vigorous.

By the 12th round, Fitz's speed had diminished. He received a couple punches on the jaw, the last sending him down for 7 seconds. This was the beginning of the end. Bob still had some cleverness, but he was very tired. He avoided the coup de grace for a while, until from absolute exhaustion he had no defense to offer any more, and Lang landed on the point of the chin and Bob was down and out for the count. The police entered to stop it, but it did not matter.

This writer said Lang was not in the championship class. He undoubtedly had improved but was not a first-class man. Fitzsimmons was unmarked, while Lang's face showed that his defense at times was ineffective. Still, Lang was able to overcome the ex-champion's wonderful headwork, ringcraft, knowledge of infighting, and machine-like guards, which might make many an excellent boxer look simple. Ultimately though, the writer concluded that Lang had vigor and strength, but not the championship skill and class.

The *Referee*'s "The Amateur" said Fitzsimmons made a great and remarkable showing, but age was defeated by youth; given the 20 years age difference. Bob had nothing to kick himself over, for he went out a great man. Excessive heat contributed to his downfall, as well as the forcing and harrying of a strong, vigorous youngster who used his 23 pounds more weight to bear up against him. It was triumph of youth, not skill. Fitz did the best that Nature would allow.

They agreed to break clean, and though the clinches were frequent, Lang often completely ignored the agreed-upon conditions. During one of the rests between rounds, Tommy Burns on behalf of Fitz called the referee's attention to the infractions.

The outstanding feature was the manner in which Bob bewildered Bill by his clever "head-stalling, ducking, and side-stepping." Time and again Fitzsimmons had Lang missing in the air. But the bulldog Lang kept coming after him. They would exchange until the inevitable clinch. Referee Arthur Scott had a warm time tearing them apart. All sides admired Fitz's skill. Many remarked, "What a wonder he must have been!" Others said what had made Bob great was not his wonderful skill but the fact that he had a weighty punch combined with the ability to absorb punishment. However, at this point in his career, his punch was lacking.

Fitzsimmons did not perform as well as he did in training, wherein he had heavier blows and more vigor and zest. Regardless, Fitz disproved those who called it a mismatch and predicted the old man's quick end. The crowd had enjoyed the contest, yelling and cheering throughout.

Sydney's *Daily Telegraph* said it was a matter of the old adage, "Youth will be served." Fitz was nearly two decades older, and there was a big handicap in weight as well, and it was all too much. Fitz was announced officially as 11 stone 2 pounds, while Lang was 13 stone 5 ¼ pounds. Still, Bob made a bold showing, and it wasn't certain he would be defeated until the 12th round. Up to and including the 11th round, Fitz's prospects of success appeared equally as good, and several rounds he clearly outpointed Lang. He easily ducked Lang's blows quite often. Lang seemed confused as to how to hit him. They had agreed to break clean, but Lang did not always observe the rules.

The *Sydney Sportsman* said age and science were beaten by youth and sheer slog. Lang was bigger and had the force and bull-like aggressiveness of youth. He simply hurled himself in and punched. Yet, more often than not, he missed. Fitz was able to move his head subtly out of the way of nearly every deadly blow. Occasionally, Bob had him bewildered. Fitz held his own until the 10th, landing solid blows combined with his good defense, but ultimately, he was bashed, biffed, and battered out in the 12th. The day had been a very hot scorcher, which did the older man no good.

The *Sydney Mail* said Fitz, in his 48th year, no longer had the stamina and vigour required. Yet, he had the skill and cleverness. His remarkable footwork and dodging capabilities helped him. Lang was 13 st 5 ½ pounds, while Fitz was 11 st 2 lb, or 2 st 4lb less. That was a handicap as well, particularly at the infighting, with Lang using his weight on Fitz.

Many remarked that Fitzsimmons put up a great fight. He had a pretty stance, erect, with head thrown slightly back. Lang crouched and twisted himself. "As an exhibition of boxing the honours went to Fitzsimmons, but in the way of a bullocking fight the laurels went to Lang." Fitz had the skill but his strength and force left him very quickly. Lang could tell that pushing the pace eventually would tell upon Bob. Afterwards, Fitz showed no signs of punishment, while Lang's face bore testimony to the fact that his defence was not equal to his opponent. "The general verdict when the fight was all over was that Fitzsimmons was justly claimed to be the king of the ring in his day."

Afterwards, in his dressing room, Lang showed no jubilation, for he was quite modest. He said,

> Fitz is a great old fighter, and sometimes, more often than not, as a matter of fact, I did not know which way to take him. He flummoxed me completely in the first few rounds, and his head work was simply wonderful. I know that not 10 per cent of my blows found any spot. I was driving at his face and often found the middle of his back.
>
> I was playing a waiting game, and so, I think, was Fitz. It was not until the eleventh round that I knew I had him. It was a left hook which caught him about an inch from the point that gave me the first advantage, and he was about tired then. But in the next round I followed up on the same spot, and one on the mark helped to finish the fight.
>
> You can say this, too, that he's a game 'un – gamer than I expected – and what would have happened had he been a stone heavier and a few years younger I wouldn't like to say.

Fitz walked in and they shook hands. Bob said, "Good luck, old man. You deserved to win."

Another paper quoted Lang as saying, "I punched him hard, and he punched me hard, and I tried to punch harder when he fooled me so badly with his fine head and foot work. Fitzsimmons must have been a wonder indeed when he was at his prime."

A third quoted Lang as remarking,

> The old-timers must have been great fighters. Bob certainly bothered me a lot to-day, and I have been thinking ever since it was no wonder he beat such a number of tough fellows. How he stalled his head! It was a revelation. No, I never felt like losing at any time, though Bob proved a hard nut, and came at me in so many different ways that a man could not rely upon any particular system of attack or defence. I had to be ready for anything and everything, no matter in what old way it arrived.

Interviewed outside, Fitzsimmons said,

> Youth must prevail. You see, I am an old man. Lang is a young man, and when youth is pitted against age, youth almost invariably must prevail. But before I went into the ring I had every confidence in my ability to win. I thought I would have won in less than six rounds, but you see my age was against me, and Lang's youth was all in his favor. ... It is a great many years since I first entered the ring, and the fight to-day, the 370th of my career, is the last. I will fight no more. But I am glad to have fought my last fight in Australia, where I learnt the art of self-defence; and I am also glad that it was an Australian by whom I was beaten. I may say here that I think Lang is a game young fellow, and with proper training should make a name in the boxing world for himself.

Bob said Lang beat him fairly and was a gentleman. Also, "I must thank the Australian crowd for the enthusiastic way in which they received me, and for their splendid impartiality and sportsmanlike attributes."

Fitz had given it another try in the hope that he might have another fight in him. "About three years ago I had what I thought would be my last ring fight. It was with Jack Johnson. He did not beat me; he fouled me."

Fitz admitted that he knew he no longer had it, even in training.

> When I was training for the contest I felt that my whole strength and agility were not what they used to be. This I particularly felt whilst running for training. There was not that same sprightliness and spring as in the days of old, and with regard to my punches whilst training I also felt that they lacked the power of old. But I did my best.

Another paper quoted Fitzsimmons as saying,

> I am convinced now, that the fighting game is too strenuous for me. In the second round I knew I had lost a lot of my vim, and I couldn't

punch at all as I used to, nor did I do so well as in my training for the match. Lang is a fine, strong fellow, and the material for a great fighter. I could make him thoroughly good if I had the chance. Yes, I felt the sun a great deal, but it's no use talking – he was too powerful, young, and heavy for me, as I am now. I'll quit the ring right here for good and aye.

Another writer said that in his dressing room, Fitzsimmons said,

I am satisfied. I thought I could make good in another battle, but have had a rude awakening to the fact that I am too old for the game, though I didn't feel so before. In the second or third round it dawned upon me that my vim was not there. I couldn't punch as I did, even while training, and I couldn't rough it with that big, strong, husky young fellow, who was always boring in and wanted a heap of shoving off. Oh, how I longed for the old vigor – the strength and speed that enabled me to hit hard when I got the chance and keep well with my opponent no matter how he rushed the pace.

Bob's motivation to take the Lang fight had been for his family. "I was fighting to-day for those three boys in America – my three lads – but it wasn't to be." Tears welled in his eyes.

Ex-champion Tommy Burns was in Fitz's corner on that day and advised the old warrior. Tommy said,

I think it was one of the most wonderful fights that could ever be seen, and Fitzsimmons is still one of the cleverest men who could enter a ring. What must he have been in his best days! It was real good to see his clever work… You see he made Lang miss him every time… If the decision had been given before the twelfth round Fitzsimmons must have been the winner, but an old man can't keep going against a big young fellow for ever. He is a great man still.

Burns said Lang was a good strong young fellow who fought well. When asked whether Lang had improved since he fought him, Burns said, "Certainly, he's improved right enough."

Another paper quoted Tommy Burns as saying Lang was nearly 100% better than he was when he fought him over a year ago, and would be hard for anyone to beat. "He is so well, so strong, and so weighty. Fitzsimmons did not shape as well as I expected him to do, or as his training indicated he would do. … yet he fought a remarkable battle against big odds, and has nothing to be ashamed of in being defeated."

Yet another quoted Burns as observing, "Fitz certainly showed a lot of skill, and he weathered a tough time extraordinarily well; he is a great old fellow beyond any manner of doubt, and as fair a fighter as ever lived, I think." Tommy liked how Bob looked in sparring, and backed him with wagers. Yet, he didn't lose that much, because the Lang people wouldn't respond.

Burns was impressed with Lang's improvement since they fought.

Lang has improved a good deal, and he has put on a lot of weight, and fights better than he did. I thought Fitz might put a right across and end the contest at any moment; but he didn't seem equal to it. Possibly the great heat affected Fitz, as the top of his head was exposed to the fierce rays of the sun while he stood in the ring. We had an umbrella over him in his corner, as you saw; but there wasn't enough time in the minute for the man to cool down.

Fitz certainly had a stiff task set him with such a husky, weighty young fellow, who is, possibly, better now than he ever was before.

Burns said he would fight Lang again if there was money in it.

Mr. W. C. J. Kelly, manager for Tommy Burns, said Lang was surprisingly strong and improved since he fought Burns. Fitzsimmons was so clever and elusive, and bewildered Lang so much, such that the Melbourne boxer did four times the work that Fitz did.

Larry Foley said, "All who saw the old man fight to-day must admit that he is still exceedingly clever, as the fight, of course, was youth against age. But it was a great go, and victory fell to the youthful man. I must congratulate Fitzsimmons on his undoubted courage and skillful tactics." Foley said Fitz was more than a wonder, for he was game too. Lang did as well as he could against such a tricky opponent.

Mick Dunn also complimented Fitz. "I think his work was simply marvellous. His head must be better than any fighting man's alive. Clever isn't a word for it."

Lang's manager said, "Fitz undoubtedly hit Bill often enough to beat him; but he didn't hit hard enough." Lang had a great chin and could take an awful lot. "I question whether there is a man in Australia to-day capable of administering the sleep-producer to the local champion. I must confess old Bob surprised me. It was a great and good fight – one of the very attractive and satisfying sort so rarely seen nowadays."

Rudie Unholz thought Fitz could have lasted the 20 rounds if he had waited more and not fought so hard during the earlier rounds. He showed glimpses of his once-great skill, and flummoxed Bill badly. Still, Lang was a good, hard, strong fighter, and would require a lot of shaking off.

Bill Squires said, "The old man fought a great fight. There can be no doubt about his cleverness, but youth was on the side of Lang, and to that must be attributed his victory." Another quoted Squires as saying, "I enjoyed Fitz's fighting better than anything in the same line I have ever seen. What a marvel the old chap must have been to have done so well to-day! Only the other man's youth, and consequent greater reserve power and speed, won the day."

Snowy Baker said it was the same old story, for it was nature that beat Fitz. At his age, it was too much to expect him to beat a bigger, younger, stronger man. Still, Bob put up a splendid fight and showed his superior ring generalship.

Youth will be served. It was good to look at Bob Fitzsimmons fighting. I enjoyed his show. Such a treat is rare in these degenerate times. Lang, too, shaped well – but his judgment was somewhat at fault compared with that of the master before him. However, he has nothing to be ashamed of. Bill Lang never shirked the hottest corner.

English lightweight Johnny Summers said,

Have I learned something? Yes, a great deal. He in the game who could watch Fitzsimmons at work and not pick up some good pointers would be more dense than a really good boxer could well be. … I thought Fitz was going to win. Why, up to the round prior to the end he had the better of the fight, and seemed as strong as at any time before.[434]

STADIUM,
RUSHCUTTERS BAY.

TO-MORROW (THURSDAY) NIGHT AT 8,
GRAND PICTURE NIGHT.
THE PICTURES OF THE GREAT CHAMPIONSHIP CONTEST
BETWEEN
(BOB) (BILL)
FITZSIMMONS & LANG
WHICH TOOK PLACE ON BOXING DAY, AND WAS ONE OF THE FINEST FIGHTS SEEN IN AUSTRALIA, WILL BE SHOWN

BOB FITZSIMMONS, the World's Greatest Glove Fighter, WILL LECTURE on the contest, and explain his sensations through the event, and illustrate the most important punches.

WILL ALSO BE SHOWN, ONE ROUND EACH OF THE FOLLOWING PICTURES :— JEFFRIES-SHARKEY CONTEST, CONEY ISLAND, U.S.A. BURNS-JOHNSON CHAMPIONSHIP MATCH, AND PICTURES OF FAMOUS BOXERS.

A TWO HOURS' SHOW OF GREAT FIGHTS
FULL BAND. ADMISSION—RESERVED CHAIRS, 3/. OTHER SEATS, 2/ and 1/.
BOOK YOUR SEATS AT HUGH D. McINTOSH'S OFFICE, CHALLIS HOUSE (6th Floor), MARTIN PLACE.
R. COVELL, Governing Director.

Fitzsimmons-Lang
Fight Pictures.

The FILMS of the GREAT CONTEST which took place on BOXING DAY at the STADIUM between the Famous Boxers BOB FITZSIMMONS and BILL LANG, the Champion of Australia, have been developed, and are the FINEST FILMS that have ever been offered to the Public.

Fitzsimmons-Lang
Fight Pictures.

The Films of the Great Contest which took place on Boxing Day, at the Stadium, between the Famous Boxer, Bob Fitzsimmons, and Bill Lang, the Champion of Australia, have been developed, and are the best that have ever been offered to the public. They are Marvellously Clear.

State Rights are for Sale
SEND BIDS AT ONCE.

EVERY ROUND of the Contest is beautifully and clearly shown.	KNOCK-OUT A GREAT PICTURE. The Knock-downs clearly shown.
EACH INCIDENT IS PLAIN. The Sensational and Clever Work of Fitzsimmons is clearly depicted.	TOMMY BURNS giving Fitzsimmons instructions.
BILL LANG'S RUSHES—Fitzsimmons' Clever Ducking.	THE MEN ENTERING the Ring—Most Exciting Pictures of Modern Times.
THE CROWD RISING TO CHEER the Fighters.	TAKEN AT ENORMOUS EXPENSE by the best operators in the Commonwealth.

All the Papers Praise the Fight.
The Best Seen in Sydney for Many Years.
Cables, Telegrams, and Letters promptly attended to.

Hugh D. McIntosh,
PROMOTER,
Challis House, Martin Place.

The films were developed quickly and started showing almost immediately. As a treat, Bob Fitzsimmons would lecture on the contest, explain important moments, and illustrate the most important punches. The films also were shown in conjunction with one round each of the fight pictures of the Jeffries vs. Sharkey and Johnson vs. Burns fights (or sometimes the first 4 and last 4 of the latter bout). Sometimes Bob would even spar a bit, including with various local boxers, such as Pat Doran of Melbourne, Dan and Mick Abbott, Bob Greenshields, Jack and Tom Jones, Harry Hayes, and Dan Morrison. Fitz traveled to different areas of the country with this show.

One summary of the fight films said Fitz put up a sterling fight. "For twelve rounds he eluded his younger and stronger opponent, and showed fine defence powers and expert ringcraft. He had the best of the early

[434] *Sydney Star*, December 27, 1909; *Sydney Morning Herald, Referee, Sydney Daily Telegraph, Sydney Sportsman, Sydney Mail*, December 28, 29, 1909.

rounds, but Lang, aided by the freshness and vigor of youth, eventually wore down the veteran and knocked him out."[435]

Bob's wife continued giving theatrical performances, being advertised as "Mrs. Robert Fitzsimmons." She often would do sketches with her husband, sometimes in conjunction with the Fitzsimmons-Lang films. It was all part of a vaudeville company entertainment show.[436]

Less than a month after beating Bob, on January 17, 1910, in Sydney, 182-pound (13st) Bill Lang knocked out 176-pound (12st 8lb) Bill Squires in the 7th round.

The Fitzsimmons vaudeville show had been in Melbourne the previous week, and his two shows there had realized over 400 pounds. He also visited Bendigo. He was scheduled to visit Castlemaine, Geelong, Ballarat, Albury, Bathurst, and Orange through the 28th, when he would return to Sydney and then leave for New Zealand.[437]

The Fitz's were well received in Timaru, New Zealand, Bob's boyhood home. Bob said he had landed in Timaru as a boy of 9 years of age, and left when he was 22. Unfortunately, his parents were no longer alive.[438]

In April, Fitz and company would tour the North Coast and Queensland, Australia with various fight films, including Fitz-Lang, Burns-Johnson, Squires-Kline, Jeffries-Sharkey, and Squires-Williams. Middleweight Les O'Donnell would accompany him as a sparring partner. They would reach Brisbane by April 23 and return to Sydney on May 6.[439]

On April 11, 1910 in Sydney, before a crowd of around 15,000, in his first fight in well over a year after losing to Jack Johnson, former world's heavyweight champion Tommy Burns, 43-4-8, weighing 181 pounds (12st

[435] *Bendigo Independent*, January 18, 1910; *Mount Alexander Mail*, January 21, 1910; *Geelong Advertiser*, January 22, 1901; *Border Morning Mail*, *Ballarat Star*, January 24, 1910.
[436] *Town and Country Journal*, February 16, 1910.
[437] *Referee*, January 19, 1910.
[438] *Referee*, March 2, 1910.
[439] *Sunday Sun*, April 3, 1910; *Referee*, April 6, 1910.

13lb), won his rematch with Australian champion 188-pound Bill Lang (13st 6lb), 21-5-1, winning a 20-round points decision awarded by referee and promoter Hugh McIntosh. The crowd supported Lang, but the decision was fair.

The *Sydney Morning Herald* wrote that there was "no question as to the absolute correctness of the decision."

> Burns established big leads on points in four-fifths of the rounds. His wonderful combination of head and foot work repeatedly nonplussed the Australian, whose attempts to get in an effective hit often ludicrously missed. … Burns gave an exhibition of clever boxing that makes his success against more formidable men than Lang comprehensible.

Tommy scored to the body and head with monotonous regularity, finishing as fit and fresh as if he could go another 20 rounds.

Given his long layoff, Tommy said he was not inclined to take any chances with Lang, and was content to box with him, feeling sure that he was well ahead on points.

The *Sydney Star* agreed, "Burns won, and won with a fair margin of points in his favor."[440]

TIVOLI THEATRE.

(By kind permission of Mr. Harry Rickards.)

TO-DAY, THURSDAY, AT 2.30.

GRAND COMPLIMENTARY MATINEE

and Public Send-off to the Departing Athletes.

TOMMY BURNS, BOB FITZSIMMONS,

BILL LANG,

who sail for America per R.M.S. Makura on Monday,

June 6.

Artists from J. C. WILLIAMSON'S COMPANY
(By kind permission of Mr. J. C. Williamson).

Artists from the TIVOLI THEATRE
(By kind permission of Mr. Harry Rickards).

Artists from the NATIONAL AMPHITHEATRE
(By kind permission of Mr. James Brennan).

FAREWELL APPEARANCE IN AUSTRALIA
of America's Dainty Prima Donna,

MRS. ROBERT FITZSIMMONS.

Sparring Exhibitions, Skipping, and Ball Punching, by
TOMMY BURNS, BOB FITZSIMMONS, and BILL LANG.

The entire proceeds of the Matinee will be devoted
to handsome testimonials and presentations to the
athletes as a small token of the esteem in which they
are held by the Australian sporting world and the
public generally.

PRICES: 3/, 2/, and 1/. No Early Doors.

Bob Fitzsimmons continued with his tour of Australia through May 1910, giving lectures, showing fight films, and sparring Les O'Donnell.

On June 2 at the Tivoli theater in Sydney, Bob Fitzsimmons, Tommy Burns, and Bill Lang gave a farewell send-off matinee, for it was the final time locals could see them before they set sail for the U.S.A. Mrs. Fitzsimmons, a high soprano "with a voice of the most brilliant and well-cultivated timbre," excited enthusiasm with her singing. Bob boxed with Les O'Donnell, and Burns sparred with Snowy Baker.[441]

On June 6, Fitzsimmons and his wife, as well as Tommy Burns, Bill Lang, and Hugh McIntosh left Sydney for America via the R.M.S. Marama. All of them wanted to see Jeffries vs. Johnson. A crowd gave the departing famous men an ovation.[442]

[440] *Sydney Morning Herald, Sydney Star*, April 12, 1910.
[441] *Sydney Morning Herald*, June 3, 1910.
[442] *Sydney Star*, June 6, 1910; *Sydney Morning Herald*, June 7, 1910.

CHAPTER 19

Back in the U.S.A.

On July 4, 1910, in Reno, Nevada, Jack Johnson fought James J. Jeffries in the Battle of the Century. Bob Fitzsimmons was present and introduced in the ring as "the greatest warrior of them all."

Bob Fitzsimmons responding to the enthusiastic calls of his admirers for a speech.

When Bob had arrived in town, he received an ovation and was greeted like a hero. Crowds followed him everywhere. "It was the admiration born of respect. ... As a fighter he was so complete."

> The craftiest general the ring has ever known perhaps, certainly one of the wittiest boxers in defending himself, and always a tiger when attacked – those characteristics made him what men call a drawing card. But there was something more than all of that. It was the fact that whenever he stepped into a ring the crowd knew that this was going to be a fight. ... He was a fighter through and through. In victory he fought fiercely, and in defeat he went down showing a lion's heart. ... Men still remember that.[443]

---

[443] *San Francisco Call*, July 4, 1910.

The Johnson vs. Jeffries fight was stopped in the 15th round after a tired and worn out Jeffries had gone down three times in that round, the first knockdowns of his entire career. It was Jeff's first fight in nearly 6 years.

Bob Fitzsimmons said there never was even a flash of Jeff's old-time self. He looked great, but had left his vitality on the road, having overtrained. He lacked vim, dash, vigor, strength, force, and power. The fight had not gone 4 rounds before Fitz was convinced of this. "He wasn't even a quarter of the man he was when he met me." Not even for an instant did Jeff show his former vim and dash. There was not even a flash of it.

Fitzsimmons gave his thoughts on the rounds. "In the first round I thought Jeffries had a shade the better of it, but he did not display the aggressiveness that I had expected of him." The 2nd and 3rd rounds were about the same. Bob kept waiting to see Jeff display his old irresistible tactics. After the 4th round, Bob realized that Jeff no longer was what he once was. "He was only the image of his former self, not the real, solid, powerful, vigorous fellow I used to know." After the 11th round, it was all Johnson. In the 13th, Bob expected to see Johnson put him out. The 15th round was the sorriest sight he ever saw. Jeff had nothing left.

Conversely, Fitzsimmons said Johnson was one of the ring's most dangerous fighters ever. The way Johnson patted Jeff on the shoulder after the rounds was as if to say, "Poor old fellow, I am sorry for you, but I have to do it." It was such a pitiful sight and sad spectacle that Bob had tears in his eyes. Fitz said of Johnson:

> He is a big, strong, clean fighter, and has a powerful punch. He is one of the cleverest fighters we ever had. I used to think that he was only a defensive fighter. He showed today that he is an offensive fighter as well. When he wants to he can be terribly aggressive. I believe that if he had forced the fighting in the first round it would not have gone four rounds. But Johnson worked along his own previously made plans. He fought a clever, cool and masterly battle from the start. He made me change my opinion of him as a fighter.
>
> I don't think there is a man in the ring today who would have a chance against Johnson. Notwithstanding that, he met a weakling compared with the Jeffries of old. He showed by his work that he is a terrific hitter, a most clever blocker and one of the most dangerous aggressive fighters the ring has ever seen.

Fitz admitted that prior to the fight, he had allowed his sentiments to carry him away and blind him to the fact that Jeff had aged and lost his vitality. Deep down he thought Johnson might win, but he pushed that thought from his mind and could only think of Jeff's former greatness. "If Johnson had met the Jeffries I met there would have been a different story to tell. ... But there's no use in speaking as to what might have happened now, for it is all over."

Bill Lang said it was a very slow bout with too much clinching and not enough exchanges. Jeff did not go after Johnson as expected. After 6 or 7 rounds, Lang concluded that Jeff was outclassed, and it would take a fluke for him to win. "It proves that an athlete cannot give up a sport and fatten up and then take off the fat and get back his former muscular strength."[444]

As Fitz previously predicted, following the fight, there was a great deal of racial unrest throughout the United States, with riots, assaults, property damage, and even murders. Many legislators, governors, and police banned the films from being exhibited. Many cracked down on the sport itself, either banning boxing or severely limiting it with legislation. Such was the case even in other countries, fearing racial unrest and unwanted symbolism. Nevertheless, Johnson earned $122,600 and Jeffries $117,066, including purse, bonus, and sale of motion picture interests, a record by far.

In August 1910, the *Buffalo Commercial* wrote that the most remarkable heavyweight fighter who ever fought under Queensberry rules was Bob Fitzsimmons. "The freckle-faced Cornishman, maker of horseshoes, and built like a reversed pyramid, was the most extraordinary fighter." He already was in his mid-30s when he won the heavyweight championship. At the same age that Bob was at the zenith of his powers, Jeffries was an old man. Jeffries was great, but by age 29 he was done. Even at 170 pounds, Fitz could knock out men weighing 50 pounds more. No one had as remarkable a career as Bob Fitzsimmons.[445]

In September 1910, Billy Delaney said Jack Johnson was the greatest heavyweight ever, for he had everything. He was fast, clever, could box, was strong, and could hit. He had all the punches. He could use his strength skillfully, stand and stall all day if he wanted and allow the other fellow to fight. "He is as great at long range as at in-fighting." There was no situation in which he was not the master, and Jack had several years before Father Time took him.

Delaney said John L. Sullivan was the hardest hitter ever, with great grit, but would be outclassed in the modern era. "Schooled in modern methods, he would have almost been unbeatable." Jim Corbett was the fastest man and a finished boxer, with a good eye, feet like a deer, and hands like a flash of lightning. He was brainy and could make a stronger man beat himself trying to hit him, but he lacked hitting power. "Had he had the punch of a Fitzsimmons or a Sullivan he would have been the peer of all the fighters."

Delaney called Fitzsimmons a "wonder." "How that old chap could hit and what a game man he was when they broke bad. He was the best middleweight who ever lived. He was too small to beat Jack Johnson, but ounce for ounce he was as good a man as ever lived."

Delaney said men like Choynski and Kid McCoy were too big for the middleweight division but not big enough to be heavyweight champions. Tom Sharkey was a bulldog, not afraid of anything, and as strong as a bear. Jim Jeffries was physically the best of all, the most powerful man of the age,

[444] *Nevada State Journal, San Francisco Chronicle, San Francisco Call, San Francisco Evening Post, San Francisco Bulletin, San Francisco Examiner, New York Times,* July 5, 1910; *Reno Evening Gazette,* July 4, 5, 1910; *Freeman,* July 9, 1910.
[445] *Buffalo Commercial,* August 1, 1910.

but he didn't like fighting, and he tried to come back when he no longer had his wonderful vitality.[446]

Bob Fitzsimmons said none of the present-day fighters had a chance to beat Jack Johnson, for he was in a class by himself. Yet, he too thought Jeffries was doped in his fight with Johnson, a claim that Jeff had made.[447]

Henry Edwards asked what had become of the fighter with the punch. The days of Sullivan, Fitzsimmons, and Jeffries were gone. Now, champions were clever boxers who depended more on science and endurance than administering a knockout quickly. "In all Bob Fitzsimmons' fistic career, he only took part in six bouts that went longer than ten rounds, as he generally won by the knock-out route before the tenth round had been reached." Edwards said Jack Johnson was not much of a puncher.[448]

On December 27, 1910, in Fond Du Lac, Wisconsin, Fitzsimmons refereed a fight between Tommy Dougherty and Frankie Conley, stopping it at the end of the 5th round, refusing to allow Dougherty to continue.[449]

Although retired from boxing, Fitzsimmons and his wife had been and would continue their theatrical and vaudeville profession.

W. C. Kelly said Fitzsimmons, as a rule, won his fights as quickly as possible, and he never backed away from anyone, always remaining in range to punch. He won admiration for his great fighting ability and willingness to meet all comers regardless of weight. In his prime, he was wonderfully fast, delivering blows from any angle, with little or no effort. "He was as crafty as a fox, and he was a past master of all the fine points of the game. He was probably the most scientific hitter ever known to the prize ring."

While in Cleveland, Ohio, on April 7, 1911, Fitz said good big fellows were scarce now. They generally did not know how to punch effectively.

> They have not learned the art of hitting. ... I learned it from Larry Foley in Australia, and he was the best tutor the world ever produced. He taught us how to hit properly and with little effort. The whole thing lies in countering and this department of the game is overlooked by a great many fighters in this country. Foley taught his pupils how to feint and how to draw a blow. He made us understand what feinting was for, and he would not stand for a boxer who would feint and not counter stiffly when he drew the other fellow's lead.
>
> Peter Jackson, Jim Hall, Dan Creedon, and a lot more of us took lessons from Larry, and out of that bunch there was not a man who was not a scientific hitter. They made no clumsy moves and never failed to beat their opponents to the punch.
>
> When Kid McCoy first came to me at New Orleans [1894] I was training to box Creedon. Kid did not know how to hit. I took a fancy

[446] *Buffalo Evening Times*, September 9, 1910.
[447] *Buffalo Evening Times*, December 1, 1910.
[448] *Buffalo Commercial*, December 9, 1910; *Buffalo Enquirer*, December 17, 1910.
[449] *Buffalo Evening Times*, December 28, 1910.

to him and showed him how it was done. I soon had him knocking his opponents cold.[450]

On April 10, 1911, in Akron, Ohio, Fitz knocked out two men larger than himself with ease, without "turning a hair." Bob and his wife had been appearing at a local vaudeville house that week. When emerging from her hotel, two men ogled and addressed Mrs. Fitz improperly. At that moment, Ruby Robert appeared, mixed it at once and laid out both with just two blows. A police officer said, "Here, you can't do that." Bob replied, "Caw'nt I? Well, my name's Fitzsimmons, and if any guy gets fresh with my wife again I'll knock his bloomin' block off." He was not arrested.[451]

Charley White said Joe Gans told him that he once saw Bob Fitzsimmons box an exhibition, and for weeks after followed Bob around the country watching his every move, trying to remember every trick he'd seen Fitz use. Gans told White that he had learned a wonderful amount about boxing by watching Fitzsimmons.[452]

Fitzsimmons told Walter Kelly of the *Cleveland Leader* that he always could beat a man quickly who rushed at him. The fellows who knew how to feint and step around bothered him the most, or at least they lasted longer. Men like Tom Sharkey were easy for Bob. But men like Jim Hall, Jack Dempsey and Jim Corbett were more troublesome to find and hit. "It made no difference how hard they could hit if they would come tearing in I liked them." Sharkey was powerful, but every time he rushed, Bob found the opening and hit him.

> I had some trouble finding Jim Corbett, for he was the shiftiest big fellow who ever pulled on a glove, and he was an adept at the art of feinting. ... I had to bide my time and do a lot of thinking before I finally got to Corbett. He was watching my right hand all the time and stepping away every time I moved it.
>
> Finally, I thought about the shift and then by feinting with the left for one side and then with the right he threw up his guard one after the other. The instant he lifted his right arm to protect his jaw I shifted my right leg in front and then let go with a left hook that landed with all my force in the solar plexus, the pit of his stomach. He went down and the fight was over.[453]

On May 2, 1911, Hank Griffin died at age 41 of either typhoid pneumonia or malarial fever. Lee Smits wrote that Griffin barred no one, had fought the likes of Jeffries and Johnson, and had been a Fitzsimmons sparring partner. He was one of the fastest and gamest fighters of the past generation. He was crafty, fearless, and tough. He held a win over and two draws with Jack Johnson, who never did beat Griffin. Bob Fitzsimmons lauded Griffin, saying,

[450] *Buffalo Commercial*, April 8, 1911.
[451] *Buffalo Evening Times*, April 11, 1911.
[452] *New York Evening World*, April 18, 1911.
[453] *Buffalo Commercial*, May 5, 1911.

He was the best all-around man to train with I ever came across. I always regarded him as a great fighter and if he'd had a fair chance in his prime he would have chased a lot of 'em to cover. … He'd do the work of three men to help put me in shape. I could get just as much as I wanted out of him in the way of boxing, let me tell you. He'd take my lead and come back as strong, no matter how hard I went into him. I never saw him show signs of wilting and I never pushed him to the limit.[454]

In mid-May 1911 in Cleveland, Ohio, Fitz and his wife were appearing every day at the Priscilla Theatre.

Bob had a great memory of his fights, including how he knocked out his foes. When asked how he knocked out Jim Hall in New Orleans, Bob immediately responded, "With a right to the jaw." Bob noted, "Hall was a pupil of mine in Australia." He had taught him to block a right for the ribs by dropping his left arm over the spot where he expected the blow. Knowing that, Bob feinted his right to the ribs, then put all his power into a right to the jaw and neck. "It was one of the hardest blows I ever landed, and it lifted Hall's feet eighteen inches from the floor and he dropped in a heap as though dead." Bob was frightened, fearing that he had killed him, because Hall did not come to for quite some time.[455]

Charley White said Fitzsimmons was undoubtedly the best as well as the cleverest man the middleweight class had ever known. He had broad shoulders and an unusually long reach of 75.5 inches. His boxing knowledge was exceeded only by Corbett, while his ability to assimilate punishment and recuperate wonderfully, combined with wonderful ring generalship, craftiness, and the power to hit harder than any other man made him the best.

Fitz was born in Helston, Cornwall, England and was one of three brothers. His father was a miner and manual laborer, and he had a roving disposition. When Bob was about 9 years old, the family moved to New Zealand, settling in Lyttleton. Young Bob walked and ran to and from school at Christ's Church, which was 3 miles from the village. Bob liked running and jumping, but not school. He worked for a grocery store for a time. At age 12, Bob was known as the best scrapper of his size in the village. He also could run faster and carry heavier loads than any other lad. His elder brother had moved to Timaru to become a blacksmith. Bob was sent there and became an apprentice to a carriage painter. Eventually, he apprenticed himself to a blacksmith. This profession suited him. He became an expert horseshoer and won a horseshoeing tournament. At age 18, he was an excellent athlete, a fleet runner and second only to the village champion at quolts.

While in Timaru, he saw a boxing match and appreciated the science, and he took up boxing, learning its fine points. Bob had a quick eye, was very agile, and possessed unusual strength. He began taking part in

[454] *Buffalo Enquirer*, May 5, 1911.
[455] *Buffalo Commercial*, May 17, 1911.

exhibitions. He eventually fought a 200-pound blacksmith while Bob was only 140 pounds. After a rough few rounds, Bob eventually was able to knock him out.[456]

In 1881 in Timaru, Fitz fought his first pro battle, under London Prize Ring rules, against Arthur Cooper. Fitz won by knockout in 3 rounds. He also beat, under LPR rules, Jack Murphy and Jim Crawford, both of whom he knocked out in 3 rounds each. He won 5 pounds or less for each contest.

Eventually, seeking more fights and better pay, he traveled to Australia. He wanted to earn enough money to set up his own blacksmith shop. He was a stowaway on the ship, but when caught, he told his story and then gave boxing exhibitions to entertain the crew.

In Sydney, Larry Foley was the proprietor of the biggest boxing hall. All the big fights were held at Foley's club. Foley gave Fitz a tryout, and he did well. The following week, he was matched with a man named Brinsted at one of Foley's regular Saturday night affairs. Brinsted weighed about 175 pounds, but Bob knocked him out in 2 rounds. He earned a 5-pound note. Next was Jack Greentree, whom he also knocked out in 2 rounds.

He then took on Dick Sandal, the amateur middleweight champion of Timaru, who traveled to Sydney to fight him. Fitz put him to sleep in 4 rounds. He earned 10 pounds.

Bob also fought Australian middleweight champion Bill Slavin, brother of Paddy Slavin, then Australian heavyweight champion. Fitz knocked out Slavin in 7 rounds. Bob earned 6 pounds, but had to pay 1 pound for training expenses.

Next was Dick Eager, who earned a draw with colored Australian middleweight champion Starlight. A job was put on Fitz. Eager wore 3-ounce gloves, while Fitz's mitts weighed 8 ounces. Bob did not even notice that the gloves were heavier than usual, and he knocked Eager out cold in 3 rounds.

Conway, the Ballarat champion, was knocked out in 3 rounds. Bob followed with victories over Pablo Frank or Fanque, the Bushman, in 2 rounds, Jack Riddle in 4, and a rematch with Eager in 2 rounds.

During this time, Fitz never received over 10 pounds to win a fight, and in most cases only 6 or 7. During these 6 or 7 years, Fitz was working at his blacksmith trade, struggling for years to earn small wages. He won many running races and won prizes at that too. He was 27 years old and married at that time.

On December 17, 1889, Fitz fought Jim Ellis, who had obtained a draw with a Māori named Lang for the New Zealand middleweight championship. Fitz, weighing only 148 pounds to Ellis's 168, still won by knockout in the 3rd round.

On February 10, 1890, Fitz fought the great Jim Hall, then Australian middleweight champion. "This fight has always been a blot on Bob's otherwise stainless career. It was a fake fight."

[456] *New York Evening World*, May 18, 1911.

Jim Hall wanted a taste of the big purses then being offered in California. He proposed to Fitz to allow himself to be knocked out. That would earn Hall sufficient money to travel to America. "This is Fitzsimmons's own story." Bob was to receive 50 pounds for taking the dive, which at that time was a lot of money for him. "Hall himself always contended that the victory was a legitimate one, but the fighting public always suspected that the affair was a fake, in which they are supported by Fitzsimmons." The defeat injured Bob's reputation, but his ability eventually prevailed.

Bob was matched for the Australian middleweight title against a colored sailor from America, Starlight, who was then the middleweight champion of Queensland. Bob knocked out Starlight in 9 rounds.

Wanting more money so he too could travel to the U.S., having heard about Jim Hall's success there, Bob went hunting for kangaroo skins, which sold for 15 pounds apiece. Once, he had to escape attacking kangaroos by climbing a tree. Another time he was struck by another's bullet, clipping one of his coat buttons off. He and his partner also had to flee a tribe of bushmen. They got lost and were without food or water for several days.

He used the money he earned to open up a blacksmith shop. But one morning he learned that his business partner had stolen all of the money.[457]

Eventually, the California Athletic Club was looking for a man who could put up a battle against Jack Dempsey. The captain of the Zealandia, who traveled back and forth from San Francisco to Sydney, mentioned Fitzsimmons. The club offered to pay for his passage over to America and give him an opportunity to show what he had. The captain returned to Australia and communicated the offer to Fitz, who jumped at the chance. Bob, his wife, and baby left in April 1890. The rest is history.[458]

Bob said he was content at this point to be known as an actor, not a fighter. "My days as a fighter are ended, but people still flock about me and want to see me box or hit the bag. I have a punch or two left, but from now on I am going to be an actor, go around with Julia, my wife, and enjoy life." Bob had a nice farm in New Jersey, where his children were being educated, and he was happy. He did not take the white hopes seriously, feeling that there was no one able to whip Johnson.[459]

Bob said he did not smoke or drink, and always remained physically active, which was the secret to his longevity.[460]

On June 18, 1911, Fitz narrowly escaped serious injury when his 90-horsepower Stearns touring car completely overturned on old Buffalo Road, about 4 miles from Batavia, New York. Bob was pinned under the car, and 12 men were required to raise the car before he could be released. His wife and chauffeur were with him. They had left Cleveland and were en route to their summer home at Bound Brook, New Jersey. The car had hit a deep rut that was covered by tall grass. Fitz was cut about the face and arms

[457] *New York Evening World*, May 20, 1911.
[458] *New York Evening World*, May 22, 1911.
[459] *Buffalo Evening Times*, May 20, 1911.
[460] *Buffalo Commercial*, May 24, 1911.

and had a deep gash in his left leg. He had thrown his wife out of danger, and she escaped without a bruise. The chauffeur was also pinned under the car but not seriously hurt.[461]

Fitz left Batavia two days later but was walking with some difficulty. Bob said it had been over two years since he had seen his three children.[462]

Upon arriving home at his farm in Dunellen, Bob said, "I've been home two months in the past four years." He was happy to have a rest and finally see his children. "I hadn't seen Bobbie for a long time. He was a little fellow when I went away, and now he's as tall as me – fifteen years old and six feet."

Bob said he didn't like cars anymore. His car turned over and fell on his chest. He barely threw Mrs. Fitz out as it turned. It would have cut him in two if soft mud had not been

BOB FITZSIMMONS, OLD GLADIATOR OF THE RING, DRIVES AN AUTO NOWADAYS

Bob Fitzsimmons, the old gladiator of the ring, is getting richer than ever by appearing in vaudeville. When he wants relaxation he climbs into his big automobile with Mrs. Fitzsimmons and they take a long tour through the country districts.

underneath. "The weight was right over my heart and I was pretty near dead when Mrs. Fitz ran around and called to me to 'wriggle,' and I wriggled and the car slid down across my stomach so I could breathe a little." A crowd finally pried it up enough to pull him and his driver out. If he ever got another car, he wanted a light one.

Regarding boxing, "No, I don't intend to fight any more. I've earned my rest. I box a little now and then, but not much. I weigh forty pounds more than I used to – not that I'm fat, you know." Robert Edgren said Bob did not show the extra weight in the least. He was the same lean-looking Fitz.

Bob said he wished he had come back from Australia six weeks sooner so he could have helped train Jeffries.

> Jeff, at his best, would beat two Johnsons. I'm not taking anything from Johnson. He's one of the best fighters I ever saw, but Jeffries was the greatest fighter that ever lived. He was twice as strong as any man that ever fought. ... Jeff could break a man in two with a punch when he cut it loose. And game – no living man was ever gamer than Jeff.

---

[461] *Buffalo Evening Times*, June 19, 1911.
[462] *Buffalo Enquirer*, June 21, 1911,

Bob said you could hit Jeffries, break his nose, cut him up, and he never whimpered or said a word, but kept coming like a bulldog until he got you. Bob said Jeff suffered more of a battering in 3 or 4 rounds against him in sparring than Jeffries did in 15 rounds against Johnson.

Fitz said Jeff was generous and loyal to his friends. After he trained Jeff for the second Corbett fight, he didn't expect anything but railroad fare and expenses, but when he was leaving after the fight, Jeffries gave him a large stack of $100 bills. Bob told him he did it as his friend and did not want any payment. But before he left, Jeff still gave Mrs. Fitz $1,000 and told her to give it to Bob when they got home. "That's the kind of man Jeff was."

Fitz was convinced that Jeffries was drugged before the Johnson fight. "As for Reno – Jeffries was drugged, and I know it from the way he acted if nothing else. I'm dead sure of it." In the ring, Jeff was stupid and slow. After the 2nd round, Jeff came to his corner and asked, "What's the matter with me, boys? I feel numb all over." "He was drugged as sure as I'm sitting here. They got him. I know how it works. ... He was drugged and dead on his feet. Some people said it was nerves. Him afraid of Johnson! Huh! Forty Johnsons wouldn't scare Jeff."[463]

Once in a while, Bob would suggest an old-man tournament, still willing to fight the men from his era, especially Corbett.

On August 10, 1911, in St. Paul, Minnesota, Bob and his wife had another one of their break-ups and make-ups. They had been reconciled for the "22nd time." "After Bob started a row at the theater where Mrs. Fitz appeared last night and was ejected by a policeman, he got in touch with her; told her he knew he had been too rough, and was forgiven." Bob said, "It's all right now. You see I am big and rough and my wife is a sensitive little thing and I guess I scare her once in a while."[464]

Although in July 1911 Jack Johnson had signed to fight English champion Bombardier Billy Wells in England for the champion's demanded $30,000 fee, by September, opposition to the fight on racial grounds put the contest on the ropes. Concerned with potential race issues and implications in its colonies throughout the world, England's Home Office, via Home Secretary Winston Churchill, refused to allow Jack Johnson to defend his title or to fight anywhere in the United Kingdom or any of its territories throughout the British Empire. A subsequent attempt to fight even black Sam McVey in Australia was thwarted.

On September 22, 1911 at Brown's gymnasium in New York, Kid McCoy was training for a comeback. Bob Fitzsimmons was seated at ringside. McCoy stopped Kid Elie, the Jersey heavyweight, in less than a round. As a result, Bob offered to climb through the ropes and engage in a friendly bout with McCoy, which was accepted. When they sparred, the Kid banged Fitz hard a couple of times, and it ruffled the old general. "The former ring marvel became a bit vexed, and suddenly tore into McCoy like a wildcat. Love taps were forgotten, and the pair slammed away at each other

463 *New York Evening World*, July 1, 1911.
464 *Buffalo Evening News*, August 11, 1911.

for dear life." Eventually, after about 30 seconds, the two were pulled apart. The crowd loudly applauded Fitz as he left the ring.[465]

On October 2, 1911, Fitzsimmons opened at the Howard in Boston in a 30-minute sketch called "The Birthmark," written by Jack London. Bob punched the bag and talked about his early career. Mrs. Fitz, a.k.a Julia Gifford, was not with him, as she had left him again.[466]

Mrs. Fitz said Bob was on probation for six months, and if during that time he neither drank nor swore, she might return to him. She subsequently claimed that Fitz had deceived her when he promised to give up liquor. Hence, Bob no longer was living abstemiously.[467]

The *Buffalo Evening Times* wrote that there was only one Fitzsimmons, whose record probably would stand for all time. Age left no defects upon him, fighting great battles long after others were past their primes. Most were on the decline after age 30, but Bob won the heavyweight championship in his mid-30s and still was effective even into his late 30s and early 40s.[468]

Word was that Bob was teaching his 16-year-old son how to box.[469]

On February 13, 1912, Gus Ruhlin died at age 40, collapsing suddenly and unexpectedly at his Brooklyn café, purportedly from a hemorrhage or rupture of the heart, or stroke of apoplexy.[470]

An indication of time possibly healing wounds, both Fitzsimmons and Corbett complimented one another. Bob said, "Jim Corbett is the cleverest man who ever stepped inside a 24-foot ring. The man who could outbox Corbett never had gloves on. Most of Corbett's cleverness was in his foot work. He could punch and get away faster than any one I ever knew." However, looking to pull back simultaneously adversely affected his punching power. But it made him very hard to hit cleanly.

Corbett said, "Fitz was as game a fighter as there ever was. When he was at his best there wasn't a man that had a harder punch, and I ought to know." Jim said although a left hook to the body stopped him, it wasn't a shift as Bob claimed, but just an ordinary left hook. Corbett noted that he punched hard enough to drop Bob in the 6th round but couldn't finish him.

Corbett said Jeffries was the greatest though. One could not outbox or outpunch him in a long fight, but boxing him carefully at long range, in and out with a lot of footwork, was the better strategy. Fitz "swapped punches with a man with whom no one had any business swapping punches." Regardless, "no matter what Fitz or I could have done it would have ended the same way." A prime Jeffries could defeat any style in a long fight.

When Corbett realized he no longer had it, he quit the game. But Fitz could not get enough, continuing to box even when past-it.[471]

Fitzimmons said none of the white hopes could beat Jack Johnson.

[465] *Brooklyn Times, Glens Falls Post-Star, New York Evening World,* September 23, 1911.
[466] *Buffalo Enquirer,* October 5, 1911; *Buffalo News,* October 8, 1911.
[467] *Buffalo Enquirer,* November 29, 1911, January 3, 1912.
[468] *Buffalo Evening Times,* January 2, 1912.
[469] *Brooklyn Daily Eagle,* February 13, 1912.
[470] *Brooklyn Daily Eagle, Brooklyn Citizen, Brooklyn Standard Union,* February 14, 1912.
[471] *Buffalo Commercial,* February 23, 1912.

In my estimate, Johnson is one of the greatest fighters that ever stepped into a ring. He has everything that goes to make a champion fighter. His defense is so marvelous that I really don't think any of the big white men now on the scene could hit him once. Some man will eventually come along and beat Johnson, but it will not be for a few more years.[472]

On March 11, 1912, in Chicago, Bob Fitzsimmons walloped college student, fraternity member, and actor Jack Taylor, giving him a black eye. Bob accused him of flirting and trifling with the affections of his wife.

Allegedly, Bob sent his wife a telegram that read, "I met your lover and handed him a wallop. Will hand you one later." Mrs. Fitz said, "Just look what my husband sent me." She admitted that she knew Jack Taylor and found him to be different from the usual run of actors. They were playing the same circuit, and they saw a great deal of each other.

Taylor sued Bob for slander and assault. Bob counter-sued for alienating the affections of his wife.[473]

Most jurisdictions in the U.S. refused to allow Jack Johnson to fight anyone, white or black. In January 1912, the New York State Athletic Commission refused to allow Johnson to box in New York.

Johnson eventually defended his title on July 4, 1912, against Jim Flynn in the remote location of Las Vegas (not Nevada), in New Mexico, which had recently become a U.S. state earlier that year and did not yet have any anti-boxing laws. Johnson won the referee's 9-round decision when the sheriff stopped the contest as a result of Flynn's incessant flagrant head butting in response to Johnson's holding or suppression tactics.

---

[472] *Buffalo Courier*, March 10, 1912.
[473] *Brooklyn Times*, March 12, 21, 1912. *Buffalo Evening Times*, March 14, 1912; *Buffalo Evening News*, March 16, 1912.

On July 31, 1912, the U.S. Congress passed, and President William Howard Taft signed a federal law banning the interstate transportation of *any* fight films. The stated goal of the prophylactic law was to prevent the dissemination of the films of Jack Johnson's fights, but the entire sport was being punished. This law cost the sport's participants hundreds of thousands of dollars, if not millions.

In August, Jack Johnson signed to fight Joe Jeannette in New York, but soon thereafter, the New York commission refused to allow the fight, for they believed Johnson's presence in the ring was bad for boxing.

In October, Mrs. Fitzsimmons denied that she was intending to file for divorce.[474]

In November 1912, Fitzsimmons and his son, Bob, Jr., gave boxing exhibitions on the stage together.[475]

Jim Jeffries was disgusted by modern boxing. "There is too much holding, clinching, and other rough work in the ring today. ... [I]n all my contests I was never warned, cautioned or censured by any referee. There never was any reason for it. I knew the rules and obeyed them at all times." Now, boxers rushed in wildly and immediately clinched. Jeff said that boxers who held were afraid of getting hit.

Jeff also noted that there were too many slappers now. Boxers today banged on each other's backs with open hands. "The slapper is fast coming to his own. When nowadays do you see a boxer hit and drop his man for the full count in one punch?" Slappers were not effective punchers. "Referees are also somewhat to blame for the backward move in the boxing game. While many thoroughly understand the rules, they are powerless, to a certain extent, when it comes to enforcing them." If more referees were less hesitant to disqualify offenders, boxing would soon be brought back to the real thing, the manly art of self-defense and effective hitting.

Jeff further said that good, effective footwork was rare. Now, many seemed to think that the more a boxer dances around the cleverer he is. A really good boxer knew how to move subtly to make a foe miss by an inch or two. Hence, effective counterpunchers were a dying breed as well, for they did not know how to make a man miss and then make him pay. Jeff won his big fights against Fitz, Ruhlin, and Corbett with counterblows. Modern fighters also did not know how to feint. Corbett could feint, draw a lead, and counter.[476]

Fitzsimmons had taken an interest in big 225-pound Jess Willard. Bob said Willard had the makings of a champion, and he was tutoring him. Fitz had "taught the Texas Cowboy how to hit at close quarters." Jess had an upcoming fight with Soldier Kearns. Bob said if Jess met the Soldier's rushing and slugging tactics with well-directed hooks and uppercuts, the fight would be short and sweet.[477]

[474] *Brooklyn Daily Times*, October 5, 1912.
[475] *Glens Falls Post-Star*, November 21, 1912.
[476] *Buffalo Commercial*, December 16, 1912.
[477] *New York Tribune*, December 23, 1912; *New York Sun*, December 25, 1912.

In another interview, Fitzsimmons said Willard showed the best natural qualities of any among the present crop of heavies and had the greatest potential to become champion. Jess said, "I have learned to hit recently, thanks to Fitzsimmons."[478]

On December 27, 1912, in New York, Jess Willard knocked out Soldier Kearns in the 8th round, winning impressively.

Tom Sharkey did not think much of present-day heavyweights.

> I've seen e'm all, Palzer, McCarty, Willard, Kearns and the others, and there ain't one o' them worth a silver quarter. ... Jeffries may have been a dead one when Johnson beat him, but when he was right – like the time he fought me at Coney Island – nobody could have whipped him. Old Bob Fitzsimmons could have stopped all these here white hopes in the same ring the same night, and the same goes for me.

Sharkey gave Jeffries the stiffest argument in his career for the first 18 rounds, but after Jeff came back in the last 7, "they had to carry the sailor away in an ambulance. Now, Sharkey admits that he was beaten..."[479]

Fitzsimmons picked Willard as the next champion. "Jess Willard has the best general idea of fighting owned by any man in the ring today. He is a born scrapper of the brainy sort, the kind that does not take a chance except when he is likely to go through with it, but who seizes the right opportunity with eagerness when it arises."[480]

Word was that Fitzsimmons, "who for his weight was probably the greatest of 'em all," had comparatively little to show for his years of labor. He was not broke by any means, but the bulk of what he had made was gone. Unfortunately, he was "an easy mark for bunco men of high and low degree ever since he first drew on a glove. The Cornishman has been flimflammed out of enough money to put half a dozen fighters and their families on Easy street for the rest of their lives."[481]

In March 1913, Julia Fitzsimmons was in Reno, allegedly to start divorce proceedings.[482] However, it appeared that this was just a rumor.

On March 15, 1913, in Wisconsin, Jim Hall died of tuberculosis.[483]

Bob's home in Plainfield, New Jersey was robbed of $1,500 in silverware.[484]

Fitz said he weighed 206 pounds and had not drunk a drop of alcohol since New Year's Eve, nor had he smoked a cigar. He wanted to fight Gunboat Smith or any other willing white man in a 10-round bout.[485]

The *Buffalo Courier* said there were many fighters, but very few like Fitzsimmons. He would always find favor with lovers of the game. He

[478] *Brooklyn Times*, December 27, 1912.
[479] *Buffalo Evening Times*, January 4, 1913.
[480] *Buffalo Evening Times*, January 13, 1913.
[481] *Buffalo Evening News*, February 18, 1913.
[482] *Buffalo Evening Times*, March 7, 1913.
[483] *New York Sun*, March 16, 1913.
[484] *Brooklyn Citizen*, March 19, 1913.
[485] *New York Evening World*, March 29, 1913.

sprang from obscurity and fought his way to three championships. He was always in condition and was the game's most dangerous hitter.[486]

Robert Edgren said the fame of great fighters was measured by their punch. Clever heavyweights enjoyed only a limited period of popularity, while men of the Fitzsimmons type, ones with the knockout wallop, always lived in the memory of fans. John L. Sullivan had the punch and knew how to land it. "Bob Fitzsimmons was as near a real champion as any man that ever climbed between the ropes. A middleweight, Bob fought men from twenty-five to a hundred pounds heavier than himself. He whipped them one after another because he had the punch." Clever heavyweights without a punch were forgotten quickly. "An old time fighter's fame can be measured by his punch. The exceptions to this rule are few."

The fans liked effective punchers who knew how to finish their man. Fitz used to say, "I never beat a man up – I knocks 'em all out gently." His idea of a gentle knockout was a sudden stunning blow that rendered the other fellow instantly senseless.

> Ten or fifteen years ago Bob Fitzsimmons was the ideal heavyweight fighting man. He never danced around. He never wasted a motion. He didn't spar and tap. Every blow he started was intended to have a certain effect. If he missed it was usually to induce or force his opponent into position where he would get the next one on the right spot.
>
> Other heavyweights lacked Fitzsimmons's business-like way of fighting. At least some of their movements were wasted. Corbett could land fifty punches on his man's chin, and only cut and annoy him. One well calculated Fitzsimmons wallop was as effective as the whole fifty.
>
> When he was getting the worst of a fight Fitzsimmons patiently worked his way in and waited for a chance to drive his terrific left or right hook home and settle things.

Fitz was cool and enjoyed fighting. "It was a joke to him to hit another fighter on the chin and knock him out for five minutes." He did it with humour and no malice. Edgren believed that up-and-coming Gunboat Smith came closest to Fitz in style and ability.[487]

The *Brooklyn Times* said no cognizance would be taken of Fitz's challenge to Gunboat Smith or any other white heavyweight. "It would be as much of a crime to let Fitz box one of the youthful heavyweights as it would be to make a match for Jim Jeffries. Fitz tried a come-back and proved a dismal failure." If he was in need of money, a benefit for him would be more appropriate.[488]

In May 1913, Fitz wrote that Gunboat Smith appeared to be the best of the heavyweights *at present*. Smith had boxing knowledge plus a punch.

[486] *Buffalo Courier*, March 31, 1913.
[487] *New York Evening World*, April 5, 1913.
[488] *Brooklyn Times*, April 23, 1913.

Smith had wins over Frank Moran, Bombardier Billy Wells, and Jess Willard. "It's possible for a boxer to win a championship without having a punch, but it isn't possible to hold it."

> Jim Corbett won the title from John L. Sullivan by dancing and jabbing. He was fast as lightning and clever, and John had passed the time when he could get into shape. In five rounds of chasing Corbett he was winded and tiring, and Corbett wore him down and got him. Then three men with a punch came along and beat Corbett. I was first, then Sharkey, then Jeffries. If Corbett had been able to hit he might have been champion for a long time.[489]

However, in another article, Fitz said Jess Willard was the most *promising* heavyweight, given that he had physical advantages over any other fighter, even though he recently lost a close 20-round decision to Gunboat Smith. With more experience and better coaching, he had a bright future. "Willard has advantages that should make him the best of all the big fellows." He was big, tall, strong, and well-proportioned.

> If Willard ever learns how to use his height and his big reach and his strength, he'll beat them all. ... Jeffries could beat me although I knew twice as much about fighting, because his weight and strength gave him a terrible advantage.

> If Willard knew a quarter as much about fighting as I do he'd go through the rest of the bunch of so-called 'white hopes' like a bullet through a chunk of cheese.

> For one thing, he's built like a lightweight, without any extra beef. He's faster than other big men. He has the longest reach in the world. He uses a good jab and there's a punch in his right hand. He's game. Smith landed a number of hard wallops and dazed him, and he came right back fighting and recovered in the same round. He isn't nervous. ... He has all the natural qualities of a fighter, but he knows about as much about fighting as a kid in a kindergarten. ...

> Willard is only a big, overgrown kid. When he has had as much experience as I got in the ring in America in one year he can beat them all unless some other man like himself comes along to fight him. ... I've fought them all, from middleweights up, and nobody knows better than I do how hard it is to fight a fast and clever man who has a big advantage in size.[490]

In another article, Fitz said men were the same physically today as 10 or 15 years ago, but the reason why boxers were not of the same class now was that the sport had changed. "It used to be all 20 or 45 rounds or to a finish. Men fighting to a finish have to know how to fight. You don't have to know so much about it boxing ten rounds without a decision." In former

---

[489] *New York Evening World*, May 22, 1913.
[490] *New York Evening World*, May 28, 1913.

eras, men could be cool and calculating, calmly focusing on effective punching and long-term strategy.

> This no-decision thing allows boxers to stall. In my championship days I never thought of such a thing as stalling, except just once. That time I stalled because I had sent my wife a wire that I was going to win in the fifth round, and the other fellow was easier than I expected, so I had to stall through a couple of rounds to keep from knocking him out too soon.

> When you have a decision to win at the end of a fight there isn't the same temptation to stall. The way it is two-thirds of the boxers are satisfied to slide through ten rounds and get the money without extending themselves or taking a chance. If the route was 20 rounds they couldn't afford to do that because the chance of losing would be greater. If they were forced to fight every time they got into a ring they'd develop great fighters just the way they used to. ...

> The reason that nearly all of the good fighters are developed in the West is that they fight long fights out there.[491]

Bob admitted that the fight he stalled and carried his foe was the 1890 contest with Arthur Upham (KO5). The next-day primary source descriptions of that fight indicate that Fitz indeed had carried and played with him, backing off and tapping whenever he hurt or dropped Upham.

The August 1911 Frawley law limited boxing matches in New York to 10 rounds with no decision, and mandated larger 8-ounce gloves instead of the usual 5-ounce gloves, none of which met with Fitz's approval.[492]

One writer said Fitzsimmons indeed not only was a staller, but one of the greatest ever, for it was part of his stock in trade. "Fitz could wabble and appear all in to draw the fire of an opponent that he might land one of his famous haymakers."[493]

The *Buffalo Times* said Fitzsimmons was a cool man in the ring, while Corbett was a hothead. Nothing ever bothered lanky Bob, but Jim often lost his temper. Supposedly, against Corbett, Bob's then-wife Rose called for him to "hit him in the slats," meaning the body, which Bob did. Others questioned whether she actually said that. Whenever Bob scored a knockdown in a fight, he calmly walked away as if he knew it was over.[494]

Jack Skelly said Fitzsimmons talked a lot about his supposedly charming farm life in New Jersey, but in reality, he rarely was there. "Night after night I have seen him of late on the great White Way in New York dallying with the bright lights and everything that goes with them. Gay Broadway is certainly a fine place for 'Fitz' to study farming, especially in the small wee hours of early morn." Bob's claims of being temperate were not true.

Skelly said when Jeffries retired in 1905, he had not really become a farmer as he claimed either. He was soon back to the "glittering lights" and

---

[491] *Buffalo Evening Times*, June 7, 1913.
[492] *New York Evening World*, June 7, 1913.
[493] *Buffalo Commercial*, July 7, 1913.
[494] *Buffalo Times*, July 13, 1913.

opened a Los Angeles café. He often puffed on a cigarette. "He was a wonderful champion at that time and could have beaten a dozen Johnsons in those days. But it was the old story."[495]

Eddie Graney picked Peter Jackson and James J. Corbett as the greatest heavyweights ever. Best middleweights – Bob Fitzsimmons and Jack Dempsey. Hardest hitters in history – Fitzsimmons, Choynski, and Kid McCoy. The gamest included Choynski and Jack Dempsey. Bob Fitzsimmons had beaten men in all of these categories.[496]

Robert Edgren wrote that present-day middleweights were a joke compared to Fitzsimmons in his prime. He could have whipped all of today's middleweights in a round each on the same night. Fitz was the greatest middleweight champion ever, but also "the greatest fighting man, weight taken into consideration, that the ring has known since the Marquis of Queensberry rules were written." He had superior power and skill combined, and could anesthetize his foes with ease, with neatly placed, well-calculated blows, including bigger men like Corbett, Sharkey, and Ruhlin. The only one he could not beat was the unmovable bulk of Jeffries, who at that time was "almost superhuman."

Edgren had first seen Fitz when he was training for the first Sharkey fight in 1896. He shifted in, out, and around, shuffling, never lifting his feet from the floor entirely, slipping around with a soft, deceiving ease. W. W. Naughton had then told Edgren, "He's the greatest in the world."

Bob had beaten the greatest in Jack Dempsey, and there were very few men who could remotely compete with him at middleweight. He was so superior that he had to fight heavyweights or go without fights. At heavyweight, he looked like an easy mark, so men were willing to fight him. He knocked out Sharkey with terrific body blows but lost on a purported foul claimed by referee Wyatt Earp in the $10,000 winner-take-all fight. "There was no foul."

When hurt, Fitz was the most dangerous man in the world. Bob showed gameness against Corbett, getting knocked down but coming back to win. He did the same with the hard-punching Choynski. Maher, another terrific puncher, staggered him. After knocking out Maher, Peter said, "He's no man; he's the divil!" Ruhlin had him staggering as well, but Bob's knockout body blows had Ruhlin thinking that he was dying for two weeks afterward. Even after Jeffries dropped and staggered Fitz, he fought like fury to the end. Jeffries mastered him only because of his tremendous advantages in weight and strength, coupled with Jeff's grim courage, marvelous endurance, and hard hitting, which made it a physically impossible task to beat him. "The greatest middleweight champion he was – and I think he'll be remembered as the greatest for many years to come."[497]

Regarding their respective weights when they fought, James J. Corbett said,

[495] *Yonkers Herald*, July 19, 1913.
[496] *Elmira Star-Gazette*, July 25, 1913. Graney's best: Welter – Joe Walcott and Tommy Ryan. Light – Jack McAuliffe and Johnny Herget. Feather – George Dixon and Terry McGovern. Bantam – Dixon.
[497] *New York Evening World*, August 2, 1913.

Now a word about Fitzsimmons and his weight. As every one but a certain sporting editor is aware, heavyweights are never required to weigh in. I don't know what Fitzsimmons weighed on the day of the fight, or what I did myself, for that matter; but this much I do know: Bob Fitzsimmons was no middleweight that day at Carson City, and I honestly believed weighed almost as much as I did!

Corbett regarded Jeffries as "the greatest heavyweight the game has known." Yet, Jeff "could not lay a glove on me for 23 rounds. The only solid punch he hit me was the one that knocked me out, when I bounded into his huge fist after backing into the ropes." Corbett said Jeff was lucky, and the only man luckier was Fitzsimmons. "I cut Bob Fitzsimmons to pieces for thirteen rounds. The fight was a joke – for me. In the sixth round I knocked Fitz down … The referee counted eight, but I and others believe that Fitzsimmons was down at least 11 seconds." Bob was nearly out. After that, "I beat him badly." Eventually, Bob caught him with an "accidental punch" in the 14th. It was like a team down by three in the 9th inning, with 2 outs, but with three men on base, and hitting a home run to win the game. "Well, that's the chance that Fitz had of beating me that day at Carson City, but he did it. He beat me fairly and squarely with the oldest blow in boxing, an ordinary punch in the stomach. Solar plexus? All a lot of rot and bosh!" Jim said Bob was only willing to rematch him after he lost his title to Jeffries, whom he erroneously thought would be easier than Corbett.[498]

Fitzsimmons still was bitter about Wyatt Earp's controversial disqualification of him against Sharkey in their first contest. He called it "highway robbery." Bob "considered Jesse James an honest man and a gentleman compared with Sharkey and Earp."[499]

Responding to Corbett's recent statements, Fitz said, "Jim Corbett's attacks on me after his stage professions of friendship for many years don't surprise me much." Corbett's reputation as "Gentleman Jim" was total nonsense. Before their fight, Jim impliedly threatened the referee with an attack by his friends around the ring should he lose. Bob said Corbett's knockdown of him was assisted by a cross buttock throw down. "The way I chased him around the ring when I got up at eight seconds showed how near 'out' I was." After Fitz knocked him out for the count with a fair body blow, shortly after Corbett recovered, he rushed at Fitz and tried to fight again, showing his poor sportsmanship. Corbett calmed down and admitted he had been defeated fairly but insisted upon a rematch. "If you don't I'll take a punch at you the first time I see you on Broadway." Bob responded, "If you do I'll kill you." Fitz remained willing to fight Corbett again and said his 17-year-old son would fight him too.[500]

Dr. Hendrick, Bob's manager, noted that the actual gentleman and fair fighter was Fitzsimmons, not Corbett. For a long while, Corbett refused to meet Fitz, and told him, "Go and get a reputation." He even refused to

[498] *Buffalo Evening News*, August 7, 1913.
[499] *Buffalo Times*, August 24, 1913.
[500] *New York Evening World*, August 28, 1913.

shake Bob's hand before the fight. Fitzsimmons won fair and square. "I saw Fitz knock his teeth out in the 13th round – the round before the knockout. Why did he allow a knocked out man to do that to him?" After they fought, Bob gave Jim a bit of his own medicine by telling him to earn his rematch. Then Corbett lost to Sharkey (who had lost to Jeffries). It was well known that Jim had his friends jump into the ring to save him from a knockout against Sharkey. Back when he was champion, Corbett fouled Charley Mitchell by hitting him while he was on his knees. Also, "It is well known that he and McCoy framed to fool the public in New York City, and that Corbett double-crossed McCoy."

Fitz was willing to wager that he could knock out Corbett within 10 rounds, if Jim really wanted to fight again.[501] Ultimately, Corbett no longer was interested in a Fitzsimmons rematch.

In October 1913, Fitzsimmons was in court in New York as a witness in a libel suit filed by Joseph Egan, boxing promoter, against Pearson's Magazine Company, because of a story suggesting that Egan took more than his fair share of the receipts from the 1902 Jeffries-Fitzsimmons rematch. When asked about that fight, Fitz said he saw Jeffries in the dressing room afterwards. "Jeff was a fright. He had eight stitches...five over his right eye and three over his left. His nose was broken in two places and he had a cauliflower ear."

Bob said he wasn't marked at all. "Jeff didn't touch me all through the fight – until the one blow in the solar plexus – the kind I handed Corbett at Reno. I was so tired out chopping the big fellow that I got careless." Bob said the blow paralyzed him. "I couldn't move a muscle."

When Jeff asked him afterwards how he was feeling, Bob said, "Fine. How're you feeling, Jeff?" "Great, never better in my life." "This made me laugh right out."[502]

Years ago, Fitzsimmons told Walter Kelly about how he helped improve Kid McCoy's punching power, saying,

> Take Kid McCoy, for instance, he could not knock down a sick man when he first came to my training quarters at New Orleans. He called there one day while I was training for my fight with Dan Creedon [in 1894] and said he would like to help me around the place just to get a few pointers from me on my knack for hitting. I took a sort of liking to the Kid right off the bat, and put him to work.
>
> I saw that he was quick with his hands and feet and that he had a good fighting eye, but he could not hit a lick. I made him punch me a dozen times as hard as he could, and I didn't feel the blows. I then took him in hand and explained to him that he could never learn to hit hard while skipping about the ring like a jumping jack. In order to get knockout impetus into your blows you must slow down, and shoot when the other fellow is coming. Get there first with your

[501] *Buffalo Commercial*, August 29, 1913.
[502] *New York Evening World*, October 22, 1913.

blow, and throw all you've got into the punch even though it has only to travel a few inches.

You take some chances of getting hit, but if you are as fast, or faster than the other fellow, there is little danger, especially if you master the trick of getting your blow there first when you see the other fellow's coming.

Bob said Corbett danced in and out and all over, jabbing, hooking, and getting away. He landed often, but almost never set, and therefore his blows did not have knockout power. Jim wanted to be safe and win without being marked. But that cost him force in his blows. "On the other hand, I tried no fancy business, but kept edging in and trying all the time to get in my full steam to his body or jaw." Fitz eventually saw his opening and seized it. "In order to hit hard a fighter has to take chances – chances of getting copped himself, and chances of hurting his hands badly. That is why you see so few knockdowns these times."

After Bob's tutoring, Kid McCoy knocked out fighters like Tommy Ryan, Dan Creedon, Peter Maher, Dick Moore, and others.[503]

On December 19, 1913, in Paris, France, world heavyweight champion Jack Johnson fought fellow black Battling Jim Johnson to a 10-round draw. The fight had been relatively tame, and champion Johnson revealed that he had broken his left arm early on in the contest. Some thought he broke it late in the fight and simply was out of shape.

BOB FITZSIMMONS, AT 51, UNDEFEATED MIDDLEWEIGHT CHAMPION, WHO WANTS TO RE-ENTER THE RING, AND HIS HUSKY SON, BOB, JR.

[503] *Buffalo Enquirer*, November 20, 1913.

CHAPTER 20

Testing the Comeback Waters Again

While at a boxing show at Madison Square Garden, New York, on December 22, 1913, Bob Fitzsimmons, "considered by many as the greatest fighter of all time," issued another one of his challenges to meet any white heavyweight in the world. Bob said,

> After looking over the crop of white heavyweights I feel it my duty to challenge any white man in the world. ... I have been out of the ring for four years and people may think I'm old, but I've forty years yet before I begin to wobble. Assisted by my son and sparring partner, I will engage to whip them all.[504]

On that card, in two 10-round no decision contests, 170 ½-pound Battling Levinsky fought 196 ½-pound Jim Coffey; and 187 ¼-pound Jim Flynn fought 190-pound George Rodel. While watching Flynn vs. Rodel, Fitzsimmons said, "Hi would bloody well like to be in the bloomin' ring with heither of those blawsted 'opes. Hi'd knock their bloomin' blocks hoff."[505]

The *New York Tribune* said Fitz was 51 years old and had not boxed since his 1909 loss to Lang, who was "little better than a fair second rater." Yet, insisting that his challenge was not mere advertising, Bob was willing to post a certified check to guarantee his appearance for a contest.[506]

However, the New York State Athletic Commission barred Fitzsimmons from boxing in New York State. The feeling was that he was too old and would get badly hurt, which would be bad for the game. Bob previously had admitted that he was too old to do himself justice. He seemed to be a shot fighter even back in 1907 when he lost to Johnson, and past-it in 1905 when he lost to O'Brien. The commission "asked" (but in truth ordered) local promoters to cancel all negotiations for a bout between Fitz and a white hope, "for humanity's sake."

One noted that since Fitz had left the ring, he had done no real training to speak of and had been careless in his habits. If he was injured, it would bring the game into disrepute. "Unscrupulous promoters would be willing to sacrifice Old Fitz for a few thousand dollars, but such a proceeding would be nothing short of brutality and the commission was appointed to prevent just such practices."

---

[504] *New York Tribune*, December 23, 1913.
[505] *Yonkers Herald*, December 23, 1913.
[506] *New York Tribune*, December 26, 1913.

However, Fitz was indignant. He said he would ask promoters in other states to arrange matches for him. Yet, "it is probable that similar obstacles will be thrown his way."[507]

Bob was insulted that the Commission allowed a bunch of "dubs" to fight while barring his ability to earn money. He had a right to earn. However, many thought it would be criminal to allow him to fight, for it either would be a farce or a tragedy.

Regardless, some suspected that Bob did not really want to box again, but was seeking free advertising, desiring "to work up new interest in himself with a theatrical tour in view."[508]

On December 30, 1913, the New York Boxing Commission formally announced that it had barred Bob Fitzsimmons from boxing. Given his age of 51, it would be too much of a risk of danger and it would be contrary to the best interests of boxing.[509]

Fitz previously had scheduled a 10-round bout to take place in New York against "white hope" Soldier Kearns. However, the New York State Boxing Commission had directed the Atlantic Garden Athletic Club to cancel any match involving Fitzsimmons.

On January 14, 1914, Bob took the matter to court to compel the commission to rescind its decision. The commission feared that Fitz, as remarkable as he was, at more than 50 years of age, might be injured by a much younger man. Fitzsimmons insisted that he was more than capable. He had affidavits to that effect and was willing to box for the court against anyone to prove it.[510]

Bob said, "I'm not quite so good as I was, but if I couldn't dispose of these white hopes I've seen I'd be ashamed of myself. They're getting money by false pretenses." Bob seemed to remember himself as he once was, not what he currently was at present, a foible of most older fighters.[511]

Fitz and the Commission were back in court again on January 16. The commissioner noted that Fitz had 12 battles since 1899 and had been defeated in 5 of them. He was not getting better with age. Fitz's lawyers argued that he had a right to earn a living and engage in a lawful profession.[512]

Bob said, "All these white hopes make me sick. I can whip any of them if they will give me a chance to do so."[513]

On January 27, 1914, Samuel Seabury, justice of the Supreme Court of New York State, upheld the Commission's decision barring Bob from boxing in New York. The commission had the right to do so given his age and the danger of the profession.[514]

In an effort to demonstrate that he still had enough to box, Fitz scheduled a 6-round bout in Williamsport, Pennsylvania at the Gilbert

[507] *Brooklyn Times, Buffalo Times, Buffalo Commercial, New York Sun,* December 27, 1913.
[508] *Elmira Star-Gazette,* December 29, 1913.
[509] *Brooklyn Daily Times,* December 31, 1913.
[510] *Brooklyn Times,* January 14, 1914.
[511] *Reading Times,* January 15, 1914.
[512] *New York Times,* January 17, 1914.
[513] *Allentown Leader,* January 24, 1914.
[514] *Brooklyn Daily Times, New York Evening World,* January 27, 1914; *Allentown Leader,* January 29, 1914.

Athletic Club. The original opponent was Terry Lambs or Lambie but was changed to KO Sweeney, a relative unknown. Some said it was Dan Sweeney, who had fought Dan Daily a season or so ago.[515]

On Thursday January 29, 1914, in Williamsport, Pennsylvania, Bob Fitzsimmons took on "Knockout" Dan Sweeney in a 6-round no decision contest. Some reported that Sweeney weighed in at 182 pounds while Fitz weighed in at 169.[516] Of course, such weights might have been self-reported.

Upon entering the ring at 10 p.m., Fitz received a tremendous ovation. Son Bob, Jr. and Fitz's manager seconded him.

1st round

The bout started cautiously. Sweeney covered up while Fitz feinted. Dan slapped Bob's back.

2nd round

Fitz landed his straight left to the jaw. Sweeney retaliated with a slap on the shoulder. He could not land on Fitz. Bob displayed his ring generalship, and it was a treat to see him circle around, once in a while sending in straight blows and following up with more rights and lefts. Sweeney kept well covered up, or else he would have been knocked out. He played it safe and covered up well whenever there was the least chance of a blow getting through.

3rd round

Fitz met him coming in and sent in lightning jabs, two of which hit the face. Sweeney fired but found Fitz out of reach. He finally landed on the jaw, but Fitz instantly retaliated with a stinging right that rocked Sweeney.

4th round

Fitz landed two quick blows that sent Sweeney through the ropes. He rose and covered his face. Bob would not waste a blow. Finally, Dan uncovered partially but instantly met a blow which sent him down again. He took a 4-count on one knee and then rose for the second time.

5th round

---

[515] A KO Sweeney from New York had fought a 15-round draw against Tommy Jones in Dayton, Ohio on January 28, but it likely was not the same man. *Harrisburg Patriot*, January 27, 1914; *New Castle News*, *Visalia Daily Times*, January 29, 1914.
[516] *Allentown Democrat*, January 30, 1914.

They mixed it up, but Sweeney could not land with the force that Fitzsimmons had in his short blows. Finally, Sweeney went down.

Sweeney rose at 6, advanced to receive a body swing that sent him down again. He rose at 7. Bob landed a terrific blow that again felled him. The referee was counting when the bell rang and saved him.

6th round

Fitz was determined to get a knockout. Sweeney again went down on his knees for a count. After a terrible body blow, he went down for 9. He clinched desperately each time Fitz was close, or he went down and took part of the count, which enabled him to last.

The crowd cheered Fitzsimmons for quite a while. It took several policemen to keep back the crowd which surrounded the ring. Sweeney had been knocked down at least 7 times.

The local *Williamsport Gazette and Bulletin* said Fitzsimmons looked good, showing many of his old-time qualities, but he had slowed down. Fitz, "perhaps the best known prize fighter the world has ever seen," defeated Knockout Sweeney in a fast 6-round go. While there was no official decision, Fitzsimmons won so cleanly that there was no question about it. Bob was very close to a knockout victory, for only the gong saved Sweeney. "Fitz looked good. That expresses it. He has lost none of his qualities of generalship and played rings around his opponent last night." He had slowed but still was fast enough to outbox and outpunch Sweeney while receiving little in return.

On five occasions, Sweeney went down in the 5th and 6th rounds for counts from four to eight seconds, seemingly to get some rest and prevent himself from being knocked out. It seemed that Fitz could have knocked him out in the 3rd round but spared him. His son, sitting in the corner, groaned. Afterwards, Bob said he knew he could win and just played with Sweeney.

Hal Sheridan said Bob showed some of his old-time fire and form and proved he still had a kick, flaying and scorching Sweeney to a mere whisper in 6 rounds. He knocked Sweeney down repeatedly and had him all but out. Only the bell saved the New Castle heavy from taking the count in the final round.

The *Scranton Tribune-Republican* said Fitz had come back. Sweeney managed to stay the limit only because he saved himself repeatedly by going to the floor for six to nine seconds. "The old man looked fit as ever and displayed his old-time ring generalship, but has lost some of his speed with advancing years. He still has a punch like the kick of a mule, is very shifty and has much good fight left in him."

The *New Castle News* said Knockout Dan Sweeney was from New Castle and had "proved a trial horse for a number of local boxers." Fitz showed good form for an old timer and "may have some battles in him yet."

The *Franklin Evening News* said Fitz "showed that he is still there with the goods. He repeatedly knocked Sweeney down and several times the latter was out for the count of nine. Bob's blows had plenty of steam behind them and he displayed his old-time skill and cunning."[517]

Pounding on a far inferior man showed that Fitz still had something, but of course it did not necessarily prove what he would do against a legitimate contender.

Nevertheless, William H. Rocap of the *Philadelphia Ledger* said Fitzsimmons had come back by whipping Dan Sweeney, a Cleveland heavyweight. Even at age 51, Fitz was far from being a wreck, but quite the contrary, against Sweeney, he "proved himself a physical marvel." He made those who said he was fit for an old man's home look ridiculous. "The writer has been the target of considerable abuse because he defended Fitzsimmons. The ex-champion has as much right to earn a living honestly as any man living." Boxing was a business, and Fitz's asset was his skill. Anyone who thought an older man could not box should go to the New York Athletic Club gym and try to last 3 rounds with Mike Donovan, who was more than 60 years old, and try to hit him. Age was not everything.[518]

However, Bub Brislin said just because Fitz decked an unknown dub four or five times did not prove that he had come back or could beat up present-day "white hopes." "In our opinion Fitzsimmons is still much in the discard" and an attempt to fight a top man would not be good. "Fitzsimmons has run his race as an athlete, and he knows it. His plan to 'come back' is simply a scheme to pick up some easy money."[519]

Bob said they might bar him, but his 18-year-old son would be a champion. "He's a natural fighter. ... Why, only Tuesday the boy landed one on my jaw and put me out. ... It was some wallop, and it took me several minutes to come to." It was only a sparring training bout, but showed how hard his son hit.[520]

On February 17, it was announced that "Jersey" Bellew, the South Bethlehem boxer, was training for a 6-round go with Fitzsimmons to be held in a few days in South Bethlehem. The *Allentown Leader* said Bellew was long recognized as one of the cleverest boxers ever developed in the Lehigh Valley.[521]

On Friday February 20, 1914 at the Market Hall municipal building in South Bethlehem, Pennsylvania, at an alleged 54 years of age (actual 50), Fitz boxed a 6-round no decision against Jersey Bellew, a.k.a Fred Bellew (but his real name was Patrick Bellew), the most notable local boxer.

According to the *Allentown Morning Call*, Bob did not look his age, and he uncorked a few of his old-time wallops to the wind. In the 2nd round, a body shot dropped Bellew in a heap. Yet, Bellew finished the round and the fight in good shape. It was not a sensational bout, but interesting.

[517] *Williamsport Gazette and Bulletin, New Castle Herald, New Castle News, Scranton Truth, Scranton Tribune-Republican, Franklin Evening News,* January 30, 1914.
[518] *Altoona Tribune,* February 3, 1914.
[519] *Scranton Tribune-Republican,* February 4, 1914.
[520] *Wilkes-Barre Evening News,* February 6, 1914.
[521] *Allentown Democrat, Allentown Leader, Mauch Chunk Daily Times,* February 17, 1914.

Afterwards, Fitz gave a speech, challenging the world in a battle of any length. He criticized the New York commission for refusing to allow him to box there, declaring that he was in better shape than the entire crop of present-day white hopes.[522]

Other papers reported that the grand old man of the ring showed that he still had much of the skill that made him a three-weight division champion. Nevertheless, this version said he and Bellew boxed to an unofficial no-decision draw.[523]

Several decades later, Bellew said he had never been knocked off his feet in 55 fights prior to meeting Fitzsimmons, and his bout with Bob was his last. He claimed to have won the popular decision. Bellew said that sometimes he boxed using the name Jersey Gordon, Paddy Fitzsimmons, or even Young Bob Fitzsimmons. Bellew subsequently became a referee.[524]

Bob Fitzsimmons, Jr.

The *Pittsburg Press* advertised that Fitzsimmons, "the most marvelous fighter of ring history," and his son, Bob Fitzsimmons, Jr., were coming there to exhibit 3 rounds with each other at each performance for a week at the Victoria theater. Although he was age 51, Fitz retained his abilities. He was awaiting a ruling on his appeal to have formal contests in New York. He was hoping to fight Battling Levinsky next, as well as Gunboat Smith and Sam Langford. Bob's son was only 19 years old and stood about 190 pounds.

Bob was still pushing for bigger fights. "Do I look like a decrepit old man? Certainly not; I am in good trim and can fight any living man. Why it was only last Friday night that I made a show of a big husky fellow named Jersey Bellew in South Bethlehem. But the boxing commission of New York would have the people think I am on the verge of going into decay."

[522] *Allentown Morning Call, Reading Eagle,* February 21, 1914.
[523] *Allentown Leader, Allentown Democrat,* February 21, 1914; *New Castle Herald,* February 24, 1914.
[524] *Allentown Morning* Call, February 14, 21, 1950; *Allentown Morning Call,* June 27, 1967.

Speaking of the current crop of white hopes, Bob said, "I can lick 'em all." Regarding the New York Commission, which had prevented him from fighting: "They're a bunch of petty grafters." Bob said he would like to box Billy Wells in England, his birth country.[525]

On March 27, 1914, the Appellate Division of the New York Supreme Court affirmed the lower court ruling prohibiting Bob Fitzsimmons from boxing in public in New York state, owing to his advanced age. The commission decided that age 50 was the limit allowed to box, and he was older than that.[526] This killed Fitz's potential for continuing as a boxer in the most populous state in the nation. Other state commissions likely would follow suit. Perhaps it was for the best.

"OLD BOB" FITZSIMMONS TRAINING HIS SON TO BECOME A CHAMPION LIKE SELF

"BOB" FITZSIMMONS AND HIS SON   COURTESY OF THE POLICE GAZETTE

[525] *Pittsburg Press*, February 22, 1914; *Pittsburgh Gazette Times*, *Pittsburgh Post*, February 23, 1914.
[526] *Harrisburg Telegraph*, *New York Sun*, March 27, 1914.

CHAPTER 21

The Final Years

On May 23, 1914, in Chicago, Bob Fitzsimmons' wife Julia filed for divorce, claiming cruelty. Fitz did not defend the divorce suit, allowing it to go through. The divorce eventually was finalized on January 20, 1915.[527]

Julia Gifford and a young Rosalie Fitzsimmons

On June 4, 1914 in New Brunswick, New Jersey, the Middlesex Grand Jury indicted Bob Fitzsimmons jointly with his "alleged housekeeper" Temo Sloan, who claimed to be a German countess living with the fighter on his Dunellen farm, on charges of open lewdness and cohabitation on May 15. The indictment was the result of testimony by the wife of Bob's former manager, Mrs. John Meek, who was caring for his three minor children at Dunellen, as well as Bob's daughter Rosalie. Mrs. Meek "averred that the children were starved and underclothed, that Fitzsimmons lived unlawfully with his housekeepers from time to time and that he earned $600 a week from fighting exhibitions and vaudeville bookings and paid an average of $100 a week to his housekeepers." Noted was the fact that "Mr. and Mrs. Fitzsimmons have been separated and Mrs. Fitzsimmons has instituted suit in Chicago for divorce." Essentially, the allegation was that he was sleeping with various housekeepers, including Sloan, and paying them a lot more than what housekeepers usually made.[528]

On June 27, 1914, in Paris, France, Jack Johnson successfully defended his world heavyweight championship with a 20-round decision victory over Frank Moran.

In late July 1914, what eventually became a global war, known as the Great War, and later World War I, began in Europe.

In December 1914, promoter James Coffroth wrote,

[527] *Brooklyn Daily Eagle*, May 24, 1914. *Buffalo Commercial*, December 24, 1914.
[528] *Perth Amboy Evening News*, June 5, 1914; *New York Sun, New York Tribune*, June 6, 1914.

Whom do I consider the greatest fighter of all time? Bob Fitzsimmons. Why? Because he was the best middleweight, the best light-heavyweight and the best heavyweight that ever drew on a glove. Fitz was the thorough master of battle tactics in the four-cornered ring. The fact that he could fight with equal facility in three different classes was because he was a physical monstrosity.

The wiry Cornishman had the shoulders and arms of a heavyweight and the legs of a lightweight. Outside of Fitzsimmons, Ketchel was undoubtedly the greatest middleweight that ever lived. He had a punch and a style of delivering it that has never been equaled. But he never would have been a match for the invincible Fitz. Nor would John L. Sullivan have stood a chance in his palmiest days.

The thing that made the Cornishman great was the fact that he was a decisive fighter. There was never the question of doubt in the mind of the fan as to who won when Fitzsimmons was in the ring. ...

The undefeated black champion, Jack Johnson, would, even with his peculiar defensive style and rangy build, have been a victim of the terrible Fitzsimmons' wallop had he fought that freckled monstrosity at a time when he was good. No, Fitz had no peer; he will always stand out in my mind as the greatest monarch of pugilism.[529]

In March 1915, when speaking about the current crop of white hopes, Fitzsimmons said, "Brains are no good unless a person knows how to use them and until the white hopes learn how to use their brains they will never amount to anything." According to Fitzsimmons, the best white hope was Jess Willard, but even he had a great deal to learn before he could stand a chance against Johnson in their upcoming encounter. "The Australian prophesied that if the bout was on the level and Johnson didn't stall for the pictures, he would put Willard away in four rounds."

Bob also declared that his son could beat all of the present-day heavies except Johnson. "The lanky one said that his boy knows more than Corbett ever did and is a better fighter than he (Fitzsimmons) ever dared to be." He expected him to turn pro in another year or so.

At that time, Bob was in Brooklyn, at the Bijou theater, showing off with the punching bag, assisted by Countess "Zillen" of Marseilles, France, who apparently was his girlfriend/fiancé.[530]

In late March, Bob applied for a marriage license to wed a 27- or 28-year-old Temo Zellin of Newark, New Jersey. Another article called her Teno Zellen. Others said Zillen. Another article said her name was Temo Simomin or Slemonin, the divorced wife of Henry Simomin of Portland, Oregon. She had been married once previously, and was born in Marseilles, France. Ancestry.com calls her Tema Zilien, a Russian. Findagrave.com says her name was Temo Ziller Selon, and despite claims to being a French Countess, she most likely was born in Russia. Another called her Temo

529 *Brooklyn Citizen*, December 6, 1914.
530 *Brooklyn Times*, March 2, 1915.

Sloan, a German who had been living with Bob on his Dunnellen farm (and previously had been indicted along with him for living with him out of sin). She was billed as "Countess Zeelin." Her divorced name was Temo Slemonin. In an official legal document, "Temo" said she was born in France and her maiden name was "Zelien."

Bob gave his age as 52, and his residence as Dunellen, New Jersey. He was born in Helston, England. His father James was born in Ireland, and his mother Jane Armstrong in England.

When asked about the age difference with Temo, Bob said it didn't matter, so long as they thought a lot of each other. "When a man gets in the limelight the dear public thinks it has the right to tell him what he must do," including how to pick a wife.

Bob's first wife was Louisa Johns (or Alice Jones). They were married in Sydney, which marriage lasted about eight years. They divorced in 1893 because of her preference for another, according to Bob. (That other happened to be Bob's manager Martin Julian.) Interestingly enough, Bob then married Rose Julian, Martin Julian's sister, who bore three children with Bob. She was a woman of the stage, a contortionist, and statuesque beauty. Her death in 1903 ended their happy marriage. Julia May Gifford was his third wife. She was a musical comedy singer. She had been married before as well.[531]

Fitz and Temo "Sloan" had been charged in June 1914 with open lewdness and living together unlawfully. However, in light of their upcoming marriage, the prosecutor dismissed the indictments.[532]

Bob said, "I married first in Sydney, Australia, in 1885, and then I married Martin Julian's sister in 1894. Then I married Julia May Gifford, and now I'm going to marry as fine a little lady as there is in the world. My children are objecting, but they can object and be hanged."[533]

On April 5, 1915, in Havana, Cuba, 33-year-old 6'6 ½" 238-pound Jess Willard knocked out 37-year-old 6'1 ½" 227-pound Jack Johnson in the 26th round (of a scheduled 45) to become the world heavyweight champion.

Fitzsimmons congratulated Willard, but also said he thought he could beat him. Bob said the outcome was one of the biggest surprises of his life.

> I thought that Johnson could trim a dozen Willards. And right now I think if Johnson had trained properly he would have beaten Willard.
>
> Don't get the impression for a minute that I'm not glad that a white man has captured the title. The fight game needs all the preserving and care it can get. Johnson's actions while champion came pretty near killing the game.
>
> Willard caught Johnson after the negro had spent five years of easy life. Johnson's extra weight around the waist line was due to his love of high life. ... The public had too much of Johnson. But you can

531 *New York Tribune*, March 17, 1915; *Elmira Star-Gazette*, March 19, 26, 1915; *Brooklyn Daily Eagle*, March 25, 1915. *Boston Globe*, October 31, 1915.
532 *Perth Amboy Evening News*, March 19, 1915.
533 *Republican*, March 26, 1915.

take it from me that in spite of his years, Johnson had ring science enough left to make a boob out of Willard if the negro had taken care of himself.

BOB FITZSIMMONS CONGRATULATES JESS

Newest Champion Shaking Hands With the Greatest Ex-Champion.

Jess Willard, new world's champion.　　　　Bob Fitzsimmons, greatest ex-champion.

Bob Fitzsimmons and his latest wife.

Bob Fitzsimmons and Temo Zelien got married on or about April 8, 1915, at the National Hotel in Washington, D.C. They were married by a reverend of the Methodist Episcopal Church. Bob said that he had given his bride jewels worth $85,000.[534]

Jack Skelly wrote that no champion of modern times was of such an erratic temperament in and out of the ring as Bob Fitzsimmons. He loved wild animals as pets, and his training camps had a circus vibe. Bob liked to wrestle. He often left himself wide open and would take many a hard punch, sometimes pretending to be knocked down or hurt. In the end, though, he would clip his gullible victim on the point of the jaw and put him to sleep. "Fitz was certainly a genius, possibly the most tricky miller of his time. He always laid for a K.O. and took many a stinger to land the winning punch." He had a fighting temperament and a fully developed, "freakish, lightning-like brain."[535]

Harry Gilmore said either Jem Mace or Bob Fitzsimmons in their primes could beat either Jess Willard or Jack Johnson if under the old-school bareknuckle rules. Willard was the biggest man who ever held the championship, and his size and strength made him formidable. However,

> In the old days we used to figure on wearing out an opponent sometimes more by our ring tactics than by the actual blows in the ring. You know every time a man went down it constituted a round. You could not go down without being hit, for that was called a foul, but you could go down if you were tapped or pushed. So fellows like Mace or Fitz would have these giants steaming and puffing chasing them. As soon as they got into close quarters they could go down after blocking a blow. And they would dart in and out with their speed until the big fellows were all tired out.[536]

[534] *Elmira Star-Gazette, Dunkirk Evening Observer*, April 9, 1915.
[535] *Yonkers Herald*, May 26, 1915.
[536] *Buffalo Commercial*, June 9, 1915.

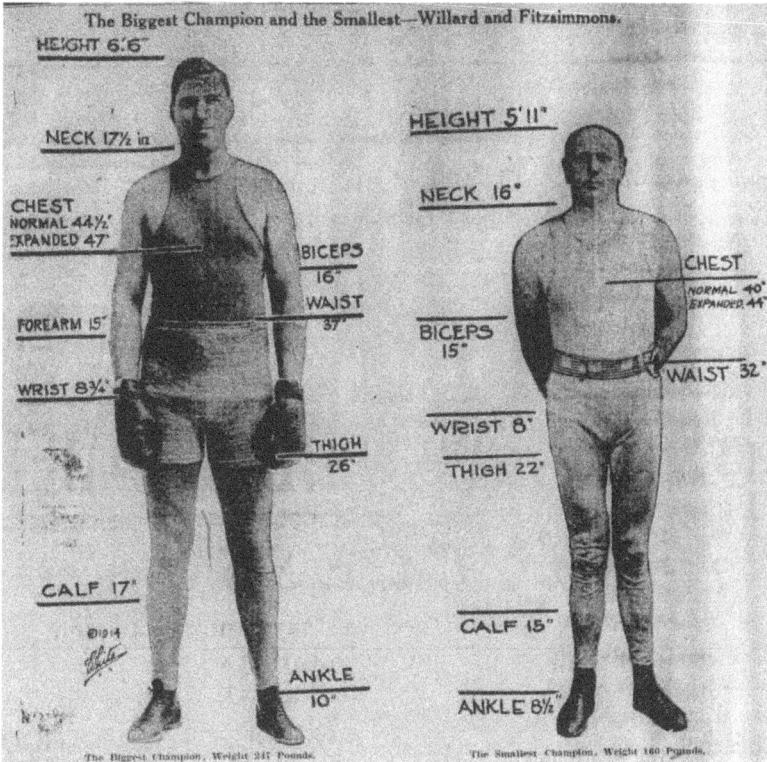

The Biggest Champion and the Smallest—Willard and Fitzsimmons.

Well-known fight referee and ring expert Ed W. Smith said that of all the fighters he ever saw with a real knockout punch, Bob Fitzsimmons was "the most spectacular of them all." "When old Bob cracked 'em with that merry old wallop of his, they fell in a heap and the referee's count usually was entirely perfunctory." Oddly enough, his knockouts all looked different, in that each man fell to the floor and took the count in some new and unusual manner. Smith saw Fitz knock out four men, including Abe Cougle in 1891, Will Mayo – a Cleveland mulatto, in 1893, Jim Corbett in 1897, and English middle Jeff Thorn in 1899. Bob could stop men with punches to either the head or body, left or right. Smith also saw Jeffries knock Fitz out cold to win the title in 1899.[537]

Robert Edgren said Fitzsimmons was one of the gamest fighters. He broke his right hand against Jeffries in their rematch, and buckled the joints of his left hand, disabling it. Yet, he kept on hitting, and hitting hard. Afterwards, when Edgren asked how he kept hitting so hard with damaged hands, Bob said, "Why, when I couldn't 'it any more with those two knuckles, I just turned my 'and up this way and 'it 'im with the two knuckles that weren't busted."[538]

In August 1915, after only about four months of marriage, Bob's fourth wife, Temo, left him. She was amongst his creditors who had sued him, including her claim for $1,000.[539]

[537] *Buffalo Enquirer,* July 15, 1915.
[538] *New York Evening World,* July 15, 1915.
[539] *Perth Amboy Evening News,* August 18, 1915.

When interviewed, Bob said, "None of the fighters nowadays amount to shucks. They don't know how to box; they don't know anything. Why, I've forgotten more than they ever knew. And say – let me tell you, my boy home can clean up the whole lot of them." He was planning to teach boxing in Buenos Aires, Argentina, in South America.[540]

Fitz was mourning the fact that his wife had left him. "I used to love her, but now I only like her. I was holding all my first wife's jewels - $80,000 worth – in trust for my children and here she up and goes to Los Angeles with them, leaving me holding the sack. Ain't women hell?"[541]

In early September, Fitz's Dunnellen farm was sold under foreclosure proceedings. He was being sued by several people, including his wife and ex-wife.[542]

The lawsuits led to assault charges against Fitz. He was placed on probation for a year and fined $10 for landing a blow on James Hendricks, who served him with a dispossess notice on his Dunnellen farm. Hendricks was acting for his brother, Dr. Joseph Hendricks, who held a mortgage on the farm.[543]

Nevertheless, the plaudits for the great Fitzsimmons continued. Robert Edgren wrote that Bob Fitzsimmons had "the greatest assortment of scientific knockout punches ever gathered by any one fighter." Peter Maher was famous for his punch as well. Hence, it was a natural for them to be matched. In their first contest, Bob outboxed and outpunched Peter until Maher retired after the 12th round. In their rematch, Bob stopped him quickly in the 1st round. Afterwards, Maher said, "I'll fight any man on earth. But this fellow isn't a man at all, at all! He's the divil himself in disguise."[544] (Yes, the "divil," meaning devil.)

KEENEY'S
ANNIVERSARY WEEK
☞ THIS is a REAL Anniversary. We have but one a year ☜
BIG CONCERTS TODAY.   1,500 SEATS AT THE MATINEE, 15c
MONDAY, TUESDAY AND WEDNESDAY
THE ONE AND ONLY ONE
JAMES J. CORBETT
(GENTLEMAN JIM)
A BEAUTIFUL WOMAN WITH A REAL VOICE
MRS.
BOB FITZSIMMONS

In January 1916, James J. Corbett was performing on stage with Bob's former wife Julia Gifford, who still called herself "Mrs. Bob Fitzsimmons" for promotional purposes.

Bob and his son Bob, Jr. were on the burlesque stage in Boston in a sketch called "The Coming Champion."[545]

[540] *Buffalo News*, August 2, 3, 1915; *Brooklyn Daily Eagle, Evening World*, August 18, 1915.
[541] *Chicago Day Book* September 2, 1915.
[542] *Daily Argus, Perth Amboy Evening News*, September 10, 1915.
[543] *Rome Daily Sentinel*, November 15, 1915.
[544] *Buffalo Evening Times*, November 22, 1915.
[545] *Buffalo Evening News*, February 19, 1916.

Approaching the Jess Willard vs. Frank Moran title fight, Bob Fitzsimmons said, "Willard is too big for the Moran type of fighter. His height, reach and 250 pounds give him big natural advantages. He is by far the best of the big fellows of to-day." Another quoted Bob as saying, "Jess looked as fresh after his fight with Gunboat Smith as he was when he started, and during the milling Smith hit him with anything he wanted at will. So Willard can handle so much punishment that I can hardly see where the challenger has a chance." Jim Jeffries said, "Willard is the ideal champion. Moran has little chance of winning the title." Jim Corbett said, "I won't be surprised if the bout goes [the scheduled] ten rounds, with Willard having a little the better of it at the end. Willard, with his great height and reach, will be a hard man to beat." Joe Choynski said, "Willard should beat Moran decisively. I don't expect a knockout." Ted Kid Lewis said, "Willard is so big and perfectly developed that I can't figure where any one has a chance to whip him." Mike Donovan said, "Willard looks invincible at this time." Jack Skelly said, "Moran is no dub. He carries a great kick, but he has never met as formidable a man as Willard. I cannot conceive of any man of Moran's size knocking out the biggest and best working champion we have ever had."[546]

On Saturday March 25, 1916, at Madison Square Garden in New York, 259 ½-pound Jess Willard unofficially but clearly won a 10-round no decision over 201 ½-pound Frank Moran. Willard landed more and harder, and emerged unmarked, while Moran had a bleeding nose and left eye. The 6'6" to 6'7" Jess said he broke his right knuckle in the 2nd round. He planned to join a 34-week circus engagement. The 6'1" Moran said, "Willard is a powerful man. He is clever and can hit, and he took advantage of every opportunity to use his weight." Bob Fitzsimmons and Jack O'Brien were amongst those in attendance who said Willard won.

546 *Buffalo Commercial*, March 17, 1916; *Evening World*, March 18, 1916.

The general verdict was that Willard was not only too big and strong for Moran, but also too clever. He jabbed and uppercut him almost at will. He eluded blows well and absorbed with ease any hard blows which struck him. The Associated Press scored it 7-2-1 for Willard. A crowd of just over 13,000 paid about $151,254. Willard earned $47,500 and Moran $23,750.[547]

One writer said Bob Fitzsimmons was an exception to the rule in that he was fighting at his best when he was near age 35, a time when most were down and out or very much passe. His career had lasted over 23 years.[548]

In November 1916, Fitzsimmons and his son signed a contract with Alexander Pantages for a vaudeville engagement from Minneapolis to Kansas City, commencing November 26, 1916.

CALL OF RING PROMPTS FITZSIMMONS, JR., TO FOLLOW STEPS OF DAD

FATHER AND SON IN ACTION BOB FITZSIMMONS, SR. AT LEFT TEACHING BOB FITZSIMMONS, JR., AT RIGHT. THE MANLY ART INSET ANOTHER VIEW OF YOUNG BOB "

Gangway for Bob Fitzsimmons, Jr The fightin' son of Ruby Robert is ready for his first big ring combat. This chip of the old block is primed for a campaign which his famous dad hopes will yield another niche in the hall of pugilistic fame for the family

"I am not entering the boxing game because I love it," said Young Bob at his quarters in Wollaston, Mass. "I don't know why I took it up unless it was I heard the call of the ring it was in my blood, I guess."

[547] Jack O'Brien, Bob Fitzsimmons, the Associated Press, International News, *New York American, New York Press, New York World, Morning Telegraph, New York Tribune, Brooklyn Citizen,* and *New York Sun* all said Willard won. Abe Attell and John L. Sullivan said Moran won. *Brooklyn Standard Union, Rochester Democrat and Chronicle, Illustrated Buffalo Express, New York Sun, Brooklyn Daily Eagle,* March 26, 1916.
[548] *Buffalo Times,* May 21, 1916.

In January 1917, the current Mrs. Fitzsimmons said she and Bob had broken up because of drink and another woman. She wanted him to stop drinking and straighten up. She had become an evangelist.[549]

Interestingly enough, that same month, Bob said he and Mrs. Fitzsimmons, Temo Zelien, from whom he had been estranged for 20 months, had reconciled their differences and decided to take up evangelistic work together. Bob said, "I can do it and get away with it. My mother started me out to be a minister and when I was a boy I attended three Bible classes a week." Fitz also was signed up for a 13-week theatrical engagement, sparring with his son Bob, Jr. for the Pantages theater circuit.[550]

When asked who was the greatest man who ever entered the ring, various experts offered their opinions. Eddie Hanlon picked Joe Gans. Tom Sharkey picked Bob Fitzsimmons. "Jeff, nor any of those fellows worried me like Bob. He wasn't only a boxer but he was game and had a knockout punch in either hand." Eddie Graney picked Peter Jackson. Young Mitchell picked middleweight champion Jack Dempsey (who Fitz dethroned). Jack Welch: Joe Gans. Sol Levinson: George Dixon.[551]

In March 1917, Bob Fitzsimmons was in Los Angeles at the Pantages theater doing a monologue, telling his life story, and giving short 3-round exhibitions with his son, Bob, Jr.[552]

That month, evangelist Bob met with James J. Jeffries at Jeff's Burbank dairy farm. The two got along well. Bob was mixing vaudeville with evangelism, traveling around giving exhibitions, stage monologues, and preaching the gospel.

Fitz received news that he had become a grandfather. His daughter Rose, who was Martin Julian's niece, gave birth to a boy.[553]

[549] *Butte Daily Post*, January 3, 1917.
[550] *Daily Missoulian*, January 11, 1917: *Bismark Daily Tribune*, January 20, 1917; *Seattle Star*, January 22, 1917; *Rochester Democrat and Chronicle*, January 28, 1917.
[551] *Buffalo Times*, February 18, 1917.
[552] *Los Angeles Times*, March 20, 1917; *Los Angeles Morning Tribune*, March 22, 1917.
[553] *New York Sun*, March 25, 1917.

JIM JEFFRIES & BOB FITZSIMMONS. ©INTERNATIONAL

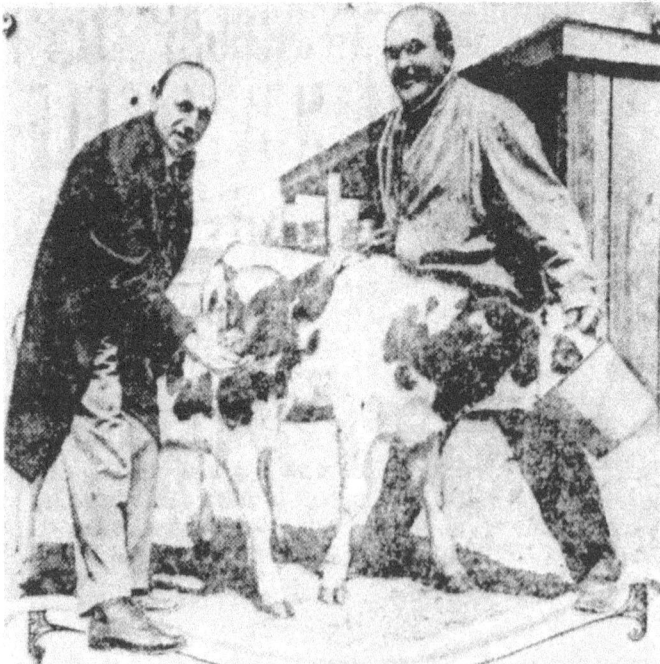

Unfortunately, in mid-October 1917, while in Chicago, Fitzsimmons was suffering from a bad case of pneumonia in his lungs.

On October 18, 1917, it was reported that Fitzsimmons was seriously ill and at death's door in a Chicago hospital. His wife was with him at the hospital. Bob had been appearing at a suburban theater until the day before, when his condition suddenly worsened. Eventually he was rushed to the hospital. He had been ill with a cold for several days, but refused steadfastly to take to his bed, until he took a turn for the worst. Physicians said he was near death and there was only a small hope for his recovery.

From Massachusetts, John L. Sullivan said, "Tell Bob for me I'm with him. He's a wonderful man. ... He was a clean fighter clear through."

Bob was at the Michael Reese hospital, and doctors gave him only 36 hours to live. He was in a stupor and had lost a lot of weight.

Mrs. Fitzsimmons said, "Bob was a great fighter and a good husband. He worked hard on the theatrical circles and I believe the exposure between acts and the drafts which blew through the wings were responsible for his present condition. I am thankful he will not be buried in a pauper's grave, like many other ex-fighters."

Mr & Mrs. Bob Fitzsimmons

Sadly, after battling pneumonia for at least a week or so, on October 22, 1917, in Chicago, at 2:45 a.m., former world middleweight, heavyweight, and light-heavyweight champion Bob Fitzsimmons died. He was only 54 years old. Purportedly, amongst his last words were, "I'm not through until I'm counted out. I never have quit and I never will." He eventually succumbed to his double pneumonia. He had contracted a cold and collapsed on Wednesday the 17th while punching the bag.

Bob Jr., who arrived after Bob died, said,

> I don't care to have anything more to do with the burial of my father
> or with the widow. I'm going to finish my deer hunt. I'm not
> welcome here. We have disagreed about my father's personal effects,
> some of which cannot be found. Then, too, I wanted him cremated,
> as I know this was his wish, but she had made up her mind to have it
> her way. Since the law is on her side, I'm going to beat it and forget.

> I have a commission as boxing instructor in the U.S.A, a lock of my
> dad's hair in my pocket, the return end of a round trip railroad ticket
> in my pocket, and deer waiting for my gun. I'm off.

He left without attending Bob's funeral.

The present Mrs. Fitzsimmons, whom Bob married two years ago, was a
French woman interested in evangelical work. She claimed that Bob had left
her very little.

James J. Jeffries said, "He was a great old general. I can speak of him
only in the best of terms. He was one of my best friends, and I am sorry he
has gone."

Edward Tranter said it was the end of one of the greatest pugilists the
world ever knew. He came to the U.S. in 1890 and was a freak to behold.
He had thin legs and massive, powerful shoulders. His youth as a
blacksmith gave him great strength, and he hit hard enough to fell an ox.
After his boxing career concluded, he had been successful in his theatrical
life.

> He earned several large fortunes that dwindled away through
> extravagance and unsound investments. Of late he had been poor.
> His fine nature, his trusting heart, his confidence in his fellowman of
> unscrupulous schemes cost Fitzsimmons his fortune more than once.
> His end was like his life – full of strife and battle, but he lost out
> despite his wonderful vitality and courage.

Another writer said 5'11 ¾" Bob Fitzsimmons had won three world
championships, more than anyone to that point – middleweight,
heavyweight, and light heavyweight. "By virtue of holding them, he must be
ranked the greatest fighter the world has ever known." He withstood the
wear and tear of the game for a remarkably long time and excelled,
regardless of his age. He was 28 in 1891 when he won the middleweight title
from the great "nonpareil" Jack Dempsey, weighing just 150 ½ pounds,
knocking Dempsey out in the 13th round; age 35 in 1897 (and 165-175
pounds) when he beat 190+-pound James J. Corbett for the world
heavyweight championship with his famous solar plexus punch in the 14th
round; and age 42 and 168 pounds in 1903 when he beat George Gardner
for the world light heavyweight crown, decking him several times en route
to the W20. He was past age 50 when "the New York Boxing Commission
arbitrarily put an end to his fighter career." He was the "freak" of the ring.
He shuffled around, but when he landed, inevitably it was curtains. He first

learned to box in New Zealand, where he got his start, but truly honed and perfected his craft in Australia. He came to the U.S. in 1890. "From the first fight that Fitz had in this country, his fighting career was comprised of a long string of ring successes, the like of which has never been equaled before or since his time." He had stopped Peter Maher twice, Jim Hall, Dan Creedon, Joe Choynski, Tom Sharkey (twice), and Gus Ruhlin. He was a blacksmith and horseshoer who kept lions as pets. Born in England, he eventually became a U.S. citizen. He was respected by everyone in the sport and admired by the entire world.[554]

The *New York Tribune* said Fitz was one of the most remarkable pugilists the world had ever known. He was a freak of build, with the waist and legs of a lightweight but chest, shoulders, and arms of a heavyweight, which enabled him to make the middleweight limit. He lost the heavyweight crown to Jeffries, a physical giant who was impervious to blows that would have finished most other heavyweights.

Others said Fitz was tough and never thought he was beaten, always believing he could bring down the other man. He was hurt and/or dropped by men such as Maher, Choynski, Corbett, and Sharkey, but got up and stopped them all. The only man he couldn't drop was Jeffries, though he busted him up.

Tom O'Rourke said, "Bob Fitzsimmons didn't have an equal. Think of the man's weight, and then reflect on his deeds and you won't place any man who ever fought above the Cornishman. No man ever hit as hard as Bob did. He brought giants down with blows that were never equaled for power.

> Could he have whipped John L. Sullivan? Could he? Let me tell you something. George Dixon could have stopped poor old Sullivan the night that Jim Corbett did, and in less time, for he wouldn't have run as much as Corbett. Corbett was scared to death. He ran until poor John was compelled to pull up from the chase, and even then Corbett was too frightened to hit him one good punch. The old fellow began to sag at the knees and fold up like an accordion. Then Corbett, afraid to really go in close for a solid blow, hit the old fellow twenty times before he finally fell exhausted on the dirt floor.
>
> Fitz? He'd have finished John L. in two rounds. He could have whipped Sullivan at his best, and a mighty short bout it would have been, for Fitz could whip any man who was crazy enough to come to him in jig time. Fitz was far ahead of Sullivan's day.[555]

Robert Edgren said Fitzsimmons made around a half million dollars but died a relatively poor man. All his possessions would not amount to $10,000. His farm at Dunellen was considerably reduced in value by judgments against the estate. Valuable jewelry had disappeared. Some said it

[554] *Brooklyn Daily Eagle*, October 18, 1917; *San Francisco Chronicle, Elmira Star-Gazette*, October 19, 1917; *Chicago Tribune*, October 21, 22, 23, 1917; *San Francisco Examiner, Buffalo Enquirer, Brooklyn Daily Eagle, Brooklyn Standard Union, New York Tribune*, October 22, 1917.
[555] *New York Evening World*, October 24, 1917.

was sold to pay debts. Bob had lived on what he could obtain from vaudeville performances. He often was cheated out of earnings, paid with bad checks, and he made bad financial decisions, often an easy mark. He lent money to folks who never paid it back.[556]

Bob's funeral took place on Wednesday October 24, 1917, in Chicago at the Moody tabernacle, North avenue and North Clark street, before 3,000 friends and admirers. Bob's father was revealed to be an Episcopal minister. Letters of condolence were read from James J. Corbett and Jim Jeffries, who also contributed flowers. Mrs. Fitzsimmons was the only member of Bob's family present.[557]

Private services were held at 810 North Clark Street. Bob was buried at Graceland Cemetery.

Robert Edgren said, "Bob Fitzsimmons was the greatest fighting man the ring ever knew." Fitz had no equal in ringcraft and skill, fighting courageously until age finally sapped his marvelous vitality. He was invincible until age finally got him. "I have seen thousands of boxers, and all the champions of the past twenty years, but not one other that combined the qualities of greatness that brought Bob Fitzsimmons fame." Fitz's punches were like hammers, but he also had a cunning brain. "If I were asked where Fitzsimmons ranked, among all the world's great boxers, in all classes from the bantams to the heavyweight, I would say that he was the greatest of them all – that among the fighting men of the Queensberry ring he stood without a peer. I expect never to see his like again."[558]

A month after Fitz's death, Edgren noted that he never did get a candid opinion of Fitz's fighting qualities from Jim Corbett, but he remembered what Corbett said in the dressing room after the Fitz fight. "I wasn't licked – I wasn't licked. He hit me and paralyzed my legs." That very well summed up Fitz's solar plexus blow. Bob Fitzsimmons knew how to put men down for the count.

After Gus Ruhlin had been defeated by Fitz, he said, "I'll fight anybody in the world, but don't ask me to fight old Bob again. For two weeks after he hit me in the body I felt sure I was going to die. I wouldn't fight him again for all the money in the world."

Tom Sharkey said, "I'd fight Jeffries every night in the week. He broke my ribs, but he couldn't lick me. But that old man Fitz! Say! I'm not a quitter or anything, but I don't want his game. Last time he hit me on the jaw I didn't remember what happened for a couple of days, and then I thought a mule had kicked me."

After the rematch with Fitzsimmons, Jeffries said,

> If I'd known what a beating the old man would hand me in that fight I wouldn't have taken it for $100,000. He broke every bone in my

556 *Buffalo Evening Times*, October 25, 1917.
557 *Buffalo News*, October 25, 1917.
558 *New York Evening World*, October 27, 1917. Edgren claimed that Bob's parents were Irish, his father an army officer and riding and fencing master, who had resided in Helston, Cornwall, England. When Bob was 3 or 4 years old, the family moved to New Zealand. Bob became a horseshoer, and won bareknuckle fights, becoming the champion there.

nose and flattened it so that I could lay my finger right across it and touch both cheek bones. He loosened every tooth in my head and nearly tore my ears off. He closed both my eyes. For a week after the fight I thought my jaw was broken. Couldn't move it, and all I could eat was soup. If he hadn't bumped into one at last I don't know what would have happened. He's a wonderful old fellow.

Kid McCoy once said, "I can outguess all the others, but nobody knows what old Fitz has in the back of his mind. When you think you know every move he can make he springs something new that you never dreamed of. I wouldn't fight that old guy if he was 100 years old."

Mike Donovan said he warned Bob that he might kill someone with his naturally powerful punch, for he did not know his own strength. He advised him to hit his exhibition partners in the body so as not to have a death on his hands. (Con Riordan later did die at Bob's hands in an exhibition.)

Peter Maher, who Fitz stopped twice, said, "I'll fight any man, but this isn't a man at all. He's the divil in disguise."[559]

Grantland Rice wrote,

> Willard, Jeffries and Johnson at their best may have been harder men to beat than Bob Fitzsimmons was. They had the big bulk which old Fitz lacked. But the main test of a fighting man should be 'inch for inch and pound for pound.' Under this arrangement there isn't any question but that Fitz was the greatest fighter that ever lived. Pound for pound he stood above them all as a fighting machine.
>
> He was more effective considering his weight than Joe Gans or Terry McGovern were. Gans and McGovern could meet and beat bigger men. But could Gans or McGovern spot a champion twenty-five pounds and knock him out?

Rice said none of the fighters of 1917 other than Willard could remain on their feet if they were to meet the Fitzsimmons who beat Corbett, Sharkey, and Choynski. "Fighters with greater bulk and greater power will come along. But as an unadulterated, unalloyed fighting man, pound for pound, the game will hardly see his equal."

Back in 1904, when Jim Jeffries was asked who the hardest puncher was that he had fought, he replied, "Fitzsimmons. He could not only hit harder than any other man I ever met, but he could hit twice as hard. He hit me on the top of the cheek bone in one fight and I thought my head was coming off. ... I thought a mule had kicked me or some one had soaked me with a lead pipe. No man living could ever hit with this fellow."[560]

Bob's son Bob, Jr. eventually became known as Young Bob Fitzsimmons, and he fought professionally from 1919 to 1931. He had some solid, competitive results against top fighters, but not quite good enough to position himself to fight for the championship. He never was stopped or knocked out, only losing decisions or no decisions. We will

[559] *Buffalo Times*, November 11, 1917.
[560] *Glens Falls Post-Star*, October 27, 1917.

never know how far he might have gone had his trainer/father not passed away.[561]

Photograph by Brown Brothers.

IF Bob Fitzsimmons had been our father we should probably have exercised more than we did, and might even have beaten the fat boy in the cross-country finals. Bob, Jr., himself is a teacher of boxing, and at one time he appeared in the ring with his father. Perhaps, knowing so well the career of a world's champion, he has no great ambition for those dizzy heights. For his father's private life was nearly as tempestuous as his life in the ring—varying from a prosperity when he had diamonds set in his teeth, to a time when he was reduced to cooking his own pork chops.

Never again did boxing see a champion like Bob Fitzsimmons, who could win world championship contests by knockout from middleweight all the way up to heavyweight. He had the perfect blend of skill, cleverness, footwork, timing, speed, power, placement, and effectiveness.

---

[561] Bob Fitzsimmons, Jr.'s results included: 1921 WND12 Erminio Spalla, WND12 Al Roberts, W8 Fay Keiser, and L15 Harry Foley; 1922 L15 Martin Burke and LND12 Charley Weinert; 1923 D12 Dan O'Dowd; 1924 DND10 Bud Gorman, WND12 Joe Borrell, WTKO10 Ted Jamieson, L10 Young Stribling, and LND10 Jimmy Delaney; 1925 WTKO10 Dan O'Dowd, WTKO3 Quintin Romero Rojas, L10 Jimmy Delaney, and LND12 Bud Gorman; 1926 L12 Johnny Risko, L10 Jack Delaney, W10 Bob Lawson, and LND10 Tiger Flowers; 1927 LND10 Chuck Wiggins and LND12 Joe Sekyra; and 1929 L10 Jack Renault.

Acknowledgments

I want to thank all those who were instrumental in assisting me with research, photographs, or promotion of my books, including but not limited to:

Gregory Speciale

Clay Moyle

Evan Grant

Matt McGrain

Tom Gerbasi

Mike DeLisa

Thomas Hauser

John Raspanti

Mike Silver

Dave Bergin

Lou Eisen

Vincent Ciaramella

Anthony Reader

Kevin Smith

Buddy Gibbs

Frank Stallone

Francis Moylan

Peter Dewar

Gary Luscombe

Kenneth Bridgham

Roy Bennett

Christopher Smith

Ismael AbduSalaam

Boxrec.com

Boxingforum24.com

Library of Congress, Prints and Photographs Division

Index